KU-307-342

SPORTING JUSTICE

101 SPORTING ENCOUNTERS WITH THE LAW

SPORTING JUSTICE

101 SPORTING ENCOUNTERS WITH THE LAW

IAN HEWITT

Published in Great Britain by
SportsBooks Limited
PO Box 422
Cheltenham
GL50 2YN
Tel: 01242 256755
email: info@sportsbooks.ltd.uk
www.sportsbooks.ltd.uk

© Ian Hewitt 2008
First Published October 2008

All rights reserved. No part of this publication may be produced or transmitted in any form or by any means, including photocopying and recording, without written permission of the publishers. Such written permission must also be obtained before any part of the publication is stored in any retrieval system of any nature.

Cover design by Alan Hunns

All photographs from Getty Images

A catalogue record for this book is available from
the British Library.

ISBN 978 1899807 68 0

Printed and bound in England by
Cromwell Press

'I have no doubt that there is a lot of popular support for the view that the law should be kept away from sport.'
– Justice Drake in *Elliott v Saunders*

'Even Hypotenuse would have trouble working out these angles.'
– Sid Waddell

CONTENTS

CHAPTER ONE

CHAPTER TWO

CHAPTER THREE

CHAPTER FOUR

CHAPTER FIVE

CHAPTER SIX

CHAPTER SEVEN

CHAPTER EIGHT

CHAPTER NINE

CHAPTER TEN

CHAPTER ELEVEN

ACKNOWLEDGEMENTS

My father introduced me to the addictive pleasures of sport. My first thanks are to him. If it involved a ball, he played it. I also learned from him that the way to read a newspaper is from the back pages first. Equal gratitude is due to my mother who encouraged me to do something 'useful' and that included becoming a lawyer.

This is certainly not an academic law book. I nevertheless acknowledge my debt to the many who have elevated sports law to a respectable discipline – and particularly to Jonathan Taylor and his team who ran the Post-Graduate Diploma in Sports Law at King's College, London which I was pleased to attend as a 'veteran' student. The seeds for the book were planted during that course. I am also very grateful to Nick Bitel of Max Bitel Greene, who kindly agreed to read through a number of chapters in draft in the light of his considerable experience in this field and yet always made constructive suggestions. Any errors are, of course, my responsibility.

Most of the 'quotes' which appear in this book, where they do not derive from the law reports themselves, come from statements or interviews widely reported in the press including in the fine sport sections of the *Daily Telegraph* or *The Times* or on the excellent website of *BBC Sport*. I acknowledge these sources. I list separately, in the Bibliography at the end, a number of books which have helped provide background on specific topics or cases.

The manuscript would not have found any shape or legibility but for the continued word processing skills of Toni Partridge to whom I am extremely grateful. And Randall Northam, as publisher, has my thanks for his encouragement and suggestions which kept the project on path.

Lastly but importantly, my special thanks go to Jenifer, my wife. Her positive support and encouragement throughout have been a vital contribution – particularly when my pace slowed.

Ian Hewitt
September 2008

INTRODUCTION

This book is a collection of stories – stories of disputes involving sport or sporting personalities which have ended up before courts and tribunals.

Most sporting disputes are resolved quickly – by a referee on the field, by an appeal body within the particular sport or by commercial negotiation. But not all disputes can be resolved easily. Some have important consequences – for an individual, a team, a competition, a sporting event, sponsors, broadcasters or the spectating public. Some involve prosecution under the criminal law. A court or appeal tribunal may be called upon to make a judgment, impose a penalty or provide a remedy. This is where sport encounters the law. This is the arena for the stories in this book.

Sporting disputes do, of course, reflect sport itself. They can be unpredictable and colourful. They can involve lively personalities, great sporting venues and extraordinary events and situations. Stories in this book involve many well-known sporting figures: Eric Cantona, Duncan Ferguson, Don Revie, Bobby Moore, Lee Bowyer, Iain Dowie, Lionel Messi and Sir Alex Ferguson among others from the world of football; Tony Greig, Hansie Cronje and Sir Ian Botham from cricket; Ben Johnson, Diane Modahl, Dave Bedford, Christine Ohuruogu and Dwain Chambers from athletics; tennis players Roscoe Tanner and Greg Rusedski; golfer Tiger Woods; Ayrton Senna and Eddie Irvine from motor racing; Lester Piggott, Adrian Maguire and Kieren Fallon from horseracing; rugby's JPR Williams; boxer Michael Watson; snooker player Stephen Hendry; ice-skater Tonya Harding; skier Alain Baxter; cyclist Floyd Landis and darts player Phil Taylor.

All make an appearance, together with many others. All have contributed, some reluctantly, to the history of sporting encounters with the law.

'Lawyers have no place in sport.' A familiar cry. Yes, but... sport does not and cannot exist without a framework of rules: rules of the game itself, disciplinary rules and procedural rules for enforcement. Sport is also subject to the laws of the land: the rules of criminal law, negligence law, employment law and laws relating to misrepresentation and unfair trading.

Without recourse to the law, the landscape of the sporting world would be very different. Or, to put it another way: bare-knuckle prize fighting might still be legal; major betting scandals in cricket and football would not have been uncovered; Kerry Packer's 'World Series' would not have changed the shape of cricket; Jenny Pitman would not have been a trainer of a Grand National winner; medical support at boxing contests would not have been substantially improved; BSkyB would have taken over Manchester United; Arsenal and Chelsea would probably not have won the FA Premier League without their foreign players; Christine Ohuruogu would not have won Olympic gold for Great Britain in Beijing; and more.

What criteria have been used to select the '101 sporting encounters with the law' in this book? I have focused on four ingredients. Did the encounter involve a leading sporting personality, venue or event? Did it illustrate or establish an important legal principle affecting sport? Were there significant consequences for the particular sport? Was it an entertaining story? Each encounter satisfies at least one of these criteria. In a large number of cases, I believe all four are satisfied. But it is a personal choice and I know that many strong candidates for inclusion have been omitted.

There has been no shortage of material. The flow of sporting disputes before courts or tribunals in recent years has been continuous including in the lead-up to the Beijing Olympics. Indeed, most of the stories in this book arise from events or incidents in the last twenty-five years – and nearly one-third from the last five years alone. 'We'll meet at the bar' has taken on a new meaning in sport.

What types of sporting dispute lead to encounters with the law?

Cases before courts and tribunals have, over the years, been rich in sporting content. This book is broken down into eleven chapters covering different categories of sporting disputes.

First, the sporting playing field is not beyond the arm of the criminal law. Many leading personalities have discovered that. On-field violence, at some level, must be subject to the sanction of the criminal law. But at what level? If a player has been punished by the sport's disciplinary authorities, should the criminal law also intervene? Eric Cantona, Duncan Ferguson, Lee Bowyer and Tonya Harding appear in Chapter One amongst a number of domestic and international cases under *Sport, Crime and the Playing Field.*

Betting and gambling have long been associated with sport. They are uneasy companions. Sometimes, too often, temptations have resulted in bribery, corruption and criminal activities which undermine the integrity of sport. Chapter Two gathers together, under *Betting, Bribery and Corruption,* a number of well-known cases from the 1919 baseball World Series to Kieren Fallon's prosecution and others pursued by the criminal authorities in football, cricket, baseball and horseracing.

Private lives of sportsmen have, perhaps too frequently, led to encounters with the courts and criminal authorities – sometimes justified, sometimes not. Just a few selected, and colourful, examples are gathered here in Chapter Three under *Sportsmen, Crime and Private Lives* including cases involving Bobby Moore, Lester Piggott, Roscoe Tanner, Navjot Sidhu and, perhaps the oddest of them all, Glen Johnson.

We return to the sporting arena under *Negligence and Personal Injury* in Chapter Four. This covers a number of unfortunate cases of personal injury resulting, allegedly, from the negligence of players, referees or event organisers. Examples come from across the field of sports: a cricket ball hit out of the ground, a badly-sliced golf shot, an ill-judged football tackle, a questionable refereeing decision in rugby, spectators injured at sporting events such as motor racing and show jumping and, perhaps most poignantly of all, Michael Watson's head injury during a world title boxing contest.

Decisions of referees and umpires have significant consequences for the outcome of sporting competitions. Victory can mean sponsorship and economic rewards, as well as sporting prizes. Promotion, relegation and championships can hinge on official rulings. At the most basic level, cries of 'that was never a penalty' or 'you can't be serious, that ball was out' are unlikely to find favour with any review body or court. But are there limits beyond which a court or arbitral body will be willing to right a clearly established wrong? Chapter Five, under *Referees, Umpires and the Olympics*, recalls a number of controversial incidents from boxing, equestrian eventing, athletics and gymnastics arising in recent years at the Olympics.

Disciplinary cases provide fertile ground for disputes. Sanctions, particularly suspensions or bans on future participation, may have a major financial effect – both for individuals (whose 'living' is sport) and teams. Efforts to stamp out doping have led to numerous cases before sporting tribunals, arbitral authorities and the courts. Chapter Six under *Disciplinary and Anti-Doping* reviews a number of disciplinary cases ranging from football, athletics, tennis, horseracing, skiing to greyhound racing, from Don Revie to Dwain Chambers.

Commercial opportunities attaching to major sporting events have transformed over the last decade or so – particularly with the value of television and other broadcasting rights. This has led inevitably to disputes. Under *Sport and Business*, Chapter Seven explores some of the cases from misleading representations of Eddie Irvine and Dave Bedford to radio broadcasts of horseracing in Australia and a commentary on a football match from an Amsterdam hotel room.

Competitive sport cannot exist in a vacuum. It depends on a structure of national and international competitions. Disputes relating to participation in leagues and competitions by clubs, teams and individuals have led to a number of high-profile cases discussed in Chapter Eight under *Leagues, Competitions and Teams*. These include the establishment of Kerry Packer's 'World Series Cricket' and players' freedom (or not) to play in 'unofficial' competitions; the establishment of the FA Premier League; the great divide in the world of darts; a conflict in snooker; the move of Wimbledon football club to Milton Keynes; and Sheffield United's claim following West Ham's breach of FA Premier League rules.

You cannot win or achieve as an individual in sport unless you are able to participate. Sport is open to all – or is it? Chapter Nine, entitled *Sex, Discrimination and Participation*, reviews a number of important cases centring on alleged discrimination in sport including Florence Nagle's fight with the Jockey Club for a trainer's licence, a female judo instructor's ambition to referee in men's competitions, the difficult case of transsexual tennis player Renée Richards, Theresa Bennett's enthusiasm to play in a mixed junior football team and Darrell Hair's allegation of racial discrimination in cricket.

Issues relating to employment of players have led to several major sporting decisions with far-reaching consequences. Contractual disputes are manifold. European laws relating to 'free movement of workers' have had a dramatic effect on the structure of player employment in football – and indeed other sports. Chapter Ten under *Sport and Employment* recalls landmark cases involving Newcastle's George Eastham, Belgian footballer Jean-Marc Bosman and Slovak handball player Maros Kolpak, along with a number of other employment disputes in football including the recent dispute with FIFA/UEFA relating to players injured whilst on international duty.

Lastly, Chapter Eleven is a personal diversion. It explores, under *A Closing Cocktail*, a few scenic detours away from the main route. They include personal battles fought in the courts by such sporting legends as JPR Williams, Sir Ian Botham and Sir Alex Ferguson. There are a number of other claims, mostly of a somewhat optimistic nature, which may not be regarded as leading sporting cases but which provide entertaining diversions to complete our journey. My own favourite is the upset Leicester soccer fan who sued for compensation for shock suffered as a result of a referee's controversial penalty decision in the last few minutes of extra time in an FA Cup tie.

This is not an academic law book. On many occasions, I have simplified the facts, and consequent legal arguments, of a particular case. I have concentrated, for simplicity and focus, on a particular aspect. I believe, though, that this approach still fairly presents the key issue for the reader. I have also interpreted widely the institutions which comprise 'the law'. The disputes discussed in this book have led to decisions not only by courts of law but also by appeal tribunals or independent arbitral bodies of which the most illustrious is the Court of Arbitration for Sport whose headquarters are in Lausanne, Switzerland. Arbitration plays an important role in the resolution of sporting disputes.

Sporting disputes before the courts can be interesting, fun and intellectually challenging. Many arise because the issues are difficult to resolve. In many cases, I have attempted to present the key issues in the form of arguments 'for' and 'against'. If you had been the judge in these cases, how often would you have made the same decision as the arbitrator, court or tribunal?

'For' and 'against' how would you decide?

The eclectic diversity of sport is reflected here in the variety of sports and sporting venues which provide the background to the stories in this book. Indeed, in one sense, this is a travel book for the sports fan. A 'whistle-stop' journey through time and across a range of sporting venues. Background scenes for our stories include: Old Trafford, Anfield, Ibrox and St James' Park; Brooklands and Imola; Augusta and the Belfry; the Oval; Roland Garros; the White City; summer Olympics at Atlanta, Seoul, Barcelona and Athens; winter Olympics in Salt Lake City; and Paralympics in Sydney. Memories of events, personalities and venues may be stirred.

In several cases, I want to exclaim the sports fan's cry: 'I was there'. I remember as a child the 1960s 'football bribery sensation' headlined in *The People* (a popular sports paper at the time); I was at the Belfry watching the Ryder Cup in 1989 and at Augusta in awe of Tiger Woods in 1997; I saw Bruce Grobbelaar play at Southampton (we thought he was a pretty good goalkeeper); I worked, as a lawyer, on the formation of the FA Premier League; I have stayed, by chance, at the Amsterdam hotel used by Talksport for their Euro 2000 broadcasting; and the incident at Buckpool golf course vividly reminds me of my own tendency to slice at golf. So, there were many personal memories as I compiled this book. May it be the same for you, the reader.

I hope you, the sports fan, enjoy this journey along the many diverse paths where sport and sporting personalities have encountered the law.

CHAPTER ONE

SPORT, CRIME AND THE PLAYING FIELD

We start with the basic question. Does the criminal law, the law of the land, apply to activities on the sporting field of play?

All major sports have disciplinary rules and procedures which enable sanctions to be imposed 'within the sport' on participants who are guilty of serious misconduct. Should the criminal law simply stay outside the touchline? How does the criminal law permit direct combat sports such as boxing? Should different rules or standards apply to sport and exempt acts of violence on the field of play which would be criminal if they took place off the field? Does it make a difference if violence occurs in a major, televised match?

Many of the encounters in this chapter are striking because of the sporting personalities involved. Others because of the important legal principle established. Our journey to explore sport's relationship with the criminal law takes us to a wide range of sporting venues including a makeshift fighting ring near Ascot, the famous football stadia of Ibrox, St James' Park and Selhurst Park, an ice-skating rink in Detroit, the Imola racing circuit in Italy and a village tennis club in France.

---

1 A PRIZE FIGHT NEAR ASCOT – WHEN IS BOXING UNLAWFUL?

Were fighters in a bare-knuckle prize fight guilty of criminal assault? Was a spectator at the fight guilty of aiding and abetting?

Our story starts near Ascot, after the races. In 1881, off the country road to Maidenhead. A surprising venue, perhaps, for a case which would settle whether bare-knuckle prize fighting was unlawful or not.

Prize fighting was still common in the early 1880s. Just over twenty years earlier, a bare-knuckle fight between England's champion Tom Sayers and America's leading fighter John Heenan had captured national attention when they fought, in Farnborough in Hampshire, for nearly two and a half hours to the point of exhaustion and broken limbs in a 'world championship'. Stories vary whether the police tried to stop the fight, but could not get through the crowd to the ring, or whether they waited until a near riot as the ring rope broke at the end. The fight was declared a draw.

Even under the London Prize Ring Rules introduced in 1838 it was a rough and violent 'sport' with very few accepted rules and restrictions. To many this form of combat had become increasingly distasteful. The Queensberry Rules, introduced in 1865, were leading to a more humane and orderly form of boxing more acceptable to Victorian society with use of padded gloves, no wrestling or throwing of an opponent, three minute rounds and the introduction of weight divisions. Amateur boxing clubs were growing in popularity.

Did bare-knuckle prize fighting involve unlawful assault or not?

Raw bare-knuckle prizefighting nevertheless continued – but under an increasing cloud of illegality. Fuelled by gambling, many fights were mismatches or fixed; others endured to the bitter end of exhaustion. Fights tended to be arranged secretly. Local police sometimes took action – but generally on the ground that such fights incited unlawful assembly and riot rather than the essential nature of the 'sport', the infliction by one person of physical injury on another. Did bare-knuckle prizefighting involve unlawful assault or not?

The issue was finally put to the Court of Criminal Appeals in 1882. And there was a surprise twist to the prosecution.

Back to Ascot. After leaving the races one afternoon in June 1881, an unnamed witness spotted a number of people coming out of a gap in the woods by the side of the road between Ascot and Maidenhead. Curious, he took a closer look. On private land, a ring of cord had been set up supported by four blue stakes. Two men, Jack Burke and Charley Mitchell, were ready to fight. Bets were exchanged between some of the 150-strong crowd. Coney was one of the spectators among the throng. Burke and Mitchell, supported by their 'seconds', took off their coats and waistcoats, went into the ring and fought for just under an hour.

The local police were alerted and decided to take action. Burke and Mitchell were charged on the basis of criminal assault. And the surprise twist to the prosecution? Coney, as a member of the crowd watching the fight, was also charged with assault. A supporting spectator, the police alleged, was aiding and abetting and that was equivalent to assault.

Should Burke and Mitchell be guilty of criminal assault even if, as consenting adults, each agreed to the risk of injury from the other's blows? If so, should Coney be treated as aiding and abetting the crime and therefore himself guilty of unlawful assault?

For: A blow struck in anger, and likely to cause physical injury, was an assault. Such an assault was a breach of the peace and unlawful. The consent of the person struck should be immaterial. Consent should not render innocent acts which were deliberately aimed at another person and were knowingly dangerous (for example, a duel). Burke and Mitchell were guilty. Prize fighting was contrary to the public interest. The presence of spectators watching the fighters, and knowing that bets were being made, encouraged these assaults. The crowd were assembled for a common purpose of a criminal character. They were therefore aiding and abetting the crime and, in the eyes of the law, Coney should also be found guilty of assault.
Against: Burke and Mitchell had agreed to fight. They were consenting adults. There should be no conviction of criminal assault where there was clear consent. Parliament, as legislature, had not made prizefighting illegal. Burke and Mitchell should therefore not be found guilty. Even if they were found guilty, Coney was only a spectator. Mere presence was not sufficient to constitute active aiding and abetting. Coney should therefore, in any event, be found not guilty.

Burke, Mitchell and Coney were convicted at the Berkshire Quarter Sessions. Given the importance of the case, however, the chairman referred the case to the Court of Criminal Appeals to review whether his direction to the jury had been correct. It was a landmark case.

An extraordinarily large eleven-strong Court of Criminal Appeals sat in judgement. Eleven judges in their full regalia. The guilty verdict on Burke and Mitchell was unanimously confirmed. Each was guilty of criminal assault on the other. Their sentences were confirmed – six weeks imprisonment with hard labour.

The deliberate infliction of physical injury by one person on another was an assault. Consent could not render it lawful. Bare-knuckle prize fighting was clearly now a criminal activity in England. Justice Hawkins summed up:

> *' ... a prizefight ... is illegal and the parties to it may be prosecuted for assaults upon each other.'*

He distinguished, rather quaintly, prize fighting from 'friendly encounters not calculated to produce real injury or to rouse angry passions' such as sparring with gloves without any intention of the parties to beat each other until exhaustion or one of them was subdued by force. Such 'friendly encounters' were on the right side of the law.

Their sentences were confirmed – six weeks imprisonment with hard labour.

As for Coney, he was more fortunate. His conviction was overturned. By an eight to three majority, the Court of Criminal Appeals decided that Coney was not guilty of aiding and abetting an assault by merely being a spectator.

Where does that leave the modern professional boxing contest?

Simply, there is no decision of the courts – or specific law of Parliament – which positively renders a boxing contest legal. It remains an anomaly. The courts have said that sparring with gloves, where boxers do not aim to injure or fight to exhaustion, is acceptable. Consent does not justify dangerous or masochistic acts beyond that level. But professional boxing is a 'sport' where blows, such as an uppercut to the jaw, are deliberately aimed at the head with the objective of causing damage. The British Medical Association, among others, continues to call for a total ban on boxing due to brain damage sustained cumulatively by boxers from blows to the head.

The modern professional bout is, apart from the wearing of gloves, the direct descendant of the prize fight. The fighters do box for money and often do so to the point of near exhaustion. They are not 'friendly encounters'. And that is without any additional violence such as Mike Tyson biting off part of Evander Holyfield's ear – an assault by any measure.

The careful regulation of boxing today as a sport under the rules of the various boxing authorities would, however, undoubtedly influence any modern-day court. It is highly unlikely, in practice, that any court would now find professional boxing illegal. The enjoyment and social role of regulated boxing would almost certainly be judged, as a matter of policy, to outweigh the risk of injury. But an anomaly it remains.

The distinctive grave of Tom Sayers, England's prize fight champion of the 1860s who died six years after that fight with John Heenan, is still prominent in Highgate Cemetery in north London. His funeral was reputedly attended by ten thousand people.

---

2 A TRAGIC FOOTBALL CHALLENGE – WAS IT MANSLAUGHTER?

Henry Moore fouled a defender in an ugly clash resulting in the death of a goalkeeper. Should he be convicted of manslaughter?

Can a footballer be liable for manslaughter as a result of a reckless tackle? The issue was, tragically, put to the test in 1898.

The case arose in Aylestone, a village south-west of Leicester. It was in the early days of association football. Football was growing rapidly in popularity. The village amateur football team in Aylestone were playing local rivals, Enderby, a Saturday scene repeated up and down the land. It was the background, though, to an incident which would give rise to the basic question: does the criminal law apply to tackles on the football field in the course of play?

A lively match was in progress. Aylestone were on the attack. John Briggs, a young forward, received a pass and pressed forward. He dribbled past Henry Moore, an Enderby central defender, and kicked the ball firmly towards the Enderby goal. Moore ran after Briggs. The chase was on. The Enderby goalkeeper ran forward to kick the ball clear and save his goal. Just as he kicked clear, the defender Moore jumped with his knees up against Briggs' back, forcing him violently forward against the knee of the advancing goalkeeper. Briggs fell to the ground, with serious internal injuries. He sadly died a few days afterwards.

Moore was charged with manslaughter. The case came before a jury trial at the Leicester Assizes. The issue was stark. Although the injury was not intentional, was Moore so reckless in using force likely to cause injury that a verdict of manslaughter was appropriate?

For: Sport, including football, was not above the criminal law of the land. The fact that the game was governed by its own rules was irrelevant. Football was a rough game and people who play it must be careful not to inflict bodily harm on another person. No one had a right to use force which was likely to injure another. If he did use such force, and death resulted, the crime of manslaughter was committed. Moore should be found guilty.

Against: Football was a physical game. The players knew this. Serious injuries did occur. There was no intention to kill. Allowance must be made for the rough-and-tumble of a contact sport even if the contact went beyond the technical level permitted by the rules. The use of the criminal law was inappropriate to apply to such an incident. Moore should be found not guilty.

Moore was found guilty of manslaughter.

The extract from the contemporary law report summarised the direction of the judge to the jury:

> *'Football was a lawful game, but it was a rough one ... No one had a right to use force which was likely to injure another, and if he did use such force and death resulted the crime of*

> *manslaughter had been committed. If a blow were struck recklessly which caused a man to fall, and if in falling he … was injured and died, the person who struck the blow was guilty of manslaughter … '*

Football was clearly a particularly dangerous game in those early days. One extraordinary feature of this case was that a young player in this same match named Veasey, who had given evidence against Moore, was himself killed a few weeks later in another football match.

What was the sentence on Henry Moore? All that is known is that the vicar of Enderby gave him an excellent character reference. Sentence was postponed and no record appears of the final outcome.

This case is a vivid illustration that the criminal law does not stop at the touchline. An earlier football case, extraordinarily also at Leicester Assizes, had resulted in a 'not guilty' verdict on a manslaughter charge – but the court had affirmed that sport was not above the law:

> *'No rules or practice of any game whatever can make that lawful which is unlawful by the law of the land.'*

The conviction of Henry Moore is the only reported case of a successful manslaughter charge arising from an on-the-ball incident during a football match. Criminal prosecution for on-the-ball incidents has become rare. Off-the-ball incidents are different. Indeed, as recently as 2006 an amateur footballer, Julian Clarke, received an eighteen-month jail sentence for manslaughter following a punch on an opponent at the end of a Birmingham Sunday League game. The opponent sadly died as a result of the head injury.

The vicar of Enderby gave him an excellent character reference.

Contact sports such as football or rugby have, however, continued to raise difficult issues for criminal prosecuting authorities. Should they intervene with lesser, but still serious, criminal charges when physical violence on the pitch crosses the boundary of acceptable behaviour? How much allowance should be made for the sporting context? Later cases would exemplify this dilemma.

---

3 TONYA HARDING – AN ASSAULT THAT GRIPPED THE SPORTING WORLD

Preparing for the 1994 Winter Olympics, leading US skater Nancy Kerrigan was struck down by a heavy blow. It was a story which would grip the international sporting world.

Now a sporting soap opera. A bizarre story which started in downtown Detroit in January 1994. It became a saga which would remain etched in the minds of all with memories of sport in the 1990s.

The Cobo Arena in Detroit was the scene for the final build-up to the Winter Olympics which began the following month in Lillehammer, Norway. Skaters were practising for the US National Women's Figure Skating Championships after which the two skaters to represent the USA in the individual event at the Olympics would be selected. The story centred on two characters, leading US skaters Tonya Harding and Nancy Kerrigan.

Tonya Harding was a feisty, fair-haired twenty-three-year-old raised from a tough background in Portland, Oregon. She had already won the US Championships twice: 1991 was her great year; second place in the World Championships and the first American woman to complete a triple axel jump in competition. Now, in 1994, her form had slipped a little although she had still come fourth in the previous year's US Championships and was seeking a shot at glory in the Olympics.

An unidentified man, wielding a metal bar, suddenly struck her on the knee.

Nancy Kerrigan, her great US rival, was a polar opposite in temperament and background. She was an elegant, dark-haired twenty-four-year-old from a well educated middle-class background in east coast Boston. She was the current US champion and the leading US medal hope.

Kerrigan had just finished her practice session at the Cobo Arena on 6th January. As she left the rink, an unidentified man suddenly ran towards her and, wielding a metal bar or club, struck her on the outside of the right knee. An eyewitness said: 'Before she could say anything, a guy ran by, crouched down, whacked her on the knee and kept running.' The man escaped as Kerrigan fell to the ground, screaming and clutching her knee.

Officials rushed to the scene. Fortunately, a doctor was on hand to treat her. Kerrigan was forced to withdraw from the US Championships in Detroit. Harding went on to win the title. Fears grew that Kerrigan would miss the Olympics.

A few days later, extraordinary rumours began to spread that the attack – which occurred just eight months after an on-court knife attack by a 'fan' of Steffi Graf on the leading tennis player, Monica Seles – might have involved associates of Tonya Harding.

Events moved quickly. On 19th January, less than two weeks after the assault, Harding's ex-husband, Jeff Gillooly, and her bodyguard, Shawn Eckhardt, were arrested along with the alleged hired attacker, Shane Stant, for an alleged plot to injure Kerrigan. Harding denied any prior knowledge of the attack.

Harding had a tempestuous relationship with Gillooly. They had married in 1990 when she was a nineteen-year-old. The marriage lasted only for three years and they were divorced in 1993. They were reconciled for a short period afterwards – but apparently not for long. On 1st February, less than one month after the attack, in a dramatic turn of events, Gillooly agreed to a plea bargain. He pleaded guilty to his role in the attack in exchange for giving testimony against Harding who, he said, was deeply involved in the conspiracy to injure Kerrigan. Harding continued to deny any involvement. Gillooly was later sentenced to two years in prison, of which he served six months, and fined $100,000.

Fears grew that Kerrigan would miss the Olympics.

Where did this leave Harding's imminent participation in the Olympics? Could the USA still select her if she was under suspicion for a criminal attack on a rival? The US Olympic Committee (USOC) sought to suspend Harding from competing in the Olympics. Harding continued to protest her innocence and threatened legal action for substantial damages against USOC if they did suspend her. USOC were in a stew.

A day or so after the opening ceremony for the Olympics had taken place in February at Lillehammer, USOC did a deal with Harding. Fearing protracted legal battles and distractions that could disrupt the Winter Olympics, USOC agreed to allow Harding to skate in the Olympics. In return, Harding withdrew her $20 million lawsuit against them. A USOC statement continued: 'We are appalled still by the attack on Nancy Kerrigan, which was not only an attack on the athlete, but an assault on the basic ideals of the Olympic movement and sportsmanship. We remain deeply concerned about this incident.'

Kerrigan, fortunately, recovered and was able to skate at Lillehammer. The stage was set for one of the most anticipated moments in Olympic history: Harding competing against Kerrigan in the women's figure skating. They even practised together in Lillehammer, under close security and watched by hundreds of the world's media. Kerrigan wore the same white lace dress she was wearing when attacked.

The stage was set for one of the most anticipated moments in Olympic history.

The attack on Kerrigan and Harding's alleged involvement had led to a media frenzy. In the US, the television coverage of the first evening of the Olympic skating competition became, at that time, the second most-watched television show in American history. Only the final episode of '*M*A*S*H*' had previously been watched by more people.

Harding performed well but, as she set out for her final session, she was involved in further drama. Struggling with a broken shoelace, she requested and was allowed to skate later in her group. She eventually finished eighth. Kerrigan, just fifty days after being struck on the knee in Detroit, then went on in the Olympic amphitheatre to give one of the most scintillating performances of her career. She missed out on the gold medal by the narrowest of judging margins in favour of sixteen-year-old world champion, Oksana Baiul, from Ukraine. Kerrigan was content with her silver medal: 'I think I skated great. I was smiling. I was happy. How can I complain?'

The Olympics did not mean the end of the saga. Afterwards, the criminal case against Tonya Harding developed.

Eventually, on 16th March, it was Harding's turn to make a plea bargain. She avoided further prosecution and a possible jail sentence by pleading guilty before an Oregon State Court to a charge of hindering the police investigation into the attack on Kerrigan. Harding was sentenced to three years' supervised probation, 500 hours of community service work and a $100,000 fine. She agreed to undergo a psychiatric examination. Asked by the county circuit judge if she had anything to say to the court, Harding said only: 'I'd just like to say I'm really sorry that I interfered.' She continued to maintain her innocence as to any prior involvement in planning or knowledge of the attack. That was the end of the criminal proceedings.

The final episode in the story came six months after the Olympics. The US Figure Skating Association conducted a full investigation. A disciplinary hearing was held in Colorado. Harding did not show up for the two day hearing. A five-member disciplinary panel of the Association decided that 'by a preponderance of the evidence' Harding 'had prior knowledge and was involved prior to the incident'. The panel acknowledged that this finding was 'based on civil standards, not criminal standards'. Her conduct had shown 'a clear disregard for fairness, good sportsmanship and ethical behaviour'.

Her conduct had shown a 'clear disregard for fairness, good sportsmanship and ethical behaviour.'

Tonya Harding was stripped of her 1994 US Championship title and banned for life from ice skating competition.

Tonya Harding was subsequently involved in numerous skirmishes with the law for a variety of personal misdemeanours. She actually made a brief comeback to skating, five years later in 1999, when she appeared in the ESPN professional competition, outside the jurisdiction of the US Figure Skating Association, held at Huntingdon, West Virginia. She finished second.

In 2002, she appeared as a boxer in a celebrity boxing event against Paula Jones, a name linked with the past of US President Bill Clinton. Harding won. She was a pretty good fighter. She subsequently competed in various official women's boxing events.

The Harding/Kerrigan saga was a dramatic and unforgettable saga of its time. It was not only a sporting soap opera, it actually inspired a chamber opera: *Tonya and Nancy: The Opera*. The lead libretto was written by a well-known author, Elizabeth Searle, and the opera was first performed in Cambridge, Massachusetts in 2006.

---

4 AYRTON SENNA – WILLIAMS TEAM ACQUITTED OF CULPABLE HOMICIDE

Ayrton Senna was killed after a crash in the San Marino Grand Prix. What was the cause? Was it culpable homicide?

The weekend of the San Marino Grand Prix in 1994 became one of the most harrowing in Formula One history.

The grand prix was being held at Imola's famous Enzo e Dino Ferrari circuit, named after Ferrari's late founder and his son Dino. Imola, one of the few Formula One circuits to run anticlockwise, is thirty miles east of Bologna and not far from the nearby state of San Marino – hence the name of the grand prix.

Ayrton Senna was racing for the Williams team that season. The thirty-four-year-old Brazilian was already a legend in Formula One. A triple world champion, he had won the drivers' world championship title in 1988, 1990 and 1991 racing with the McLaren team. After the introduction of restrictions on active suspension and traction controls in Formula One by the racing authorities, Senna had moved from McLaren to the Williams team for the 1994 season in an effort to meet the challenge of the Benetton-Ford of Michael Schumacher. It was Senna's third race for Williams. Despite pole positions in the season's opening two races, he had failed to finish. His Williams Renault FW16 was not yet handling well. Was this to be the breakthrough?

The weekend started dramatically. During Friday's practice, fellow Brazilian Rubens Barrichello hit a kerb and flipped his car into the top of a tyre barrier. It looked a bad crash but, fortunately, he was not seriously injured. In Saturday's qualifying, tragedy struck. Austrian Roland Ratzenberger crashed head-on into a wall after a front wing failure. He was taken to hospital but later died. It was the first fatality in Formula One for twelve years. Senna secured pole position for the next day's race.

Senna was deeply concerned by Ratzenberger's death and led a drivers' meeting the following morning to establish a safety group. He seriously thought of withdrawing from the race. He prophetically remarked: 'There are no small accidents on this circuit.'

Motor racing's governing body, the FIA, and Italian authorities later rejected allegations that Ratzenberger had been killed instantly at the track at Imola. If Ratzenberger's death had been certified at the track on the Saturday, under Italian law Sunday's event would have had to have been cancelled.

Sunday, 1st May 1994. The grand prix began. Senna took the lead from his pole position. Back on the grid two drivers, Pedro Lamy and JJ Lehto, were involved in a starting-line accident. Track officials deployed the safety car to slow down the field and enable the debris to be cleared. Senna urged the safety car to go faster, but it would not. On the sixth lap, the safety car left and the race was restarted.

On the seventh lap, Senna was leading with Schumacher just behind. Senna entered the notorious Tamburello corner. It was a flatout left curve with little room between the track and a concrete wall which protected a creek which ran behind it. Senna's car entered the corner at 192 mph ... and went off the track. His car struck the unprotected concrete barrier. On impacting the wall, the right front wheel of Senna's car was torn off including a piece of metal suspension. The car bounced back on to the run-off area and came to a halt. It was clear that Senna was seriously injured. The visor in his helmet had been pierced by a piece of metal. Senna had suffered a fatal head injury. A surgeon performed an emergency tracheotomy. Senna was rushed by helicopter to the Maggiore Hospital in Bologna. In the evening, he was declared dead.

'There are no small accidents on this circuit.'

When track officials examined the wreckage of Senna's car, they found a furled, blood-soaked Austrian flag which Senna was going to raise in honour of Ratzenberger at the finishing line.

The 1994 San Marino Grand Prix itself was restarted thirty-seven minutes after Senna's accident. The race was won by Michael Schumacher.

The world of Formula One entered a state of shock and disbelief on news of Senna's death. Three days of national mourning took place in Brazil. Over a million people lined his funeral cortège in his hometown of São Paulo.

What was the cause of the accident? Many theories were expounded.

Was it driver error? Did Senna simply lose control of the car?

Was there a failure in the power-steering as Senna tried to check an over-steer at the corner?

Was the accident caused, in part, by the fact that the lengthy use of the safety car meant that tyres were not yet fully hot and the car was lower and more vulnerable to bumps on the track coming into the Tamburello corner?

Was there negligence behind the scenes at Williams?

Inspection by the Italian authorities revealed damage to the steering wheel column. Did it occur on impact with the concrete wall? Or did it occur before Senna left the track? Senna had earlier in the year requested that the steering column be modified in order that he could fit more comfortably in the car and have a clearer view of the instrument panel. A new column could not be manufactured before the start of the grand prix season. The existing column had been cut, welded and reinforced by two metal plates. Had this failed? We shall never know. Unfortunately, in-car videotape footage of the last second or so of Senna's drive which might have revealed more has never become publicly available.

Six people were charged with culpable homicide.

The Italian authorities decided to bring a criminal prosecution. It was led by state prosecutor, Maurizio Passarini, zealous to make a name for himself. Six people were charged with culpable homicide. Three members of the Williams team were singled out – team principal Frank Williams, technical director Patrick Head and car designer Adrian Newey. Also charged were the FIA circuit director Roland Bruynseraede, the Imola circuit director Giorgio Poggi and Federico Bendinelli, head of the company that operated the Imola track. It seemed that the Italian authorities were determined to blame someone.

Culpable homicide in Italy was a different concept from manslaughter under English law. It could be alleged on the basis of relatively little negligence – certainly not the same recklessness required for manslaughter under English law – and prosecutions were not uncommon in Italy after a major accident. Punishment could range up to five years' imprisonment although a fine was more likely for prosecution after a racing death. However, to most international observers, it sounded the same as manslaughter.

The implications for the individuals charged were considerable. The potential ramifications for motor racing were also major. A guilty verdict, and the risk of prosecutions in the event of any subsequent accidents, would have made it likely that the FIA would withdraw its support for motor racing in Italy. No more Formula One in the home country of Ferrari?

The trial began in Imola in February 1997, nearly three years after the accident, under Judge Antonio Costanzo. The local courthouse was not big enough. A ballroom, converted from a Saturday night dance spot, became the venue for what would turn out – with frequent intervals and mini-hearings – to be a ten-month trial.

Passarini contended that a substandard modification had been made to the steering column of Senna's car. 'A modification to the steering column which had been poorly executed caused it to break.' The column suffered from metal fatigue as a result of poor workmanship. This led to steering column failure as Senna entered the Tamburello curve. Unable to steer, so the state prosecutor alleged, Senna was unable to brake sufficiently due to the design of the track surface. His superb driving skills could not save him.

Engineers from the Williams team, for the defence, said that the problem was most likely an over-steer as Senna's car went over a bump on the asphalt surface of the Imola track. Senna countered by steering away but the car appeared to bump and skid to the right, with Senna unable to brake and hold the line.

Evidence emerged that the steering column in the other Williams car, driven by Britain's Damon Hill, had also been modified in a similar way before the season began. The work was done in March. Both drivers had raced two grand prix events with the modified cars without any problem. Damon Hill himself gave evidence. Whilst some of his recall was rather vague, his opinion was that Senna had been attempting to correct over-steer. After seeing the film, Hill said: 'The steering wheel is exactly the way I would expect to see it to correct over-steer.'

The steering column in the other Williams car, driven by Damon Hill, had also been modified.

Extraordinarily, neither Patrick Head nor Adrian Newey was allowed to examine the wreck of the car. It remained impounded by the Italian police throughout the trial.

On 7th November, Passarini made his closing submission to the court. He continued to maintain that a defective steering column had been the cause. But without warning, he recommended that all charges against Frank Williams and also officials Bruynseraede, Bendinelli and Poggi should be dropped. Williams merely dealt with the administrative side of the business. Head and Newey were the people, he alleged, ultimately responsible for the design changes made to Senna's car. Defence counsel for the Williams team argued that the prosecution's case simply had no basis in proof. Senna's steering column was the same as Damon Hill's. The case was unfounded.

Judge Antonio Costanzo gave his verdict on 16th December 1997. In a ninety-second statement, he cleared all six defendants of culpable homicide in relation to Senna's death.

It was not until June 1998, six months after the verdict, that Judge Costanzo's full written official report was published. This gave the prosecutor, Passarini, zealous to the end, some scope to appeal since Costanzo did cite the breaking of the modified steering column as a cause although no direct fault could be attributed to the particular defendants. The appeal was heard in Bologna in November 1999. It was short. After three days, the appeal court again absolved the defendants. There was no new evidence. Williams had also appealed on the factual finding and the appeal court said there was insufficient evidence to support the original judge's view that a broken steering column was the cause. The Williams team had been vindicated on all fronts.

We will never know for sure the cause of Senna's death.

As a replacement for Senna in the 1994 season, Nigel Mansell returned to race for the Williams team. Damon Hill eventually lost the drivers' title to Michael Schumacher by just one point. Would Senna have won the title had he lived? With Mansell taking victory in the final race after an infamous collision between Schumacher and Hill in the Australian grand prix at Adelaide, Williams won the constructors' championship.

Back at Imola, the flat out Tamburello curve has since been reduced and reshaped as a fourth gear left-right chicane. In 2006, the FIA decided that Imola would not host a Formula One grand prix in 2007 and it was not included in the 2008 calendar.

---

5 DUNCAN FERGUSON – CRIMINAL ASSAULT AT IBROX?

Duncan Ferguson was seen headbutting an opponent. Should he be prosecuted under the criminal law?

We return to the football field and an incident in April 1994 involving a moment of violence by a well-known participant on a sporting field. It would later give rise to an orchestral symphony.

The scene was Ibrox, one of the great, atmospheric football stadia of the world; home of Glasgow Rangers and their fanatical supporters. Rangers, who were destined to be champions that year, were playing Raith Rovers in the Scottish Premier Division. Duncan Ferguson was the home club's main striker and a crowd favourite. Ferguson always had a fiery temperament. At 6 feet 4 inches tall, strongly built and with a competitive nature, he was a centre forward of the old school.

Ferguson turned to McStay, grabbed him by his jersey and deliberately butted him in the left side of his face.

It was a lively first half-hour of the match. Rangers were on the attack again. The ball was crossed by a Rangers player. Ferguson and experienced Raith defender, John McStay, challenged for it. A tussle took place involving a certain amount of arm pulling. The referee awarded a free-kick to Raith. Ferguson was not happy. He turned to McStay, grabbed him by his jersey and deliberately butted him in the left side of his face. McStay fell to the ground clutching his face. The injury was a flesh wound but not sufficiently serious to prevent him resuming the game.

The referee, Kenny Clark, and his linesmen missed the headbutt but the incident was reported to the Scottish FA by the referee supervisor. The Scottish prosecution authorities decided to take a close interest in this incident. They believed that football was not controlling its players and that they should intervene. Ferguson had an existing criminal record. It included two previous, but not football related, convictions for breach of the peace and assault. Importantly, he was still on probation for one of the offences. Enough was enough. Despite the Scottish FA imposing a twelve-match suspension on Ferguson, the police decided to prosecute Ferguson for criminal assault for his challenge on McStay.

It raised the general question: should the criminal law apply to on-field incidents in sport? Was Ferguson being punished twice for the same offence? Manslaughter is one thing – but should punishment for other on-field misconduct be solely a matter for disciplinary bodies within the sport itself? The case of Henry Moore, nearly a century earlier, may have made it clear that certain cases such as manslaughter could not be ignored – but should the law intervene with lesser offences?

The case came before the Sheriff Court in Glasgow. Should Ferguson be found guilty of assault? If so, what should be the punishment?

For: Sport is not above the law. There was no reason why an act of violence which would otherwise constitute criminal behaviour should be exempt simply because it was committed in a sporting context. Violent conduct on the field of play encouraged others (particularly younger players) to follow suit. The seriousness of the conduct should be reflected by the assertion of the criminal law. Ferguson had committed a deliberate assault and should be punished by the criminal law.

Against: Judgments on on-field incidents should be left to the disciplinary authorities within the sport. Contact sports inevitably involved a degree of excitable, and sometimes 'over-the-top', behaviour. The disciplinary authorities within the sport were well able to impose serious penalties, fines and suspensions. Introducing the criminal law would be arbitrary, intrusive and unnecessary.

Ferguson was convicted. He was sentenced to three months' imprisonment by Sheriff Eccles. This was both 'in the public interest' and to bring home to him that such behaviour could not be tolerated.

Ferguson appealed against the sentence to the High Court of Judiciary in Scotland. Ferguson's defence counsel claimed that the incident had happened 'in the heat of the moment'. Ferguson 'was a young man now maturing after a period in which he had been less well equipped to handle pressures'.

The appeal was unsuccessful. The Scottish appeal court said that it had no wish to intervene in physical contact sports such as professional football but, when acts were done which went well beyond what can be regarded as normal physical contact and an assault was committed, the court had a duty to condemn and punish such conduct. A footballer who assaults another player on the football field is not entitled to expect leniency just because the incident occurs during the course of a match. Indeed, the court said:

> *One of the factors which may indicate the gravity of the offence is the fact that the assault has been committed in public before so many spectators. This fact becomes all the more important where the player is a public figure and the incident occurs during a game which has such a high profile as a league match in the Scottish Premier Division.*

The sheriff had described Ferguson as having a 'quite appalling record of previous violent offences.' Importantly, Ferguson was on probation at the time. The Lord Justice-General summed up: 'The sentence of three month's imprisonment which was intended to be a deterrent to others, cannot be described as excessive.'

Ferguson was the first professional footballer in the UK to be given a prison sentence for an assault on the pitch.

Ferguson was the first professional footballer in the UK to be given a prison sentence for an assault on the pitch. He served forty-four days in Glasgow's infamous Barlinnie prison.

Ferguson was transferred by Glasgow Rangers to Everton before his jail sentence had been completed. His appeal against his twelve-match suspension was rejected by the Scottish FA. Following his release from prison and completion of his suspension, Ferguson played his first match – for Everton reserves. These reserve matches rarely attracted more than 1,000 spectators. Ferguson's return attracted a crowd of 10,432. He was saluted by a Scottish pipe band and banners protesting his innocence.

Later, the Evertonian terrace chant could be heard for their new hero: 'Dunc and disorderly.'

This remains a relatively rare case of a criminal prosecution for conduct during a professional football match. Indeed, Scottish prosecuting authorities have often appeared readier to intervene than their English counterparts. Terry Butcher was another example; charged and found guilty of a breach of the peace for violently pushing a Celtic player in the chest after a goalmouth collision in a lively 'old firm' Glasgow derby match also at Ibrox.

Those 'off-the-ball' incidents which have attracted the attention of the English prosecuting authorities have usually resulted in fines for unlawfully causing bodily harm under the Offences against the Persons Act. There have been numerous prosecutions in amateur rugby and football. In the professional game, Chris Kamara, then of Swindon, was in 1988 the first English footballer to be convicted of causing grievous bodily harm after breaking a Shrewsbury Town's player cheekbone in a fracas in the tunnel after the match; he was fined £1,200.

James Cotterill of non-league side Barrow AFC became the first English professional footballer to be given a prison sentence (four months) for an assault during a match – a punch 'off-the-ball' which broke an opponent's jaw during a first round FA Cup match in November 2006 against Bristol Rovers. The punch, not seen by the referee, was caught by the BBC and shown on *Match of the Day*. The police then intervened.

Duncan Ferguson's story attracted attention in one unlikely follower. It inspired a piece of classical music – entitled 'Barlinnie Nine' – by one of Finland's most famous composers, Osmo Tapio Raihala, who happened to be an Everton fan. Raihala said: 'I got the idea for it when [Ferguson] was facing jail and had just become something of a cult figure for Everton. It takes into account the contradictions in him: he has an aggressive side but there is a lyrical undertone to him, as the fact that he keeps pigeons shows.' The night that the orchestral symphony premiered in Helsinki was the same night that Ferguson scored the only goal in an Everton victory against Manchester United.

' ... there is a lyrical undertone to him, as the fact that he keeps pigeons shows.'

In 2003, Ferguson's 'hard man' image was maintained when he stopped a burglar who was breaking into his house in Formby,

Merseyside. The burglar required two days of hospital treatment following the incident.

---

6 ERIC CANTONA – THE KUNG FU KICK THAT SHOCKED FOOTBALL

Should Eric Cantona's Kung Fu attack on a spectator at Selhurst Park be prosecuted as a criminal offence?

Less than a year after Duncan Ferguson's headbutt, English football and the criminal law met in extraordinary circumstances on a Wednesday night in January 1995 at Selhurst Park in south London. The match was a highlight fixture for the capacity Crystal Palace crowd of 18,000, a Premier League match against Manchester United – led by the charismatic but temperamental Eric Cantona. The twenty-eight-year-old Frenchman, also captain of his country, was in his pomp and prime.

The incident was triggered just three minutes into the second half of a scrappy game with the score still at 0-0. Little did the crowd realise that about to occur was one of the unforgettable scenes of 1990s football. Cantona was in a tussle with Palace defender, Richard Shaw, who, unnoticed by the referee, pulled Cantona's shirt. The ball was cleared upfield. Cantona kicked out at Shaw and was sent off.

Matthew Simmons, an unruly twenty-year-old Palace fan, ran down eleven rows to the front of the main stand to the touchline to shout at Cantona as he left the field and walked along the touchline in front of the main stand. The words were disputed but they appeared to include: 'F*** off back to France, you French b*******'. The red mist descended on Cantona. There followed a scene never before witnessed on a football ground, a violent attack by a player on a spectator.

Cantona executed, dramatically and perfectly, a Kung Fu kick with both feet into the chest of Simmons in front of the stunned fans. This was followed by punching and fighting. Paul Ince also got involved. Other players and officials attempted to intervene and the brawl was eventually broken up. Cantona was escorted off by ground stewards and the United kit man. The match itself ended 1-1.

The incident made front and back page news. Manchester United took prompt action. The club suspended Cantona for nine months until the end of the season and fined him two weeks' wages. The Football Association also brought disciplinary action as a result of which he was fined a further £10,000 and banned from playing until October, two months into the following football season. FIFA supported a worldwide ban.

Was this ban, imposed within football's own disciplinary procedures, sufficient? Should Cantona also be punished under the criminal law? Should Cantona be prosecuted for assault? If so, was a custodial sentence appropriate?

The criminal authorities did decide to prosecute. Cantona appeared in March 1995 before the magistrates' court at Croydon.

For: There is a level of violence which the law cannot tolerate or ignore. The fact that it occurred on a football field was irrelevant. Cantona was a role model for youngsters. The incident occurred in a public arena. The crowd were incensed. A criminal punishment to affirm the role of the criminal law and to deter others was appropriate. The punishment imposed internally by the football authorities was not sufficient. It was a clear and violent assault by Cantona. The criminal law must demonstrate that such conduct cannot be tolerated, wherever it occurs. A serious penalty, including a custodial sentence, should be imposed.
Against: The act occurred in the heat of the moment. There was considerable racial provocation. No lasting injury was suffered by 'the victim'. The football authorities had acted quickly and efficiently. Their punishment was heavy. The nine-month football ban would have a significant effect on Cantona's ability to play football – his living. The matter had been dealt with adequately within the sport. Any additional penalty of the criminal law was unnecessary.

The prosecution claimed that, but for efficient policing and stewardship, the incident could have escalated into major public disorder. A large number of people were horrified by it. Cantona expressed his regret. The decision to send him off had been correct although he thought he had been 'repeatedly and painfully fouled' in the course of the match. The insults and taunts from Simmons added to his frustration.

Cantona was found guilty of criminal assault. He was initially sentenced to two weeks in prison. The chairman of the bench, Jean Pearch, a retired teacher, told Cantona:

> *You are a high profile public figure with undoubted gifts, and as such you are looked up to by many young people. For this reason the only sentence that is appropriate for this offence is two weeks' imprisonment forthwith.*

Cantona's lawyers immediately lodged an appeal. After three anxious hours in a cell, Cantona was freed on bail. His sentence was reduced on 31st March to 120 hours community service.

The incident, extraordinary and regrettable as it was, did at least provide the opportunity for a memorable press conference after the appeal verdict. Cantona walked in, referred to the British press and carefully expounded a depth and mystery of philosophy not often encountered in English football: 'When the seagulls follow the trawler, it's because they think sardines will be thrown into the sea.' He then left the room.

'When the seagulls follow the trawler, it's because they think sardines will be thrown into the sea.'

The courts have continued to stress that 'the criminal law does not stop at the touchline' or, in this case, the front row of the crowd. At the extremities of behaviour, the criminal law has a role to demonstrate that certain kinds of violence are unacceptable and should result in the sanction of the criminal law. The occurrence of such incidents before a large crowd in a high profile, and often televised, arena undoubtedly influences the authorities in the exercise of their discretion whether or not to take action. Similar themes can be detected in the cases involving Duncan Ferguson, Terry Butcher and, more recently, Lee Bowyer.

There must remain, though, considerable doubt whether the use of the criminal law really acts as a deterrent or, indeed, was a meaningful punishment in most of these situations. The disciplinary structure within football imposed a serious penalty – one that really hurt. What did such a prosecution and sentence against Cantona really achieve?

Cantona duly served his community service. This included helping coach schoolchildren and working with juvenile offenders in Salford.

Matthew Simmons, a window fitter with a previous conviction for assault, was later convicted of threatening behaviour for his role in the incident. He was fined £500 and banned from all football grounds for one year. In an extraordinary sequel to the original incident, after the verdict was announced at Croydon magistrates court Simmons leapt over a table and lunged at the prosecution lawyer. He grabbed him by the neck and appeared to kick him in the chest. Six police officers rushed to restrain him. Simmons was jailed for a week for contempt of court but freed after twenty-four hours.

Paul Ince was also charged with assault and threatening behaviour following the Selhurst Park incident but was acquitted.

Manchester United, in Cantona's absence, lost the Premier League title by one point to Blackburn that year.

Cantona returned to the Manchester United side in October in the following 1995/96 season in glorious form. The charismatic Frenchman was voted Footballer of the Year by the Football Writers' Association. He scored the winning goal in the FA Cup final to give Manchester United the 'double' for the second time.

During his lengthy ban from football in 1995, Cantona returned to France and started his film-acting career. He appeared as Lionel, a rugby player, in a comedy *Le Bonheur est dans le Pré* (Happiness is in the Field). The film was a box-office success in France.

In his latest film project, *Looking for Eric* directed by Ken Loach, Cantona returns to Manchester. The film, co-produced and starring Cantona as himself, tells the story of a United fan who imagines that Cantona is by his side, helping him to cope with life's challenges. The film aims to capture the special relationship Cantona had with the United fans – not those from Crystal Palace.

---

7 PUNCH & JUDY – A TWO-FOOTED TACKLE IN THE THANET & DISTRICT LEAGUE

A bad tackle in an amateur match in the Thanet & District League led to the Court of Appeal laying down the law.

In 2002, the full authority of the Court of Appeal led by the Lord Chief Justice, Lord Woolf, was called upon to opine on the role of the criminal law on football's 'field of play'. Not in a glamorous Premier League match but an incident at the recreation ground at Minster in Kent in an amateur match in the Thanet & District Football League. It may have been an amateur match but it was an ugly foul.

Minster were leading 2-0 with just over ten minutes left. A tussle took place near the corner flag as Minster striker, Chris Bygraves, attempted to waste time in the professional manner. Punch & Judy defender, Mark Barnes, fouled him clumsily. Barnes was told to 'grow up' by the referee.

Barnes was told to 'grow up' by the referee.

Shortly afterwards, Bygraves received a through ball near the penalty area which set up another goalscoring chance for Minster. Running towards the goalmouth, he shot with his left foot into the net. Just after he kicked the ball, Barnes tackled Bygraves crudely from behind; a bad two-footed tackle which caught the right ankle of the Minster striker. Bygraves heard a snapping noise and fell to the ground, suffering a serious injury to his right ankle and right fibula. Barnes allegedly said words to the effect: 'Have that.' Barnes was sent off for the crushing tackle.

Barnes was charged at Canterbury Crown Court of inflicting grievous bodily harm. The prosecution described it as a 'crushing tackle which was late, unnecessary, reckless and high up the legs.' Barnes claimed it was a 'fair, if hard, challenge' in the course of play and that any injury caused was accidental. Barnes was found guilty and ordered to give 240 hours community service.

Fortunately for Barnes, he was rescued by the Court of Appeal. His conviction was overturned because the judge's direction to the jury was not sufficiently clear as to the threshold to be reached before the criminal law applied. This was the important long-term aspect of the decision. Ruling the conviction 'unsafe', the Lord Chief Justice, Lord Woolf, stressed the significance of the case:

> *The issue which this appeal raises is an important one. It goes to the heart of the question of when it is appropriate for criminal proceedings to be instituted after an injury is caused to one player in the course of a sporting event, such as a football match.*

Most organised sports, he said, had their own disciplinary procedures for enforcing their particular rules and standards of conduct and therefore, in the majority of instances, there was no need for – and it was undesirable that there should be – any criminal proceedings when a player injured another player in the course of a sporting event. Lord Woolf said, a little unhelpfully, that a criminal prosecution should be reserved for 'those situations where the conduct is sufficiently grave to be properly categorised as criminal.' Importantly, he laid down the latest guidelines for deciding whether a criminal offence should be prosecuted:

The criminal law should not be triggered unless there was contact which 'was so obviously late and/or violent that it could not be regarded as an instinctive reaction, error or misjudgement in the heat of the game.'

A criminal prosecution should be reserved for situations where the conduct is sufficiently grave and goes beyond what the injured player could reasonably be regarded as having accepted by taking part in the sport in question – in other words, actions which are clearly outside 'the playing culture' of the particular sport. Factors to be taken into account include 'the type of sport, the level at which it is being played, the nature of the act, the degree of force used, the extent of the risk of injury' and the defendant's intention.

... a criminal prosecution should be reserved for those situations where the conduct is sufficiently grave to be categorised as criminal ...

Fine and sensible words but deciding when acts of violence or misbehaviour go beyond the 'playing culture' or 'the norms' of the sport is difficult. Does the playing culture of ice hockey include high stick challenges and brawling? How much 'hurly-burly' is acceptable in rugby? The judgment suggests that a significant degree of allowance within the criminal law should be made for the sporting context. As a result, it is probable that criminal prosecutions for 'field of play' incidents will be fewer in future and reserved only for very exceptional cases of violent behaviour – or where there is a public audience and a serious risk of public disorder or 'breach of the peace' arises as a result of the incident.

---

8 AN OBSESSED TENNIS FATHER – DOPING AN OPPONENT: A TRAGIC TALE

Christophe Fauviau's attempt to help his son to a victory in a local tournament led to a tragic death – and a manslaughter charge.

Parents of sporting children can be very demanding. Tennis parents can be notoriously pushy, intrusive and troublesome for tennis clubs and authorities. Jimmy Connor's mother was pretty outspoken. Mary Pierce's father, Jim, was so abusive he was banned by the Women's Tennis Association from attending tour events. Jelena Dokic's father, Damir, was amongst the most troublesome. At Wimbledon, Dokic was escorted by the police off the grounds after a brawl in which he smashed a journalist's telephone. Later in the year, he was banned from the US Open for unruly behaviour – one incident beginning with his outrage over the price of salmon in the players' cafeteria.

But a story from France went way beyond that level. It ranks as one of the saddest of sporting tales.

The background scene was a tennis club in Dax in south-west France, a sleepy town around thirty miles from Biarritz. It was the summer of 2003. Cristophe Fauviau, a forty-three-year-old former military officer, had become obsessed with the fortunes of his children as promising tennis players and often practised with them at the Dax club.

His thirteen-year-old daughter, Valentina, showed real promise and was amongst the highest ranked junior players in France. She had special coaching in Paris and was a junior international player; she later reached the top 500 in the junior world rankings. His son, Maxime, was two years' older. He was keen but not as talented as his sister. He was playing a number of local tournaments that summer.

Suspicions of foul play were first aroused in a semi-final of a competition in the nearby village of Bascon. A young player, due to play Maxime, apparently spotted Fauviau senior tampering with the player's drinks bottle shortly before the match. He decided not to drink from the bottle. He lost but still alerted officials after the match of the father's suspicious behaviour. Then, the following day, Maxime's opponent fell ill after the match (which Maxime won) and was taken to hospital where he was kept for two days. The local police investigated and took away suspect bottles for analysis.

Before detectives had completed their enquiries, the next week's evening tournament in a village near Dax was underway. Maxime was in the quarter-final and due to play Alexandra Lagardère, a popular twenty-five-year-old primary school teacher who was hoping in due course to become a qualified tennis umpire.

Fauviau accompanied his son. It was a muggy July evening. Fauviau offered to get water for the players as they prepared to go on court. After the first set of the match, Lagardère pulled out. He was feeling exhausted with the heat. He had a two hour nap at a friend's house before driving home at 11 p.m. He set off; his car left the road, hit a tree and he was killed. There were no skid marks.

The first prize was a modest sum of money and a leg of ham.

Maxime, incidentally, went on to win the tournament. The first prize was a modest sum of money and a leg of ham.

The laboratory tests on the water bottle taken from Maxime Fauviau's previous match revealed traces of Temesta, an anti-anxiety drug that can cause extreme drowsiness. Police then made the link between Fauviau and Lagardère. Postmortem tests showed that Lagardère's drink also had traces of Temesta.

Fauviau was arrested. He admitted to the drugging of Lagardère. He also admitted to doping the drinks of at least twenty-five players during matches against his son and daughter over a three-year period. It was never his intention to kill, he said. He realised that he had harmed people and that he would carry the burden of Lagardère's death for the rest of his life. His children knew nothing about their father's activities.

At his trial in Mont-de-Marsan in France, Fauviau was found guilty by a jury of manslaughter – unintentionally causing death by deliberately administering a toxic substance. He was sentenced to eight years in prison.

---

9 LEE BOWYER – BRAWLING WITH HIS OWN TEAM-MATE

Lee Bowyer's clash with his own Newcastle team-mate was an unedifying sight – but should the law intervene?

St James' Park, home of Newcastle United, has been the scene of many high points. In April 2005, Newcastle were losing 3-0 against Aston Villa before a crowd of 52,000 frustrated spectators. The next few minutes became one of the low points in Newcastle's history.

There were ten minutes left. Newcastle midfielder, Lee Bowyer, had not for the first time lost his temper. Extraordinarily, he suddenly headed – literally – towards his own team-mate, Kieron Dyer, on the halfway line. Bowyer pushed his head in the direction of Dyer's face. Brawling and punching took place between the two team-mates. Bowyer's frustration had reached boiling point. The reason? Apparently, Dyer had failed to pass to Bowyer when Bowyer thought he was in a good attacking position. Bowyer later said: 'Just a moment of madness and it happens.'

Dyer had failed to pass to Bowyer when Bowyer thought he was in a good attacking position.

Both players were sent off. Bowyer was banned by the Football Association for a further three matches in addition to his automatic four game suspension following his dismissal. He was also fined £30,000 by the FA and six weeks' wages by Newcastle, around £200,000. Bowyer was a 'bad boy' of football. The media had a field day reporting the latest incident.

Should the criminal authorities also intervene? What would be the purpose?

Well, they did. The case dragged on – partly because Bowyer tried to go to court to get the initial decision to prosecute overturned. Bowyer was eventually brought before the Newcastle Magistrates Court in July 2006, over twelve months after the incident. Although a charge of assault was considered, the Crown Prosecution Service eventually charged Bowyer with the lesser public order offence of using threatening behaviour likely to cause alarm or distress. He was found guilty and fined £600.

What was the point? Bowyer's counsel told the court that the prosecution was 'a bewildering response to what was a minor spat in which no one was injured and not one of the 50,000 people at the match complained.' Bowyer had pleaded guilty to avoid a lengthy trial which would have involved a number of his fellow professionals. Gordon Taylor, chief executive of the Professional Footballers' Association, criticised the court action as a 'total waste of public money. The incident was blown out of all proportion. Far more serious incidents occur almost weekly in sport and go unpunished.'

Police and the Crown Prosecution Service defended the decision to prosecute Bowyer. They had a duty to investigate after receiving complaints. 'The incident was not something arising from competitive contact sport. It was an argument that could just as well have arisen in the street.'

The police's concern was public order and, allegedly, the risk of such behaviour causing crowd disorder. This was the factor which took the case beyond the guidelines laid down by the Court of Appeal in the earlier Barnes case. As with the assault by Eric Cantona at Selhurst Park, the decision shows that disciplinary action 'within the sport' by an employer club or by a sporting regulatory body does not make a player immune from prosecution under the criminal law. The Chief Crown Prosecutor for Northumbria declared publicly after the decision:

> *The criminal law doesn't cease to operate once you cross the touchline of a sports field. Neither does being disciplined by an employer or a sport governing body make an athlete immune to the law. It's not only the spectators who have a responsibility to behave themselves, but also the players on the pitch.*

No doubt Bowyer's previous 'bad boy' disciplinary record and the high profile of the incident contributed to the decision to prosecute. But did the use of the criminal law really serve any useful purpose? To most, this was simply a waste of time.

In the summer of 2006 Lee Bowyer was transferred from Newcastle to West Ham. In one of football's ironies, West Ham under new manager Alan Curbishley made further signings in August 2007 to build up his team. One of his first signings was ... Kieron Dyer.

Curbishley said: 'I spoke to both players and have been assured that it was a one-off, and they both actually speak to each other regularly.'

Another, more serious, 'team-mate' incident in football concerned Manchester City's Joey Barton. Barton was charged with assaulting City team-mate Ousmane Dabo in a training ground bust-up in May 2007 which left Dabo with injuries to his eye, nose and lip requiring hospital treatment. This led to a suspended four-month jail sentence, £3,000 compensation order and 200 community hours service. Barton was transferred for £5.8 million in June 2007 ... to Newcastle.

---

10 AN ANGRY DANE – A COSTLY ATTACK ON A REFEREE

A drunken Danish fan was outraged at the referee's decision in the last minute of the Euro qualifier. The consequences were dramatic.

In England in 1995, Cantona leapt off the pitch, attacked a spectator and caused a furore. In Denmark in 2007, it was different. A spectator leapt on to the pitch, attacked a referee and caused a furore. It turned out to be a costly attack.

It was a Euro 2008 qualifier at the Parken Stadium in Copenhagen in June 2007. This was the first time that neighbouring Scandinavian rivals, Sweden and Denmark, had played each other in a European qualifying match. The match was never completed on the pitch. A drunken twenty-nine-year-old Danish 'fan' saw to that.

Sweden had taken a commanding 3-0 lead but a spirited Denmark fight-back in the second half brought the scores level at 3-3. The game entered the eighty-ninth minute. At least a draw had been salvaged to keep Denmark's hopes of qualifying alive. Swedish forward Markus Rosenberg and Danish defender Christian Poulsen were in an 'off-the-ball' tussle in the Danish penalty area, unseen by the referee. Rosenberg apparently elbowed Poulsen in the face. Poulsen retaliated by punching Rosenberg in the stomach and Rosenberg fell to the ground. The German referee, Herbert Fandel – who refereed the 2007 Champions League final between Milan and Liverpool – consulted his linesman. Fandel sent off Poulsen and awarded Sweden a last-minute penalty.

The spot-kick was never taken. As Fandel lowered his red card, the Danish fan, fuelled by beer and outraged by the referee's decision, managed to leap the low fence and headed towards the referee. Given his rather wobbly physique, the attacker moved with surprising speed. He attempted to grab the referee by the neck and started to punch him. He was restrained by Danish defender Michael Gravgaard and made it hurriedly back to the stands before being seized by ground stewards and the police. The referee, shaken by the incident, walked off with the other match officials and abandoned the match.

The Danish fan, fuelled by beer and outraged by the referee's decision, headed towards the referee.

What would be the consequences? For Denmark, it was all bad news. UEFA announced that Sweden would be awarded a 3-0 victory. The Danish FA were fined around €65,000 and ordered to play their next four home games at least 250 kilometres away from Copenhagen, with the next match against Lichenstein being played behind closed doors. One difficulty emerged. There was virtually no ground outside that radius, and still in Denmark, which could hold an international fixture.

'It seems that they didn't look at the geography when they made their decision. Denmark is a small country,' said a bemused spokesman from the Danish FA. On appeal, the fine was halved and the revised order was for two matches to be played at least 140 kilometres from Copenhagen – in fact allowing matches against Lichenstein and Spain to be played in Aarhus, just on the permitted limit. Sweden's 3-0 victory stood, however, rendering Denmark's chances of qualifying effectively at an end.

The attacker, when sober, rued his drunken interference. 'I haven't slept all night in my cell. The last thing I ever wanted was to hurt the national team. I want to say sorry to everyone in Denmark.' His identity was kept secret, for his own safety. One newspaper ran a campaign for information about him. 'Do you know this crook? This man is responsible for the Danish loss against Sweden.' He was later revealed as Ronni Norvig, a Dane working in Sweden.

Norvig was charged with attempted assault and trespass. He pleaded that, due to the consumption of between fifteen to twenty beers prior to the incident, he could remember little about the attack. He was initially sentenced to a thirty-day suspended prison sentence and ordered to serve forty hours community service. In December, he was less fortunate. A Copenhagen appeals court overturned the original sentence and replaced it with a straight jail sentence of twenty days.

This was not the end for the attacker. The Danish FA announced that it was seeking civil damages from Norvig of around €255,000 representing its lost income due to Denmark's next two Euro 2008 qualifiers being played, untelevised, behind closed doors together with legal costs. And the cost to Norvig could be even higher; the owners of the Parken Stadium were also reported to be claiming civil damages of around €940,000 for their loss of ticket sales as a result of the altered venue.

Crime on the playing field can be costly.

The plight of the referee was quickly turned in Denmark into an on-line video game shared over the internet. Translated: 'Try the game that lets you experience what referee Herbert Fandel witnessed in the now famous game between Denmark and Sweden. Watch out for the mad attacker and avoid being hit by Christian Paulsen. Avoid the mad attacker by shooting him using your left mouse button. Avoid being hit in the stomach by the footballer by moving with the arrow keys.'

A referee must be alert for the unexpected.

CHAPTER TWO

BETTING, BRIBERY AND CORRUPTION

The criminal law's interest in sport extends beyond acts of violence. More insidious and corrupt behaviour can undermine sport and fall foul of the criminal law. Many sporting scandals involving betting, bribery and corruption have, over the years, led their perpetrators – or alleged perpetrators – to the criminal courts.

Betting and sport have long been close, but uncomfortable, companions. The uncertainty of the outcome of a match or competition lies at the heart of sport's excitement. Gambling can, though, lead to temptation – the temptation to find improper ways of reducing that uncertainty, at worst of manipulating the result, for the benefit of the 'insider'. Bribery and corruption are great dangers which threaten the integrity of sport.

Our review in this chapter brings together scandals from across a range of sports: the 1919 baseball world series; the 1960s betting scandal which shook English football; a horse-switching scam in a race at Leicester; the revelations of Hansie Cronje regarding Test cricket; modern-day betting scandals in English, German and Italian football and, most recently, the prosecution of leading jockey Kieren Fallon.

---

11 1919 CHICAGO WHITE SOX 'PLEASE SAY IT AIN'T SO, JOE'

It was baseball's World Series. Was there a fix? The story, if true, would be shattering to the millions of followers of America's national game.

October 1919. Baseball enthusiasm was gripping the American nation after the war. At Redland Field, Cincinnati more than 30,000 spectators were excitedly awaiting the opening game in the World Series between the Cincinnati Reds and the Chicago White Sox.

The White Sox had one of the best teams ever to play the game with such players as star pitcher Eddie Cicotte, lead hitter Buck Weaver and one of the greatest hitters of his era, left-fielder 'Shoeless' Joe Jackson (nicknamed because he once played part of a game in blistered feet without shoes). Chicago were the hot favourites to win the Series. The game was a sell-out.

Cicotte pitched the first ball to Cincinnati's opening batter, Maurice Rath. It was called a strike. The second pitch was wide and hit Rath in the back. Was it deliberate? Was it a pre-arranged sign? Back in the lobby of the Ansonia Hotel in New York, reading the telegraphed play-by-play account of the game, Arnold Rothstein smiled. He was a prominent gambler. He knew the fix for the first game was on. A syndicate had financed a scheme involving up to eight Chicago players. All had been vulnerable to temptation – not only due to greed but also resentment. Although amongst the best players in the game, they were paid less under Chicago's dictatorial owner, Charles Comiskey, than players on many other inferior teams.

The White Sox had one of the best teams ever to play the game.

With the scores level in the opening game, a messed-up piece of fielding allowed Cincinnati to take the lead. The game ended with a 9-1 victory to the Cincinnati Reds. A similar sequence occurred in the second game. Chicago came back in the third and fourth games of the nine-game series. Was it because the players were unsure that they would be paid? Had the fix come unstuck? Or was it to make the score more respectable? Game five was notable for a throw from left field by Joe Jackson which was intercepted, clumsily, by Eddie Cicotte, preventing an 'out' and leading to a Cincinnati score. Cincinnati took the lead in the series. The Cincinnati Reds went on to win the World Series 5-3.

Rumours about the fix continued within the game through the winter months and into the 1920 season. The story finally broke publicly during an investigation into alleged match-fixing at a lesser league game. A player gave evidence which implicated the 1919 World

Series. It created a furore. The American sporting public was stunned. Baseball was the national game and the World Series was its pinnacle. A criminal grand jury investigation commenced. Eddie Cicotte decided to talk. 'Shoeless' Joe Jackson also confessed, in testimony to the grand jury, that he had been involved and that he had been given $5,000. He later asserted that he did not directly participate in any deliberate match-fixing.

On 22nd October 1920, indictments on counts of conspiracy to defraud were named against five gamblers (but not Rothstein) and eight Chicago players – Eddie Cicotte, 'Shoeless' Joe Jackson, Claude 'Lefty' Williams, Oscar Felsch, Arnold Gandil, Fred McMullin, Charles Risberg and Buck Weaver.

The case was heard in July 1921 in the Criminal Court of Cook County in Chicago before Judge Hugo Friend. The prosecution set the scene: 'The spectators wanted to see the great Cicotte pitch a ballgame. Gentlemen, they went to see a ballgame. But what they saw was a con game.'

'... they went to see a ball game... what they saw was a con game.'

However, certain of the players' confessions, including those of Cicotte and Jackson, had mysteriously been stolen or mislaid in the lead-up to the trial. (Many turned up later, after the trial, in the offices of Comiskey's lawyers.) The formal evidence available in court for the prosecution was thin. The trial lasted five weeks.

The jury took only two hours to reach their verdict. Not guilty. Hats and confetti flew in the courtroom from the still faithful supporters.

The consequences of the saga were considerable. With the game's integrity under severe question following the initial investigation, a new structure for the organisation of US baseball was created with the appointment of the first Commissioner of Baseball, the splendidly-named Judge Kenesaw Mountain Landis. As one of his first acts, Landis announced that, despite the jury verdict, all eight players were barred from organised baseball for life.

> *Regardless of the verdict of juries, no player who throws a ball game, no player who undertakes or promises to throw a ball game, no player who sits in confidence with a bunch of*

> *crooked ballplayers and gamblers, where the ways and means of throwing a game are discussed and does not promptly tell his club about it, will ever play professional baseball.*

The saga became known as the Black Sox scandal. To this day, participants in the scandal have been denied entry into the Baseball Hall of Fame.

The innocence of America's great game had been lost. One sad, and probably untrue, story was told in a local newspaper of a youngster going up to 'Shoeless' Joe Jackson on the steps of the courthouse after his grand jury appearance. He was tearful, pleaful, disbelieving, still holding on to his dreams: 'Say it ain't so, Joe. Please say it ain't so.'

The story of the 1919 series is written indelibly into America's sporting history. *Eight Men Out*, released in 1988, dramatised the scandal in a popular film based on Eliot Asinof's book published in 1963. Kevin Costner's 1989 movie *Field of Dreams* also revived the memory of the 1919 team. The film centred on a vision which the lead character, Ray Kinsella, had on his farm. He saw a baseball field in place of a cornfield and his father's hero, 'Shoeless' Joe Jackson, standing in the field. Ray uprooted his crop to make room for a baseball pitch. One summer night, 'Shoeless' returned in the vision along with other members of the 1919 Chicago White Sox team and they played a supernatural night game on Ray's pitch.

'Say it ain't so, Joe. Please say it ain't so.'

'Shoeless' Joe Jackson's career batting average is still one of the highest in baseball history and, although not inducted into the Baseball Hall of Fame, he is still ranked amongst the sport's greatest players. Jackson's last words before his death in 1951 were reportedly: 'I'm about to face the greatest umpire of them all and He knows I am innocent.'

---

12 SWAN, KAY AND LAYNE FOOTBALL'S SHOCK SIXTIES BETTING SCANDAL

It was a story which, in the 1960s, astonished the footballing public. Three players from Sheffield Wednesday, a top first division side, were accused of match-fixing.

A conversation took place one morning in late November 1962 over a cup of tea after training at top first division side Sheffield Wednesday. It was a conversation which, fifteen months later, would lead to the headline: 'THE BIGGEST SPORTS SCANDAL OF THE CENTURY.'

Sheffield Wednesday were then a top-ten first division side – and runners-up two seasons previously, in 1960/61, to the magnificent double-winning Tottenham Hotspur. David 'Bronco' Layne, Wednesday's centre-forward and one of the most prolific goalscorers in English football, led the conversation. He was sitting with Peter Swan and Tony Kay. Swan was the club's centre-half – a strong, talented player, superb in the air, with a trademark look of shorts hitched up at the waist. He was a regular England player; a first-choice member of the squad that travelled to Chile for the World Cup in 1960 although struck down by illness and destined not to play. Kay, red-haired, hard-tackling and full of energy, was a highly promising wing-half.

Rumours of match-fixing in the lower divisions of the Football League started to circulate in the 1960s. There had always been talk of isolated end-of-season promotion or relegation matches being suspect. Now, there were wider allegations and suspicions of more matches being 'fixed' to take advantage of the increase in betting on football – particularly after on-street betting shops were made legal in 1961. Betting firms offered 'fixed odds' for particular matches. A group of three matches, a 'treble', could offer more attractive odds. The bookmakers thought, though, that the risks of a 'treble' of matches being fixed were low. But were they? Despite certain rumours and questioning by the Football League, nothing concrete or widespread had surfaced.

Layne told the others that he had the previous evening been to see a match at his last club, Mansfield. He had bumped into an old team-mate, Jimmy Gauld. Gauld, originally from Scotland, had been around at a number of clubs including Charlton, Everton, Plymouth Argyle, Swindon, St Johnstone and Mansfield. He was a proven goalscorer until his career came to a premature end with a broken leg at Mansfield. It appeared that he was now using his network of contacts to assist a betting syndicate. Discussing the rumours that were around, Gauld confirmed that there was money to be made out of betting on football – especially 'fixed odds' betting on particular matches. Gauld put a proposal to Layne.

Gauld confirmed that there was money to be made out of betting on football.

Layne discussed the proposal with Swan and Kay over that tea-break. Gauld had arranged with players to fix matches at two lower-division games which he did not disclose (actually, Lincoln to lose at home against Brentford and York to lose at Oldham). He wanted a treble. No one would suspect a first division match. If Sheffield Wednesday were to lose their forthcoming match against Ipswich at Portman Road, they could make some money. A £50 bet would produce at least twice that sum in winnings.

Layne asked the others what they thought. 'Well, we usually lose anyway at Portman Road!' Each player agreed to stump up £50 for Layne to give Gauld to make the bet.

The first division match against Ipswich took place a few days later on 1st December 1962. Sheffield Wednesday were outplayed and lost 2-0 at Ipswich to two goals from Ray Crawford. Swan later said that he was trying throughout – but he did not know what he would have done if Wednesday had not been losing. Ipswich won fairly. Kay was named Wednesday's man-of-the-match by *The People*. The three players thought no more about it. It was a 'one-off' for them.

In 1963 *The People* started running a series of articles about bribes and match-fixing in football. They were, though, isolated cases. Three players confessed to throwing a Third Division match (Bradford Park Avenue against Bristol Rovers) and were each fined £50 at Doncaster Magistrates Court. One more case, Ken Thomson, of Hartlepool United, was exposed. The series of articles ended and most people thought that was the last of it.

Then, on a Sunday in April 1964, the dramatic headline appeared on the front page of *The People*: 'TOP SOCCER STARS BRIBED.' It was named: 'THE BIGGEST SPORTS SCANDAL OF THE CENTURY.' The paper had returned to its investigations. A sudden and totally unexpected new dimension had appeared. Now the paper named players with national reputations, players at the height of their careers in the first division. The unthinkable. *The People* had strong evidence against Gauld, the alleged ringleader. The paper wanted 'big names' for the story. Gauld had decided to go for a last big pay-day. In return for a fee in excess of £7,000, a small fortune then, he had told the story of that Sheffield Wednesday first division match and, in 'a shattering exposure', given the paper the top names they wanted.

'The Biggest Sports Scandal of the Century.'

The newspaper's evidence was handed to the police and the Director of Public Prosecutions. Supporters and footballers throughout the land waited, amidst growing tension and astonishment, to see whom would be prosecuted.

Bookmakers had allegedly lost more than £35,000 that December weekend. Swan, Kay, Layne and Gauld were charged with a criminal conspiracy to defraud. All four were found guilty at Nottingham Crown Court. Justice Lawton described Gauld as 'an unpleasant rogue' and 'the spider in the centre of the web'. Gauld was sentenced to four years' imprisonment and ordered to pay £5,000 costs. Swan, Kay and Layne were each sentenced to four months in prison and fined £150. Each was subsequently banned for life by the FA from playing football again. Six other players from clubs in the lower divisions, who were more deeply involved in betting activities than the players from Sheffield Wednesday, received sentences ranging from six months to fifteen months. The scandal has, nevertheless, always since been associated with the Sheffield Wednesday trio.

It was later revealed that Jimmy Gauld had been one of the players interviewed by the Football League when rumours started in 1961. No concrete evidence emerged, although Alan Hardaker later remarked: 'Although Gauld denied any knowledge of anything wrong, the firm impression was that he was not telling the truth.'

Before sentencing Gauld, Justice Lawton said:

> *Your crime has been great. It is my duty to pass a sentence on you to make it clear to all evil-minded people in all branches of*

sport that this type of activity is a crime and a serious crime ... You are responsible for the ruin of footballers of the distinction of Kay and Swan.

The People declared in its inimitable style: 'December 1st 1962 – soccer fans, and all who cherish the good name of British sport, should write that date in bold, black letters. It was the Day of Infamy for British football ... the ugly cancer of corruption spread its evil growth right up to the highest strata of soccer.'

Swan, Kay and Layne later played together for Thorp Arch Open Prison football team, much to the delight of the soccer-mad governor.

Swan's ban was lifted by the FA after seven years following support from such figures as Matt Busby and Joe Mercer who wrote to *The Times*. At the age of thirty-six, Swan had one further year at Sheffield Wednesday. He received a great welcome from the crowd on his return against Fulham, which Wednesday won 3-0. He then transferred to Bury where he helped them to promotion from the old third division. He later led Matlock Town to the FA Trophy as player-manager.

Kay was transferred in that same 1962 season to Everton for a fee of £60,000. It was a record fee, making him England's most expensive footballer. He played forty-four times for Everton, when they won the league title in 1962/63, before the exposé broke.

Evidence at the trial included tape-recordings of incriminating conversations with Layne and Kay which Gauld had secretly obtained for the newspaper. This was one of the first times that such taped evidence, obtained in secret, had been used in a criminal court. Kay apparently later spent a day in London – at the invitation of the Kray twins – explaining how such evidence had been obtained and used.

---

13 *FLOCKTON GREY* – A 20-LENGTH WIN – BUT FOR WHICH HORSE?

The grey galloped away to win a two-year handicap race at Leicester. But was the horse a two-year-old?

A cold, wet Monday at Leicester was the setting in 1982 for a horse-racing 'who-dunnit' worthy of a Dick Francis novel.

The Flat season had just begun in March. The first race on the card at Leicester was the Knighton Auction Stakes over five furlongs for two-year-olds. One of the ten runners was *Flockton Grey*. The horse, a gelding by *Dragonara Palace* out of *Misippus*, was entered for his first race as a two-year-old.

'It would make a very good book, a good detective story.'

Flockton Grey was trained by Stephen Wiles, a thirty-four-year-old former jump jockey, at Langley Holmes Stables in Flockton, Yorkshire. Wiles' record as a trainer was undistinguished. He had never had a winner on the Flat. *Flockton Grey* had been bought as a yearling for 1,700 guineas by its current owner, Ken Richardson, a Yorkshireman whose self-made fortune had been founded on a sacks and paper business. Despite the horse's lacklustre background, there seemed to be plenty of betting interest and *Flockton Grey* was surprisingly well-backed at Leicester at a starting price of 10-1.

To even greater surprise, including that of his jockey, *Flockton Grey* galloped away to win the race by twenty lengths. Or did he? The exceptional margin of victory caused suspicion and the Jockey Club launched an investigation. As Judge Henry Bennett QC later addressed the jury in York Crown Court: '... this case is both curious and fascinating and you may have thought more than once this would make a very good book, a good detective story.'

George Edmunson, an investigator with a security firm on behalf of the Jockey Club, arrived at Langley Holmes Stables. There was a grey two-year-old gelding at the yard. A blood test established, almost certainly, that the horse's blood line was *Dragonara Palace* out of *Misippus*. But it was not the horse that won at Leicester! The 'passport' for the *Flockton Grey* at Leicester described a horse with a conspicuous scar on its off-fore leg below the knee. The grey in Wiles' yard had no such scar.

Wiles told the investigator that *Flockton Grey* was probably at another stables, seventy miles away, owned by Richardson. Another stables to visit. Edmunson drove there. But there was no sign of a grey gelding. *Flockton Grey* had vanished.

Then, a stroke of luck. Subsequent examination of one of the official photographs at Leicester revealed a photograph of the winning horse of the Knighton Auction Stakes with its mouth wide open. Teeth are a distinctive guide to age in a young horse. Veterinary examination of a blown-up photograph indicated that the winner was almost certainly a three-year-old horse – not a two-year-old. The search was now on for a three-year-old with a scar on its off-fore leg!

The search was now on for a three-year-old with a scar on its off-fore leg!

Certificates, forms and records were examined in the search for such a horse. Candidates were eliminated – leading to one probable 'suspect'. After further investigation, it was discovered with virtual certainty that the winner at Leicester had been an experienced three-year-old grey named *Good Hand,* a horse owned by an associate of Ken Richardson, a horse with a respectable racing record. The mystery was nearly solved. It appeared that a naming form and certificate had been signed, and a passport subsequently issued by Weatherbys in January 1982, for a horse in the name of *Flockton Grey* bearing the markings of *Good Hand* but with a date of birth indicating that the horse was a two-year-old. By a complex set of arrangements, the horse racing at Leicester under the name of *Flockton Grey* had not been the unpromising foal but the experienced *Good Hand. Good Hand* was eventually traced to a remote field at Glaisdale, near Whitby, eight months after the race.

Further investigations revealed that bets, spread around betting shops in Yorkshire and placed by associates of Richardson, had backed 'the ringer' to win over £200,000.

Richardson, along with his racing manager and his horse-box driver, was charged with conspiracy to defraud. The case rumbled on until a five-week trial at York Crown Court ended in June 1984. Richardson was convicted by a majority verdict of the jury. He was given a suspended nine-month prison sentence and fined £20,000.

Following the conviction, the Jockey Club announced that Richardson had been 'warned off' from racing for an unprecedented period of twenty-five years.

No suspicion was attached to the jockey, Kevin Darley. A former champion apprentice, Darley would surely have won by less than twenty lengths if he had been part of the scam.

Ken Richardson, as many in Doncaster will remember without pleasure, later re-surfaced as the benefactor of Doncaster Rovers Football Club in the 1990s. Although not a director, his friend Ken Haran (who had placed a number of bets earlier for Richardson on *Flockton Grey*) was chairman. Richardson's daughter and niece were directors. His influence at the club was all-pervading.

In June 1995 there was a fire in the main stand at Doncaster. Arson was suspected. After a search of the club's offices, Richardson was arrested and charged with conspiracy to burn down the stand in order to collect the insurance money. Sheffield Crown Court was told that Richardson had offered £10,000 to a former SAS soldier to start the fire. Unfortunately for Richardson, his accomplice left his mobile phone at the scene and was easily traced. Richardson was convicted and sentenced to prison for four years.

... his accomplice left his mobile phone at the scene and was easily traced.

Extraordinarily, in 2006 – twenty-one years after his conviction – Richardson obtained leave to appeal the original verdict from the *Flockton Grey* 'ringer' trial. He claimed that the prosecution had failed to disclose evidence which would have cast doubt on the accuracy of the photographs identifying the 'ringer' as *Good Hand*. The Court of Appeal listened but said there was no meaningful new evidence. The conviction stood.

---

14 BRUCE GROBBELAAR – BRILLIANT SAVES – INSPIRED OR UNINTENTIONAL?

The headlines in The Sun *were astonishing. Were there really links between Bruce Grobbelaar and an Asian betting syndicate to fix matches?*

The sell-out crowd enjoyed a dramatic match at Anfield between Liverpool and Manchester United in January 1994 in the FA Premier League. It was a match to be remembered – a match which would later be replayed, on videotape, in Winchester Crown Court.

Liverpool were losing 3-1 at one stage but pulled back to level the score. Bruce Grobbelaar was Liverpool's long-standing and sometimes eccentric goalkeeper. Who could forget his 'wobbly-legs' routine as Roma's Francesco Graziani missed his crucial kick in the penalty shoot-out when Liverpool won the European Cup Final in 1984? Grobbelaar made two terrific second-half saves against Manchester United: first from a shot from Ryan Giggs and then a powerful half-volley from Roy Keane struck his hand as United were thwarted. The result was a thrilling draw.

It was a match which would later be replayed, on tape, in the Winchester Crown Court.

After the end of the 1993/94 season, though, Grobbelaar's fantastic career at Liverpool had come to an end. Thirteen seasons, more than 600 appearances, six league titles, a European Cup victory, three FA Cups and three League Cups had made him, in his words, 'the most decorated goalkeeper in the league'. Grobbelaar had been transferred to Southampton and was enjoying an extension to his playing career. In another lively match in early November that year, at Maine Road, Southampton drew 3-3 away with Manchester City.

Then, four days later, the world of football was astonished. *The Sun* published a series of articles concerning Grobbelaar. *The Sun* alleged that Grobbelaar, along with Wimbledon goalkeeper Hans Segers, had been accepting payments through middlemen – including former Wimbledon and Aston Villa striker John Fashanu and a Malaysian,

Heng Suan Lim – on behalf of an Asian gambling syndicate. Tipped off by a former business partner of Grobbelaar with whom he had also served in the Rhodesian army, Chris Vincent, the paper contrived a 'sting' operation resulting in secret audio and videotape evidence of an extraordinary meeting between Grobbelaar and Vincent in a hotel room in Southampton.

Grobbelaar was seen apparently taking cash from Vincent.

The conversation seemed to be evidence of corruption. Was Grobbelaar building a 'nest egg' for his retirement? After initial talk about women, football and the old days of their failed safari business in Zimbabwe, the conversation turned to other matters. Grobbelaar appeared to be admitting that he had accepted a payment of £40,000 from a syndicate to make sure Liverpool lost to Newcastle in a league match the previous year. He also said that he blew the chance of making £125,000 when he 'accidentally' made two 'blinding saves' to defy Manchester United in that match at Anfield.

When with Southampton, he said that he had deliberately let in an early goal against Coventry before Southampton stormed back. Vincent was trying to interest Grobbelaar in 'working' for another Asian syndicate. Grobbelaar was seen apparently taking £2,000 in cash from Vincent as first of a series of advance payments for rigging future matches.

It was devastating. It appeared that Premier League matches were being fixed. It was the biggest media story of betting and alleged corruption in football since the scandal of the 1960s. An investigation, called 'Operation Navaho', was launched by the police. In March 1995 Grobbelaar was arrested and, along with Lim, Fashanu and Segers, charged with conspiracy to corrupt by giving or accepting money for improperly influencing or attempting to influence the outcome of certain football matches. Grobbelaar alone faced a separate charge of accepting a corrupt payment, on the basis of the 'sting' operation, on behalf of another (in fact fictitious) syndicate. The case went for jury trial before Justice Tuckey at Winchester Crown Court.

The trial started in January 1997 in Court Three, the same courtroom used for the Rosemary West mass-murder trial a year or so earlier, amidst continuing media frenzy. Grobbelaar pleaded not guilty. He claimed, rather extraordinarily, that he was only stringing Vincent along in order to gather evidence on his former associate's affairs with the intent of taking it to the police. He was himself trying to entrap Vincent. 'I was returning to my days in the bush. As a tracker, you are out in front, doing your own thing, trying to find people.' As for his dealings with Lim, he said that he only gave 'advice' or 'forecasts'. He never 'fixed' or threw a match.

'I was returning to my days in the bush.'

Curtains were drawn in the courtroom. The jury were entertained to excerpts of the goalmouth action in a number of matches, including the full ninety minutes of the 3-3 draw against Manchester United at Anfield. No evidence was produced that Grobbelaar had actually played in a way which amounted to match-fixing. Witnesses included 1966 England goalkeeper Gordon Banks. (Grobbelaar's counsel raised laughter in the court when he asked Banks why he had not caught the ball when making his famous save from Pelé in the 1970 World Cup!) Banks, in his statement, said that he had studied the videotapes of the relevant matches and that, in his opinion, Grobbelaar had played in a 'thoroughly professional and competent manner.' Jimmy Armfield could see nothing untoward. Southampton manager and former World Cup player, Alan Ball, said that he had had no hesitation in continuing to pick Grobbelaar after his arrest. Other witnesses included Ron Atkinson, Alan Hansen, Nigel Clough and Bob Wilson. The Wykeham Arms in Winchester became a popular meeting point after the day's events.

After a trial lasting eight weeks, the jury were out for nearly eleven hours. They failed to reach a verdict on any of the charges. A re-trial was ordered. It began again in June 1997. After a forty-five-day retrial of evidence, followed by more than twenty-six hours of deliberation spread over five days, the second jury of six women and five men eventually reached a verdict on the main charges. The atmosphere was tense. 'Not guilty.'

The jury were still undecided on the separate charge against Grobbelaar based on the £2,000 received during the 'sting' operation. After a further three hours deliberation the following day, still no agreement. Judge McCulloch directed the jury to be dismissed and the prosecution withdrew the charge. That, after all the media frenzy, was the end of the criminal case.

Subsequently, Grobbelaar made (as it later turned out) a major mistake. In the light of the criminal verdict, he decided to proceed with a libel action against *The Sun*. It opened in the High Court in July 1999. The jury found in Grobbelaar's favour with an award of damages of £85,000.

The Sun appealed. The Court of Appeal overturned the lower court's decision on the grounds that the jury's verdict was 'perverse'. Lord Justice Simon Brown said that it represented a 'miscarriage of justice which this court can and must correct'. He found Grobbelaar's explanation 'quite simply incredible'. It was the first time that a jury verdict in a libel case had been set aside as a perverse finding. But this was not the end. The case was eventually appealed to the House of Lords, the highest court in the land.

The House of Lords technically re-instated the verdict of libel – but gave Grobbelaar nothing. They decided that, although the specific allegations of match-fixing had not been proved, there was strong evidence of dishonesty on Grobbelaar's part. Grobbelaar had acted 'in a way in which no decent or honest footballer would act'. It was a damning verdict. Grobbelaar no longer had any reputation which could be damaged.

Lord Bingham remarked:

> *It would be an affront to justice if a court of law were to award substantial damages to a man shown to have acted in such a flagrant breach of his legal and moral obligations.*

The House of Lords slashed Grobbelaar's award of damages to £1 and ordered him to pay *The Sun*'s legal costs, estimated at £500,000.

Grobbelaar was unable to pay the costs and was later declared bankrupt in England. 'The Britons bankrupted me. I came to their country with £10 in my pocket and they gave me £1 back. But in between I had one hell of a ride.'

Grobbelaar was never far from incident. During his initial trial at Winchester, he was permitted by the judge to go to Harare one weekend to play for Zimbabwe against Ghana in an Africa Nations' Cup qualifying match. The game, which ended in a draw, was notable for being halted just before half-time when a swarm of bees flew over the ground – forcing the players to crawl off the pitch with shirts over their faces to avoid being stung.

A month after being cleared, Grobbelaar was appointed head coach of the Zimbabwe national team and returned to South Africa. He came back to England in 2006 to play, for charity, in a replay of the 1986 FA Cup Final against Everton. Liverpool won 1-0.

---

15 FLOODLIGHT PLOT AT THE VALLEY – STRANGE GOINGS-ON AT EVENING MATCHES

Floodlights suddenly failed at matches at Upton Park and then Selhurst Park. Was this a coincidence?

We stay in football and we continue with an extraordinary tale of floodlights, fixing and another Asian betting syndicate.

The story started at Upton Park, home of West Ham United, in November 1997. An exciting evening match in the Premier League was in progress against relegation-threatened Crystal Palace. Crystal Palace had surprisingly taken a 2-0 lead. West Ham fought their way back to 2-2 with an equaliser in the sixty-fourth minute. One minute later, the lights at Upton Park suddenly failed, plunging players and fans into darkness. The referee finally called the match off after a thirty-minute wait.

Next, to Selhurst Park in south London later in the same year for another Premier League match. Lowly Wimbledon were playing against Arsenal. A dogged Wimbledon were holding on to a 0-0 scoreline at half-time. Suddenly, just fifteen seconds into the second half, the floodlights failed. Despite a restart, they went out again – and the match was abandoned.

Just fifteen seconds into the second half, the floodlights failed.

Then on to The Valley, again in south London, in February 1999. Charlton Athletic were due to play Liverpool. The police received a tip-off. Three days before the evening match, three men were caught 'red-handed' by the police on the premises at The Valley and were arrested on suspicion of burglary. They were Wai Yuen Liu, from west London, and two Malaysians, Eng Hwa Lim and Chee Kew Ong.

A search of Liu's car and the Malaysian pair's hotel room revealed electrical devices designed to sabotage the floodlights and capable of being triggered by remote control. There was enough equipment to wreck the lights at another eight matches. It now seemed likely that the earlier events at Upton Park and Selhurst Park had been part of a pattern of sabotage.

How did the gang gain access? At The Valley, the criminal gang were assisted by a local security supervisor, Roger Firth, who was paid £20,000 for letting the saboteurs into the ground. His failed attempt to bribe a fellow security guard led to the uncovering of the plot.

Little did fans in England realise at that time that the earlier floodlight failures at Upton Park and Selhurst Park had almost certainly been part of a plot hatched thousands of miles away in Malaysia. The international popularity of Premier League football as a subject of betting in Asia was becoming apparent. The floodlight plot was a scam by an Asian betting syndicate to fix English premiership matches. How did the 'fix' work? Under Malaysian betting custom, the result – and bets made – stood if a match was abandoned at any stage after half-time. This allowed the betting syndicates 'in the know' to rake in huge sums on rigged matches – particularly where a small club was doing well against a large club.

The floodlight plot was a scam by an Asian betting syndicate.

The FA ordered immediate checks to be carried out of floodlights at all Premier League grounds prior to the following weekend's fixtures.

The scale of the crime started to become clearer to the Metropolitan Police Organised Crime Group investigating the case. The insatiable appetite in Asian countries for sports betting, perhaps disillusioned by the blatant match-rigging and corruption in Malaysian football prevalent during the 1990s, had now focused on the Premier League. The police believed that, after the unwelcome publicity of the match-fixing trials involving Bruce Grobbelaar, Hans Segers and John Fashanu, the efforts of certain Asian gangs had moved to technical sabotage. If the floodlight plot had succeeded, it could have netted millions for the criminals.

The saboteurs caught in England, along with the Charlton security guard, were eventually charged with conspiracy to cause a public nuisance. The trial was held at Middlesex Guildhall Crown Court. They were convicted. Ong and Lim were each jailed for four years, Liu for thirty months and Frith for eighteen months. Judge Evans told Lim and Ong:

> *People who live within the jurisdiction of this court derive much pleasure from following professional sport... You were partners in a highly professional, technical criminal operation for which you were no doubt going to be paid a substantial financial reward...*

The FA, perhaps a little optimistically, declared: 'With the outcome of today's trial, a clear message has been sent to anybody intending to use football as a vehicle for criminal activity.'

In both replayed matches, normal service was resumed. West Ham beat Crystal Palace 4-1 and Wimbledon lost 1-0 against Arsenal. Arsenal went on to become champions that season and Crystal Palace were relegated.

---

16 HANSIE CRONJE – A FALL FROM GRACE AND CRICKET'S SHAME

An alleged mobile phone call between Hansie Cronje and an Indian bookmaker would have a shattering effect on the world of cricket.

'Hansie is a god-fearing, intense cricketer. He would never succumb to such a thing. It beggars belief.' Bob Woolmer, then South Africa's coach, expressed the opinion of virtually everyone in cricket.

Rumours of match-fixing in cricket had by the late 1990s been circulating for a number of years. Stories proliferated as one-day matches became ever more popular. Many of the rumours involved players or gambling syndicates in the subcontinent of India, Pakistan and Sri Lanka. How much of this was real? How far did match-fixing extend in the game?

It was the fifth and final Test of the series between South Africa and England in January 2000 which first raised questions in the minds of some English observers that irregularities might also lie closer to home. The match was at Centurion Park, near Pretoria, with South Africa 2-0 up in the series. The Test, with South Africa opening the batting, was badly affected by rain with three days lost. A draw was certain. Before the final day's play, Hansie Cronje, the South African captain, surprisingly offered to declare and forfeit South Africa's second innings if England would do likewise and, in effect, forfeit their first innings. England's captain, Nasser Hussain, accepted the unexpected opportunity to salvage a win. South Africa declared leaving England to chase 249 runs. This was the first time in Test cricket that each side had forfeited an innings. England went on to win the match by two wickets in a dramatic finale. Many applauded Cronje's initiative. Others were not so sure.

It was the first time in Test cricket that each side had forfeited an innings.

Hansie Cronje was one of the most respected men in cricket. Known for his strong religious beliefs, he wore a wristband inscribed with the letters WWJD for 'What Would Jesus Do'. The thirty-year-old South African captain was regarded as embodying the true spirit of the game: unrelentingly competitive but always sporting. A shrewd strategist and an inspirational leader, he was a sporting ambassador for post-apartheid South Africa.

Cronje's record as captain was very good. Under his 53 tests as captain, South Africa won 27 Tests and only lost 11. His captaincy of one-day internationals resulted in 99 wins out of 138 with one match drawn. He had the best win-ratio of all contemporary national captains in one-day internationals during this period. Bob Woolmer, as South African coach, would later say: 'He was the best captain I had the pleasure of working with. He was a real leader of men. They would have walked off Table Mountain for him.'

On 7th April 2000 came the bombshell. Police in Delhi revealed that, after a tip-off, they had taped a mobile phone conversation between Hansie Cronje and an Indian bookmaker, Sanjay Chawla, during the one-day series earlier that year between India and South Africa. The transcript revealed a corrupt plan to 'rig' performances by certain players in one of the matches. The astonishment was not just the revelation of possible corruption but total disbelief that Cronje could be involved. Delhi police confirmed that three other players, Herschelle Gibbs, Nicky Boje and Pieter Strydom, were also under investigation.

Cronje firmly denied the allegations. Ali Bacher, managing director of South Africa's United Cricket Board (UCBSA), backed his captain: Cronje was known 'for his unquestionable integrity and honesty'. Four days later came the defining moment. Cronje called Ali Bacher at 3 a.m. to inform him that he had not been 'entirely honest' about his comments and that he had accepted money from an Indian bookmaker for 'providing information and forecasting'. Bacher was shattered.

Cronje called Ali Bacher at 3 a.m. to say that he had not been 'entirely honest.'

Cronje was promptly sacked as South African captain. Bacher said: 'We in South African cricket are shattered. We... have been deceived.'

The police investigation in India triggered an international reaction. Over the next weeks and months, numerous enquiries and investigations took place worldwide. Criminal charges were brought against Cronje in Delhi alleging cheating, forgery and criminal conspiracy. The charges have never been closed. Back in South Africa, the criminal authorities questioned Cronje. He was granted immunity from criminal prosecution there but only on condition that he told the whole truth about his involvement in the affair.

UCBSA, together with the South African Government, set up a commission to carry out an enquiry into match-fixing and related matters affecting South African cricket. The enquiry was led by Judge Edwin King. It was standing-room only in the wood-panelled room as the hearings of the King Commission commenced in June. The next few weeks were sensational. Hansie Cronje read out his statement. He told Judge King that he had 'an unfortunate love of money'. He admitted that he had been talking to bookmakers and others involved in match-fixing since 1995 and had accepted around $140,000 from bookmakers over this period. Amongst his confessions:

He had been asked for match information and had supplied team selections and daily forecasts when India toured South Africa in

1996-97. In the second Test, Cronje had told the score at which South Africa would declare.

Cronje admitted that he had accepted money (around $7,000) and a gift (a leather jacket) in January 2000 during that fifth Test with England at Centurion Park. Cronje said he had been approached by a bookmaker named 'Marlon' to make an early declaration to ensure the game had an outcome. He was promised a larger sum, to be paid into a charity, but it never materialised.

He had offered bribes to certain players to underperform in a one-day international in India's Nagpur City during South Africa's 2000 tour: Herschelle Gibbs (by scoring less than 20 runs) and Henry Williams (by conceding more than 50 runs as a bowler).

Cronje said that he had 'taken his eyes off Jesus' when Satan approached him. He continued to deny, though, that he had ever fixed a result or deliberately lost a game. Was all revealed to the King Commission? Or was it worse? Was Cronje simply being more honest than most others in his admissions and the scapegoat for more widespread troubles in the game?

In October, Cronje was banned for life by the South African Cricket Board from playing cricket and having any future involvement in cricket-related activities. UCBSA said:

> *Hansie Cronje acknowledged accepting money from bookmakers as well as attempting to induce others in his team to underperform. The actions... cut across the foundation of trust placed in a person in such a position of integrity. In our opinion, his actions have harmed the good name of cricket in South Africa.*

President Nelson Mandela met him: 'It is my duty to say to him 'you have made a serious mistake'.'

The only legal action involving Cronje which actually reached the courts was his challenge to this lifetime ban. He argued that it constituted an unreasonable restraint of trade. In September 2001 his campaign opened in the Pretoria High Court to get the life ban overturned. He claimed that he had not been given a fair hearing and that the ban interfered with his attempts to earn a living including by coaching at grass-roots level. The UCBSA contended that it was perfectly entitled to decide that neither it nor its affiliates would associate with Cronje any longer.

Judge Frank Kirk-Cohen upheld the life ban. However, the court clarified that the ban could not apply to coaching at schools not affiliated to UCBSA. It also confirmed that Cronje was free to attend matches as a spectator and report as a print journalist – although he could be denied media accreditation and associated facilities.

The effect on cricket worldwide was traumatic. The game examined its very heart and soul. Investigations were held by the cricket authorities in Pakistan, Australia, India, England, New Zealand, Sri Lanka and the West Indies. Two other former national captains, Mohammed Azharuddin of India and Salim Malik of Pakistan, were also banned for life. Importantly, an Anti-Corruption Unit was set up under Lord Condon by the International Cricket Council (ICC). It reported on 'silence, apathy, ignorance and fear' in the game and gave a wide-ranging and disturbing analysis of corruption in international cricket.

The ICC announced new regulations and potential bans which would apply to any player, umpire, referee, team official or administrator involved in betting on any match in which he takes part or in which his country is represented. Attempting to contrive the result of a match (i.e. match-fixing) would result in a life ban.

Wisden summed up the saga simply. Hansie Cronje's 'admission that he took bribes from bookmakers to provide information and fix matches exposed the extent of a corruption scandal that cricket authorities had signally neglected to confront.'

In June 2002 a light plane, carrying Hansie Cronje as a passenger, crashed during bad weather into a mountain near George in South Africa's Western Cape province. Cronje and the two pilots were killed. Despite conspiracy theories, an inquest eventually judged that the air crash had been due to pilot error.

Nelson Mandela said in a statement: 'Here was a young man courageously and with dignity rebuilding his life... The manner in which he was doing that... promised to make him once more a role model of how one deals with adversity.'

---

17 ROBERT HOYZER – 'THE REFEREE'S BEEN BRIBED!'

Questionable decisions helped a German third division side beat Hamburg in the Cup. Had the referee been bribed?

Ante Sapina and his two brothers were well-known at the Café King in Berlin. It was a popular night spot. Sapina, a Croatian, ran a sports betting agency. The police had been keeping any eye on the Sapina family. They were key members of a gambling syndicate suspected of criminal activities. But who was the tall fair-haired man who often joined them for cocktails?

Most football fans have thought it when refereeing decisions go against their team: 'The referee's been bribed.' In 2004 a story broke of actual bribery of a referee at the heart of German football. It was Hamburg's visit to play Paderborn which triggered the discovery of the scandal. Paderborn, close to an army base in northern Germany for American and British forces, was a focal point for American sports in Germany. Its baseball, American football and basketball teams had all achieved considerable success – but not its soccer team. Paderborn was then just a third division side in the German league.

The 21st August 2004 was, however, a big day for Paderborn football club. Their supporters were looking forward to a first-round cup tie against Hamburg SV, a leading Bundesliga club. The referee was Robert Hoyzer. Twenty-five-year-old Hoyzer, 6 feet 5 inches tall and a distinctive figure with his fair hair, was one of Germany's best young referees although he had not yet refereed in the top division of the Bundesliga.

The match started predictably. Hamburg pressed forward and swept into an early 2-0 lead. Then, the course of the match changed. Late in the first half, after an innocuous foul, Hoyzer sent off Hamburg's Belgian international striker, Emile Mpenza, for repeatedly protesting the referee's decisions. Spurred on by having an extra man, Paderborn made a fight back. Hoyzer awarded them two questionable penalties in the second half. Paderborn went on to record an unexpected 4-2 victory, much to the delight of the local fans.

Behind the scenes, Hoyzer's performances had started to arouse questions. Four referees went to officials at the German football association with their suspicions. What did enquiries reveal? It was Hoyzer who had been having regular meetings at the Café King in Berlin with Ante Sapina and other members of a Croatian gambling syndicate.

The German FA were very concerned as they investigated further. They took the precaution of changing officials for many matches the day before the games were due to be played. They discovered that large sums of money had been bet on matches in which Hoyzer had refereed. Certain other referees and players also came under similar suspicion. Hoyzer was questioned by the German FA.

Hoyzer had been having regular meetings with members of a gambling syndicate.

After initial denials, Hoyzer broke down. He decided to co-operate with both football and criminal investigators. In late January 2005 he admitted to being paid to manipulate a number of games. He had received payments of more than €65,000 and an expensive new television set. In exchange, he agreed to help the authorities to uncover schemes implicating other officials, players and Croatian-based gamblers. The German FA fined Hoyzer €50,000 and banned him for life from German football.

Criminal action was also taken. Hoyzer was charged and convicted of fraud. The prosecutor sought only a suspended sentence in the light of his co-operation. However, the Berlin court was not impressed. Judge Gerti Kramer sentenced Hoyzer to prison for two years and five months. 'It wasn't a youthful misdemeanour but a serious crime.' Ante Sapina, who was alleged to have made more then €750,000 from Paderborn's victory, was also convicted and given a 35-month sentence. His brothers, Milan and Filip, were given suspended sentences. One other referee, Dominik Marks, was given a suspended eighteen-month sentence. There would be a few empty seats at the Café King in the months to come.

Hoyzer appealed against his sentence and was supported by the State prosecutor. However, a court in Leipzig did not agree. It confirmed Hoyzer's conviction and length of sentence. The President of the German FA, Theo Zwanziger, commented: 'The threat of two years in prison will make one or two people think before trying to influence a football match.'

It was Germany's biggest match-fixing scandal. The scandal was even more damaging since Germany were due to host the 2006 World Cup a year later. How deep did the rot go? The German FA acted promptly to reassure the public. Berlin prosecutors investigated a total of twenty-five people. Charges were only brought in respect of matches in the lower leagues. The scandal, it conveniently appeared, did not affect any matches or referees in the top division of the Bundesliga.

As a result of the Hoyzer case, the German FA decided to adopt new policies to prevent any similar betting schemes in the future. They imposed, effective for the 2005/06 season, a complete ban on betting on soccer matches by anyone associated with the sport – players, coaches, referees and other officials. Also, referees were assigned to matches with only two day's notice.

After review by the German FA, two of the suspect matches were replayed, with one match producing a win for the previously 'victimised' team, but most results were allowed to stand. By the time of discovery of Hoyzer's conduct, Paderborn had already been eliminated from the German Cup. The German FA paid Hamburg €2 million compensation for their loss in the 'rigged' match and agreed, in addition, to hold a friendly international at Hamburg. The German FA later filed a legal claim for damages (initially around €1.8 million) against Hoyzer to recover their legal costs and the settlement paid to Hamburg.

The German FA paid Hamburg €2m compensation for their loss.

After a hearing before a Berlin court, an out-of-court settlement was reached in 2008. Hoyzer agreed to pay a monthly sum of €700 for fifteen years as compensation to the German FA. The total will add up to €195,600 and will be given to charity by the federation.

All this exposé came too late for the Hamburg coach, Klaus Topmoeller. He was sacked a month or so after the defeat at Paderborn.

German supporters now have another term of abuse. When a referee makes a wrong decision, the fans chant 'Hoyzer!'

---

18 SERIE A SCANDAL – CALCIOPOLI: A TANGLED WEB WITHIN ITALIAN FOOTBALL

Secret recordings of conversations between Luciano Moggi, the general manager of Juventus, and refereeing organisations were released by the police. They revealed a scandal at the heart of Italian football.

The story broke in public in May 2006 as Juventus were heading for their twenty-ninth Serie A championship and Italy were preparing for the World Cup. A scandal at the heart of Juventus. A scandal, calciopoli, at the heart of Italian football. And at the centre of it all, a balding sixty-nine-year-old man with a taste for fine cigars and tailoring.

The scandal was exposed, to a large extent, by chance. The breakthrough came from investigations started by the criminal authorities – but into different allegations. In Naples, inquiries were taking place into an alleged illegal betting ring involving players and referees. Investigating magistrates had ordered phone taps on various people including a number of mobile phones belonging to Luciano Moggi, general manager of Juventus. In Turin, investigations also involving phone taps were taking place into doping allegations involving players from Juventus. In the meantime, in Rome, magistrates were investigating the affairs of GEA World, a footballing agency with close links to Juventus.

The phone taps revealed more than anticipated. Exposed by the recordings were conversations between club presidents and executives with representatives of refereeing organisations and with referees themselves. Conversations about appointments of referees for matches, favours to be done, help to be given. It was widespread and sinister. And everyone seemed to be friendly with Moggi. No club appeared to be more affected or involved than Juventus, the Old Lady of Italian football, the most glamorous and successful team in Italy.

The central figure was Luciano Moggi. He had become one of the most powerful figures in Italian football. Having worked as a deputy railway station master in a small Tuscan town in the early 1970s, he had moved into football. His charm, his successful scouting methods for a number of clubs (he is credited with helping to discover Paolo Rossi and Gianfranco Zola) and his good relationships with players and officials had enabled him to move to the top of the game. He was a good friend to have – and an enemy to avoid.

He was a good friend to have – and an enemy to avoid.

Juventus were the main club involved. Juventus were used to coming first. By 1994, they had won the Italian championship a record twenty-two times – but, by their standards, they were in a slump with only one championship success in nine seasons. Backed by the influential Agnelli family, owners of Italian car maker Fiat and a major shareholder in Juventus, the club turned to Moggi as new general manager and one of a fresh team to help bring them success. Along with chairman Antonio Giraudo and former player Roberto Bettega, the triad led Juventus over the next twelve years to seven Serie A titles and a Champions League trophy. In May 2006, another Serie A title was just a few days away.

Then, transcripts from the secretly recorded conversations were released to the public by the Italian police. The publication of a conversation between Luciano Moggi and Pierluigi Pairetto, the vice-chairman of UEFA's referees' committee, was a typical and stunning example. It was evidence of a 'Moggi system' more sinister than ever previously imagined, evidence of a system to appoint match referees who would favour Juventus.

Pairetto began: 'I know you've been forgetting about me, but I've been remembering you. I've put in a good referee for the Amsterdam game [against Ajax].'

'Who?'

'Meier.'

'Terrific,' said Moggi.

In alliance with other Juventus officials and key members of the Italian football federation, Moggi appeared to be influencing – and even controlling – the appointment of referees and other match officials for Italian and European matches through a vast network based on influence, pressure and reciprocal favours. He appeared to know about the appointment of some referees before their names were released by the Italian federation. The transcripts of more than

100,000 conversations, over eight months, were to provide the bulk of the evidence in the subsequent trials.

Police investigations in Naples and Turin revealed similar discussions involving other clubs. It became increasingly apparent that this was not just a one-club affair. It was all evidence of a tangled network of relationships between referee organisations and other major Serie A clubs such as AC Milan, Fiorentina and Lazio. The scandal had spread throughout Serie A. The investigating magistrates in Naples described it all as 'a cupola of power marked by alliances between the managers of some big clubs, agents and referees.' The presiding figure was Moggi.

Naples prosecutors later revealed that another series of telephone calls had been discovered involving Moggi and several referees. During the twenty-four-hour period before one match in 2004 between Juventus away at AC Milan, prosecutors discovered a series of thirteen telephone calls between Moggi and the referee. The match ended 0-0. Many calls were made using mobile phones with foreign SIM cards – Moggi alone was discovered to have had at least five foreign SIM cards.

The police handed all the materials to the Italian footballing authorities. The ramifications were wide-ranging, immediate and at the highest level. On 5th May, four referees were suspended. On 8th May, Franco Carraro, President of the Italian Football Federation, resigned. Two days later, his vice-president, Innocenzo Mazzini resigned; next, Tullio Lanese, the President of the Referees' Association. Even the presenter of a TV football show was forced to stand down after it appeared that slow-motion replays had been adjusted to suit Moggi's requests. At club level, the entire board of directors of Juventus resigned on 11th May.

The entire board of directors of Juventus resigned on 11th May. The club clinched their Serie A title three days later.

Meanwhile, just three days later, Juventus clinched their Serie A title with victory. Joyful celebrations took place amongst the crowd and the players. But it was an uneasy celebration. That same day, a tearful Luciano Moggi resigned and told the press: 'I miss my soul. It has been killed. From this day the world of football is no longer my world.'

On 23rd May, a seventy-six-year-old retired Italian judge, Francesco Borelli, was asked to take over the investigative affairs of the football federation. The criminal investigations continued in Naples, Turin and Rome. Italy was consumed by the scandal – even as the World Cup approached. Media interest was insatiable. Pages and pages were given over to the scandal. To some, the existence of such a web of corruption was not a shock – but, to most, the details of the extent of the network of influence, alliances and corruptive associations were astonishing. Some revelations were almost amusing – including referee Gianluca Papresta being locked in the dressing room by an angry Moggi after failing to award a penalty to Juventus in a match in 2004.

Borelli quickly completed his initial investigations and passed his findings to the sporting public prosecutor, Stefano Palazzi. In Italy, interestingly and effectively, prosecutions in sport are heard by a special sporting tribunal, a court where the level of proof required is less than in a criminal court. The sporting court was presided over by an eighty-one-year-old former judge, Cesare Ruperto.

The sporting trial began in Rome on 29th June, right in the middle of the World Cup in Germany. Palazzi laid out his charges to the court and asked for each of Juventus, AC Milan, Lazio and Fiorentina to be relegated – with Juventus' relegation being not just to Serie B but to Serie C. No witnesses were allowed. Each party argued its case. Each of the clubs professed its innocence – except Juventus who argued that a fair punishment would simply be relegation to Serie B.

In the World Cup, a few hundred miles away, Italy were meanwhile beating Germany in a spectacular semi-final with a winning goal from Alessandro Del Piero – of Juventus – to set up a final with France in Berlin on 9th July. In the final, with the score at 1-1 at full-time and Zidane sent off for his head-butt on Italy's Materazzi, the match went to penalties. France missed one and it was left to Fabio Grosso to smash in the winning spot kick. Italy had won their fourth World Cup. Captain Fabio Cannavaro – of Juventus, of course – lifted the trophy in his 100th game for Italy. Which league would he be playing in next season?

Juventus had been stripped of two Serie A titles and relegated to Serie B with a massive points deduction.

Just five days later, on a hot Friday evening in Rome, Cesare Ruperto read out the sentences of the trial. The shock was great. Juventus had been stripped of their two Serie A titles for seasons 2004/05 and 2005/06 and relegated to Serie B to start with a massive thirty-point deduction. Lazio and Fiorentina were also relegated. AC Milan avoided relegation but with a points deduction which removed them from European competition.

The verdict of the court was that this was not a case of match-fixing as such. There was, however, a network or system which operated outside of the rules in order to 'alter the impartiality of referees' and was 'contrary to the spirit of loyalty and integrity' which should be at the foundation of sport. Juventus were credited with at least getting rid of the culprits and promising a new ethical code. No players had been charged.

Each of the clubs appealed against their punishments, first to the football federation's appeal court and subsequently to the Italian Olympic Committee's Court of Arbitration (CONI). The final appeal verdicts were announced in July 2006. Each of the clubs received better news. The points deduction for AC Milan was reduced and they qualified for the Champions League. Lazio and Fiorentina were back in Serie A but with heavy point deductions. Juventus, though, remained relegated to Serie B but with a much lower points deduction (nine rather than the original thirty). Juventus briefly considered taking a further appeal to the courts but withdrew.

Punishments had been given to around twenty individuals. Luciano Moggi himself was given a five-year ban from football and fined around €50,000 with a further recommendation that he be banned for life from membership of the Italian football federation at any level. Antonio Giraudo (the Juventus chairman) was also given a five-year ban. Pierluigi Pairetto was given a two-and-a-half year ban from football.

Inter Milan were designated champions of Serie A for the 2005/06 season in place of Juventus. The saga was formally over. The Italian football public, most of the nation in other words, had been shocked by the scandal. Football would go on – but speculation would continue. Was all uncovered? Would Serie A recover? Would Juventus return to the top?

Other footballing consequences of the saga were considerable. Faced with significantly reduced revenues in Serie B, Juventus could not retain all their best players. They were forced to transfer such stars as Patrick Viera, Gianluca Zambrotta, Emerson and Lilian Thuram.

Fabbio Cannavaro, Italy's World Cup winning captain, joined Real Madrid. Manager, Fabio Capello, had also resigned and left for Real Madrid as the crisis unfolded – perhaps, but for calciopoli, he would not have become available to take over as England's manager at the end of 2007?

Over at rivals AC Milan, owner Silvio Berlusconi experienced mixed fortunes. The appeal verdict had conveniently enabled AC Milan to retain their place in the UEFA Champions League for 2006/07 – and, in one of football's ironies, the club went on to triumph in that competition beating Liverpool 2-1 in the final. As owner of television company Mediaset, though, Berlusconi saw the consequences of Juventus' relegation to Serie B – a significant drop in pay-TV revenues and a depreciation in the value of rights to its Serie A highlights. So much so, that Berlusconi threatened to sue the Italian FA!

As the 2006/07 season got underway, Juventus showed that they still had sufficient depth to overcome the nine-point penalty in Serie B. They won back their place in Serie A for 2007/08 after their one and only season in the lower division. The 2007/08 season ended with Juventus back in the top three in Serie A – and with fresh investigations, and charges, underway into Moggi's activities and those of other teams and officials. Have things really changed in Italian football?

---

19 KIEREN FALLON – RACING'S 'TRIAL OF THE CENTURY': A NON-RUNNER

Six-time champion jockey Kieren Fallon was facing charges of conspiracy to defraud. It was an investigation which cast a dark shadow of suspicion over the integrity of British racing.

It was a thrilling finish to the Prix de l'Arc de Triomphe at Longchamp in October 2007. Kieren Fallon showed all his riding skills and determination as he hit the front in the final furlong to win on *Dylan Thomas*. Waving an Irish flag, the man from County Clare received an emotional ovation in the winner's circle. Trainer Aidan O'Brien, for whom it was a first Arc triumph, was delighted: 'Kieren gave him a masterful ride and he is a master in the saddle.'

Less than twenty-hours later, on a Monday morning, the forty-two-year-old Irishman was in court 12 of the Old Bailey, London's Central Criminal Court, before Justice Forbes and a twelve-person jury in racing's 'trial of the century'. Fallon, six-time champion jockey on the flat in Britain and widely-regarded as one of the finest riders since Lester Piggott, was facing the trial of his life. His co-defendants were two jockeys, Fergal Lynch and Darren Williams, and three members of an alleged betting syndicate led by a professional gambler, Miles Rodgers. They were all charged with a conspiracy to defraud – a conspiracy to 'rig' the running of twenty-seven horse races and defraud punters betting on the online betting exchange, Betfair.

Fallon, perhaps the most talented horseman of his generation, had never been far from controversy. A shy man in public, he seemed to court trouble. He was suspended in 1994 for six months for pulling another jockey, Stuart Webster, from his horse in a race at Beverley. In 1998 he won a successful libel case against the *Sporting Life* over the riding of a horse called *Top Cees*. Public splits from leading trainers Henry Cecil and Sir Michael Stoute for personal reasons were to follow. But this was now a trial which could lead to the end of his career – and a trial which threatened the reputation and integrity of racing generally.

Fallon, perhaps the most talented horseman of his generation, had never been far from controversy.

It had already been a long-running saga by the time it came to the Old Bailey. A BBC *Panorama* programme in October 2002 on corruption in racing led to investigations by the Jockey Club. Materials and reports were handed over by the Jockey Club's investigation team to the police. Fallon and others were first arrested in September 2004. A long dark cloud of suspicion would hang over British racing for the next three years.

He was released on bail and not formally charged until 3rd July 2006 by the Crown Prosecution Service. Fallon was, three days' later, suspended by the Horseracing Regulatory Authority (HRA) from racing in Britain. An appeal board upheld this decision. Fallon took his challenge to the High Court. Why not innocent until proved guilty?

Having regard to the nature of the charges and the apparent evidence, the High Court decided that the HRA were entitled to conclude that there was sufficient substance to justify the suspension. The court recognised the HRA's 'duty to enhance the public perception of the integrity of the sport'. It was, with the benefit of hindsight, a hard decision. Fallon could not ride here in Britain – but was free to do so in Ireland and France which he did with continuing success culminating in his triumph at Longchamp.

At the Old Bailey in October 2007, the Crown Prosecution set off. At least the defendants were permitted to sit in the body of the court. A copy of the *Racing Post* was within reach. The prosecution's claim was that twenty-seven races were involved in the 'conspiracy' during a period from December 2002 to September 2004 and that a total of £2.12 million had been gambled by the syndicate on these races. Fallon had ridden in seventeen of these races. A system existed, it was alleged, whereby Fallon, Lynch and Williams would tip-off members of the syndicate and enable bets to be laid, through a large number of Betfair accounts, on specified horses to lose.

The most dramatic race spotlighted by the prosecution was at Lingfield in March 2004. The video was shown to an enthralled jury. Fallon came into the home stretch on *Ballinger Ridge*. He was leading by five or six lengths with two furlongs to go. Fallon dramatically slowed his momentum, never to recover, allowing another horse to win. Was it a deliberate fix – or an innocent blunder? On the day of the race, it was alleged that Fergal Lynch had been an intermediary for phone calls and text messages between Rodgers and Fallon. Rodgers had placed £72,000 on *Ballinger Ridge* to lose, allegedly winning him £26,599. A stewards' inquiry had later been held and Fallon was suspended for twenty-one days for easing up.

Was it a deliberate fix – or an innocent blunder?

Other evidence of supposedly rigged rides, and sinister off-course activities, was relayed to the court. There was a story of a plain-clothes officer being spotted one evening by Rodgers who was apparently on his way to Fallon's home near Newmarket and who changed his course when he thought he was being followed.

On another occasion, associates of Rodgers did visit Fallon shortly after Fallon, allegedly, had made a 'mistake' when he rode *Russian Rhythm* to victory in a prestigious race at Newbury in May 2004.

Rodgers had lost over £100,000 which he had laid on six Betfair accounts backing the horse to lose. Fallon's visitors, it was alleged, sought 'a more reliable working arrangement' with Fallon for stopping horses in the future.

Evidence was given of numerous phone calls from Fallon and Lynch on the eve of races to associates of Rodgers and others, many made on mobile phones not 'registered' with the racing authorities as required by rules introduced to protect the integrity of racing. Intriguingly, amongst many others, these included almost daily phone and text messages between Fallon and soccer's Michael Owen. Was this all evidence to support a conspiracy – or was it, in the later words of Justice Forbes, 'consistent with normal social interchange and innocent transmission of racing tips or information by the jockeys'?

The prosecution case foundered in three major respects. First, of the seventeen races in which Fallon was allegedly involved in a 'fix', Fallon actually won five of them. His win-ratio for these races (29.4%) was higher than his average overall win-rate (19%) during the period of the alleged conspiracy. Fallon's counsel made the most of this: 'The very fact... that the greatest jockey of his generation ends up being unable to help winning more often than when he is trying to win is simply ridiculous.' Rodgers' betting syndicate had actually lost £338,000 over these races! Secondly, there was no evidence that Fallon had himself profited in any personal way from the alleged conspiracy.

...there was no evidence that Fallon had himself profited

Thirdly, and crucially, the only expert witness for the prosecution was an Australian, Ray Murrihy, chief racing steward in New South Wales. He had studied all the videos of the races and determined that the rides were 'suspect'. Under cross-examination by Fallon's counsel John Kelsey-Fry QC (regarded by most as 'man of the match'), Murrihy admitted that he was not an expert nor knowledgeable in British racing rules, practices and culture. It was the turning-point of the trial. In the words of Justice Forbes:

> *This is an extraordinary admission, given that he was purporting to give evidence about twenty-seven races run in the UK according to UK racing rules. In my opinion, that was tantamount to Mr Murrihy disqualifying himself in giving evidence in relation to*

> *the suspect races... It is abundantly clear that his evidence fell far, far short of establishing a prima facie breach of UK racing rules... very little value can be attached to it.*

On 7th December 2007 the eleven-week trial suddenly collapsed. Justice Forbes formed the view that there was simply 'no case to answer'. The jury were so instructed and they formally declared Fallon and the other defendants 'not guilty'. The trial, which had cost an estimated £10 million, was over. The case had been thrown out. It was a non-runner.

The investigation had not all been a hardship for the police. Two police officers travelled to Australia to interview Murrihy, the expert witness. 'I remember it was December,' he said. 'They went to Bondi Beach and got sunburn.'

The collapse of the trial was both a relief and an embarrassment for British racing. A betting 'fix', involving one of Britain's leading jockeys and threatening serious damage to the reputation of British racing, had not been proven. The ability of the authorities to monitor betting patterns and to prosecute racing cases in court had, though, been thrown seriously into doubt. The reputation of the economic fraud unit of the City of London Police had suffered a major blow – the same unit investigating alleged corrupt dealings in football.

Kieren Fallon, who had been unable to race in Britain for seventeen months, expressed his anger but was less ebullient than might have been expected at the following press conference. 'I am of course relieved and delighted but outraged. There was never any evidence against me.' 'I am devastated at having lost over a year's racing at the top level. I have missed out on considerable income.'

'I am of course relieved and delighted but outraged.'

Within the day, it was announced that Fallon was in further trouble. It was reported that he had tested positive for cocaine following a race in August at Deauville in France. The B sample was still to be tested. Fallon had previously served a six-month ban in France for a similar offence in June 2006. An eighteen-month worldwide riding ban, and perhaps the effective end of his career, still loomed for the forty-two-year-old jockey.

CHAPTER THREE

SPORTSMEN, CRIME AND PRIVATE LIVES

Sportsmen have high profile lives. And yet they are as prone to stray into criminal activities, or to be a victim of crime, as any other individuals in their private lives.

Many sportsmen have found themselves in the criminal courts for private activities unconnected with their sport. Some for assault and other irresponsible acts of violence; some for drunken driving; some for more surprising misdemeanours. A number of offences have deservedly led to jail sentences and are sad and depressing tales.

Here is just a small collection of criminal investigations where high profile sportsmen, some unjustly or unfairly, have over the years made the headlines on the news pages rather than the sports pages – including the story of St Leger Goold, the Wimbledon trunk murderer; a false claim of theft against Bobby Moore which threatened England's World Cup chances; and a group of footballers challenging for 'the oddest crime of all'.

---

20 THOMAS ST LEGER GOOLD – A WIMBLEDON FINALIST AND THE TRUNK MURDER

It was a gory tale, a dismembered body in a trunk at a railway station in Marseilles. And the murderer? A former Wimbledon finalist.

In August 1907, the dramatic headline appeared in *The Times*: 'A WOMAN'S BODY IN A TRUNK.' It was reported that Vere Thomas St Leger Goold had been arrested for murder. He was later convicted.

Who was he? Eighteen years earlier, Goold, or St Leger as he was known, had been a finalist in the third year of the Wimbledon Championships.

The younger son of an Irish baron from Waterford in County Cork, St Leger was a popular player with flamboyant shots and an attacking style which appealed to spectators. As inaugural Irish champion earlier in the year, he entered Wimbledon for the 1879 Championships, then held at the Worple Road ground, and made a strong impact. He won his way through to the All-Comers Final losing, a little tamely, 6-2 6-4 6-2 to the Reverend John Hartley.

St Leger was a popular player with a flamboyant style.

Hartley had only just made it through his semi-final. He was the vicar in a Yorkshire village and, not expecting to get so far in the tournament, he had not arranged a replacement to take Sunday services before his Monday semi-final. So, he had to travel back to Yorkshire on Saturday, take Sunday services, breakfast early on the Monday, ride by horse to Thirsk station, travel by train to King's Cross, London and get a horse-drawn cab to take him to Wimbledon by 2 p.m. for his semi-final. Somewhat tired, a rain-break refreshed him and his win put him in good shape for his final against St Leger the following day. Perhaps life for St Leger would have been very different if Hartley had not won that semi-final.

St Leger disappeared from the tennis scene in the early 1880s. He married Marie Violet, a French woman, in 1891. It was her third marriage. They emigrated to Montreal, Canada but returned to the United Kingdom in 1903 where they started a laundry business in Liverpool which failed. They were in financial trouble.

It was the move to Monte Carlo which really proved their undoing. The couple apparently assumed the title of Sir Vere and Lady Goold. Trying to make their fortune on the gaming tables, they sunk even more heavily into debt. They came across Emma Liven, a wealthy Danish widow and also a frequent gambler at the tables. One evening, she turned up at the Goold's flat in Monte Carlo. It is unclear whether she had lent the Goolds money which she wanted back or whether the Goolds invited her over knowing her penchant for wearing expensive jewellery.

The following day, the Goolds caught the 5.38 a.m. train from Monaco to Marseilles. They left a trunk and a large bag in the station cloakroom at Marseilles and asked a railway porter to send the luggage on to London. The porter noticed a distinctive smell from the luggage. The police were informed. When the trunk and bag were opened, the police found the dismembered remains of a woman – the victim was Emma Liven.

The Goolds were arrested. They pleaded innocence at first, saying that the victim had been killed by her lover and they had panicked to avoid being implicated in the crime. But the story did not stand up. St Leger confessed to the crime. His wife denied actually being involved in the killing, but there were too many stab wounds for one person alone to inflict.

The murder trial was held in Monte Carlo before presiding judge Baron de Rolland. Both were convicted. St Leger was sentenced to penal servitude for life. His wife was initially condemned to death but, on appeal, this was reduced to life imprisonment. Marie Violet was sent to jail in Montpelier where she died six years later. St Leger was sent to Devil's Island, the notorious French penal colony off the South American coast. He died one year later, aged fifty-five, thirty years after being a finalist at Wimbledon.

St Leger was sentenced to penal servitude for life.

---

21 BOBBY MOORE IS INNOCENT OK! THE CASE OF THE STOLEN BRACELET IN BOGOTA

Bobby Moore was arrested in Bogota. Was it a conspiracy to prejudice England's chances of retaining the World Cup?

It was a criminal investigation which dominated the front page headlines. There was disbelief and concern throughout the nation. Even the Prime Minister felt that he should intervene. England's preparations for the World Cup were thrust into turmoil. Bobby Moore, England's captain, the man who four years earlier had lifted the World Cup at Wembley after England's triumph, had been arrested.

The incident happened in Bogota, the capital of Columbia, in May 1970. The England team were due to play a friendly match against Columbia later in the day as part of their preparation for the World Cup finals soon to be held in Mexico. Bobby Moore and Bobby Charlton, two of England's greatest players, were in the Fuego Verde (Green Fire) jewellery shop off the foyer of the Tequendama Hotel in Bogota where the team were staying. They were looking for a present for Bobby Charlton's wife, Norma.

Moore and Charlton left the shop and sat a few yards away in the foyer of the hotel. Suddenly, the shop assistant, Clara Padilla, came out and accused Bobby Moore of stealing an emerald and diamond bracelet (then worth around £600). The police were called and statements taken. Moore and Charlton offered to be searched but this was not taken up. Manager Alf Ramsey, not known for his diplomatic skills, was called. He spoke to the players and then to the police. The matter appeared to have been resolved.

Moore and Charlton rejoined their team colleagues. England went on to beat Columbia 4-0 in the friendly, with two goals from Martin Peters and one each from Alan Ball and Bobby Charlton.

The England party then flew to Quito for another friendly, against Ecuador, to gain further experience playing at altitude. After beating Ecuador 2-0, they headed off to Mexico for the start of their defence of the World Cup – but via Bogota because there was no direct flight. They returned to the Tequendama Hotel. He and other team members were watching the film *Shenandoah* in the hotel when Moore was tapped on the shoulder. The police had come to arrest him.

After diplomatic discussions involving the local British Charges d'Affaires, Moore agreed voluntarily to go later in the day to a police station to make a further statement. After hours of questioning, Moore was formally arrested. He was about to be placed in jail when the Colombian government intervened. Moore was, instead, placed under more civilised house arrest at the home of Alfonso Senior, the Director of Colombian Football. He was accompanied by two armed guards.

After hours of questioning, Moore was formally arrested.

The following day, a reconstruction was held at the jewellery shop. Moore was dressed in the England jacket which he had been wearing at the time of the alleged incident. Part of the shop assistant's evidence was that Moore had taken the bracelet and put it in his inside-left pocket. Moore demonstrated to the judge that there was no such pocket!

After the reconstruction, Moore returned to Alfonso Senior's house and asked if he could go training. Accompanied by his guards, he used a public playing field nearby – much to the delight of a crowd of local boys who were soon organised by Moore, as if marshalling his defence, into two teams along with the guards.

Moore was held under house arrest for four days. More diplomatic pleas and interventions were tried – including from Britain's Prime Minister, Harold Wilson. They were finally successful. On 29th May Moore was released and allowed on a flight to Mexico subject to a promise to return if required.

England's opening match in the World Cup was four days later in Guadalajara against Romania which, in sweltering heat, England won 1-0 with a goal from Geoff Hurst. In the next game, nine days after his release, Moore was playing in the classic 1-0 defeat by Brazil, one of the greatest games of his career. His tackle, cleanly sweeping the ball away from Jairzhino, was a defining example of defensive skill. Moore and Pelé ... swapping shirts at the end of the match remains an iconic image.

England qualified for the next stage but went out 3-2 in extra time to West Germany in the quarter-finals in Léon after holding a 2-0 lead with little more than twenty minutes left.

The case against Bobby Moore lingered on. In November 1972 a Colombian judge decided that the charges against Moore were to be shelved, but the case was re-opened in 1973. On 2nd December 1975 Moore was finally sent a letter by the UK Foreign Office stating that the case had been closed.

A further twist to the story occurred nearly thirty years later. A UK Foreign Office document released by the Public Record Office in March 2003 revealed that even the head of Columbia's police had believed all along that Moore was not guilty. In June 1970, within weeks of Moore's arrest and four days after Moore's legendary display against Brazil, a British Embassy official had reported in writing to the Foreign Office that the police in Columbia had traced the bracelet, which had been 'hawked around the underworld during the previous week'. The police had also 'established the identity of the thief, a woman, and hoped to make an arrest shortly'. The background of the jeweller and the witnesses had been thoroughly scrutinised and 'some suspicious circumstances established'.

Why was Moore placed under arrest? Was there a conspiracy to hamper England's chances of retaining the World Cup? Was it simply a case of mistaken identity? We will never know. But Moore's legacy remains intact.

---

22 LESTER PIGGOTT – CENTAUR BRINGS DOWN BRITAIN'S GREATEST JOCKEY

Lester Piggott had failed to declare substantial amounts of riding and bloodstock income to the Inland Revenue. He was exposed by an investigation codenamed 'Centaur'.

Lester Piggott remained stony faced as Justice Farquharson delivered his sentence at Ipswich Crown Court in 1987. The fifty-one-year-old former champion jockey, one of the great figures of British sport, had been found guilty of an alleged tax fraud involving over £3 million of undeclared income.

Memories were still recent of his fabulous racing record. He had retired as a jockey just two years earlier. A winner all over the world with thirty Classic victories to his name in England, including nine in the Epsom Derby where, as an eighteen-year-old in 1954 on *Never Say Die,* he had been the youngest ever jockey to win the event. His rides on horses such as *Sir Ivor, Nijinsky, Roberto* and *The Minstrel* were the stuff of sporting legend. He rode 5,300 victories in more than thirty countries during his unparalleled career. He was awarded the OBE in 1975.

But Piggott had failed to declare income from the fruits of his success to the Inland Revenue. It was alleged that he had signed false declarations during three successive investigations into his tax affairs by the Inland Revenue between 1970 and 1985. The largest

Tonya Harding (right) and Nancy Kerrigan avoid each other during practice before the 1994 Winter Olympics in Lillehammer, six weeks after a physical attack on Kerrigan in Detroit. Harding was alleged to have links with the attack. [3]

Ayrton Senna's fatal crash in Imola in the San Marino Grand Prix in 1994. Was it culpable homicide? [4]

Duncan Ferguson confronts referee Steve Bennett. At Glasgow Rangers, he became the first professional footballer in the UK to be jailed following an assault on the pitch. [5]

Newcastle's Lee Bowyer brawls with team-mate Kieron Dyer during a match at St James' Park in 2005. Dyer had not passed the ball to Bowyer. Team-mate Stephen Carr and Aston Villa's Gareth Barry try to stop them. [9]

'Shoeless' Joe Jackson was the lead hitter for the infamous 1919 Chicago White Sox. Were the World Series that year a fix? [11]

Bruce Grobbelaar attends Winchester Crown Court during his trial into alleged corruption. [14]

South African newspapers react in April 2000 to the confessions of former cricket captain, Hansie Cronje. [16]

German referee Robert Hoyzer's decisions stunned top Bundesliga side, Hamburg, who lost 4-2 at lowly Paderborn in a cup-tie. [17]

Kieren Fallon declares victory in the Prix de l'Arc de Triomphe on *Dylan Thomas* in October 2007. The following day he was at the Old Bailey facing his trial for alleged race-fixing. [19]

Luciano Moggi, director-general of Juventus, was at the shadowy heart of the calciopoli scandal. The story broke as Juventus were heading for the Serie A title in 2006. [18]

England captain Bobby Moore at Mexico City airport in 1970. Moore had been released from house arrest in Bogota. [21]

Lester Piggott at Leicester for his first race after returning to the track, having retired five years previously and served a year in prison for tax fraud. [22]

Indian cricketer-turned-politician Navjot Sidhu addresses a press conference in 2006 after appealing to India's Supreme Court to stay his imprisonment for manslaughter. [25]

Colombian defender, Andrés Escobar, lies on the ground after scoring an own goal in a World Cup match against the USA in 1994. Ten days later he was shot dead. [24]

The Pakistan cricket team in silence during the 2007 World Cup after the unexplained death of coach Bob Woolmer. [26]

Glen Johnson is in trouble with referee Phil Dowd in 2008 – and earlier at B&Q. Was his the oddest crime of all? [27]

The Bradford City fire disaster, which killed 56 people, unfolds in May 1985. [32]

A Bentley practises for the Double-12 hours event at the famous Brooklands racetrack in 1930. The race became the scene of an unexpected accident — and a first for the courts. [28]

Twelve years after being paralysed in a world title fight with Chris Eubank, Michael Watson (centre) takes part (right) in the London Marathon. He was joined by Eubank (left) for the final mile. Former European champion Spencer Oliver is on the right. [35]

Paul Elliott is carried off after a tackle by Dean Saunders in a Liverpool fixture against Chelsea in 1992. It led to the first negligence lawsuit for a tackle in top-division football. [36]

Bernardo Segura, of Mexico (2569), is joyful as he crosses the line in the 20 kilometre walk at the Sydney Olympics. He was less happy later when he was disqualified, leaving Robert Korzeniowski of Poland (2711) the winner. [40]

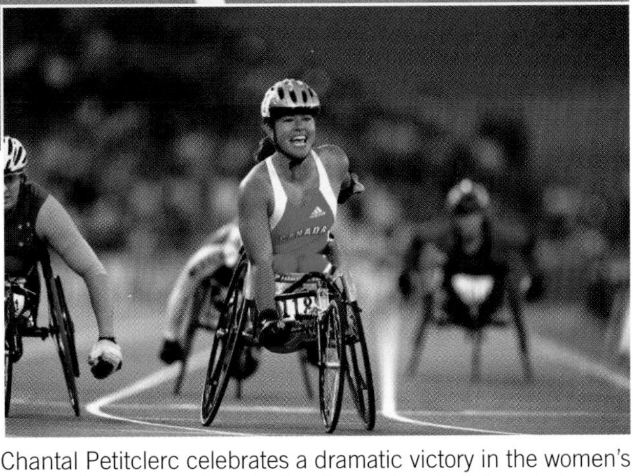

Canada's Chantal Petitclerc celebrates a dramatic victory in the women's T54 wheelchair 800 metres final during the Sydney Paralympic Games. The race was, controversially, ordered to be re-held. [41]

Canada's Jamie Salé and David Pelletier skate to music from *Love Story* at the 2002 Winter Olympics. They reacted to the marks with astonishment — as did the crowd. [42]

Bettina Hoy on her way to a clear round in Athens to give Germany the team gold medal in equestrian eventing at the 2004 Olympics – or so she thought. [44]

Brazil's Vanderlei de Lima is pushed into the crowd by an interloper, a former Irish priest, when leading the 2004 Olympic marathon. Did it rob him of gold? [45]

Yang Tae Young, of Korea, performs on the parallel bars in the 2004 Olympic gymnastic final. Was he denied the gold medal? Should it be corrected? [43]

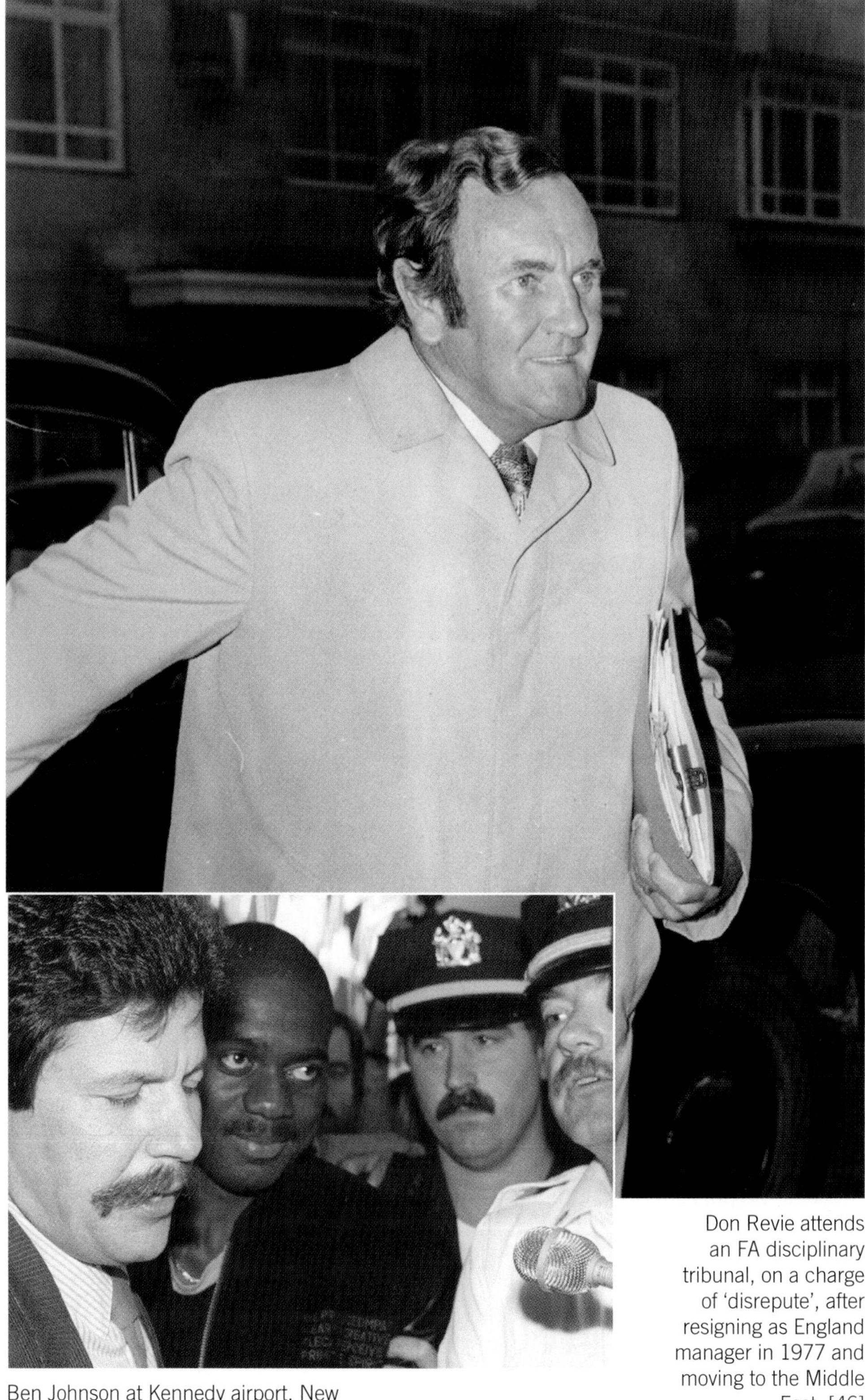

Don Revie attends an FA disciplinary tribunal, on a charge of 'disrepute', after resigning as England manager in 1977 and moving to the Middle East. [46]

Ben Johnson at Kennedy airport, New York, on his way home in disgrace from the Seoul Olympics. [47]

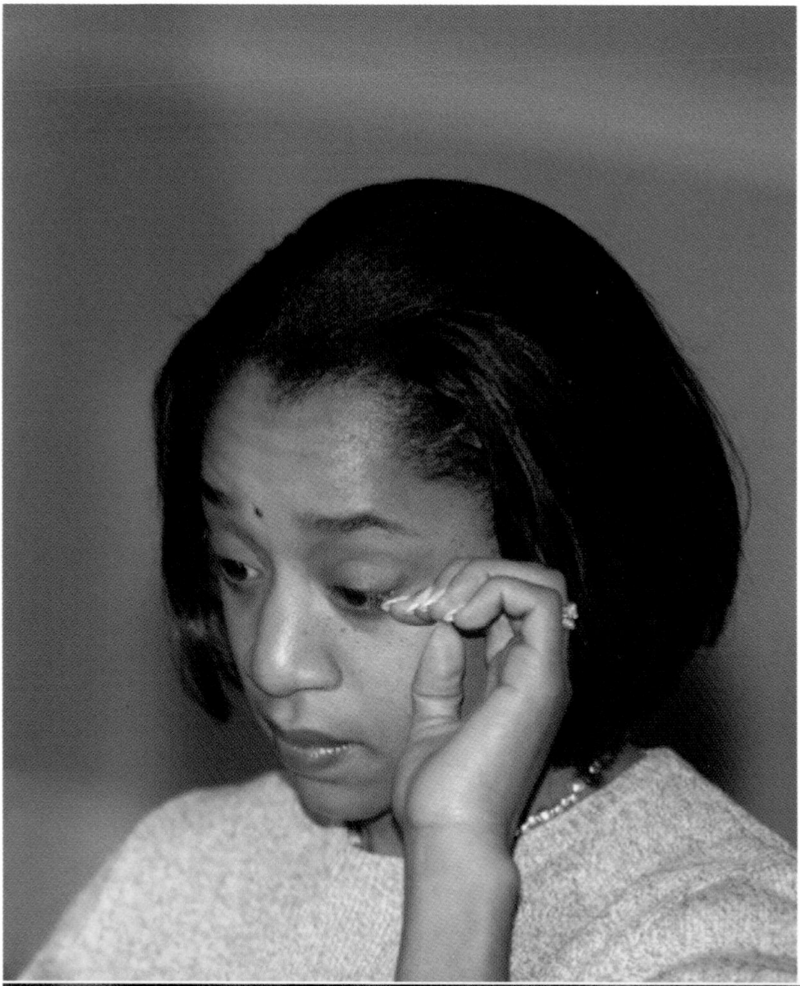

Diane Modahl gives a tearful press conference after the results of a drugs test were revealed.... and before her £1 million claim when eventually cleared. [48]

Greyhound racing at Wimbledon Stadium. A poor performance by a pre-race favourite, *Knockeevan King*, in a heat of the English Greyhound Derby in 2002 led to contentious disciplinary proceedings. [50]

Mariano Puerta in action in the 2005 French Open final. Was his later ban for a doping offence unfair? [53]

The Winter Olympics 2002. Scotland's Alain Baxter displays Britain's first-ever skiing medal But would he have to give it back because of a nasal inhaler? [49]

sum on the charge sheet related to nondisclosure of £1.3 million or more of riding income. Another charge alleged that, during a period of fourteen years, he had omitted to declare over £1 million income from bloodstock operations. The prosecution claimed that he had used different names to channel his earnings to secret bank accounts in Switzerland, the Bahamas, Singapore and the Cayman Islands.

Piggott was charged following a joint investigation by Customs and the Inland Revenue codenamed 'Centaur' after the half-man, half-horse beast of mythology.

The sentence delivered by Justice Farquharson was severe. Three years imprisonment. It was at that time the largest individual tax evasion charge to be prosecuted in England, and the heaviest sentence to be passed, for a personal tax fraud. Appeals for leniency were rejected. The judge said that he could not ignore the scale of Piggott's tax evasion without an invitation to others to cheat.

It was at that time the highest sentence to be passed for a personal tax fraud.

Piggott was stripped of his OBE in 1988 following his conviction.

Lester Piggott served 366 days in prison – first in Norwich and then a prison near Haverhill, about ten miles from Newmarket. He was sent the *Racing Post* each day. Many had questioned his ability to cope. But the taciturn demeanour he always had in public, attributable in part to partial deafness and a minor speech impediment, served him well. 'I kept my nose clean and stayed out of trouble. The year passed.'

Piggott is not alone among leading sportsmen to have run into serious trouble over his tax affairs. Although not jailed, perhaps fortunately, Boris Becker was sentenced in 2002 to two years' probation by a Munich court for failing to pay €1.7 million in German taxes over a ten year period of his tennis career, after concealing a continued residence in Germany while purporting to have moved to Monte Carlo. More recently, Guus Hiddink, the manager of Russia's football team, was given a six month suspended sentence and a €45,000 fine for evading more than €1.4 million in Dutch taxes by claiming to be resident in Belgium.

Two other sporting figures have been stripped of honours following criminal misdemeanours. Boxer 'Prince' Naseem Hameed was stripped of his MBE in December 2006 following his fifteen-month prison sentence for dangerous driving. The world darts champion, Phil Taylor, was relieved of his MBE in 2006 after being convicted of an assault on two female fans.

As for Lester Piggott, he returned as a jockey in 1990 at the age of fifty-four. Less than two weeks after picking up the racing reins again, he won a famous victory on *Royal Academy* in the Breeders' Cup Mile at Belmont Park, one of the most prestigious races in America. It was a second coming. The flair, the skill and the drive were undiminished by time. Even Lester Piggott found a smile.

---

23 ROSCOE TANNER – THE FALL OF THE FASTEST SERVE IN TENNIS

Roscoe Tanner was a Wimbledon finalist in 1979. Twenty years later, it had become a sorry tale of fraud, debt and jail.

Roscoe Tanner, the left-hander from Chattanooga, Tennessee, had the fastest serve in tennis in the 1970s. Winner of the Australian Open in 1977, the American was a Wimbledon finalist in 1979 – giving Bjorn Borg a serious fright as Borg won his fourth title in a five-set thriller 6-7, 6-1, 3-6, 6-3, 6-4.

'It's a sad, sad story.'

What happened to Tanner afterwards? His former coach at Stamford University, Dick Gould, summed it up: 'It's a sad, sad story. He always saw his glass as overflowing. He just kept screwing things up.' He certainly did.

Tanner seemed unable to adapt to an ordinary life. 'He just doesn't understand money' said his former coach. His first marriage ended in a bitter divorce. He fathered a child by Connie Romano, an artist, whom he met when she was working for an escort service. He agreed a large lump sum payment to support the child. He failed to pay. During a senior tennis event in Naples, Florida in 1997, he was arrested after failing to show up before a New Jersey court and jailed for the first time.

Four years later, deep in debt, he was arrested again during a senior tournament in Atlanta and jailed for failing to pay agreed monthly amounts to his second wife, Charlotte, with whom he had two daughters.

Worse was to come. A year previously, in 2000, he had bought – none of the reports tell us why – a thirty-two-foot yacht in Florida from a man named Gene Gammon for $39,000. Tanner handed over a deposit and paid a cheque for $35,595. It bounced. Tanner used the boat to secure a personal loan. Several years later, in 2003, Gammon tracked Tanner down after he had gone, with his third wife, to Germany to earn some money playing club tennis there. The US government sought an extradition order against Tanner who was jailed in Karlsruhe, Germany, before being transferred to a jail in Florida and later New Jersey for nine months. In November 2003, undertaking to mend his ways, he was sentenced to ten years' probation for the earlier yacht fraud in 2000. He failed again to make agreed payments to Gammon and, this time, in 2006 was arrested and sentenced in Clearwater, Florida to two years in prison for violating his probation.

'I was broke but I was still trying to put up the front as a successful guy'

Tanner, when asked how it all went wrong, said:

> *It was a multitude of things. When I was in jail, I was thinking about all the things I had been blessed with and given, and wondered: how did I end up in this spot?' 'I'm not proud of what I've done. I made a lot of money, but I also made some bad deals and had some unfortunate marriages and liaisons. I was broke, but I was still trying to put up the front as a successful guy.*

---

24 ANDRÉS ESCOBAR '– GOOOOOOOL'

An own goal in the World Cup led to tragic consequences in one of the sport's saddest tales.

Andrés Escobar, the Colombian footballer, was with his girlfriend as they left the El Indio bar in a suburb of Medillín, his hometown, and went to the car park. There was an altercation with some 'supporters'. Suddenly, he was shot and killed by a sequence of twelve bullets. After each bullet, the killer is said to have shouted 'Gooooooool'. It was surely the most tragic case of a sporting victim of crime.

Twenty-seven-year-old Escobar had been a regular international player for the successful, if unpredictable, Colombian national side. He played in both the 1990 and 1994 World Cup sides. He is remembered in England for his goal in the 1-1 draw at Wembley in 1988. He was a gentlemanly player, nicknamed 'El Cabellero del Futbol' in Columbia.

The 1994 World Cup campaign promised well for Columbia. They were playing exciting football, including an astonishing 5-0 win over Argentina in their South American qualifying group. Players such as Asprilla (later remembered well at Newcastle), Valderrama and Rincon were adding spark and dazzle to the team. The footballing world was taking notice. Many experts fancied them to do well in the World Cup in America. But their preparations were conducted against a backdrop of rumours of South American betting syndicates and drug cartels. Coach Hernán Gomez was reported to have received death threats.

It was surely the most tragic case of a sporting victim of crime.

The opening match against Rumania was a shocker for Columbia. They looked edgy and uncertain. It was a surprising, and deflating, 3-1 defeat to begin their campaign. Worse was to follow in the second match against the USA before a 93,000 crowd in the Rose Bowl in Los Angeles.

For Escobar, he was desperately unfortunate in the thirty-fourth minute of the match against the USA. A cross came over from the left. Positioned around the penalty spot, Escobar stretched out his leg towards the goal to cut out the cross. The ball caught his boot and deflected firmly towards the near post of the Colombian goal. The goalkeeper was wrong footed. The own goal set the USA on the path to a surprise 2-1 win and the Colombians were out of the World Cup in the first round.

Just ten days later, back in Columbia, Escobar was shot. His murder was widely believed to be a retribution for the own goal.

Subsequently charged, and convicted a year later, was Humberto Muñioz Castro. He was sentenced to forty-three years in prison. This was later reduced and he was eventually released in 2005 after serving approximately eleven years. It has never been established whether he acted alone or at the direction of one of the gambling syndicates.

South American soccer has had other excitable and dramatic consequences in the past. Notably, riots in a match between El Salvador and Honduras in June 1969 came at a time of deteriorating diplomatic relations between the two countries over immigration and border disputes. This led two weeks later to open warfare between the two countries with many casualties: the 'Soccer War'.

But the tragic tale of Andrés Escobar must be the saddest individual story.

---

25 NAVJOT SIDHU – AN OPENING BATSMAN, POLITICS AND A CHARGE OF HOMICIDE

A former opening batsman for India and a well-known TV commentator, Sidhu's political future looked bright. But a dark cloud from the past would return.

It was a peculiarly Indian tale – a story of a Test opening batsman and TV commentator, a promising political career and a charge of culpable homicide.

The central figure was Navjot Sidhu. Born in Patiala in the Punjab, Sidhu became one of India's best known and successful batsmen in the 1990s – frequently opening the batting in partnership with the legendary Sachin Tendulkar. Making his international debut in 1983, it was not until the 1990s that Sidhu blossomed as a Test cricketer. His finest moment in Test cricket was his 201 innings against West Indies in 1996–97. Often steady and dour, sometimes flamboyant, he was known for his liking, and ability, to attack spinners – even the great Shane Warne – earning him the nickname 'Sixer Sidhu'. He retired in December 1999 having played more than fifty Test matches, with a batting average of 42.13, and a further 100 one-day internationals.

Sidhu was a natural. He moved easily into work as a cricket commentator and analyst. Sidhu's forthright and lively style made him a popular TV personality and famous for his one-line wisecracks, all delivered with a touch of humour. They became known as 'Sidhuisms'. Some were quaintly philosophical: 'One, who doesn't throw the dice, can never expect to score a six.' 'The cat with gloves catches no mice.' 'You may have a heart of gold, but so does a hard-boiled egg.' Others were graphic and awkward metaphors: 'The Sri Lankan score is running like an Indian taxi meter.' 'The Indians are finding the gaps like a pin in a haystack.' 'He has a backlift like an octopus falling out of a tree.'

'One, who doesn't throw the dice, can never expect to score a six.'

Inspired by his ever increasing popularity, Sidhu turned to politics. He became a candidate for the main opposition Bharatiya Janata Party (BJP) in the Indian general elections and comfortably won his seat in the Lok Sabha (India's lower house of Parliament) for Amritsar in the Punjab. His political future was bright.

But a dark cloud was looming.

Back in 1988, while still a Test cricketer, Sidhu had been involved in a nasty private incident. He and a friend became involved in a quarrel with another man over a car parking space in a restricted zone in Patiala. He was alleged to have ended up hitting Gurnam Singh, a sixty-five-year-old, who sadly died later. Sidhu was not charged with any offence at the time.

Then, shortly before Sidhu retired from cricket in 1999, the relatives of Gurnam Singh succeeded in getting a charge brought against Sidhu for causing his death. In September 1999, eleven years after the incident, the case was heard before a district court in Patiala. Medical evidence did not conclusively establish that the victim died as a result of the alleged blow to the head. Sidhu was acquitted.

Sidhu was free to pursue his plans for a political career – he would, under Indian law, have been ineligible to contest political elections for six years if he had been found guilty of such a criminal offence. But there were many twists and turns still to occur in the saga.

Singh's relatives were determined to pursue the matter. In December 2006 the case against Sidhu was reheard by the Punjab and Haryana High Court. Shock when the court announced its decision. Sidhu had been found guilty of culpable homicide. The former cricketer and Member of Parliament received his sentence. Three years in prison. His sentence was, though, suspended until 31st January 2007 pending Sidhu's appeal to the Supreme Court of India. He was released on bail in the meantime.

After the guilty decision, Sidhu promptly resigned as a Member of Parliament. Was his political career over?

Sidhu's appeal was heard by the Supreme Court of India in New Delhi a few weeks later in January 2007. The Supreme Court decided in his favour. Justices Mathur and Raveendran observed that Sidhu would suffer 'irreparable injury' if he was not able to contest the political seat he vacated purely on moral grounds. This was a 'fit case to suspend the order of conviction passed by the High Court'. His conviction and sentence were 'stayed' – if not indefinitely at least until a further appeal hearing.

Forty-year-old Sidhu was free to continue his political career. Had his reputation and standing been irrevocably damaged? He recontested an election for the Amritsar seat in the Lok Sabha in February 2007. He successfully defeated his nearest rival, State Finance Minister Surinder Singla, by a substantial margin of 77,626 votes. He resumed his bright and promising political innings.

But is there still a cloud lurking on the horizon for 'Sixer Sidhu'? We may not have heard the end of this unpredictable Indian story. Or to recall another Sidhuism: 'Nobody travels on the road to success without a puncture or two.'

---

26 BOB WOOLMER – AN OPEN VERDICT

Bob Woolmer, Pakistan's coach, was found dead the morning after the team's shock exit from the World Cup. Was it death by natural causes – or murder?

Bob Woolmer, Pakistan's fifty-eight-year-old cricket coach, could scarcely believe his eyes. Pakistan, ranked fourth in the world in one-day internationals, had lost to Ireland. It was one of the biggest upsets in cricket history. Pakistan were out of the 2007 World Cup at the initial group stage.

Woolmer attended the post-match media conference. He spoke of the stresses of the job. 'Doing it internationally, it takes a toll on you – the endless travelling and the non-stop living out of hotels.' He went back, around 8.30 p.m., to his room on the twelfth floor of the Pegasus Hotel in Kingston, Jamaica. Perhaps he thought about the past and how he had arrived here. Almost certainly he thought about the future and his family back in England. Should he resign?

Born in India to English parents, cricket had always been in Woolmer's blood. He developed into a fine all-rounder for Kent and then for England – remembered for his six-and-a-half-hour defence against Lillee and Thomson in a 149 innings in his second Test for England at the Oval in 1975. He was not averse to controversy. He had joined the rebel 'Packer circus'. Although he continued to play for England, he never really recovered his form of the 1970s and retired as a player in 1984.

He became an innovative and well-respected coach. It had become his life. Appointed to coach South Africa in 1994, he had many successful years working closely with captain Hansie Cronje and his team. He had also been through, his reputation untouched, the turmoil of the betting and bribery crisis. After a brief return to England, the travelling began again when, in 2004 and to the surprise of many, he accepted the appointment to coach the Pakistan team. He had experienced many highs and lows in that role, including the ball-tampering disputes and now this shock World Cup defeat. He knew that the reaction back in Pakistan to the team's performance would be highly critical. He sent an email to his wife saying he was 'a little depressed. Our batting performance was abysmal. I could tell the players were for some reason not able to fire themselves up.'

At 10.45 a.m. the following morning, a Sunday, a maid entered his room to find Woolmer's body – he was a big man – sprawled on the floor by the bathroom door. Blood and vomit were on the walls. Woolmer was taken to the University of the West Indies Hospital but pronounced dead. Speculation was immediate and unconstrained. Natural causes? Suicide? Murder? The following days and weeks would rank amongst cricket's darkest times.

The Jamaican police, headed by deputy police commissioner, Mark Shields, investigated. An early autopsy report was given by government pathologist, Dr. Ere Seshaiah. A spokesman announced the dramatic news on 22nd March:

> *The pathologist's report states that Mr Woolmer's death was due to asphyxiation as a result of manual strangulation. In these circumstances, the matter is now being treated by the Jamaican police as a case of murder.*

Theories and speculation abounded throughout the press and the cricket world:

There was no sign of any forced entry into the room. He must have known his assailant. There were rumours of arguments with members of the Pakistan team.

There was 'very little' sign of a struggle. Had he first been drugged or poisoned? Rumours of a snake venom and, later, traces of a weedkiller in his stomach started to circulate.

Had Woolmer been murdered as retribution for the World Cup defeat – remember Andrés Escobar?

Was he killed at the direction of a gambling syndicate? Rumours continued of match-fixing and dubious 'hangers-on' in Jamaica from the ubiquitous Asian betting world. The spectre of corruption in cricket loomed darkly again.

Was he about to write a book recording 'secrets' of his time with South Africa and Pakistan which others did not want to become public? Barry Richards, one of South Africa's greatest cricketers and best man at Woolmer's wedding, remarked: 'There was a feeling around that Bob was going to expose something. There is a dark side to cricket. Bob was passionate about the game. Perhaps too passionate.'

Should the World Cup be cancelled? These were sad, mysterious and troubled days. The Pakistani team were finger-printed and interviewed. Many were outraged by their treatment and the innuendo of suspicion. Others called for a major review of cricket. Lord MacLaurin, former ECB chairman, said: 'When you've got something like this happening, which has really besmirched this World Cup, we've got to look at absolutely everything … to make sure we do the very, very best for cricket around the world.' The World Cup continued but under a dark cloud of disinterest, accusations and chaos.

The Jamaican authorities struggled to cope with an investigation in the spotlight of the world's media. It had all become front-page news, worldwide. Representatives from Scotland Yard and a British pathologist were invited at the end of March to assist in the investigation.

No real leads emerged to solve the 'crime' and doubts gathered as to the correctness of the original autopsy report. The weeks passed. On 12th June, the Jamaican police declared that, after all, it was not a case of murder. South African and Canadian pathologists had also joined the medical team and concurred with a finding by the British forensic team. 'Mr Woolmer died of natural causes.' In later toxicology tests 'no substance was found to indicate that Bob Woolmer was poisoned'.

'Mr Woolmer died of natural causes.'

That was not, though, the end of proceedings. A coroner's inquest had been ordered in Jamaica back in April and the process was still to be completed. Investigations continued. Several members of the Pakistan team had refused to travel to Jamaica for the inquest, including captain Inzamam-ul-Haq. There was still lingering resentment at some of the accusations and treatment directed at the Pakistan team in those initial days. The inquest in Kingston finally concluded in November 2007. It had heard from over fifty witnesses. Coroner Patrick Murphy gave his final summation. He listed several possible verdicts available to the jury – death by natural causes, accidental death, suicide, murder and involuntary or voluntary manslaughter.

The verdict was inconclusive. The eleven member jury decided that there was insufficient evidence of either a criminal act or death by natural causes. They were unable to decide an outcome. It was an 'open verdict'. The jury's foreman was reported as saying: 'We had no choice. We came to an open verdict because the evidence was too weak. There were too many what ifs and loopholes.'

The inquest therefore did not rule out the controversial strangulation theory of the Jamaican government's pathologist. But the Jamaican police decided that it was the end of their investigation: 'We do not intend to go any further with these investigations,' said deputy police commissioner Mark Shields.

The saga was at an end. Shocking, sad and disturbing for all concerned – for Bob Woolmer's family and for the world of cricket. For a time, a long time, they had seemed cricket's darkest hours. Many of cricket's troubles, prejudices and potentially destructive influences had surfaced again menacingly. The crime that never was? Probably, death by natural causes of a much travelled, big man of cricket suffering from diabetes and stress. But, in the end, an open verdict.

---

27 GLEN JOHNSON – THE ODDEST CRIME OF ALL?

Which footballer has committed the strangest crime of all? Portsmouth's Glen Johnson became a contender in 2007.

Sportsmen (and indeed they do all seem to have been men) have been caught in some pretty odd activities in their private lives which have fallen foul of the criminal law.

There have been some unpleasant and sad tales. Footballers have been prominent. A strong football team could be assembled from players given a jail sentence for private assault and similar violent offences (Jonathan Woodgate, Gary Charles, Joey Barton and Dennis Wise, the latter being later acquitted) or for drink or dangerous driving offences (including Lee Hughes, George Best, Tony Adams, Terry Fenwick, Mick Quinn, Jan Molby and Jermaine Pennant).

As for the challenge for the strangest crime of all, Mickey Thomas is a strong contender. The long-haired ex-Welsh international winger was a popular player with clubs such as Wrexham, Manchester United,

Everton and Chelsea. In 1993, Thomas found himself in court before Justice Gareth Edwards on a charge of passing counterfeit £10 and £20 notes to trainees at Wrexham when he was a player there. Despite his illustrious Welsh name, the judge had little sympathy for Thomas. The judge thought Thomas was a 'flash and dashing adventurer' and decided to make an example of him. Perhaps he had heard Thomas joking with reporters as he arrived at court: 'Anyone got change of a tenner for the phone?'

'Anyone got change of tenner for the phone?'

Thomas was sentenced to eighteen months in jail, spent in Walton prison in Liverpool. It did not subdue Thomas, who later became popular as a pundit and after-dinner speaker. 'So, Roy Keane is on fifty grand a week. Mind you, I was on fifty grand a week until the police found my printing machine!'

For a collection of unusual offences, Peter Storey, the hard-tackling midfielder for Arsenal's double-winning side in 1971 and holder of 19 England international caps, had a distinctive and unenviable record. In 1979 he was fined £700 and given a six month suspended jail sentence for running a brothel in east London. A year later, he was jailed for three years for involvement in a plot to counterfeit gold coins. In 1990 he completed his collection with a twenty-eight-day jail sentence for attempting to import twenty pornographic videos from Europe which he had hidden in a spare tyre.

But in January 2007, a new contender for 'the oddest crime of all' appeared in the shape of Glen Johnson. An England international left-back with Chelsea, and reportedly earning £30,000 a week, twenty-two-year-old Johnson was on loan to Portsmouth. An extraordinary report appeared. Glen Johnson had been arrested by the Kent police on suspicion of stealing a toilet seat and tap fittings from a B&Q store in Dartford, Kent.

Johnson, and fellow footballer Ben May, a striker on loan at Millwall from Chelsea, were seen on CCTV putting the toilet seat in a box marked with a cheaper price tag and hiding the taps underneath a sink at the check-out to avoid paying for them. They were spotted by a seventy-four-year-old security guard at the DIY store. Police were called and both Johnson and May were given on the spot £80 fixed penalty fines.

A worker at the B&Q store told reporters: 'We all recognised Johnson. No one could quite believe a bloke like him, with all that money, would be moronic enough to nick a toilet seat. They seemed to find the whole thing funny.'

The following week, Johnson turned up for training at Portsmouth. He found two toilet seats on his peg in the changing room put there by his team-mates. 'He's taken a lot of stick but he took it all in good heart,' one of them said.

CHAPTER FOUR

NEGLIGENCE AND PERSONAL INJURY

Injuries occur, sadly but inevitably, in the course of sport. Potential causes of accidents are varied and numerous. They include a dangerous sliding tackle in football, a collapsing scrum or head-high challenge in rugby, a badly sliced golf shot, reckless horseriding, a defective grandstand and even poor crowd control. Serious injuries can result – not only to participants but also to spectators.

Who should bear the risk of injury? Should the principle of liability for negligence apply to injuries in the course of sport? If so, what level of care is required? Who can potentially be liable – players, referees, event organisers, club owners, spectators, governing bodies within sport, the police? A wide range of disputes have come before the courts which have explored these questions, particularly during the last twenty years – and we see how major court decisions have significantly shaped the law in this area. Would you, the reader, have made the same decisions?

Sporting accidents included in this chapter have occurred at such famous and varied sporting venues as Brooklands racetrack, White City Stadium, White Hart Lane, Anfield, Hillsborough, Buckpool Golf Club, Llanharran rugby ground and Hexham racecourse.

---

28 BROOKLANDS – SPECTACULAR CRASH ALONG THE FINISHING STRAIGHT

An extraordinary accident during a race at Brooklands resulted in death and injury to spectators. Were the track operators liable?

The Talbot racing car was thrown high into the air before crashing into the crowd. The accident, in 1930, was of a kind never seen before at Brooklands. It became a first for the courts: were the track operators, the Brooklands Automobile Racing Club (BARC), liable to spectators for injuries arising from the sporting action?

The famous Brooklands racetrack in Surrey, just twenty miles south-west of London, had been associated with motor racing since 1907. It was the birthplace of British motorsport. Constructed by wealthy landowner, Hugh Locke King, it was the world's first purpose built motor racing circuit and in 1926 was the scene of the first ever British grand prix. The two-and-a-half mile circuit, with its massive and distinctive concrete banking on two sides, had captured the public's imagination. It represented the epitome of speed.

The track was oval in shape. There was a long straight stretch, the finishing straight, which was more than one hundred feet wide and bounded on its outer side by a six-inch high cement kerb and, beyond that, an iron railing 4 feet 6 inches high. Spectators could view from stands higher up, although many preferred to be much closer to the track and stand by the railing.

The race meeting in May 1930 was held under the auspices of the Junior Car Club, a long-standing and distinguished racing club. It was a long distance race under handicap, the JCC Double-12 hours event with the two twelve-hour races being held on consecutive days. Christopher Hall was a student at the Royal Naval College at Greenwich. He went excitedly with some friends to see the racing on the first day. Being an enthusiast, he had taken up a viewing position close to the railing towards the end of the finishing straight.

Christopher Hall went excitedly with some friends to see the racing.

It was just after 6 p.m. and the day's racing was in its closing stages. A small Austin came along the straight at around eighty-five miles per hour. Gaining on it, and about to overlap it, were three larger cars racing at around one hundred miles per hour. One was an Alfa Romeo followed just behind, on each side, by two Talbots (number 22 was a car's length behind on the left and number 21 was on the right, in effect 'slip-streaming' the Alfa Romeo).

Hall watched keenly. At the end of the straight, tightly packed, the group of cars came to a sharp left-hand bend which was best approached from the right side of the straight. Talbot 22, driven by Colonel Rabagliati on the left of the group, appeared to swerve its course to the right. The hub of its left rear wheel touched the hub of the near front wheel of the Talbot 21. The blow, startlingly, threw the Talbot 22 high into the air. It struck the top of the railings, turned upside down and rolled into the crowd of spectators. Some managed to flee but most were struck before they could move. No accident of this kind had occurred before at Brooklands.

The blow, startlingly, threw the Talbot 22 through the air.

Two people died, one being the riding mechanic accompanying the driver in the Talbot 22 and the other a spectator. Twenty other spectators were injured, some seriously. The injured were taken to the Weybridge cottage hospital. One of them was Christopher Hall who suffered scalp wounds and contusions.

At the inquest four days later, the jury concluded that the deaths were by misadventure. The clerk of the course said that 'nothing less than fortification' would have withstood the impetus of a car weighing a ton and going at eighty miles per hour. The coroner remarked, nevertheless, that arrangements should be made to keep the spectators further back.

Christopher Hall subsequently brought a claim to get compensation for his injuries. No negligence was alleged against the driver of the Talbot but Hall instead sued the BARC, lessees and operators of the track, for negligence. He alleged that they had provided insufficient protection for spectators watching such a highly dangerous sport or had, at the least, not given sufficient warnings of danger.

This was the first time that the courts had been called upon to consider the duties of a sports event organiser or venue owner to spectators arising out of the actual sporting action itself – rather than, for instance, the more obvious physical risks of a defective grandstand.

Should the BARC be liable to compensate the injured spectators? What was the extent of the duty owed by an event organiser or venue owner to paying spectators?

For: Motor racing was known to be a dangerous sport. Accidents could occur. The track operators should have ensured that paying spectators were kept a safe distance from

the track or, at least, that sufficient warnings were given. It became an implied term in the contract of admission that the event organiser should use reasonable care to ensure safety of spectators. The railings were not strong enough to resist such a collision at high speed. The kerb was useless. Reasonable care for the safety of spectators had not been taken.
Against: This was the first time, since the track at Brooklands had opened, that any spectator had been injured by a car leaving the track. No car had ever gone through the railings. A spectator must appreciate that there was a risk of an accident inherent in motor sport notwithstanding that all usual precautions were taken. A spectator voluntarily took that risk. The duty was simply to use reasonable care. It was not an absolute warranty of safety. Reasonable care did not require the track operators to strengthen a barrier against a danger which had never happened in twenty-three years.

Hall lost his claim.

Hall won in the lower court but the case went to the Court of Appeal. The Court of Appeal decided that the operators of the racetrack, the BARC, were not liable. They were not 'insurers' against accidents 'which no reasonable diligence could foresee, or against dangers inherent in a sport of which a reasonable spectator takes the risk'. Lord Justice Greer summed up:

> *I do not think the defendants are under any obligation to provide safety under all circumstances, but only to provide against damage to spectators which any reasonable occupier in their position would have anticipated as likely to happen.*

There is a certain level of risk, inherent in many sports, which a spectator must accept. The sports event organiser owes a duty of 'reasonable care' not a 'warranty of safety'.

In relation to its facts, this is a decision of an earlier age. The modern-day compensation culture had not yet taken root. The level of 'reasonable' care expected of an event organiser has moved with the times. It is probable that, today, the interests of safety of spectators would require a higher standard of care from an event organiser than those accepted in the early days at Brooklands. It is a useful reminder, though, that the law does not impose an absolute guarantee of safety. Motor sport is dangerous. Attending a sports event is not 'riskfree'.

In January 1946, the circuit at Brooklands was sold. The Junior Car Club absorbed the Brooklands Automobile Racing Club. It changed its name, retaining the same initials as the latter, and became the British Automobile Racing Club.

---

29 CHEETHAM CRICKET CLUB – A STRAIGHT SIX AND A SURPRISED PEDESTRIAN

Bessie Stone, peacefully standing outside her house, was unexpectedly struck by a cricket ball. Was the local cricket club liable?

In August 1947 postwar Britain was enjoying a hot summer. In cricket, Denis Compton was in glorious form for England and his swashbuckling style was captivating the sporting nation. Locally, cricket was being played at Cheetham cricket ground on the outskirts of Manchester. It was a typical scene repeated throughout England.

The cricket club at Cheetham had been in existence, and matches played regularly on its ground, since around 1864. The ground was bounded at one end by Beckenham Road. The road was built in 1910. At that time, a small strip of land was given up by the cricket club in exchange for a strip at the other end, so that the Beckenham Road end was a few yards nearer the batsman than the opposite end. The cricket field was protected by a seven-feet high fence which, in effect, was even higher above the pitch because of the sloping ground.

She was suddenly hit on the head by a cricket ball – a huge six.

Bessie Stone lived at 10 Beckenham Road near the cricket ground. She had stepped from her garden onto the pavement. She was suddenly hit on the head by a cricket ball – a huge six struck straight down the ground by a player on the visiting team during a game against the Cheetham 2nd XI. Miss Stone was injured. She had been standing not far short of one hundred yards from where the blow was struck.

A neighbour, at 11 Beckenham Road which was slightly nearer the pitch, said that he had known balls hit his house, or come into his yard, a number of times over the previous few years although his evidence was not very strong. Others said balls had been hit out of the ground only about six times over thirty years.

Bessie Stone claimed damages against the cricket club to compensate her for her injury. It became a major issue. Another first for the courts. The case was fought all the way up to the House of Lords.

Should the cricket club be found guilty of negligence in failing to take sufficient precautions to prevent cricket balls being hit out of the ground? More generally, what was the duty of a sports event organiser or club to prevent balls escaping and causing injury?

For: When the boundary was altered in 1910, the club should have taken into account the increased risk of balls being hit out of the ground. Cricket balls were not hit out of the ground accidentally. If a motorist on the road had been hit, it could have resulted in a serious accident. This was an accident which could have been avoided. The pitch should have been moved further away from the Beckenham Road end or the fence at that end should have been raised.

Against: Cricket was a lawful game. Every person using the highway must accept some risk from the lawful activities of others on their own property. The cricket club did not have to guard against every conceivable risk but only those which were reasonably probable or foreseeable. The club's duty was to guard against balls being constantly hit out of the ground or hit out by an ordinary stroke, but it was not necessary to provide against an extraordinary or exceptional stroke. One must stay in the realm of practical life and common sense. The club were not negligent and should not be liable to pay damages.

Bessie Stone lost her claim.

A first judge dismissed her case at the Manchester Assizes but she was successful on appeal to the Court of Appeal. A majority of that court decided that the cricket club (which, since it was an unincorporated club, meant that the persons responsible were the members of the club committee) had been negligent since they were aware of the potential risk.

The House of Lords came to the rescue of the cricket club. They concluded that Bessie Stone had no claim after all. The hitting of a cricket ball out of that ground was an event which could have been foreseen might occur and it was a conceivable possibility that a person might be injured. In order for liability in negligence to arise, however, 'there must not only be a reasonable possibility of its happening but also of injury being caused'.

In this case, the risk of injury had been so remote that a reasonable person would not have anticipated it. Lord Normand summed up the view of the court:

> *It is not the law that precautions must be taken against every peril that can be foreseen by the timorous.*

Lord Normand, one suspects a cricket fan, set out the ultimate dilemma which would have faced the club: 'The only practical way in which the possibility of danger could have been avoided would have been to stop playing cricket on this ground.' Implicitly, such a step was too extreme to contemplate at this time in the context of a cricket loving nation.

Cheetham cricket club were more fortunate with the court's judgment than many golf clubs – including St Augustine's Links in Ebbsfleet, Kent where a passer-by in 1922 was struck by a golf ball driven from the thirteenth tee while he was driving on a road adjacent to the course. The court was influenced by the fact that balls had for some time, and frequently, been sliced on to the road. Or were our judges more predisposed in favour of cricket than golf?

---

30 *WORK OF ART* – AN ACCIDENT AT THE NATIONAL HORSE SHOW

A photographer was injured by a horse galloping off course during a competition at the White City. Should the rider be held liable for negligence?

The heavyweight horse galloped dramatically towards a photographer and his companion. The horse's rider had lost control. The unfortunate, if bizarre, accident at the White City Stadium raised another first for the courts: what liability does a player or other sporting participant have for an injury to a spectator?

The stadium at the White City had been built for the London Olympic Games in 1908. The running track was the site in 1954 of Chris Chataway's famous win over Vladimir Kuts to break the world 5,000 metres record. Five years later, the White City was the arena not for an athletics event but for the National Horse Show organised by the British Horse Society.

Although the equestrian arena was over 100 yards long and 70 yards wide, it was quite tight for the gallop. The famous running track surrounded the equestrian arena. The competitors entered at one end. At the other, they rounded a bend and turned right into a straight in front of a bandstand. The competition this time at the National Horse Show was for heavyweight hunters.

One of the leading horses was *Work of Art* owned by Hugh Sumner and ridden by an experienced horseman, Ron Holladay. For this competition, the horses were required to walk, trot, canter and gallop. The gallop was the strength of *Work of Art* and Holladay was anxious to display his horse's abilities to the full. He started his round. *Work of Art* took the bend at the far end at a fast pace – too fast. Holladay tried to straighten him but lost control. A few feet off line, *Work of Art* set off down the straight on line with a set of flower tubs on the edge of the arena by the running track.

Edmund Wooldridge was a photographer for the event. He had, with permission, taken up position with his camera and tripod close to a bench seat between two of the flower tubs – towards which *Work of Art* was now hurtling at speed. Unfamiliar with horses,

Wooldridge took fright at the approach of the galloping heavyweight horse. He was particularly concerned, gallantly, for the safety of Miss Smallwood, a director of the company which employed him, who was sitting on the bench near him. Wooldridge attempted to pull Miss Smallwood off the bench out of the line of the horse. As he did so, he stepped or fell back onto the cinder running track. Unfortunately, this was directly into the path of the galloping *Work of Art*. The horse had veered to the left on to the cinder running track and past the bench where Wooldridge had been standing, rather than to the right on to the grass arena. Wooldridge was knocked down and severely injured.

Wooldridge fell back onto the cinder track.

Wooldridge later brought a legal claim against Holladay for negligence in the riding of *Work of Art*. The Court of Appeal wrestled with the issue.

Should Wooldridge be entitled to recover damages, to compensate for his injury, from Holladay on the grounds of negligence? More generally, what was the extent of the duty which a competitor in a sporting event owed for the safety of spectators?

For: Holladay had ridden his horse too fast round the corner of the arena. Trying to bring it back in line, he carried the horse too close to the bench seats where he knew people were positioned. He knew, or should have known, that this would be likely to endanger them. The fact that Holladay was participating in a sporting competition was irrelevant to the underlying duty to take reasonable care not to injure others – and that included injury to spectators. As rider of *Work of Art*, he failed to discharge that duty. **Against:** Allowance must be made for the sporting context. It was not the same as a motoring accident. The duty of care which a competitor in a sporting event owed to spectators was no greater than that owed by him to other competitors. He must not act recklessly but, short of reckless disregard, he should not be held liable for an accident which occurred in the course of sporting competition. A horse was an unpredictable animal. A spectator voluntarily assumed such risks as there might be inherent in a competition. An error of judgment, in a fast-moving sporting event, fell short of the threshold for any claim in negligence.

Edmund Wooldridge lost. The Court of Appeal decided that Ron Holladay was not negligent. He was not liable to compensate the injured photographer.

By riding too fast around the bend in these circumstances, Holladay might have been guilty of an error of judgment in 'the agony of the moment' but this did not amount to negligence. In the sporting context, a higher threshold was required before liability arose for negligence. The court concluded that a spectator attending a game or competition took the risk of an act of a participant causing injury to him even if this involved an error of judgment or lapse of skill.

Lord Justice Diplock summed up:

> *A person attending a game or competition takes the risk of any damage caused to him by any act of a participant done in the course of the game .... unless the participant's conduct is such as to evince a reckless disregard of the spectator's safety ... The most that can be said against Holladay is that he was guilty of an error of judgment or a lapse of skill ... That is not enough to constitute a breach of the duty of reasonable care which a participant owes to a spectator.*

The courts had not previously been called upon to consider the liability of a participant to a spectator. Eric Cantona had not yet made his appearance! The court upheld the general principle that everyone, organisers and participants, should use reasonable care not to cause injury. However, the courts would be reluctant to find that the threshold had been crossed, giving rise to liability, unless the act of carelessness had reached a level tantamount to reckless disregard for safety. An error of judgment 'in the heat of battle' or in 'the flurry or excitement of the competition' is not sufficient. This theme or principle runs through a number of cases in this chapter.

Ron Holladay, although he had apparently been unconscious for a short time after the accident, returned to the arena to ride again on *Work of Art* and triumphed to become champion in class on the same horse later in the evening.

---

31 VIOLENCE AT ELM PARK – HOOLIGANISM, MISSILES AND INJURY

A policeman was injured by a concrete missile as a result of spectator violence during a football match at Reading. Could the club be held liable for his injuries?

Elm Park was the scene for Reading's fourth division home match in April 1984 against regional rivals, Bristol City. Each club was a promotion hopeful. Hooliganism, the scourge of football, was sadly about to scar the game again.

The crowd was one of the largest of the season – around 8,500 spectators compared with an average gate at Elm Park for Reading's home matches of less than 4,000. Many Bristol City fans had travelled. Some violence was feared and, indeed, there was some sporadic fighting between rival supporters before the match and during the first half.

Soon after the start of the second half, violence erupted. There was a lot of fighting and a large number of missiles were thrown from the east terrace occupied by the Bristol fans. It was frightening. The missiles were thrown into the police and towards Reading supporters. They included sharpened coins and a considerable number of pieces of concrete, some heavy lumps, apparently loosened from the rather dilapidated terraces. A number of fans, mainly from the terrace occupied by Reading supporters, invaded the pitch. The referee stopped the match and took the players off. Police, including handlers with dogs, went on to the pitch to clear it of invaders.

A number of police officers were injured. Extra police, on panda control in the town centre, were called to the ground. A twenty-eight-year-old recently promoted sergeant, by the name of Cunningham, went to the terraces to help settle the commotion.

He came across a man, in his fifties, kneeling and busily engaged in breaking up the concrete terrace. Cunningham reached down to arrest him. The man turned and struck him hard on the right side of his skull with a lump of concrete. Cunningham slumped to the ground, barely conscious. He was then punched and repeatedly kicked by various youths. Other police officers were struck by concrete missiles and injured. The scenes were later described as amongst the worst violence seen at any football ground in Britain.

With the arrival of further police called to the ground, order was restored. The pitch was cleared and, after seventeen minutes stoppage, play was resumed. The police considered that abandoning the match could have led to even greater violence. The match itself ended in a 2-0 victory for Reading.

Following the referee's report, the FA brought disciplinary charges against both football clubs alleging failure to take all reasonable precautions to prevent misconduct by supporters. Despite previous FA warnings after a less serious incident at a Reading match earlier in the season, also involving concrete missiles, the FA disciplinary commission came to the conclusion that 'Reading had taken all reasonable precautions in accordance with the requirements of [the rules] and therefore no disciplinary action was to be taken.'

Cunningham himself suffered from post-traumatic stress following the incident. He felt he was unable to face again a very violent situation. He retired from the police force in October 1984. Together with a number of other police officers, he decided to pursue a civil claim against Reading FC for breach of a legal duty to ensure reasonable safety for visitors to the ground.

Should Reading FC be liable for the injuries to the police officers? Or were the violent, criminal activities of the hooligans outside the responsibility of the club?

For: Reading FC owed a duty to take reasonable care for the safety of visitors, who included police officers on duty at the match. The club knew from previous experience that hooligans would be likely to be there and might attempt to break up the terraces and use pieces of concrete as missiles. They should have provided more stewards to assist with crowd control. It was a match that was particularly likely to lead to violence. The club did not take sufficient steps to repair the terraces despite the warnings earlier in the season. The fencing designed to segregate rival supporters was also inadequate. This all amounted to negligence. **Against:** The club should not be held responsible for acts of hooligans who were the cause of any injuries. Such behaviour was a 'new cause' beyond the control of the club. The club relied on the police for policy and advice in relation to safety matters. Operational decisions on the day were exclusively taken by the senior police officers present and not the club. The FA disciplinary commission had found that the club had taken all reasonable precautions. The club should not be held legally liable for the violent acts of spectators.

Cunningham won his case. Reading FC were liable.

The court rejected Reading FC's arguments. The court decided that a reasonably prudent occupier would have taken greater steps to remove or minimise the risk. The club knew that there was a reasonable possibility of violence. They had failed to repair adequately the condition of the ground. The intervention of hooligans and the use of concrete missiles, loosened from the terraces, were 'very easily foreseeable'. The finding of the FA disciplinary hearing was irrelevant. The club had been negligent. Justice Drake summed up: 'I am satisfied that those responsible for the Elm Park ground failed in [their] duty ... to see that ... visitors to their grounds – spectators and others alike – will be reasonably safe ... '

Cunningham and the other police officers were entitled to damages to compensate for their injuries.

Social expectations had changed since, for example, the accident at Brooklands racetrack in 1930. Clubs and event organisers should take great care for the safety of visitors. They should normally insure against this risk. Here, a football club should be under a duty to ensure that its ground was in good condition and to take measures to prevent hooliganism – or, at least, hooliganism which could lead to serious injury as a result of dilapidated terracing.

The final match at Elm Park took place on 3rd May 1998, a 1-0 home defeat as Reading were relegated from Division One. Reading then moved to their new £45 million Madejski Stadium which opened for the following season.

---

32 BRADFORD FIRE DISASTER – LITTER, FIRE AND TRAGEDY AT VALLEY PARADE

Fifty-six supporters lost their lives in the dreadful fire tragedy at Bradford City. Was there liability for negligence?

It was a hot, sultry day with a light, but gusty, wind blowing. Saturday, 11th May 1985. The day should have been a celebration. It became a tragedy.

Bradford City were playing their final match of the season, against Lincoln City. They were already assured of the Third Division Championship. There 11,076 fans present at Valley Parade, Bradford City's home ground. Locally born captain, Peter Jackson, was presented with the championship trophy before the kick-off. It marked City's promotion to the second tier of English football for the first time since before the Second World War.

At 3.40 p.m., shortly before half-time, the first signs of a fire were noticed beneath the wooden bench seats at the Kop End in Block G of the antiquated Main Stand, built in 1909 in a golden era for the football club. The stand was holding 2,150 supporters.

According to later forensic investigation, the likely cause of the fire was the accidental dropping of a match or a cigarette stubbed out in a polystyrene cup and setting light to rubbish and debris under the stand. Within a few minutes, flames were clearly visible and the police began to evacuate people. The match referee, Dan Shaw, stopped play three minutes before half-time with the score still 0-0.

Although onsite fire equipment was brought into action immediately, the blaze engulfed and destroyed the wooden structure of the Main Stand within a few terrible minutes. Supporters at the front spilled on to the pitch. Others towards the back were trapped by the locked gates. There were many acts of heroism. Numerous police officers and supporters later received bravery awards. But fifty-six supporters tragically lost their lives and approximately 265 people were injured.

A cruel irony was that steel to replace the wooden roof of the stand was lying in a car park behind the stand for erection the following week.

Amongst the dead were John Fletcher and his son Andrew. Subsequently, his wife, Susan Fletcher, brought an action for negligence against Bradford City FC and the West Yorkshire County Council. The purpose of the claim was primarily for the respective insurance companies of the two defendants to be able to apportion liability for the compensation costs between them.

Evidence emerged at the High Court that an inspector for the Health and Safety Executive had written to the club several years' earlier in which he had warned of the dangers of a build-up of litter under the stand seating. Firemen searching through the charred remains of the wooden grandstand found papers dating back to the late 1960s.

An earlier visit from a representative of the county council's engineers department, in connection with an application for an improvement grant, had resulted in a written warning to the club about the potential fire risk of a carelessly discarded cigarette. Also contributing to the loss of life were locked exit doors and turnstiles and the absence of an emergency evacuation system. The council's fire department received significant criticism during the court hearing. Any warning letters received by them appeared to have been filed with no action being taken. The court concluded that 'either the letter was not considered at all or ... an irresponsible decision was made without proper consideration'.

Warnings had been given of the dangers.

Who should bear the liability? The claim was brought before the High Court in 1986.

The court decided, after a three-week hearing, that both Bradford City FC and the West Yorkshire County Council were negligent. The club should be apportioned with two-thirds of the blame and one-third of the liability should be borne by the West Yorkshire County Council.

The tragedy itself had very significant consequences for football – and for all sports grounds throughout the country. An inquiry, set up by the government, was chaired by Sir Oliver Popplewell into Crowd Safety and Control at Sports Grounds. The inquiry also took into account the events at the Heysel Stadium in Belgium, just eighteen days after the Bradford fire, in the European Cup final between Liverpool and Juventus. The final Popplewell Report was published in 1986.

Its recommendations resulted directly in new legislation governing safety at sports grounds across the UK, principally the Fire Safety and Safety of Places of Sport Act 1987. Any stand at a sports ground, with covered accommodation for 500 or more spectators, would now need a Safety Certificate from the local authority. A complete revision took place of the Green Guide issued by the Home Office regarding safety measures at sports grounds.

Bradford City played all their 'home' fixtures for the 1985/86 season and the first half of the following season at adopted grounds – at Bradford Northern Rugby League Club (Odsal Garden), Huddersfield Town (Leeds Road) and Leeds United (Elland Road).

On 14th December 1986, a full house 15,000 crowd saw a commemorative fixture to open the redeveloped Valley Parade when Bradford City defeated an England XI 2-1. The ground has been further redeveloped substantially since. A new £1.5 million stand was completed in 1996 and officially opened by Her Majesty the Queen in March 1997.

---

33 A GOLFER'S NIGHTMARE – A BADLY-SLICED DRIVE AT THE FIFTH

It was a golf society day at Buckpool golf club. During the afternoon round, a badly sliced drive by John Shipley injured another golfer. Was he liable for negligence?

The links golf course at Buckpool lies close to the fishing town of Buckie in the north-east of Scotland. It is, for many, one of Scottish golf's best kept secrets. Folklore has it that Robbie Burns, Scotland's national poet, must have crossed the land, where Buckpool's course is now set out, in order to reach the welcoming inn where, in one of his poems, he commented on the good ale of Lady Onlie:

'Lady Onlie, honest Lucky
Brews gude ale at shore o'Bucky.

I wish her sale for her gude ale.
The best on a'the shore o'Bucky.'

There are wonderful views across the Moray Firth towards the hills of Caithness. Sea breezes whip up from the Firth between shots and add to the test. Built on sand, Buckpool has fast rolling fairways, often lined by tall mature gorse bushes. It is a challenging course. Paul Lawrie, later an Open Champion in 1999 at Carnoustie, had his first professional win at Buckpool in 1986 and has played the course several times.

Sea breezes whip up from the Firth between shots and add to the test.

In September 1987 the local cricket club had a golf society day at Buckpool. The morning round was completed without incident. A good lunch was followed by an afternoon round; a very common scene at golf clubs around the land.

Thirty-two-year-old John Shipley was an occasional player and a 24-handicapper. He had been playing well by his standards. Having holed out at the long par 4 fourth, Shipley's group moved to the fifth tee. It was aptly named Morven since the distinctive hill on the north side of the Moray Firth dominated the skyline as the golfers stood on the elevated tee. It was a slight dogleg to the right, with a row of four bunkers to the right of the fairway and gorse and broom to the left. The ideal line for the drive was to the left of the bunkers.

As Shipley's group prepared to drive off, Paul Lewis and his group reached the fourth green. For golfers playing from the fifth tee, the fourth green was forward and to the right. The nearest part of the fourth green was around twenty yards away; the furthest part around fifty yards.

One member of Shipley's group drove off down the fifth fairway. Shipley went next. Shipley took his stance and drove. Unfortunately, the ball came off the toe of the club and went at an angle of thirty degrees to the right. It struck Paul Lewis as he reached the fourth green and injured him.

Lewis later claimed damages from Shipley. The case was heard, on appeal, by the Sheriff Court at Elgin in the Grampians.

Should Lewis be entitled to claim against Shipley for negligence? What is the extent of the duty which a golfer owes to fellow golfers on the course?

For: Shipley was negligent in driving off while Lewis and his group were on the fourth green. He could see that they were within range of a ball driven in that direction. As a 24-handicapper, Shipley knew or should have known that there was a real risk when he hit the ball that it would not go straight down the fairway but at an angle towards the fourth green. It was a risk which was reasonably likely to happen. Shipley was negligent.
Against: None of the players involved thought that there was a real risk. One of Shipley's group had driven off immediately before him without mishap. Shipley had not previously that day mishit a shot by striking the ball with the toe of the club. Although the layout of the fourth and fifth holes had been unchanged for 60 years, there was no record of any similar incident having happened. The risk of being hit by a golf ball in the circumstances of the accident was simply a risk Lewis impliedly accepted by playing the game of golf. This did not amount to negligence.

Lewis won his claim.

The Scottish court decided that Shipley was negligent in driving off in these circumstances. A reasonably careful player, conscious of some lack of skill and aware of a real risk that he might mishit the ball and cause injury, would have delayed before driving off.

> *If there is a real risk that the event will happen, as distinct from a mere possibility which would never influence the mind of a reasonable man, it is negligent to neglect such a risk if it can be avoided without difficulty.*

Golfers beware! Court decisions are unpredictable. The message is clear: personal injury insurance, including liability insurance will always be sensible for golfers.

---

34 HILLSBOROUGH – ENGLISH FOOTBALL'S WORST DISASTER

The tragedy at Hillsborough resulted in mental shock and injury for many. Could they also claim damages against the police for negligence?

It became one of the saddest days in football. 15th April 1989. The day of the Hillsborough disaster.

Hillsborough Stadium, home of Sheffield Wednesday, was the neutral venue for the FA Cup semi-final between Liverpool and Nottingham Forest. The same teams had met the previous year at the semi-final stage, also at Hillsborough. It was again a sell-out. The opposing fans were segregated as was customary for all large matches, the Liverpool supporters being assigned to the smaller Leppings Lane End as in the previous year.

Owing to a variety of factors, including traffic delays on the route to Sheffield from Liverpool, many of the Liverpool fans were late in arriving for the 3 p.m. kick-off. This resulted in a considerable build-up of fans at the Leppings Lane End. This End was divided into six 'pens'. The outside turnstile entrances led people more naturally into the central pens 3 and 4 although, once just inside the ground, it was possible to enter the other pens, at the sides, rather than the central pens.

Shortly before kick-off, the police decided to open a set of exit gates, Gate C, at the Leppings Lane End in order to relieve the extreme pressure outside the ground where fans were seeking to enter and a very dangerous situation had built up. Unfortunately, the natural next move of these late entering fans was to try to get into the central pens, 3 and 4, which were already overcrowded – rather than the outside pens where, if they had known, there was more room. The resulting influx of hundreds, or possibly thousands, of fans anxious to see the match resulted in a terrible crush at the front of the central pens where people became heavily pressed against high steel perimeter fencing (fencing

Shortly before kick-off, the police decided to open a set of exit gates.

introduced, ironically, at most grounds to prevent pitch invasions by hooligan spectators which had once plagued the sport).

For a time the severe problem at the Leppings End was not noticed by anybody other than those affected. It was 3.06 p.m. when the referee, after being advised by the police, stopped the match. A total of ninety-six fans died as a result of the disaster and more than 750 received physical injuries. It was the worst ever disaster at a sports ground in the UK.

The Hillsborough disaster led to a public inquiry, chaired by Lord Justice Taylor. It analysed the causes of the disaster and apportioned blame. There were a number of factors: the choice of ground was ill-considered; the local authority and the club were criticised for certain safety procedure defects; poor sign-posting outside the turnstiles and on the concourse contributed; and a minority of the fans were unruly and had drunk too much. The Taylor Report found, however, that 'the principal cause of the disaster was the failure of police control'.

A number of legal claims were brought following the tragedy including a failed private prosecution against two individual senior police officers. The Chief Constable of South Yorkshire, responsible ultimately for crowd control at the ground, formally admitted civil liability in respect of the deaths and personal injuries physically suffered.

The principal legal case which came before the courts related not to fans suffering direct injury but to another class of claimants, those suffering psychiatric injury or shock:

One claimant, Robert Alcock, lost his brother-in-law. He was in the West Stand with his nephew, his brother-in-law's son. He witnessed, with horror, the tragic scenes without realising at the time that his brother-in-law had swapped his ticket and was involved. A visit at midnight to the mortuary led to identification.

Another was at the ground and knew his brothers were in the central pens behind the goal.

One other claimant had watched the tragedy unfold on live television knowing that his children were in the ground.

Each of the claimants in this group did not suffer direct physical injury. However, each had suffered 'nervous shock' resulting in a form of psychiatric injury. In a group of test cases, actions were brought on behalf of each of these claimants against the Chief Constable. Were they entitled to recover damages as well as those suffering direct personal injury?

The House of Lords decided 'no'. The claims failed. Where the claimant had not suffered physical injury, the court decided that shock induced psychiatric illness, nervous shock, was a category of loss which in these circumstances fell outside the scope of damage or injury for which the police could be held liable. It was, in effect, a policy decision that the law could not or should not go that far.

Lord Justice Taylor's Final Report was published in January 1990. It made a total of seventy-six recommendations designed to improve the state of safety at football grounds in Britain. Specific recommendations of the Taylor Report led to two vital changes. First, fences in front of fans at the perimeter of pitches were removed. Secondly, and even more fundamental, standing terraces should be replaced with seated areas in all league football grounds by the end of the century – with all first and second division stadia becoming all-seater by the start of the 1994/05 season and all third and fourth division stadia by 1999/2000. Numerous other detailed recommendations were made, and implemented, which have led to far greater regulation on the safety of sports stadia and crowd activities.

Football stadia could never be the same again.

---

35 MICHAEL WATSON – A TRAGIC NIGHT FOR BOXING

Michael Watson suffered a brain haemorrhage at the end of a boxing title fight. Was the British Boxing Board of Control liable to him for not ensuring better medical support?

It was a tragic and unforgettable evening in 1991 at White Hart Lane in north London. An evening which would have a profound affect on boxing. An evening which would have profound implications for the legal responsibilities of all sports governing bodies.

Normally the home of Tottenham Hotspur, White Hart Lane on

that September night was the setting for a WBO super-middleweight title bout, an all-British fight between Michael Watson and Chris Eubank. It was a cool evening, with a blustery autumn breeze, for the open air fight. The boxers arrived to a ringside atmosphere which was intense and partisan.

Twenty-six-year-old Michael Watson was a popular, classy boxer from London. His fights with Nigel Benn and then Chris Eubank had excited fans and TV audiences throughout Britain. Just over three months earlier, he had fought a classic encounter with Eubank at Earl's Court for the WBO world middleweight title. Eubank, born in England but brought up in Jamaica and later in New York, retained his title although most observers thought Watson, the 'people's champion', had done enough to win. This was the rematch. It was a night which would change boxing.

It was a savage fight, tough but fair. Eubank was behind on most scorecards until, shortly before the end of the eleventh round, a fierce uppercut from Eubank caught Watson square on the chin and threw him back against the ropes seconds before the end of the round. It was clear that Watson was in difficulty. Less than a minute into the twelfth and final round, he appeared unable to defend himself. The referee, Roy Francis, stopped the fight. Watson had in fact suffered a brain haemorrhage and, returning to his stool, he lapsed into unconsciousness.

Chaos erupted inside and outside the ring. Seven minutes elapsed before Watson was examined by one of the doctors in attendance. He was taken by ambulance to North Middlesex Hospital. Nearly thirty minutes elapsed between the end of the fight and reaching the hospital. He could then be given oxygen and blood – but had to be transferred to St Bartholomew's hospital in central London for treatment in their neurological department. By this time, he had sustained serious brain damage. Watson sadly remained in a coma on a life-support machine for forty days and underwent multiple surgery to remove two blood clots from his brain. He was left paralysed down the left side and with other physical and mental disabilities. His neurosurgeon, Peter Hamlyn, doubted that Watson would ever be able to walk again.

Chaos erupted inside and outside the ring.

Watson later claimed damages against the British Boxing Board of Control (BBBC) for negligence on the grounds, he alleged, that there had been an inadequate level of medical support. It was the first time a claim for damages had been brought against a sports governing body for injury sustained by a competitor in the course of the sport. The issue went to the Court of Appeal.

Should the British Boxing Board of Control, as the regulatory body responsible for boxing in the UK, be liable for negligence in not regulating for better medical support at such a boxing event?

For: The fight had taken place in accordance with the rules of the BBBC. The resuscitation treatment received at the hospital should have been available at the ringside. If it had been, Watson would not have sustained such serious brain damage. The Board, as governing body, had regulatory control over a sport where physical injury was foreseeable, including regulation over the level of medical care to be available. The Board failed in its duty of care to see that all reasonable steps were taken to ensure that a boxer received immediate and effective attention if injured during a fight.
Against: The Board was a non-profit making body. It did not itself organise boxing contests or employ medical staff at contests. Indeed, the fight was organised by the World Boxing Organisation (WBO). The Board was simply a UK regulatory body. In legal terms, there was not sufficient proximity between the Board and individual boxers to give rise to a direct duty of care owed to each boxer. There was no evidence of any other boxing authority in the world imposing regulations requiring the degree of medical support contemplated. There had in fact been an ambulance close to the ringside staffed by an adequately trained paramedic. The Board should not be liable in negligence for Watson's injury.

Watson won his claim.

The Court of Appeal decided that the British Boxing Board of Control was liable. The Board was the regulatory body for boxing in Britain. The court, in haunting words for sports governing bodies, said that:

> *[T]he Board was in a position to determine ... the measures that were taken in boxing to protect and promote health and safety ... of professional boxers at fights held in the UK. This*

> *gave rise to a duty of reasonable care owed by the Board to each boxer. The Board had access to specialist learning in the field. A reasonable standard of care required the availability of resuscitation facilities at the ringside and of medical staff who knew how to use them. If they had been available, the outcome would probably have been different.*

Watson was subsequently awarded damages of around £750,000.

This was truly a landmark case, the first in which a governing body had been judged negligent for failing to regulate properly for the safety of participants – even though it had no direct role in the organisation of the contest itself. It was a decision which really made sports governing bodies sit up and take notice of their potential legal liabilities. Governing bodies, generally, have become much more alert to their potential liabilities to participants as well as spectators.

The plight of Watson forced the sport to introduce a number of safety measures which have since helped to save other fighters. Indeed, many believe that British boxing has now probably the best safety procedures in the world of boxing, including a requirement to have an ambulance available with the necessary resuscitation equipment at the venue and trained teams of paramedics at the ringside.

For the British Boxing Board of Control (BBBC) itself, the case was a financial disaster. It was a non-profit organisation and inadequately insured. They had thought liability insurance was 'too expensive and inappropriate'. Facing legal costs of around £300,000 and the prospect of substantial compensation to be paid to Watson, the BBBC was placed into administration in 1999 in a bid to secure its long-term survival as the regulatory body of the sport. Two partners of the accounting firm, Hacker Young and Partners, were appointed joint administrators.

The BBBC eventually sold its London headquarters to finance the damages settlement and is now headquartered in Cardiff.

In 2003, twelve years after his accident, the sporting world was uplifted at the sight of Michael Watson walking the London Marathon. He completed the 26.2 mile course in just over six days, raising funds for the Brain and Spine Foundation. Watson's neurosurgeon described it as 'one of the greatest physical achievements the marathon has ever seen'. He was joined for the final mile by Chris Eubank.

Michael Watson was awarded an MBE in the New Year's honours list in 2004 for his work for disabled sport.

---

36 DEAN SAUNDERS – A CAREER-ENDING TACKLE AT ANFIELD

A clash between Dean Saunders and Paul Elliott led to the end of Elliott's playing career. Did a claim lie in negligence against Saunders?

Liverpool were at home at Anfield against Chelsea in September 1992. Two fiercely competitive teams. A nasty clash early in the game led to a first for the courts: the first legal claim by a footballer for damages resulting from a tackle in a top flight game. Could a professional player sue another player if he was injured as a result of a bad tackle?

The score was 0-0 after ten minutes. The ball was played out of the Chelsea half into open space near the halfway line. Dean Saunders, a Liverpool striker and Welsh international, ran toward the ball – as, from a different direction, did Chelsea's highly regarded defender, Paul Elliott. Saunders was just favourite to reach the ball. Elliott made a leap towards the ball with his right leg forward in a kind of scissors action. Saunders saw this and, a brief fraction of a second later, responded by jumping with both feet off the ground. Saunders' feet landed on Elliott's outstretched leg in the area of the knee. Elliott was seriously injured, the cruciate ligaments in his knee were severed. The incident, in effect, brought Elliott's playing career to an end.

It was the first legal claim by a professional footballer for damages for an alleged negligent tackle.

The match ended in a 2-1 win for Liverpool.

Elliott later brought a legal claim for damages against Saunders for negligence. It was the first legal claim by one professional footballer against another for damages based on an alleged negligent tackle during a match.

Was Dean Saunders guilty of negligence by making a challenge which intentionally or recklessly risked serious injury? What is the duty of care owed by a professional footballer in making a challenge in a match at the level of the Premier League?

For: The video evidence suggested that Saunders jumped at Elliott rather than the ball. He appeared to have changed his mind, checked and slowed down, waiting for an opportunity to jump at Elliott. Saunders could have taken evasive action to avoid the collision. He acted recklessly in going 'over-the-top' at the man rather than the ball. **Against:** Saunders claimed that he was always going for the ball. His actions in that moment were governed by instinct rather than careful thought. He jumped to avoid injury without intending to land on Elliott's outstretched leg. His eyes were focused on the ball. The referee had a good view of the incident and, in fact, gave a foul against Elliott for dangerous play.

Paul Elliott lost his claim.

The case came before the High Court. Justice Drake observed:

> *Dry legal language hides the drama which has led to the appearance in this court of two top ranking professional footballers who, with numerous supporting witnesses, have over a period of about nine days, replayed an incident which, in real life, lasted less than a second.*

The court acknowledged that 'there is a lot of popular support for the view that the law should be kept away from sport'. It reaffirmed nevertheless that the law of negligence did apply to injuries on the sporting field. The question was: did Dean Saunders break the standard of care required?

A series of well-known players and commentators gave evidence. As the judge remarked, they brought 'their individual colour into the witness box'. Much of the witness evidence, on both sides, was based on study and analysis of the slow motion video replay.

In the witness team put out by Paul Elliott were such illustrious figures as Dennis Wise, Dave Beasant, John Hollins, Don Howe, former eminent referee Ken Aston, and reporters Brian Glanville and Patrick Barclay. Even Ken Bates, Chelsea's colourful chairman, gave evidence based on the video replay. All suggested that Dean Saunders had paused momentarily and, recklessly or intentionally, jumped in a way which went 'over-the-top' at the man rather than for the ball. Some purported to have a view from the pitch, including Dennis Wise who was about twenty yards away and said that he had not seen many worse tackles than this one by Saunders. Justice Drake did not, though, find Wise 'reliable as an eyewitness'.

Vinnie Jones was a reluctant witness. Officially recognised by Justice Drake as 'a player with a considerable reputation as the hard man of football', Jones in the end could not say for certain that Saunders deliberately went over the top. 'The whole thing took place at lightning speed.' 'Football is a man's game and people can get hurt.' Justice Drake was impressed by Jones as 'a very good reliable and honest witness.'

Lined up as witnesses for the defence of Saunders were former players Larry Lloyd, Garry Birtles and Geoff Hurst. Hurst thought that, once committed, Saunders could not avoid Elliott's challenge and acted reasonably in jumping as he did. Saunders himself said: 'Instinct told me to get my feet off the floor and that was the only way I was going to get the ball without getting seriously hurt.'

Justice Drake was impressed by Vinnie Jones as a 'very good reliable and honest witness.'

The strongest evidence came, in the end, from the officials. The referee, John Key, was only about ten yards from the incident. He thought Saunders was attempting to play the ball. He awarded a free kick not against Saunders but against Chelsea because of Elliott's dangerous play. The nearest linesman raised his flag for the same reason. Journalist Brian Glanville said the referee was 'inept', but the Football League referee assessor at the match thought the referee's decision to penalise Elliott was correct.

On the basis of the evidence, Justice Drake had little difficulty in reaching the judgment that Elliott had failed to prove that Saunders was in breach of his duty of care. He was not guilty of dangerous or reckless play.

It would be another day before a professional player would succeed in a claim for negligence against a fellow player.

The first successful claim by a professional footballer was in 1996 when Stockport County's Brian McCord was awarded £250,000 in damages against Swansea's John Cornforth after a career-ending high tackle. This was followed by Gordon Watson's claim. When playing for Bradford City, Watson suffered a double leg fracture in a clash with Huddersfield defender Kevin Gray in a Division One game in 1997. Watson was awarded over £950,000 – importantly, not only against Gray but also Huddersfield Town FC as his employer.

Clubs beware! For several years, the courts became reluctant to impose liability for field-of-play incidents. But the potential liability of an 'employer' for the misdeeds of its players took a significant turn in 2008. First Redruth Rugby Club were ordered by the Court of Appeal to pay £8,550 in damages (plus substantial legal costs) when one of their players, second row forward Richard Carroll, hit and injured an opponent after 'a melée of the kind which frequently occurs during rugby matches'. The incident was, the court said, sufficiently connected with his employment for the club to be liable – even if deliberate and he was only a part-time employee. Clubs must be encouraged to 'eradicate, at least minimise, the risk of foul play which might cause injury'.

Later in 2008, Ben Collett, a young promising Manchester United player (described by Sir Alex Ferguson as an 'A-class' player with an 'outstanding chance' of being awarded a professional contract) succeeded in a claim after his career had been ended by a reckless 'over -the-ball' tackle by a Middlesbrough player in a reserve match. His damages? An extraordinary, and record, £4.3 million. They will be met by Middlesbrough or, more particularly, the club's insurers. Was this a one-off ? Many clubs – and lawyers – wonder where all this will lead. Insurance premiums will no doubt rise.

His damages? An extraordinary, and record, £4.3 million.

As for Paul Elliott, in 2003 he was awarded the MBE for his work with young players and his involvement with anti-racism initiatives in football. In 2006 Elliott was appointed to serve on the disciplinary panel of the Football Association.

---

37 ADRIAN MAGUIRE – INJURY IN A TWO-MILE HURDLE AT HEXHAM

It's not just football or rugby where players cause accidents. Careless riding in a race at Hexham by leading jockey, Adrian Maguire, led to an injury to a following jockey. Did a claim lie in negligence against Maguire?

Hexham racecourse is in a superb country setting, perched on Yarridge Heights high above the historic market town of Hexham. It has been the home of National Hunt racing in Northumberland for more than a century.

A two-mile novice hurdle race at Hexham in September 1994 involved twenty-three-year-old Adrian Maguire, one of the country's leading jump jockeys. The Irishman had, in 1992, won a stirring victory in the Cheltenham Gold Cup aboard *Cool Ground* and then, the following year, the King George VI Chase on *Barton Bank*. In the two-mile hurdle at Hexham he was on *Master Hyde*. Grand National winner, Mick Fitzgerald, was riding *Mr Bean* and Derek Byrne was on *Royal Citizen*.

It was a close race. These three horses were together as they jumped the second last hurdle. *Royal Citizen*, on the inside, jumped badly. Ahead, they approached a left hand bend. *Mr Bean* and *Master Hyde* pulled three-quarters of a length ahead of *Royal Citizen*.

Both Maguire and Fitzgerald moved their horses inside, taking a line which left Derek Byrne on *Royal Citizen* no room on the bend. Byrne, though, was seeking to make up the lost ground and was urging *Royal Citizen* forward between the rail on his near side and *Mr Bean*. *Royal Citizen* shied away from the closing gap and veered to the right behind *Mr Bean* and *Master Hyde*. This manoeuvre unseated Byrne.

Byrne's fall brought down the immediately following horse, *Fion Corn*, ridden by jockey Peter Caldwell. Caldwell fell to the ground and suffered serious injury, breaking his back.

A stewards' inquiry was held following the race. The stewards found that Maguire and Fitzgerald had been guilty of careless riding on the grounds that they had left insufficient room for Byrne to come along the inside rail on *Royal Citizen*. Each jockey was suspended for three days.

Later, Caldwell brought a claim in the courts against Maguire, and also Fitzgerald, to recover damages for negligence to compensate for his injuries. It was the first case of its kind in horseracing. It brought into sharp focus the question: how high is the standard of care owed by a participant in competitive sport to other participants?

> **How high is the standard of care owed by a participant in a competitive sport to other participants?**

Should Maguire be found guilty of negligence and liable to pay damages to Caldwell? The case eventually went up to the Court of Appeal.

For: A participant in a sporting activity owed each other participant a duty of care. Maguire and Fitzgerald were guilty of careless riding under the rules of racing. Both jockeys should have looked to their left to see that *Royal Citizen* was no longer in contention. They had not satisfied the standard of care required in the circumstances. It was foreseeable that injury could result to a jockey on a following horse if they failed in that duty. They should be liable for damages in respect of the injuries caused by that negligence.
Against: Account must be taken of the special circumstances of competitive sport. Decisions are taken in the heat of the moment. Each participant was expected to compete for the best possible placing, if not for a win. Accidents and misjudgements inevitably occurred. Careless riding was a relatively common offence in racing. The threshold before a legal claim could be brought in the courts for negligence should be much higher than a mere error of judgment or lapse of skill. The standard should be equivalent to deliberate or reckless disregard of the consequences. Maguire and Fitzgerald were not guilty on that test.

The courts decided in favour of Maguire and Fitzgerald. Caldwell's claim for negligence failed.

In the High Court, evidence was given – including by fellow jockey, John Francombe – that they should not have taken the inside line unless and until they were one length clear of *Royal Citizen*. Double Grand National winner Carl Llewellyn was also called as an expert witness. He agreed that the two jockeys should have known Byrne was on their inside, but said: 'It happens every day of the week. These things happen all the time.'

In the High Court, the judge decided that the riding of the two jockeys had not been reckless or negligent.

> *This incident reflected the cut and thrust of serious horseracing. In theory avoidable but in practice something that is bound to occur from time to time, no matter how careful is the standard of riding.*

On appeal, the Court of Appeal was of a similar view. The test for negligence, in this context, must take into account the circumstances of competitive sport including the inherent dangers, the customs and conventions of that sport and the skills and standards reasonably to be expected of participants in a fast-moving horse race.

Lord Justice Tuckey summed up:

> *... participants in competitive sport owe one another a duty of care ... [but] it is not possible to characterise momentary carelessness as negligence. [There should be] no liability for errors of judgment, oversights or lapses of which any participant might be guilty in the context of a fast-moving contest. Something more serious is required.*

Lord Justice Judge said similarly:

> *... in the context of sporting contests it is ... right to emphasise the distinction to be drawn between conduct which is properly to be characterised as negligent ... and errors of judgment, oversights or lapses of attention of which any reasonable jockey may be guilty in the hurly burly of a race.*

Maguire and Fitzgerald had not broken that level of duty.

Adrian Maguire had, unwillingly, helped to clarify the law. This was an important judgment. The decision reaffirmed that civil claims between playing participants in a competitive sport can only be brought in extreme circumstances. The law makes considerable allowance for the 'rough and tumble' of competitive sport. The courts will be reluctant to support a civil claim for damages for accidental injury unless the defendant has, in effect, been guilty of a level of recklessness which is outside the 'playing culture' of the sport.

Adrian Maguire narrowly lost out to Richard Dunwoody in the race for champion jump jockey in that 1993/94 season – 194 winners to Dunwoody's 197. Maguire later became one of the elite group of jump jockeys to win over 1,000 winners in his career.

---

38 WHO'D BE A REFEREE? A COLLAPSING SCRUM AT DAISY FIELD

Do referees owe the players a duty of care for their safety? A tragic incident in an amateur Welsh rugby match would lead to the answer.

Daisy Field, home of Llanharran rugby football club in south Wales, was the scene of a tragic incident late in an amateur match in 1998. It gave rise to another first for the courts: could an amateur referee be liable for injuries suffered by a player in an adult match?

Llanharran moved to Daisy Field in 1990. The ground was so called because of the adjacent milk processing plant which closed in the late 1960s after more than fifty years. In January 1998 a local derby match was being played between the amateur Llanharran 2nd XV and neighbouring Tondu 2nd XV. It was a hard-fought match on a boggy pitch.

After half-an-hour's play, Llanharran lost their loose-head prop through injury. They had no trained front row forward on the bench or the field to replace him. The referee, David Evans, told the Llanharran captain that they could provide a replacement from within the scrum or, if they wished, opt for non-contestable scrums. If they opted for the latter and won the match, the points would not count towards the league competition.

Llanharran flanker, Chris Jones, said that he would 'give it a go' as front row forward. He was not asked by the referee about his experience for that position. When the match resumed, set scrummaging deteriorated and the scrum collapsed a number of times. The lack of technique and experience of Jones as a prop forward was a significant factor.

The match moved into the final minute. Llanharran were leading 3-0 but Tondu were attacking strongly. There were a number of set scrums five metres from the Llanharran line. Tondu were looking for a pushover try which, if converted, would have enabled them to snatch victory.

There was a final scrum. The Llanharran pack did not crouch as a unit. Twenty-four-year-old Richard Vowles was the Llanharran hooker. The front rows failed to engage properly. The referee blew his whistle. As the scrum parted, Vowles collapsed to the ground. It was clear that it was a serious injury. The referee brought the match to an end. Vowles was taken by ambulance to hospital. He had suffered a dislocated neck which led to paralysis.

As the scrum parted, Vowles collapsed to the ground. It was clear it was a serious injury.

Confined to a wheelchair following the injury, Vowles later brought a legal claim for negligence against the referee, David Evans, and the Welsh Rugby Union (WRU) who appointed him. The basis of the claim was that Evans, the referee, ironically a practising solicitor, had breached his duty to safeguard the safety of the players by not satisfying himself that Jones was sufficiently trained or experienced for the front row. Evans and the WRU resisted saying that, at most, it was an error of judgment. It was the first time a claim had been brought against a referee for negligence in an adult match (one earlier claim against a referee had been made following an accident in a youth match).

Did an amateur referee owe the players a duty of care? Should Evans have satisfied himself that Jones was sufficiently trained or experienced to be tried in the front row? Was he negligent and liable to compensate the injured player?

For: One of the responsibilities of a referee is to safeguard the safety of the players. He does owe the players a duty of care. He should apply the laws of the game with this in mind. The evidence suggested that Evans did not satisfy himself that Jones was suitably trained or experienced for the front row. He abdicated responsibility by simply leaving it to the Llanharran captain to elect whether or not to proceed with non-contestable scrums. This constituted a breach of his duty. **Against:** Evans was an amateur referee. It was not fair or reasonable to expose such a referee to the risk of ruinous legal liability. If referees were to become potentially liable for damages claims, the supply of amateur referees might well diminish significantly – contrary to the interests of the game. If a referee is to be held liable, the threshold for liability should be very high and not simply an error of judgment. Moreover, whilst the scrummaging had deteriorated after Jones had entered the front row, it was not totally unsatisfactory. A finding of negligence would be excessive.

Richard Vowles won his claim for damages.

In the Swansea County Court, the court recognised that it was making an important judgment in the context of amateur officials. Justice Morland nevertheless said:

> *... it is just and reasonable that the law should impose upon an amateur referee of an amateur rugby match a duty of care towards the safety of the players.*

The Court of Appeal confirmed the finding of the lower court that the referee, David Evans, had been guilty of negligence and was liable to compensate Vowles for his severe injury.

The court concluded that a primary cause of the accident to Vowles was that the referee, in breach of the laws of the game and negligently, had permitted a player who lacked suitable training and experience to play in the Llanharran front row. Lord Phillips stated:

> *... Mr Evans abdicated ... responsibility ... of deciding whether ... to insist upon non-contestable scrummages. This constituted a breach of his duty to exercise reasonable care for the safety of the players.*

The court emphasised that the referee's decision was made when play was stopped. Very different considerations would apply where it was alleged that a referee was negligent because of a decision made during play itself. Lord Phillips was aware of the implications of the decision.

He said:

> *In my judgment when rugby is funded not only by gate receipts but also by lucrative television contracts I can see no reason why the Welsh Rugby Union should not insure itself and its referees against claims and the risk of a finding of a breach of duty of care by a referee where the threshold of liability is a high one which will not easily be crossed ... Insurance cover for referees would be a cost spread across the whole game.*

This was another landmark case. It was the first time that an amateur referee in any sport had been held liable for injuries arising in an adult amateur game. The WRU accepted responsibility for the referee whom they had appointed and therefore became liable for payment of the damages to Vowles.

This important decision caused deep concern in many quarters. It seems a very hard decision on the facts – and undoubtedly influenced by the fact that the WRU was known to be standing behind the individual referee for payment of any damages. Who would be a referee? Many fears were expressed that the decision could have a serious effect on the willingness of amateurs to referee matches and, indeed, on coaches, teachers and volunteers of all kinds who assist in amateur sport.

The court's decision had a serious effect on the finances of the WRU which only had limited insurance cover. Subsequently, the WRU's insurers insisted that only qualified referees should referee in matches at all levels. This led to the cancellation of many matches in Wales the following season. The WRU were given a grant by the Sports Council to assist in increasing the number of trained referees in Wales.

Better times in Llanharran's history occurred in 2003/04 when, under the off-pitch leadership of Welsh legend Gareth Edwards, the club's first team won a thrilling race to win the first division championship and earn the club a place in the top tier of Welsh club rugby.

CHAPTER FIVE

REFEREES, UMPIRES AND THE OLYMPICS

We move to the heart of the competitive action. Referees, judges, umpires and panels are constantly making decisions in the course of play (or, sometimes, at the end of play) which are crucial to the outcome of the match or competition. Common sayings sum up the traditional standards of sport: 'the referee is always right', 'the umpire's decision is final', 'there must be a winner on the day'. The ordinary courts are, rightly, very reluctant to become involved in reviewing purely 'field of play' decisions. But when should a court or arbitral tribunal intervene to correct a proven mistake or apparent injustice?

The Court of Arbitration for Sport (CAS) has become the most important arbitral tribunal in sport. It was set up in 1984 by the International Olympic Committee (IOC) under the initiative of President Juan Antonio Samaranch, with the objective that the growing number of sports-related disputes should be resolved 'within the family of sport' rather than the more hostile and costly environment of litigation in the traditional courts. Its headquarters are in Lausanne, Switzerland. Its panel of arbitrators from more than eighty countries are chosen for their experience in arbitration and sport. Operating independently of the IOC, CAS is recognised by the international legal system as a true independent court of arbitration.

CAS derives its authority from the rules of a large number of international and national sporting bodies which provide for CAS to be the ultimate appeal body for disputes under that body's jurisdiction. CAS has developed a special role in the Olympic Games. A panel of arbitrators is available at short notice to hear any disputes which need resolution during the Games. Whilst its decisions only apply to the particular facts or rules in the dispute before it, principles expressed by CAS are widely respected and influential in future sports' cases worldwide. The establishment of CAS has been a major success.

This chapter takes us to challenges before CAS in a wide range of sports, including disputes challenging the results in the 20 kilometre walk, the marathon, gymnastics, and equestrian eventing at the Olympics and a wheelchair race in the Paralympics.

---

39 CHRISTOPHE MENDY – A HIT BELOW THE BELT?

Could Christophe Mendy use video evidence to get a referee's decision to disqualify him overturned and his Olympic boxing bout re-held?

'I've sacrificed years of my life for this. Why stop that fight? Why?' A heavyweight boxing contest was the setting for a major controversy at the 1996 Olympic Games in Atlanta. It was a quarter-final bout between Christophe Mendy, a twenty-five-year-old highly fancied French boxer, and Canadian David Defiagbon. The winner was assured of at least a bronze medal.

Mendy was much admired in the boxing world. He was a bronze medal winner at the 1995 World Amateur Championships when he narrowly lost to reigning Olympic champion, Félix Savón from Cuba. Mendy, a stylish boxer, was the strong favourite and regarded by many experts as the most likely challenger to the legendary Savón who was seeking to retain his Olympic title. Defiagbon, born in Nigeria, was an All-African champion who fled to Canada for political reasons in 1992 and obtained citizenship.

The fight was closer than expected. Mendy led after the first round and well into the second. Defiagbon then recovered to take a 10-8 lead on the judges' scores by the end of the second round. The third round started. Mendy attacked strongly, boring in on Defiagbon and slinging punches as Defiagbon was pinned to the ropes. Mendy was now just one point behind. There were nearly two minutes left for Mendy to assert his superiority.

Then, after a punch to the body from Mendy, Defiagbon suddenly dropped to the canvas as if his legs had been removed from under him. He rolled on the floor, clawing at his groin with his glove and claiming a low blow. Mendy looked down in disbelief. Defiagbon continued writhing, his face contorted with pain for several minutes.

A doctor was called. He examined Defiagbon in the ring and accepted the Canadian's word that he was unable to continue. Mendy was disqualified by the referee, Abduk Samad. The fight was over. Mendy was astonished, angry and near to tears.

The French team were outraged. Mendy, through an interpreter, made his plea: 'This is sacrilegious. This is dishonest. Why stop that fight? Why?' The French team leader made a written protest and delivered a videotape of the fight to officials, claiming that Mendy should not have been disqualified. It was not a low blow but a legitimate punch to the liver. Defiagbon could in any event have continued.

'This is sacrilegious. This is dishonest.'

Should videotape evidence be used to alter the referee's decision and the result? The Amateur International Boxing Association (AIBA) rejected the protest. The French team persisted and appealed to the ad hoc panel of the Court of Arbitration for Sport (CAS) which was available at the Olympics. The panel met before the semi-final round.

Should CAS review the decision made by the referee that the punch was below the belt and that Mendy should be disqualified?

For: The French team argued that the videotape indicated that the blow was not low. Defiagbon was in any event greatly exaggerating the effect of the blow. He could have continued. A clear injustice had occurred and the decision of the AIBA to reject the protest should be overturned. **Against:** The referee's decision made at the time, on the application of technical 'game rules' to the circumstances, must be treated as final. That was an essential element of sport. The protest had in any event been considered by the appropriate body within the AIBA. It would be wrong for it to be reviewed or overturned by an outside arbitral tribunal.

Mendy lost again. CAS decided that, although it did have power to review the case, it would not intervene.

It was the first time that a claim to review a referee's decision had come before CAS. CAS laid down the fundamental principle. It was not appropriate for an arbitral panel to review a referee's decision regarding the application of a technical rule specific to the sport concerned. Such decisions were the responsibility of the referee or the federation concerned:

> *... the referee's decision ... is a purely technical one pertaining to the rules which are the responsibility of the federation concerned. It is not for the ad hoc Panel to review the application of those rules.*

The arbitral panel was less well placed to decide than the referee in the ring or the ring judges. Intervention with a referee's decision should only be considered if there is evidence of an error of law or of a malicious act. It was for each sport to decide to what extent, and how, within its own rules a player or team should be able to challenge a refereeing or sporting decision. CAS would not, in the absence of evidence of bad faith, go beyond that and itself hear again or review a 'field of play' decision of a referee or umpire.

It was not appropriate to review a referee's decision regarding the application of a technical rule.

There has been no reported case in England of a legal challenge to a referee's decision aimed at altering the result of the game or competition itself – as opposed to a disciplinary consequence of a referee's decision, such as a sending off. In the Paul Elliot/Dean Saunders case (see Chapter 4), the court affirmed: 'Unless and until video is introduced by the governing body of a sport as an aid to the referee or umpire [as part of the game's rules], his decisions on the field must be final as regards what happens during the game.' If the referee says the ball did not cross the line for a goal, it is no goal. The English courts would almost certainly take the same line as CAS and not interfere with any 'field of play' decision unless bad faith or fraud is demonstrated.

Defiagbon went through to the semi-final – which he won and so became assured of at least the silver medal. In the final, he was well-beaten, 2-20, by the great Félix Savón.

---

40 BERNARDO SEGURA – MEXICAN OUTRAGE AT 'OLYMPIC ROBBERY'

Could Bernardo Segura claim that his disqualification was contrary to the rules and that his Olympic marathon gold medal should be re-instated ?

It was a warm September evening. The Olympic Stadium in Sydney would be the scene of many dramatic finishes during the 2000 Olympics. None more so than in the first track event, the 20 kilometre walk. Who was the winner?

The spectators in the stadium were excitedly awaiting the climax as the walkers entered the stadium for the final lap. The crowd had followed the race on the large television screens. It was going to be the closest finish ever in Olympic race walking. The race had been at a fast pace throughout. An Olympic record was in prospect.

Thirty-year-old Mexican Bernardo Segura, holder of the world record, was making a challenge for the lead. Just in front were the reigning 50 kilometre walk Olympic champion, Poland's Robert Korzeniowski, and another Mexican Noe Hernandez. They were ten metres ahead when Segura began his challenge to overtake the two leaders as they left the loop around the stadium and began to enter the long tunnel into the stadium itself.

It was going to be the closest finish ever in Olympic racewalking.

In race walking, at least one foot must remain in contact with the ground throughout. Competitors are assessed by highly experienced judges at many points along the race. A judge may give either a caution directly to a competitor or an official warning. The same judge may only give one warning. Warnings are not given to a competitor but are posted on a signboard and the competitor does not know which judge has given a warning. If a competitor receives two official warnings, a third warning leads to disqualification. Disqualifications can, though, only be notified by the chief judge. A disqualification must, under the rules of the sport, be given as soon as practical during the race or 'immediately' after the finish.

Segura knew that he had already received one warning, after one hour fifty-one minutes of the race. His second warning, of which he was apparently unaware, came eight minutes later as he left the loop outside the stadium for the final time and began accelerating to catch the leaders. Then, as Segura entered the tunnel into the Olympic Stadium and just four minutes and four hundred metres from the finish, another judge spotted a further loss of contact.

Segura and the crowd were completely unaware of the situation and its implications. Segura pressed forward to finish ahead of Korzeniowski by just two seconds in a dramatic neck-and-neck finish. It was a new Olympic record. Mexico rejoiced. Segura conducted his victory celebrations, draped in the Mexican flag. He was interviewed by television. With the cameras rolling, he received a congratulatory telephone call from President Ernesto Zedillo of Mexico.

Then, a full fifteen minutes after he had crossed the line, the chief judge interrupted. He showed an astonished Segura a red card for disqualification. Mexican officials launched an official protest, but it was rejected. They felt victimised. A further appeal against the disqualification was made by the Mexican officials to the Court of Arbitration for Sport (CAS). The matter was heard at short notice by the ad hoc panel of CAS which sat at the Olympics.

Segura conducted his victory celebrations, draped in the Mexican flag

Should Segura's disqualification be set aside on the basis that it was not given 'immediately' after the finish as required by the rules?

For: The rules must be interpreted strictly where a disqualification is concerned. 'Immediately' means promptly after the finish of the race. In an event as important as the Olympic final, it was known that any disqualification would dramatically affect the result and that victory celebrations would be televised worldwide. In these circumstances, it was vital that the rule should be strictly interpreted.

> **Against:** Segura had been judged to have lost contact on three occasions. Official warnings had been given in accordance with the rules. At the finish, the chief judge was engaged in giving a warning to another competitor still racing. Discretion was then exercised not to interrupt the televised interview which Segura was giving (until it went on longer than anticipated). The delay was unfortunate. However, the rules had been broken. The disqualification should stand.

Segura's disqualification was confirmed by CAS.

The three warnings had been duly given. 'Immediately' must be read as qualified by a notion of 'reasonable under the circumstances'. There was no evidence of malice or bad faith by the judges. The arbitrators stressed that it would be unfair on the other competitors if the result was altered:

> *The panel must have regard to the interest of competitors who did not infringe the rules ... The undoubted disappointment and embarrassment suffered by Mr Segura do not begin to outweigh the fact that he merited disqualification under the applicable rules; his competitors are entitled not to be deprived of their places.*

The delay was unfortunate but the disqualification must stand. Arbitrators should be very reluctant to review a determination made 'on the playing field' by officials charged with applying the rules of the game unless the rules are applied in bad faith.

It would be unfair on all competitors who had abided by the rules if the result was altered. The panel ruled that the disqualification must stand.

Robert Korzeniowski was confirmed as the winner of the gold medal. He went on to win the double, retaining his 50 kilometre walk title.

This was another clear example of the reluctance of courts or tribunals to intervene in decisions made by referees, umpires, judges or panels 'on the playing field' when applying the rules of the game. Any other decision would have been unfair on other competitors who had raced in compliance with the rules. Even if the manner of disqualification was unsatisfactory, the underlying substance must prevail. The interest of maintaining the integrity of sporting competition led inexorably to the 'fairness' of disqualification.

Last-minute disqualification at the point of victory was not a new experience for Segura. He had also been disqualified five years earlier after winning the 1995 Pan American Games in Mar del Plata, Argentina. Ironically, Korzeniowski recalled that he had also suffered a fate similar to the Mexican while in the silver position in the stadium finish to the 50 kilometre walk at the 1992 Barcelona Olympics. He said: 'I have made it a rule since then never to accelerate over the last stages of the race, since the judges can disqualify you in the last four-hundred metres without warning.'

The decision did little to quell the sense of outrage amongst the Mexicans. Feelings were so great in Mexico itself that the Australian embassy in Mexico City even felt compelled to issue a statement denying any official conspiracy by the Australian government. One of Mexico's leading daily newspapers described it as 'an Olympic robbery'.

---

41 CHANTAL PETITCLERC – COLLISION IN THE WHEELCHAIR 800 METRES

Could Chantal Petitclerc overturn a chief referee's decision ordering a wheelchair race in the Paralympics to be re-run after a crash earlier in the race?

Kylie Minogue sang to the crowd. Australia embraced the 2000 Paralympics with the same enthusiasm as the summer Olympics earlier in the year. An audience of 87,000 spectators enjoyed a party atmosphere at the opening ceremony with the parade of nations involving 4,000 athletes from more than 120 countries. But competition was as fierce as in the summer Games. None more so than in the women's 800 metres wheelchair race.

The Paralympic flame was ignited at the opening ceremony by one of Australia's best-known wheelchair athletes, Louise Savage. Savage, the reigning World Sportsperson of the Year with a Disability, had won seven gold medals at the previous Barcelona and Atlanta Games. She had not been beaten in a wheelchair race for eight years.

Her great rival for the women's 800 metres was Canada's top wheelchair racer, thirty-one-year-old Chantal Petitclerc. After an accident in 1983 had left her with paraplegia, Petitclerc had turned to sport. Her intense dedication and skill had won her universal recognition. In 1999 she was honoured for her contribution to the advancement of women in track and field by the International Amateur Athletics Federation (IAAF). Petitclerc had already won silver medals in both the 100 and 200 metres at the Sydney Paralympics. She was looking forward to the 800 metres and her race with Savage. 'I have dreamt about Louise more than I have about my boyfriend', she said.

The racers were ready. It was a fast start. Petitclerc and Savage were soon in the leading group as they fought for the lead. Further back, a collision occurred after 198 metres between three athletes. The official starter allowed the race to continue. Out at the front, Petitclerc and Savage fought a thrilling battle. In a dramatic finish, Petitclerc held on to beat Savage and win the gold. A famous victory. Or was it?

'I have dreamt about Louise more than I have about my boyfriend'

A protest was made after the race by one of the other competitors, Wakacho Tsuchida of Japan, who was bounced out of her chair in the earlier collision. She felt that, but for the collision, she would have had a chance of a bronze medal. The chief referee, considering the protest, decided to disqualify an Irish athlete who caused the collision. More significantly, he ordered the race to be reheld the following Thursday. The Canadian Paralympic Committee protested. Petitclerc's victory, they argued, should stand. 'Chantal won that race. She won it fairly. We will go to all lengths to ensure that Chantal is treated justly.'

Under the rules of the IAAF and the International Paralympic Committee, the starter had entire control of the start. He could choose to 'stop the race within the first 200 metres if a collision takes place'. The Canadians argued that his decision at the time to continue the race was the official decision and should stand. The race should not be re-held. 'We do not understand the decision to deny our protest.

It is illogical and a contradiction of the IAAF Handbook and the IPC rules,' said the Canadian head coach.

The Canadian team appealed to the ad hoc panel of the Court of Arbitration for Sport (CAS) who heard the case just two days after the original race.

Should the decision of the chief referee to order a re-race be overturned? Should the decision of the starter to allow the race to continue be upheld? Should Petitclerc retain her gold?

For: The collision occurred within the first 200 metres. The starter had, under the rules, the sole power to decide whether or not to stop the race. He decided not to stop it. The leading pack were ahead of the collision and the starter judged it right to let them continue. It was not within the power of the chief referee to overrule the starter's decision. Petitclerc won fairly.

Against: The race had ceased to be within the first 200 metres when the leading group were beyond that mark. It was within the chief referee's power to decide whether or not to order the race to be re-held. It could not be certain where innocent racers, affected by the collision, might have finished. It was the chief referee's decision. He properly exercised his power to order a re-race.

Petitclerc won her case.

CAS decided that, for the purposes of the rules, ' ... a race is within the first 200 metres if some athletes are within 200 metres of the start even though some ... are beyond the 200 metres.' The starter should have been the sole judge, under those rules, whether or not the race should be stopped when there was a collision within the first 200 metres. The chief referee had no power under the rules to overturn the starter's decision.

The chief referee had no power under the rules to overturn the starter's decision.

The decision of CAS was not a case of subsequent intervention in a 'playing decision'. It was a case of upholding the rules and the decision of the 'field of play' official who, under those rules, had the responsibility for making the decision. Louise Savage accepted the decision gracefully. 'The court's decision is fine. I had nothing to do with it. We didn't disagree with anything that happened. That's the way it goes.'

Petitclerc retained her victory and the 800 metres gold.

The two great rivals met again later in the 2000 Paralympics in the wheelchair 1500 metres. Savage gained her revenge, winning gold with a fine tactical race. Petitclerc came fifth.

In 2005 Chantal Petitclerc was named Canada's female athlete of the year – as well as being given the prestigious Laureus Award by sports journalists around the world to the disabled athlete of the year.

She won a further five gold medals at the Beijing Paralympics in 2008, making a total of fourteen Paralympic victories in her career.

---

42 OLYMPIC 'SKATEGATE' SCANDAL – THE FRENCH JUDGE AND THE SECOND MARK

Could the Canadian skating pair get the Olympic decision overturned on the grounds that one of the judges had unfairly prejudged the result?

It promised to be a great night. The Russian, Canadian and Chinese pairs were amongst the most talented ever assembled in competition. The capacity 17,000 spectators in the high, imposing stands of the Salt Lake Ice Center were excitedly anticipating the finals of the pairs figure skating event at the 2002 Olympic Winter Games. It became one of the most controversial events in Olympic history.

Russian skaters had long dominated this high profile event in world skating. The Russian pair, the graceful Yelena Berezhnaya and Anton Sikharulidze, were in the lead after the short programme. Not far behind in the scoring were the crowd favourites, Canada's pair of Jamie Salé and David Pelletier. The scene was set for the all-important long or 'free' programmes.

For the nine judges, this was their own Olympic final. It was the pinnacle of their own careers. The youngest was judge number four, Marie-Reine Le Gougne from France. With her striking red hair and stylish glasses, she looked sophisticated and very French. This was her second Olympics. She was one of the rising stars of her generation of judges and already a candidate for appointment to the prestigious technical committee of the International Skating Union (ISU). She looked a little nervous. There was no French competitor. She was aware that her scoring was likely to be important, possibly even a 'swing vote'.

The youngest judge was number 4, Marie-Reine Le Gougne from France. She looked a little nervous.

Berezhnaya and Sikharulidze went first. The Russian pair moved with awesome grace and power. Their programme was one of the most difficult ever attempted, with dramatic throws and advanced choreography. But they were prone to minor mistakes. It was clear that they stumbled during their double axel. The judges' marks (potentially up to 6.0) for technical merit were good but included some 5.7s and 5.8s. The second marks, for presentation, were high including seven 5.9s. The door to gold was nevertheless open for Salé and Pelletier if the Canadian pair could skate a 'clean' programme.

The Canadian pair set off. They were not as fast or powerful as the Russian pair but there was an easy, fluent feel to their skating programme. They were a couple, on and off the skating rink. They glided movingly to the music from the film *Love Story*. Although skating a slightly less difficult programme than the Russians, the Canadians performed flawlessly. The crowd adored them and clapped in time to the music. They were given a standing ovation. Most expert commentators thought they had done enough to win. The judges' marks went up.

The marks for technical merit were good but six of the nine scores were 5.8s. Slightly ahead. It all depended on the second mark for presentation. The scores went up. There were only four 5.9s and no 6.0s. The scoreboard flashed: second place. The crowd erupted in boos. David Pelletier described the second mark as a 'punch to the stomach'.

Monitors then revealed that judges from the United States, Canada, Germany and Japan had scored the Canadians higher. Judges favouring the Russian pair were from Russia, the People's Republic of China, Poland, Ukraine ... and, to complete a 5-4 split in favour of the Russians, the judge from France. There was clear disbelief and astonishment from the crowd. Salé and Pelletier accepted their silver medal with disappointment.

Then the story started to unravel. After the event, Marie-Reine Le Gougne, the French judge, walked into her hotel. Waiting for her was the head of the ISU's technical committee, Sally Stapleford, who gave her an angry look and spoke about integrity and honesty. Le Gougne began to cry. Two other members of the technical committee joined her. They left convinced that the French Federation had forced Le Gougne to vote as she did as part of a deal with the Russians to help their pair and, in exchange, get support for the French dance team which had a good chance of the gold medal the following week.

There was clear disbelief and astonishment from the crowd.

A judges' event review was held the following day. The referee told the judges that those who had voted for the Russians had made a serious mistake. It had been a miscarriage of justice. Le Gougne broke down again. Sobbing, she said that her federation president, Didier Gailhaguet, had pressured her to vote for the Russians and that it was not her own choice. She pleaded that the ISU must 'help us' break free from the pressure of the federations.

Events moved swiftly. The ISU president, in a press conference, admitted that the referee had received an allegation of misconduct. The Canadians officially appealed the decision in the pairs event. They formally proposed that Salé and Pelletier should have a dual gold medal with the Russians. If not, the Canadians would go forward with an appeal to the Court of Arbitration for Sport (CAS).

Although the original decision of the judges was not challenged in court or before an arbitral tribunal, the situation revealed a type of bad faith or corruption which would surely justify intervention with the 'playing decision' of a referee or judge in accordance with the guidelines for intervention pronounced from time to time by CAS. The ISU and IOC acted without this being necessary.

The ISU Council met and voted to declare Le Gougne's vote void. The pairs event was declared a tie and, with the approval of the IOC, a gold medal was given to Salé and Pelletier at a second awards ceremony. The Canadians dropped their appeal to CAS.

For skating, the saga had significant consequences. The ISU substantially changed the judging rules for figure skating. The new system was designed to overcome many of the risks demonstrated at the 2002 Olympics. Under the new system, a more complex and objective system for awarding marks for each skating element was introduced. Each judge's mark is anonymous; the scoreboard hides their identities. Importantly in this context, the panel of judges has been increased to twelve – but marks are averaged by randomly selecting nine judges, discarding the highest and lowest marks, and averaging the remaining seven. 'Nobbling' a single judge is now far less likely to be effective.

Two months after the Olympics, the ISU Council held an internal disciplinary hearing in relation to Marie-Reine Le Gougne and Didier Gailhaguet. It was a limited affair. With the exception of Le Gougne, none of the judges who voted for the Russians were present. Le Gougne claimed that she had made her confession while in an overwrought emotional state. Le Gougne and Gailhaguet were found guilty of pre-judging the Olympic pairs event. Each received just a three-year suspension and a prohibition from taking part in the 2006 Olympics. Le Gougne vowed to appeal her suspension all the way up to CAS. She later dropped her appeal.

In May, Didier Gailhaguet easily won re-election to the presidency of the French ice skating federation.

Both the Canadian and Russian pairs retired from amateur competition shortly after the Games and embarked on a professional career. In December 2005, Jamie Salé and David Pelletier were married in Banff.

---

43 YANG TAE YOUNG – A JUDGE'S MISTAKE ON THE PARALLEL BARS

Could Yang Tae Young overturn the result of the gymnastics final which had been reached after a clear error had been made by the judges?

The men's individual all-round gymnastics final in Athens in August 2004 was destined to be the closest men's all-round competition in Olympics history – and the most controversial. An error was made by the judges – bona fide but crucial to the result. Could it be corrected?

After the first four events, several gymnasts were in contention as they entered the parallel bars routine which was the penultimate session of the six-rotation event. Twenty-four-year-old Yang Tae Young was the hope of South Korea. Lying in third place, the parallel bars was one of his major strengths.

Judging in gymnastics is complex. One group of judges assess the start value, the technical difficulty of the routine. Another group of judges assess the execution, the performance of that routine. The combined marks, according to an appropriate formula, determine a competitor's final score for that event.

Yang's routine on the parallel bars, it later transpired, was given a start value of 9.9 rather than a 10 which was technically correct under the rules of the International Gymnastics Federation (FIG). (For the expert, it appears that the judges had failed to spot that Yang had performed a Belle in his routine rather than the less difficult Morisue.) Yang had been given a 10 for the identical routine earlier in both the team qualifying and team finals sessions at the Olympics.

This error was not noticed at the time of the competition. Yang performed strongly on the parallel bars and received a high mark overall. In fact, he took the lead in the overall competition after that event. However, the USA's leading gymnast, Paul Hamm, had moved into close contention and, with a sensational performance in the sixth and final rotation on the high bar, Hamm became the winner of the gold medal. Yang came third for the bronze.

The earlier judging error was then discovered after a videotape review. FIG officials confirmed that one-tenth of a point had been wrongly deducted from the difficulty value of Yang's routine. Yang should have been awarded a start value of 10. He had scored 9.712 points on the parallel bars but, with the higher start value, he would have finished the overall competition with 57.874 points and defeated Hamm by 0.051 points. FIG suspended the three judges involved.

The South Korean delegation formally protested: 'We want this obvious misjudgment to be corrected. We want fairness and justice.' Yang claimed that the result should be corrected and that he should win the gold medal or, at least, receive a shared gold medal with Hamm.

Bruno Grandi, the President of FIG, personally supported this claim and actually wrote to Paul Hamm in the week after the event. The score had been miscalculated, Grandi wrote, 'the true winner of the all-round competition is Yang Tae Young.' He suggested that Hamm should give up his Olympic title, saying that he would view the gesture as the 'ultimate demonstration of fair play.' Neither the US team nor the International Olympic Committee agreed.

' ... the true winner of the all-round competition is Yang Tae Young.'

Yang and the South Korean federation took their claim to the Court of Arbitration for Sport (CAS). The hearing lasted nearly twelve hours and CAS deliberated over this difficult case for several months.

Should the error of the judges be corrected, the result changed and the gold medal awarded to Yang? More generally, in what circumstances should a court or arbitral tribunal review an error made by judges 'on the playing field'?

For: The error by the judges was clear. If the error had not been made, Yang's overall score would have been greater than Hamm's. The President of the International Gymnastics Federation himself acknowledged that Yang was 'the true winner'. This was a case where it was right to correct the result.

Against: The formal protest by the Korean federation was not made until after the competition had ended. If it had been made earlier, a mechanism existed within the rules of the sport for reviewing the result. After the event, it was not appropriate for a court or tribunal to review retrospectively decisions made by officials on 'the field of play'.

Yang's claim failed.

CAS decided that the result should not be changed. The rules of the competition, in the view of CAS, did not permit a challenge after the event. Even if it had jurisdiction, a court or tribunal should only interfere with an official's 'field of play' decision if it had been tainted with fraud, arbitrariness or corruption. The panel should abstain from correcting the results of an admitted error by an official.

In addition and crucially, CAS stressed that there was no certainty that Yang would have gone on to win. The reactions of leading competitors under pressure in the final event could have been different if the score or competitive circumstances were different. Any solution or method for dealing with a judging error should be left to mechanisms within the framework of that sport's own rules. The considered judgment of CAS clearly sets out this fundamental position:

> *An error identified with the benefit of hindsight … cannot be a ground for reversing a result of a competition. We can all recall occasions where a video replay of a football match, studied at leisure, can show that a goal was given when it should have been disallowed (the Germans may still hold that view about England's critical third goal in the World Cup Final in 1966), or vice versa or where in a tennis match a critical line call was mistaken.*
>
> *For a court to change the result would on this basis still involve interfering with a field of play decision. Each sport may have within it a mechanism for utilising modern technology to ensure a correct decision is made in the first place (e.g. cricket with run outs) or for immediately subjecting a controversial decision to a process of review (e.g. gymnastics) but the solution for error … lies within the framework of the sport's own rules; it does not license judicial or arbitral interference thereafter.*

Hamm kept his gold medal.

In the 2008 Beijing Olympics in contrast, there were just seconds to go in the quarter-final of the taekwondo event when the judges missed a clear points-winning kick to the head by Britain's Sarah Stevenson against a Chinese opponent. An immediate and exceptional appeal was, after discussion, not contested by the Chinese federation. Stevenson won a bronze medal.

As for Yang Tae Young, he was still treated like a champion in his own country. The Korean Olympic Committee awarded him a symbolic gold medal. Their president said: 'The Korean Olympic Committee has decided to treat Yang Tae Young as a gold medalist – regardless of the verdict of the Court of Arbitration for Sport.'

---

44 BETTINA HOY – A FALSE START IN ATHENS

Could the French and British equestrian teams overturn a successful appeal decision which awarded Olympic gold medals to Bettina Hoy and the German team ?

It was chaotic. The gold medal seemed to be changing hands by the hour. The 2004 Olympic Games in Athens provided one of the most thrilling equestrian eventing competitions in Olympic history – and controversial.

Equestrian eventing comprises three events: dressage, cross country and showjumping. The final showjumping phase at the Markopoulo Olympic Equestrian Centre on the outskirts of the capital was coming to its climax. France were ahead in the team event and top French rider, Nicolas Touzaint, was leading in the individual event. Poor rides in the jumping by the French team, however, then left Germany with a strong chance of the team gold medal.

The leading German equestrian rider was forty-one-year-old Bettina Hoy. Her next round, if a clear round, could clinch the team event. It would also count towards the individual event and set her up with the prospect of a personal gold.

Bettina Hoy set off on her grey gelding, *Ringwood Cockatoo*. Under the rules of the International Equestrian Federation (FEI), she had forty-five seconds to reach the start line and then ninety seconds to complete the course after crossing the start line. The bell rang. Hoy started her warm-up circle. She unintentionally crossed the start line, well within the initial forty-five second time limit. Unknown to her, this automatically triggered the computerised timing device for the start of her round. But the stadium clock, visible to the competitors, did not re-start.

Hoy, still apparently thinking she was in her warm-up circle and with time in hand, made a wide turn shortly before the first fence and this brought her once again behind the start line for her 'real' round. As she crossed the start line this time, the stadium clock re-started. It was a glorious clear round. Hoy, judging her timing by the stadium clock, completed the triumphant round two seconds inside the ninety second time requirement. Germany celebrated the team gold medal.

With tears of joy, Bettina fell into the arms of her Australian husband, Andrew, who was competing for his home country. They were a rare married couple, competing for different countries in the same event. There were more tears to follow as the saga unfolded.

It was discovered that, during Hoy's round, the computerised timing device had continued to measure her time from the first crossing of the start line. The timing device indicated a total time which was 12.61 seconds over the ninety second limit. The French team formally protested. After deliberations, the stewards of the Ground Jury ruled that Hoy should be penalised with fourteen time penalties. The team gold medal was gone. The German team slipped from gold back to fourth place outside the medals. The French had now won the team medal.

Hoy completed a glorious clear round.

Chaos ensued. Hoy and the German team appealed instantly to the FEI Appeals Committee – who met promptly and decided on the grounds of 'fair play' that Hoy should not suffer because of a timekeeping mistake by the organisers. 'Bettina Hoy had no way to believe that her round had started,' explained a member of the Appeals Committee, 'as the clock was restarted when she crossed the line for the second time.' 'When errors occur in the management of a competition, it is right to make sure the rider doesn't pay the consequences.' The Appeals Committee rescinded the time penalties. The team gold medal had been won again by Germany. Win, loss, win – all within the same day.

After the chaotic finish of the team event, the best-placed riders overall had a final round of jumping to decide the individual gold. There was still a sense of turmoil. Was Hoy now going for a double gold or was her earlier ride still in doubt? Hoy on *Ringwood Cockatoo* had one rail down in the final round and, assuming the earlier round stood, was in second place, awaiting the final round of the leading twenty-four-year-old French rider, Nicholas Touzaint, who could afford one error. Dramatically, Touzaint knocked down a pole at the first jump, then another, and another. Britain's Leslie Law moved into second place. Hoy had won the individual gold ... or had she?

The medal ceremony went ahead. The medals were presented by HRH Princess Royal, an IOC member and a former Olympian in eventing. Hoy and Germany proudly celebrated. Nevertheless, it was now the turn of representatives of the French, British and American teams to object. The chaotic issue was referred to the ad hoc panel of the Court of Arbitration for Sport (CAS).

Should the decision of the FEI Appeals Committee be over-ruled and the time penalties imposed by the Ground Jury on Hoy be reinstated?

For: Hoy crossed the start line and the timing of the round should commence from that first crossing. The computerised timing device should be the prevailing mechanism. The Ground Jury was the body set up under the FEI rules with authority to settle all problems within its jurisdiction. Appeal bodies, such as the FEI Appeals Committee and indeed CAS, should not interfere with the initial 'field of play' decision of the Ground Jury. **Against:** By any test, Hoy was the fastest individual rider in the competition. She had seen the stadium clock and had clearly been misled by the timing shown by it. Hoy should not suffer because the starting procedures of the organisers were at fault. The FEI Appeals Committee's decision should be followed. The FEI Appeals Committee was not second-guessing the facts. It was interpreting the rules. It was authorised to apply a principle of fairness. The gold medals should remain with Hoy and Germany.

Hoy and the German team lost.

CAS decided, three days after the event itself, that neither it nor the FEI Appeals Committee should interfere with the judgment of the Ground Jury. This was the 'field of play' decision made by the official body on the spot. The FEI Appeals Committee 'had no jurisdiction to entertain the appeal'. Its decision was 'null and void' and 'the decision of the Ground Jury is reinstated'. The time penalty on Hoy should stand. France won the team gold medal, not Germany. Leslie Law of Great Britain won the individual gold medal, not Hoy.

Bettina Hoy was aboard a flight from Athens to Germany, with her gold medals safely packed, before she learnt of CAS's decision taking them away for the second time in three days. As for Leslie Law, he was competing in horse trails in Solihull when he heard that he had become Britain's first eventing gold medallist since 1972. He was so shocked he withdrew from the competition. 'My concentration level was zero.'

In one sense, this was a narrow decision based on the specific rules of the FEI which, in the view of CAS, left the matter to be decided by the Ground Jury and not the FEI Appeals Committee. In a more fundamental sense, this was another important example of the reluctance of courts and tribunals to interfere with 'field of play' decisions. In most sports, there is a decision of the referee or umpire during the course of play. Here, as in a number of other sports, it is the judgment of officials made immediately after the competition. In either case, the hurdle for challenging decisions made by referees, judges or panels at the 'field of play' in sport is great. It will always depend on the rules of the particular sport but intervention is very rare.

And yet there is a lingering feeling in this case that, although the right decision was reached on the merits and the computerised time device should have prevailed, this was indeed an issue of interpretation of the rules which could properly have been decided 'within the sport' by the FEI Appeals Committee.

After the 2004 Olympics had ended, a small gold-plated statue of Bettina Hoy was modelled to mark her success and can be seen in the city hall of her birth-town of Rheine in Northern Westphalia. The FEI said: 'The FEI wishes to emphasise that the decision taken by its Appeals Committee was based on fair play and the best interest of the sport, as well as a different interpretation of the rules.'

---

45 VANDERLEI DE LIMA THE OLYMPIC MARATHON AND THE IRISH PRIEST

Could Vanderlei de Lima claim a joint gold medal after being stopped by an interloper when leading the Olympic marathon?

It was the last day of the summer Olympic Games in Athens 2004. The men's marathon was in progress. No one could have foreseen the extraordinary incident which would take place. How should the intervention of a former Irish priest affect the result?

The marathon, in line with the historical setting of the 2004 Games, was due to finish in the 108-year-old marble Panathinaiko Stadium where the first modern Olympics were held in 1896. Beginning in the town of Marathon, the race followed a steep and difficult course. Legend had it that this was the course along which the Greek messenger, Pheidippides, carried the news in 490 BC that the Greeks had defeated the Persians ... and then dropped dead after delivering it.

The leader in 2004 was Vanderlei de Lima from Brazil, an experienced marathon runner and winner of the 2003 Pan American Games. Just 5 feet 6 inches tall, he was attempting to become the first Brazilian to win an Olympic gold in the men's marathon. De Lima had been in the leading pack throughout the race and had held a clear lead since the halfway mark, at times almost by a full minute. After thirty-five kilometres and with less than ten kilometres to the finish, de Lima still held a lead of forty-eight seconds over his closest pursuers, Italy's Stefano Baldini and America's Meb Keflezighi. Was glory beckoning for the Brazilian?

Suddenly, an interloper appeared, dressed extraordinarily in a kilt, green beret and wearing knee-high socks. He was later identified as Cornelius Horan, a former Irish Catholic priest. Horan, originally from County Kerry but living near London, was an established troublemaker. The previous year he had been jailed for running on to the track and disrupting the British grand prix at Silverstone. This time, in Athens, he was bearing a placard declaring: 'THE SECOND COMING IS NEAR SAYS THE BIBLE GRAND PRIX PRIEST'.

Suddenly, an interloper appeared, dressed in a kilt, green beret and wearing knee-high socks'

Horan hurled himself at de Lima, shoving him sideways into the kerbside and the adjacent crowd. It was fully fifteen seconds before de Lima, stunned beyond belief and helped by a spectator, could struggle free to start again. With his rhythm badly shaken and slightly dazed, de Lima gathered himself and continued – joined by a posse of police motorcycle outriders. His lead had been cut to around ten seconds. Within minutes, he was passed by Baldini and Keflezighi. Baldini went on to cross the line first and win the gold.

When de Lima entered the Panathinaiko Stadium, it was to great acclaim from the 70,000 strong crowd who had been watching the earlier incident in amazement on the large television screens in the stadium. De Lima sprinted joyously to the line, smiling broadly, spreading his arms and blowing a kiss to the crowd, to take the bronze medal. His time was seventy-seven seconds behind Baldini.

The Brazilian track foundation launched an official appeal, claiming that a second gold medal should be awarded to de Lima. De Lima himself said afterwards about the incident:

> *I was scared, because I didn't know what was going to happen to me... If you stop in a marathon, you struggle the next three or four kilometres. It's hard to get your rhythm back. I don't know if I could have won, but things would have been different.*

The International Association of Athletics Federations (IAAF) rejected the appeal. The Brazilian Olympic Committee and de Lima appealed to the Court of Arbitration for Sport.

De Lima was clearly hampered. Should the result be altered or, at least, a second gold medal awarded to de Lima?

For: De Lima was still in a clear lead. He was physically and seriously affected by an event beyond his control – and one which the race and security authorities might have done more to prevent. He could have held on to his lead and won. The Olympic ideals should recognise the special circumstances and award a second medal to de Lima. **Against:** It was impossible to calculate how much energy and momentum was lost by the attack. There was no certainty, or indeed probability, that de Lima would have won. It was an act of 'force majeure' which had to be accepted. The result could not be changed under the rules.

De Lima failed in his claim.

The Court of Arbitration for Sport (CAS) decided that the result could not be changed. It had 'no power to remedy his legitimate frustration'. The circumstances were unfortunate, but it could not change the results of a sporting event unless there was evidence of bad faith or arbitrariness. 'The results of the marathon race of the Athens Olympic Games must stand.'

Baldini kept his gold medal and de Lima his bronze.

Should CAS have attempted to impose a 'fair' solution? Unless the rules of competition give an appeal body scope to impose, retrospectively, a 'fair' solution, then neither the IAAF nor CAS could do so. 'Rules are rules.' But what if, theoretically, de Lima had been within yards of the finishing line? Would a different decision have been reached?

Horan was taken to the General Police Division in Attica and held overnight. He was later given a twelve-month suspended jail sentence.

Considerable sympathy was felt for de Lima. De Lima was later asked why he was so joyous when he crossed the line at the end of the race. Through an interpreter, he explained: 'It is a festive moment. It is a unique moment. Most athletes never have this moment, very few have the privilege to live such moments.'

At the closing ceremony of the Games, the International Olympic Committee gave de Lima a medal named after the founder of the modern Games, Pierre de Coubertin, in recognition of his 'exceptional demonstration of fair play and Olympic values'. De Lima also later won the nationwide poll for 'Brazilian athlete of the year' for 2004.

CHAPTER SIX

DISCIPLINARY AND ANTI-DOPING

All competitive sports have rules requiring minimum standards of conduct from the participants. These rules aim to establish 'a level playing field' for competitors. Anti-doping rules, in particular, aim to ensure that certain participants do not cheat by gaining artificial advantage over others through the use of drugs. Decisions of disciplinary bodies (not always 'men in blazers') who enforce these rules can seriously affect the livelihood of a player or athlete and his or her opportunity to win medals, prizes or competitions – and, in a team sport, a ban may affect the fortunes of a team deprived of a star player.

This is fertile ground for legal challenge. Sporting bodies strain to keep legal challenges to a minimum, strongly preferring that these issues should be settled 'within the sport' and not the law courts. Many appeals, under the rules of sport governing bodies, now make their way to specialist tribunals or ultimately to the Court of Arbitration for Sport (CAS) – but many have also found their way to the ordinary courts.

We visit in this chapter a kaleidoscope of different sporting events and venues including the athletic stadia of Seoul, Sydney and Lisbon, Wimbledon greyhound stadium, the tennis courts of Roland Garros and long distance swimming in Brazil.

---

46 DON REVIE – RESIGNATION INCITES THE FURY OF THE FA

Could Don Revie challenge a ten year ban on the grounds of apparent bias in the FA's disciplinary tribunal?

Don Revie was sitting down with his wife, Elsie, one evening in July 1977. He knew he was about to make an announcement that would astonish the world of football.

As England manager for three years following the caretaker regime of Joe Mercer which took over from Sir Alf Ramsey, Revie had never been able to produce for England the successful record which he enjoyed as manager of Leeds United during their glory years. Perhaps he reflected again on those early 1970s: winners of two First Division titles, the FA Cup and the League Cup; European Cup semi-finalists and more; and a personal award of an OBE in 1970.

For Revie, it was probably England's 2-0 defeat the previous November in Rome in the Group Two World Cup qualifying match against Italy which made up his mind. Goals from Antognoni and Bettega made it highly unlikely that England would qualify for the finals in Argentina. There followed a depressing series of home internationals with dismal defeats at Wembley against Wales (1-0) and Scotland (2-1).

The newspapers and the fans were on his back, relentlessly. Revie was convinced that the Football Association, his employer, were building up to dismiss him – probably later that year after the return match at Wembley against Italy which would complete the World Cup group stage. Revie had had enough:

> *I sat down with Elsie one night and we agreed that the job was no longer worth the aggravation. Nearly everyone in the country seems to want me out.*

Revie had always been a planner. In his playing days, he was best known for his role as a deep-lying centre-forward at Manchester City based on the style of the Hungarian forward, Nándor Hidegkuti, a pivotal player in the great Hungarian team which destroyed England in 1953 and 1954. In English football it became known as 'the Revie plan'. Now, Revie had prepared his plan for his resignation.

The following morning, on 11th July 1977, the news first broke in the *Daily Mail* to an astonished public. Revie had quit. Secretly, without the FA's knowledge, he had secured a lucrative role as supremo of football in the United Arab Emirates on a four-year contract with a reported tax free remuneration of £340,000. Revie had denied the FA the satisfaction of sacking him. He also made a useful sum from the sale of his story to the *Daily Mail*. He was off.

The reaction was almost hysterical. The leaders at the FA were furious, especially since they did not receive Revie's letter of resignation until later in the morning after the *Daily Mail*'s publication. The press labelled Revie 'a traitor'. Revie's secret plot to run away, for a Middle Eastern pot of gold, was condemned. One columnist said: 'He should be castrated for the way he left England.' Alan Hardaker, then secretary of the Football League, sarcastically remarked: 'Don Revie's decision doesn't surprise me in the slightest. Now I only hope he can quickly learn to call out bingo numbers in Arabic.'

'He should be castrated for the way he left England'

The FA, under the chairmanship of Sir Harold Thompson, were deeply offended by the manner of Revie's resignation. Thompson was a 'donnish' figure. A passionate supporter of the amateur game, Thompson was a chemistry fellow at St John's College at Oxford and had been Chief Scientific Adviser to the Home Office Civil Defence in the 1950s. Involved with Oxford University Association Football Club for most of his life, he became the University representative on the FA Council in 1941. He represented the epitome of the amateur game. Thompson became the Chairman of the FA in 1976. Revie's behaviour was anathema to his ideals.

The FA, under Thompson's leadership, decided to charge Revie under FA regulations with bringing the game into disrepute. Revie refused to attend the hearing. When he finally did meet the FA to discuss the matter, his objections were ignored. The FA's disciplinary tribunal met and decided to ban Revie from English football for a period of ten years. It was a lengthy punishment. And who was one of the members and a dominating presence at the tribunal? Sir Harold Thompson.

Revie challenged the ban. He alleged bias in the disciplinary tribunal which had banned him. He took the matter to the High Court. Should Revie's ten year ban be quashed on the grounds of bias in the disciplinary tribunal?

For: The tribunal was biased. The Chairman of the FA was effectively acting as prosecutor, witness, judge and jury. This inevitably destroyed the tribunal's impartiality. It was a basic breach of natural justice and the ban should be declared illegal.
Against: The case was considered carefully and objectively by the tribunal. The length of the ban was reasonable in the circumstances This was an internal matter for the football authorities and there was no reason for the courts to intervene.

Revie won this one.

The High Court reluctantly agreed with Revie's case. The judge, Justice Cantley, thought Revie was 'a very prickly man' and was highly critical of his behaviour: 'He held the highest post of its kind in English professional football and he published and presented to the public a sensational and notorious example of disloyalty, breach of duty, discourtesy and selfishness. His conduct brought English professional football, at a high level, into disrepute.'

... the tribunal's procedure was contrary to natural justice ...

Nevertheless, the court agreed that the tribunal's procedure was 'contrary to natural justice'. Such a disciplinary tribunal must not be constituted, or behave, in a manner which creates the likelihood of bias.

Revie's ten year ban was quashed.

The principle of the court's decision in favour of Revie was an important one. It was one of the first to confirm that disciplinary tribunals, particularly those whose decisions can affect people's livelihoods in sport, must observe basic rules of 'natural justice' in their proceedings. These basic rules include not only a right to a fair hearing of the defendant's case but also the absence of any clear predetermined bias in members of the panel – or, just as important, the appearance of real bias. The theme of natural justice is one which we see repeated in many later cases.

Revie never returned to English football. He served three of the four years of his contract with the United Arab Emirates, his contract being terminated by mutual consent in 1980. Shortly afterwards, he became manager of the UAE first division team, Al Nasar, and later managed Egypt's Al-Al FC. He came back to the UK in 1984 seeking the post as manager at Queens Park Rangers but it never transpired. He died in 1989.

---

47 BEN JOHNSON – FIRST IN SEOUL AND THEN IN MONTREAL

Could Ben Johnson successfully challenge his lifetime ban as being an unreasonable restraint of trade?

The Olympics 100 metres final in Seoul, South Korea. 24th September 1988. It was the showdown between Ben Johnson and Carl Lewis.

Ben Johnson, the twenty-six-year-old Jamaica-born Canadian, was the 1987 World Champion and current 100 metres world record holder. Carl Lewis, America's golden athlete, held the 1984 Olympic 100 metres title amongst his glittering array. There was no love lost between Lewis and Johnson. Their rivalry will go down in athletics history. Millions around the world turned on their television sets, many of us in the western world in the middle of the night, to witness the most anticipated sprint race in history.

With a sensational start, Johnson led from the starting blocks to the finish, destroying the field and clocking a new world record of 9.79 seconds. Forty-six strides; the fastest man in history. He later remarked that the time would have been even faster had he not, in that iconic gesture, raised his hand in triumph just before the finish. A race that all spectators and viewers will never forget.

It became the race when athletics lost its innocence.

And yet it became the race when athletics lost its innocence. The integrity of sport at the highest level was shattered. Previously, in public perception, the problem of drugs abuse had been largely confined to weightlifting and other field events.

Now, it was centre stage – in one of the signature events of the Olympic Games.

The telephone call came to Johnson in the early hours of 27th September. His urine sample after the race had been found to contain traces of Stanozolol, a prohibited anabolic steroid. He was disqualified. His gold medal was forfeited by the International Olympics Committee. He was sent home in disgrace. The gold medal was awarded to Carl Lewis.

Johnson was subsequently banned by the International Amateur Athletics Federation (IAAF) for two years.

The story started to unfold more fully. An in-depth Canadian governmental investigation in 1989, the 'Dubin' Inquiry under Chief Justice Charles Dubin, heard hours of testimony about the use of performance enhancing drugs by athletes. It appeared that the use of drugs was widespread throughout athletics. Johnson was not alone. He was just one of the first to be caught. Charlie Francis, Johnson's coach and also Canada's national sprint coach for nine years, told the inquiry that Johnson himself had been taking steroids since 1981. Johnson's 1987 world record was annulled in the light of this investigation.

After his two-year ban ended in 1990, Johnson was re-instated. He started competing again but never recovered his former speed. Indeed, he took part in the 1992 Olympics in Barcelona as a member of the Canadian team, but failed to make the 100 metres final.

After his come-back, he was tested after every race in which he participated. All was well on that front until January 1993 when he competed in an indoor event in Montreal. His urine samples, following a test at that event, revealed a level of testosterone greater than the permitted level. Hearings took place. Time for appeal ran out. In April 1993, Johnson was advised that he was now banned by the IAAF from competition for life. It was this decision that led to the court case before a three-judge panel of the Ontario Appeal Court.

Johnson challenged the decision on the grounds that a lifetime ban from competition was an unlawful restraint of trade. Should he succeed?

For: The ban restricted Johnson from carrying on his livelihood as a runner. It was a restraint of trade. A lifetime ban was more than was reasonably necessary to protect the public interest. It was excessive and unlawful.

Against: The ban, even if technically a restraint of trade, was reasonable in all the circumstances. It was necessary to protect not only Johnson himself but, importantly, the public interest in fair competition. The integrity of the sport must be protected. The influence of elite performers on young athletes should also not be ignored. Most major sports impose a lifetime ban for a second offence.

Johnson lost again.

The Ontario Court held that, even though the ban was a restraint of trade, a lifetime ban was reasonable and lawful in the circumstances. The interests of the parties and the public required the maintenance of integrity in the sport. As the defence counsel put it vividly, the public had a right 'to know that the race involves only an athlete's own skill, his own strength, his own spirit and not his pharmacologist'. The court's function was not to review the merits of decisions reached by tribunals in specialised fields. Johnson's lifetime ban was upheld.

'The race should involve only an athlete's own skill, his own strength, his own spirit and not his pharmacologist.'

To many, the sport has never recovered since that race in Seoul.

Johnson would never race again. Whilst he admitted to the extensive use of steroids, Johnson later maintained that his test at Seoul in 1988 was sabotaged by a 'third party' as part of a conspiracy against him. He says that Stanozolol was not a steroid that he used.

In 1999, Johnson made surprising headlines again when it was revealed that he had been hired by Libyan leader, Colonel Gaddafi, to train his son who was a promising soccer player. His son eventually joined an Italian team but was sacked after one year, it is alleged, for failing a drugs test.

In 2006, Johnson appeared in an advertisement in the USA for an energy drink, Cheetah Power Surge. In a mock interview, Johnson was asked: 'Ben, when you run, do you Cheetah?' Johnson replied: 'Absolutely. I Cheetah all the time.'

---

48 DIANE MODAHL – A REMEDY FOR BEING INNOCENT?

Could Diane Modahl sue for damages when suspended by the governing body for a doping offence for which she was subsequently exonerated ?

Diane Modahl was one of Britain's leading athletes. The year 1994 promised to be a great one for her. The women's 800 metres champion in the 1990 Commonwealth Games, the twenty-seven-year-old was a leading contender to retain her title at the forthcoming Games in Canada. No one could have foreseen that the year would end in high controversy and that British athletics would be on a path to bankruptcy.

In June 1994 Modahl was competing in an athletics meeting at the Lisbon University Stadium in Portugal shortly before the Commonwealth Games. She was asked, under the doping control procedures of the International Amateur Athletics Federation (IAAF), to provide a routine urine sample. Part of the sample, the A sample, was tested by a laboratory in Lisbon. It reported a level of testosterone well above any permissible level. Modahl was, by this time, in Canada. She was informed of the result and asked to return to Lisbon. The B sample, tested by the same laboratory, later showed similar results. She was suspended from the Commonwealth Games.

Modahl was the first British woman athlete to have tested positive in a drugs test.

It was a high profile case. Modahl was the first British woman athlete to have tested positive in a drugs test.

An initial hearing in December, before a five-man disciplinary committee of the British Athletics Federation (BAF), concluded that she had committed a doping offence and banned her from competition for four years – the length of sentence applicable under the rules adopted by BAF and IAAF at that time. Modahl strongly protested her innocence and appealed.

Before the appeal body, Modahl claimed that the initial committee proceedings had been biased against her. Backed by scientific advisers, she was also able to produce new evidence that mishandling of the samples at the Portuguese laboratory may have led to the contamination. Delayed refrigeration of the sample could have kick-started a bacterial growth in the urine, a by-product of which could have been an increased level of testosterone in the sample. The appeal body decided in Modahl's favour and lifted the ban in July 1995. It was not until March 1996, though, that the IAAF also accepted the report and cleared her to compete internationally.

But Modahl was still angry. She had been unable to compete internationally for nearly two years at the peak of her career. She brought a legal claim for damages against the British Athletics Federation (BAF). With echoes of the Revie case in the background, Modahl alleged that the initial disciplinary panel had been biased against her since certain members had publicly presumed her to be guilty. This bias had prevented a fair and impartial hearing. This was, she alleged, a breach by the BAF of its contractual duty to her to conduct a fair and impartial hearing.

She claimed almost £1 million in damages, legal and medical costs. This was the first time that an athlete had sued a governing body in Britain for damages as a result of a disciplinary decision. Modahl's claim resulted in much complex litigation lasting many years. Eventually, this issue came before the Court of Appeal.

Modahl claimed almost £1 million in damages, legal and medical costs.

Should Diane Modahl be entitled to recover damages from the BAF to compensate for the period of the ban which resulted from the initial disciplinary hearing and which was subsequently overturned?

For: As a member of an athletics' club affiliated to the BAF and as a competitor in BAF-governed events, Modahl was bound to abide by the relevant rules of the BAF and, in particular, the governing body's disciplinary procedures. On the part of the governing body, there was an implied contractual obligation to administer those rules through disciplinary proceedings which were fair and impartial. In this case, two members of the initial disciplinary committee were either biased or appeared to be biased. It was this faulty hearing that resulted in Modahl's disqualification – which lasted until the ban was lifted internationally by the IAAF in March 1996. Modahl was entitled to damages as a normal remedy for breach of contract. **Against:** Athletes accept the disciplinary jurisdiction of the BAF simply by competing and not through a formal contractual relationship. In any event, there was no evidence that members of the original disciplinary committee were actually biased. Even if they were, there was no evidence that this affected the result. The difference between the first disciplinary hearing and the appeal, at which Modahl was cleared, was the new scientific evidence that the samples could have been degraded through the handling procedures at the Lisbon laboratory. In any event, a fair result had been reached. Modahl was cleared. A governing body should not be liable in damages for a defect in part only of the proceedings if the eventual result was fair.

Diane Modahl lost her claim.

The Court of Appeal decided that, where 'a sensible appeal structure' has been put in place by a governing body, the parties must 'accept what in the end is a fair decision.' In fact, the court decided that there was no actual bias in this case – and the apparent bias of one member did not taint the process or influence the decision. It did not amount to a breach of the obligation to provide a fair hearing overall. 'The test is to ask whether, having regard to the course of the proceedings, there has been a fair result.' The principal reason for the change in the decision at the appeal stage was the new scientific evidence available.

So, no monetary compensation for Modahl.

At the sporting level, a highly important consequence of the Modahl case was the tightening-up of criteria for accreditation of laboratories for drug testing in sport, together with more rigorous procedures for taking samples and their subsequent laboratory analysis.

For sports governing bodies generally, this was a wake up call. It stressed the importance of having fair disciplinary procedures. This was the first time, in the UK, that an athlete had brought a legal claim against a governing body for damages following a disciplinary decision.

In the US, American Harry 'Butch' Reynolds, the 400 metres world record holder, had brought an $18 million claim for damages against the US athletics governing body when his suspension for a drugs offence was lifted. After extended litigation, he failed in his claim.

Modahl also failed – but only because the court could point to the important new scientific evidence as being the reason for the appeal decision rather that a defect in the proceedings themselves. The potential threat of litigation, these days, is never far away. All sports governing bodies must now take extra care to ensure that their disciplinary processes are fair and properly conducted.

For the governing body, the BAF, the high cost of litigation proved overwhelming. Effectively bankrupted, after a period of turmoil, the BAF went into administration and was later re-incarnated as UK Athletics.

Diane Modahl returned to competition in 1996 and won a bronze medal in the 800 metres at the Commonwealth Games in Kuala Lumpur. But she never recovered her previous best form. In 2004, following the example of her cousin, boxer Chris Eubank, Modahl appeared in the reality TV show *I'm a Celebrity, Get Me Out of Here!*

---

49 ALAIN BAXTER – A NASAL INHALER AND A BRONZE SKIING MEDAL

Should Alain Baxter be disqualified if doping was accidental and not sufficient in quantity to be performance enhancing?

People knew when Alain Baxter was around at the 2002 Winter Olympics in Salt Lake City in Minnesota, USA. Proud of his Scottish background, twenty-eight-year-old Baxter sparked some early controversy at the Games by dying his hair blue and white in the cross of St Andrew, the flag of Scotland. The British Olympic Association, wanting to project an image of 'Britishness', asked him to remove it.

Baxter, from Aviemore in Scotland and known as 'the Highlander', was Britain's best alpine skier. Named after the 1970s French skiing star, Alain Penz, Baxter first represented Britain in 1991 and had steadily moved up the world rankings. He was looking forward to the challenge of the 2002 Winter Olympics.

Baxter frequently suffered from nasal congestion, a long-standing medical condition. In the UK, he normally used a non-prescription Vicks vapour inhaler for relieving the congestion. The inhaler was a permitted substance under UK athletic anti-doping rules. There had never been any issue.

His nasal problem resurfaced in Salt Lake City. He asked his coach, Christian Schwaiger, to pick up a Vicks inhaler when he was out shopping. He came back, instead, with a liquid Sinex recommended by the British team doctor but Baxter found that this did not work satisfactorily.

Baxter then crashed during training and took the next day off – and went shopping in nearby Park City where he was staying. He spotted a Vicks vapour inhaler in the chemist section of the supermarket. 'I saw the inhaler that I wanted Christian to buy in the first place because I had been using it since I was a kid.' He bought it, not consulting the team doctor or reading the back of the package, since it appeared to be exactly the same product as the one he regularly used in the UK.

When competition began, on the slopes at the Olympics, Baxter was in excellent form in the slalom. He performed well on his first run, finishing in eighth place. On his second run, Baxter had a brilliant run and moved into second position. There were a number of skiers left to complete their second runs. Would Baxter's time be sufficient for a medal? One by one, the remaining competitors struggled on an increasingly rutted and difficult course.

Finally, with only American home favourite, Bode Miller, and first-run leader, Jean-Pierre Vidal of France, left to go, Baxter was assured of at least fourth place. Then Miller sensationally crashed and Baxter was certain of a medal – which became a bronze when Vidal clinched the gold for France. Baxter and the British team were ecstatic. This was the first ever alpine skiing medal for Britain at an Olympics.

This was the first ever alpine skiing medal for Britain at an Olympics.

As a medallist, Baxter then underwent a routine doping test for which he submitted a urine sample. He returned to Scotland the following morning where he received a hero's welcome. The next day, as Baxter was celebrating in his home village of Aviemore, the shock telephone call came. The laboratory report had revealed a very small trace of methamphetamine, a prohibited substance under the IAAF anti-doping rules. A disciplinary hearing was held and reported to the IOC Executive Board. A month later in March, it was announced that Baxter had been disqualified from the men's alpine skiing slalom and had lost his medal. He was banned from competition for three months.

How did this occur? It transpired that the composition of the US version of the Vicks inhaler which Baxter had bought was slightly different from the version sold in the UK and included a level of levmetamphetamine, a form of the prohibited substance methamphetamine. It was accepted by all, though, that the minimal quantity was not sufficient to be in any way a performance enhancing stimulant. It made no difference to the result.

Baxter challenged the decision and the matter was referred to the Court of Arbitration for Sport (CAS).

Baxter argued strenuously that the drug was taken entirely innocently and was not sufficient to have any effect whatsoever on his performance. Should Baxter be entitled to his bronze medal, and the disqualification lifted?

For: Baxter did not take the drug intentionally. His use was consistent with the medication he had always taken in the UK. The levels of levmetamphetamine were so low that it would not have had any stimulant effect on athletic performance. The IOC doping rules failed adequately to distinguish between the different types of methamphetamines as prohibited substances. Disqualification was a disproportionate remedy in the circumstances. He should not be stripped of his bronze medal and suspended.

Against: Levmetamphetamine was within the scope of substances prohibited under the IOC rules. It was irrelevant whether or not he took it intentionally or negligently. Athletes are strictly responsible for substances placed in their body. Results achieved by a 'doped athlete' at a competition must be cancelled irrespective of guilt. The level was also irrelevant. It was simply a question of whether it was a prohibited substance or not under the rules. The fight against drugs, and fairness to all athletes, required that the rules be strictly enforced. Baxter should, of course, have read the back of the package and was not entirely without fault.

Baxter lost. CAS dismissed Baxter's claim.

The drug was a prohibited substance under the rules of the IAAF. Disqualification was the minimum sanction under the rules, irrespective of whether ingestion of the substance was intentional or negligent or entirely innocent. Disqualification applied irrespective of whether or not the actual dosage in fact had any performance enhancing effect.

Rules were rules. CAS was unsympathetic to any argument that it should overturn the rules. CAS confirmed that the rules could not be ignored unless 'they were so overtly wrong that they would run counter to every principle of fairness in sport'. That was not the case here.

CAS was unsympathetic to any argument that it should overturn the rules.

The panel accepted that Baxter was 'a sincere and honest man' who did not intend to obtain a competitive advantage in the race. However, the consequence of this doping violation must be disqualification and the loss of his bronze medal.

The case brought home to the British sporting public the severity of the anti-doping laws at the Olympics. Were they too severe?

The fight against doping in sport requires tough laws. They have been built on the concept of so-called strict liability. Each athlete must be responsible for any substance which enters his body – irrespective of whether it has been taken knowingly or innocently. Was it inevitable that there would be a few 'hard' cases in the cause of ensuring tough and effective laws to 'clean' the sport? Or did this case go too far? Did it show that the anti-doping rules were excessive and unjust? Two significant criticisms could be made:

There should be a burden on the anti-doping authorities to ensure that substances are only prohibited at a level which genuinely leads to a 'performance enhancing' advantage for a competitor or is a substance harmful to the health of the athlete. The doping regulations should have distinguished between the different types of methamphetamines. (The latest regulations now do this. Baxter would not have contravened the rules as they now stand.)

If a substance exceeds the prohibited level, then the fairness of 'a level playing field' for all competitors probably means that disqualification is inevitable. But any subsequent suspension of an athlete from competing or additional penalty for the offence must surely be proportionate to the offence? A ban was too much.

Baxter was very unlucky. This was a 'hard' case.

---

50 TOM FLAHERTY – *KNOCKEEVAN KING* AND A STEWARDS' INQUIRY

Was there sufficient bias, or apparent bias, in the disciplinary proceedings to justify a claim by dog trainer, Tom Flaherty, to overturn a doping decision?

Next, a visit to the dogs.

Wimbledon greyhound stadium is one of the most popular greyhound venues in the country. The English Greyhound Derby is a particular highlight. The 9.15 p.m. race on an evening in May 2002 at Wimbledon was one of the heats in the second round of the Derby. The favourite was *Knockeevan King*, owned and trained by Tom Flaherty, a well-known and experienced trainer based in Scotland.

Knockeevan King had convincingly won its first heat at Wimbledon a week earlier. The two-year-old greyhound had returned to Scotland and been brought down from Edinburgh on the morning of the race. He appeared to be in good condition. He was placed in kennels at the Wimbledon stadium around 6.15 p.m. – three hours before the race.

The dogs were paraded on the track shortly before the race. Betting had been strong. Although it had drifted back slightly in the betting before the start, *Knockeevan King* was still 5-4 starting favourite. The traps opened ... but there was no repeat of its success in the first round. *Knockeevan King* finished last of the five runners.

A urine sample, taken from a random test on *Knockeevan King* prior to the race, revealed traces of hexadrine which was a drug often used to treat a urinary infection. It was a prohibited substance under greyhound racing rules. A charge was brought by the governing body, the National Greyhound Racing Club (NGRC), against Flaherty for administering a prohibited substance. It was heard by an independent stewards' inquiry in September.

Flaherty protested his innocence. He alleged that the substance must have been administered during the period of kennelling and he expressed strong views that the security arrangements at Wimbledon stadium were inadequate. Security at the open room kennels was 'akin to running a busy pub with a biscuit tin instead of a till and expecting no pilfering'. An independent stewards' inquiry, nevertheless, declared him guilty and fined him £400.

Flaherty continued to assert that he was innocent. He claimed that the inquiry had been conducted unfairly and that it had stained his reputation. Amongst a number of alleged defects suggesting possible bias, Flaherty learnt that the chief executive of the NGRC (in effect, the prosecuting authority), Frank Melville, had remained present during the private deliberations of the independent stewards after the hearing even though he was not a member of the tribunal. Flaherty brought a legal action to have the decision of the inquiry set aside.

Should a disciplinary hearing by a sports governing body be conducted in a way which is free of any apparent bias? Did Melville's presence in the private deliberations create a bias, or at least an appearance of bias, which was sufficient to render the inquiry procedurally unfair and invalid?

For: A disciplinary hearing set up by a sports governing body must be conducted in accordance with basic rules of natural justice – including in a manner which is not only free of actual bias but in a way which avoids any appearance of bias. Melville was a senior employee of, and clearly associated with, the NGRC. He was not a member of the stewards' tribunal which was meant to be independent. His presence at the post-hearing stage of private deliberations of the stewards, in the absence of Flaherty, would be perceived by most people as likely to influence the tribunal. The decision must be set aside. **Against:** Melville's presence did not actually influence the decision of the tribunal. There was no evidence that he had contributed to the tribunal's substantive deliberations. He was there simply to assist the tribunal with any queries or information. Even if Melville's presence was not in line with good practice, it did not affect the outcome which was still a fair result overall on the merits. The courts should be very reluctant to intervene in decisions made by disciplinary bodies within the sport itself.

Flaherty won before a lower court. The NGRC appealed to the Court of Appeal. Flaherty lost this time.

The Court of Appeal upheld the decision of the stewards' inquiry. The court decided that an informed observer would have concluded that there was no real possibility of bias arising through Melville's presence. There had been a fair result overall and the court should not intervene. In words that are music to the ears of members of sports governing bodies, the court said:

> *It is of paramount importance that sporting bodies should be given as free a hand as possible, consistent with the fundamental requirements of fairness, to run their own disciplinary processes without the interference of the courts.*

These are words which are likely to be quoted often in future cases involving challenges to disciplinary proceedings of sports governing bodies.

Flaherty's £400 fine was reinstated.

After a number of 'natural justice' decisions from Revie onwards, this case seemed to reflect a turning of the tide in favour of non-intervention in the internal disciplinary workings of sports governing bodies. The court clearly did not believe Flaherty's claims and, no doubt thinking that justice had in effect been done, seems to have gone to the outer limits of non-intervention. Any presence of such a senior executive of the governing body, which is in effect the prosecutor, would surely be viewed by most people as leading to a significant risk of bias? But the Court of Appeal decided not.

The NGRC, nevertheless, did amend its disciplinary procedures for the future. It decided to introduce an independent Appeal Board to provide a further right of appeal from NGRC stewards' decisions in order to avoid going through the courts 'which is costly for all concerned'.

Flaherty himself was not amused. He refused to pay the £400 fine imposed by the stewards and, in protest, surrendered his licence to train greyhounds for racing in England.

---

51 GREG RUSEDSKI: A SELF-INFLICTED PROBLEM FOR TENNIS?

Should Greg Rusedski be charged for a doping offence if the suspected cause was supplements supplied by trainers employed by the ATP?

'It is absolutely clear that something is very wrong here.' Greg Rusedski was stunned when he heard the result of a routine drug test at a tournament in Indianapolis in July 2003. Canadian-born Rusedski was proud of his career. Runner-up in the US Open final in 1997, BBC Sports Personality of the Year that same year and still Britain's number two ranked tennis player, he could not believe the result of the test.

Yet his sample had revealed a level of nandrolone of more than five nanograms per millilitre, not likely to affect performance but in excess of the two nanogram level permitted by the anti-doping rules administered by the Association of Tennis Professionals (ATP).

The ATP decided to call a disciplinary hearing. The likely result, if Rusedski was found guilty, would be a two-year ban for this first offence. For twenty-nine-year-old Rusedski, this would effectively mean the end of his career.

But the story had really started earlier. Tennis had until then been considered a 'clean' sport with little history of drug abuse. There had been one or two incidents. Perhaps the most high profile case had concerned Petr Korda, the Australian Open champion in 1998, who tested positive for nandrolone at Wimbledon later that year. The circumstances did not appear to be deliberate and, under the rules then applying, he was banned for one year. There were a few other isolated cases – mostly of players using 'social' drugs.

For Rusedski, this would effectively mean the end of his career.

Then, from August 2002 to May 2003, extraordinary results emerged in men's tennis. Many tests, some reports say affecting more than forty of the top players on the professional tour, revealed enhanced levels of nandrolone. The results for seven players were in excess of the two nanogram threshold permitted by the anti-doping code. A crisis for tennis appeared to be looming. One player, Bohdan Ulihrach from the Czech Republic, was named and banned by an ATP disciplinary panel for two years. However, concerned by the unusual spate of findings, the ATP were forced to investigate further.

What was going on? The astonishing fact was that all these cases bore the same analytical 'footprint' and appeared to come from an identical source. A commission enquiry appointed by the ATP concluded that Ulihrach and the six other players might have tested positive because of contaminated electrolyte supplements handed out in tablets by the ATP's own trainers to help players recover after long matches!

ATP decided that Ulihrach's ban should be rescinded and that the six other unnamed players should not be prosecuted. The ATP eventually, in May 2003, ordered their trainers to stop distributing these supplements. The ATP announced on their internet site, in their newsletter and on dressing room notice boards at tournaments that there was a danger in using them.

The problem was that Rusedski's positive test occurred two months after this edict. Many other players also continued to record higher than usual levels of nandrolone – but not in excess of the two nanogram level that required reporting as a potential offence. Yet, evidence suggested that Rusedski's sample bore the same 'footprint', and came from the same source, as the previous cases reported prior to May. The ATP, nevertheless, decided to proceed against Rusedski.

Usually, a doping investigation would not be made known publicly until after the ATP disciplinary hearing and only if a 'guilty' verdict was passed. In an unprecedented stance, fearing that the investigation would become public anyway, Rusedski himself made the charge known. It was a bold move. He fought a vigorous public defence through the media in advance of the hearing scheduled for February 2005 in Montreal.

He issued a public statement:

> *It is absolutely clear that something is very wrong here. We now have over 47 samples demonstrating elevated levels of nandrolone. These 47 samples emanate solely from the 120 or so top players on the ATP main tour ... If it was unfair and unreasonable to proceed to prosecution of the previous cases, equally I consider it will be wrong and unfair to proceed with mine.*

It was a delicate and unusual issue for the ATP. Since identical previous cases had not been pursued and the 'guilty' source may well have been supplements supplied by trainers employed by the ATP itself, should the case against Rusedski be dropped?

For: The source of Rusedski's 'doping' was clearly the same as the previous cases, including that of Ulihrach, which the ATP had decided not to pursue. It would be grossly unfair for the ATP then to proceed against Rusedski. The likely source was still from supplements provided by ATP trainers and it would be inequitable for the ATP to prosecute. Insufficient notice, given the importance, had been given to the players of the risk from these supplements. It would be wrong to discriminate against Rusedski.
Against: Rusedski, along with all other athletes, must have responsibility for any substances taken by him. Warnings had been duly given by the ATP and their trainers had stopped supplying the suspect supplements. Rusedski's case arose after these warnings had been given. Rusedski's case was above the permitted limit and the principle of 'strict liability' should apply.

Rusedski was successful.

The disciplinary tribunal said that his exoneration rested 'upon the unique circumstances of the case and ... the unique circumstances pertaining in tennis'. Rusedski had taken exactly the same substances as Ulihrach. 'It was unfair that the ATP should seek to prosecute him for substances which they themselves had given him, and which in all probability had caused him to test positive.' The ATP should have taken more steps to notify its players in a 'meaningful' and 'direct' way of the reasons for stopping the distribution of the electrolyte tablets. Having not proceeded in earlier cases, the ATP 'could not in fairness prosecute this case' as, on the best available scientific evidence, 'it created the underlying situation in the first place.'

Greg Rusedski's was a highly prominent case. It was the first time a player had gone so public in the period prior to the initial hearing. It saved Rusedski's career. Perhaps his upfront outspoken north American background served Rusedski well, after all?

Rusedski could continue competing. 'It's an enormous relief for me and my family and I look forward to resuming my career.'

The exoneration of Rusedski fitted uneasily with the anti-doping code's principle of strict liability and, if pleading lack of fault, the burden on an athlete to demonstrate the particular 'innocent' source of any prohibited substance. A particular difficulty was that it was no longer certain that the ATP-administered supplements were to blame. Indeed, the source has never been satisfactorily explained.

On the other hand, there would have been a clear and distinct unfairness if the ATP had proceeded against Rusedski after not prosecuting six other players when all cases had the same 'footprint' and appeared to derive from the same source. This was a very unusual case. In the end, fairness and consistency rightly proved more important than the principle of strict liability.

Rusedski's bold defence led not only to his own exoneration but also, ultimately, to much improved administration of anti-doping cases in tennis. It was clearly wrong that the ATP should have the potentially conflicting roles of representing players as the players' union, administering and prosecuting the anti-doping programme and appointing the disciplinary panel. In 2005, administration of the anti-doping programme, including responsibility for setting the rules, testing and prosecution of cases arising at ATP-sanctioned events, moved away from the ATP and became the responsibility of the independent International Tennis Federation (ITF). Similar arrangements have also since been established with the WTA Tour in respect of the leading women's tournaments.

Greg Rusedski continued his career including playing in the Davis Cup and helping Great Britain to win back a place in the World Group. He retired in 2007.

---

52 THE BALCO SCANDAL – WALKIN' FISH, A SYRINGE AND A SPORTING EARTHQUAKE

A syringe turned up, anonymously, at the US anti-doping agency. It contained a 'clear' substance. It triggered a sporting earthquake.

It was a simple plastic syringe. It arrived, in June 2003, at the US Anti-Doping Agency (USADA) from an anonymous source. The sender described himself over the phone as a high-profile track coach. He said the syringe contained a drug given to a number of leading US athletes. He named the owner of BALCO, Victor Conte, as the source of the steroid in the syringe. It started a sporting earthquake. Its tremors are still being felt worldwide.

It started a sporting earthquake. Its tremors are still being felt worldwide.

Who was Victor Conte? He was a session musician for many years. He played bass guitar. With a laid-back style earning him the nickname 'Walkin' Fish', he played in a few bands around the San Francisco area. One was a trio calling themselves, ironically, the Pure Food & Drug Act. The most successful was the horn-based soul and rock band

Tower of Power with whom he appeared for a few years in the late 1970s – he played on the cult band's 1978 album *Come Play With Me*. He would later say that he 'was one of the few band members who weren't on drugs'.

Conte had big ideas. He became a self-taught pharmacist. He developed contacts in sport and saw an opportunity to make money by providing nutritional supplements to swimmers and athletes. He founded in 1984 the Bay Area Laboratory Co-Operative (BALCO). The obscure nutrition laboratory off US Highway 101 near San Francisco Airport initially offered blood and urine tests for athletes and supplied nutritional supplements for them, particularly a zinc and magnesium replacement supplement which Conte termed ZMA. Many top athletes and baseball players became clients and advertised the, perfectly legal, product. He termed them his 'ZMA track club'.

One of his key clients was US sprint star Marion Jones, coached by Trevor Graham, the former Jamaican sprinter. Jones became the triumphant athlete of the 2000 Sydney Olympics – her 'Drive for Five' resulted in gold medals in the 100 metres, the 200 metres and the 4x400 metres relay as well as bronze medals in the long jump and the 4x100 metres relay. Five medals – a feat never before achieved by a female athlete. After divorcing her first husband (and college coach) shot-putter CJ Hunter, she became attached to promising US sprinter Tim Montgomery. In September 2002, in Paris at the IAAF Grand Prix finals, Montgomery stepped into the public limelight himself when he sensationally broke the 100 metres world record with a time of 9.78 seconds. They were the 'golden couple' of world athletics.

They were the 'golden couple' of world athletics.

Marion Jones gave birth to a son by Montgomery in June 2003. It was the same month that the plastic syringe arrived at USADA.

The syringe was half-full of a 'clear' substance. USADA arranged for scientists at the Olympic drug-testing laboratory in Los Angeles to determine its chemical structure. It turned out to be a steroid – tetra-hydrogestrinone or THG – previously undetectable in drug screening tests. The term 'designer drug' entered the sporting lexicon.

Then came a critical step. Four months later, in September 2003, a joint raid on the offices of BALCO was made by government agencies with powers of criminal prosecution – the San Mateo County Narcotics Task Force, the Food and Drug Administration, representatives of USADA and agents of the Internal Revenue Service. At an off-site storage facility, they found numerous vials and containers of steroids, human growth hormone and testosterone. They seized computers and documents listing athletes who had been clients. BALCO had been exposed.

BALCO had been exposed.

Criminal prosecutions followed. Damning evidence of the scale of BALCO's operations emerged during grand jury and other pre-trial investigations under the US criminal system. Numerous witnesses from the world of athletics and baseball testified before the grand jury. It was evidence which would provide the basis for later criminal trials – including charges of perjury.

In February 2004, the US Attorney General announced a forty-two-count indictment against four men (the BALCO four): founder Victor Conte, the mastermind behind the scheme; executive James Valente; track coach Remi Korchemny; and trainer Greg Anderson. Among the charges were conspiracy to distribute anabolic steroids, conspiracy to defraud through misbranded drugs and money laundering.

Victor Conte chose his only escape route and agreed to a plea bargain with the US federal prosecutors. He pleaded guilty to steroid distribution and money laundering in a deal to help the prosecutors with their investigations. He was sentenced in July 2005 to just four months in prison and four months of house arrest. James Valente, BALCO's vice-president, received probation. Greg Anderson, long-time friend and trainer of US baseball star Barry Bonds, received a six-month prison sentence. Conte has since described his sentence as 'the wrist slap heard "round the world".'

The effects of the BALCO scandal were devastating. It became the biggest drugs scandal in sport. New tests for drug screening athletes were developed and past samples reviewed. The roll call of athletes caught up in the aftermath of the scandal has been extensive. Amongst notable athletes caught within the early trawl for THG or a similar drug, modafinil, were world title holder for the women's 100 and 200 metres, Kelli White and Britain's leading sprinter, Dwain Chambers. Chambers was banned for two years.

Victor Conte, founder of BALCO and the central figure in track and field's biggest drug scandal, at the 2008 Tribeca Film Festival in May 2008 in New York City. [52]

Marion Jones and her then partner Tim Montgomery in 2002. Both US sprint stars were involved in the BALCO affair and later punished for drug offences. [52]

Floyd Landis testifies at his arbitration hearing following his disqualification in the 2006 Tour de France. [55]

Dwain Chambers arrives at the High Court in London He was attempting to overturn a British Olympic Association bye-law banning him from competing in the Beijing Games. [56]

Tiger Woods wins the 1997 Masters at Augusta. He was less pleased with an artist's commercial painting celebrating his victory. Did it breach his personal rights? [59]

Manchester United fans protest against the board's deal with Rupert Murdoch's BSkyB. BSkyB's bid looked unstoppable. [60]

Eddie Irvine enjoying the limelight as Ferrari driver in 1999. In a commercial dispute it was claimed that he 'would not get out of bed for less than £25,000'. [61]

England's Steve McManaman hurdles over Portugal's Paulo Bento during Euro 2000. They were playing in Eindhoven. Talksport's 'live' commentary came from Amsterdam. [62]

London Marathon race director Dave Bedford in his running days. He was surprised, along with many others, in 2003 to see runners advertising the 118 118 telephone enquiry service. [66]

FIFA's Sepp Blatter in reflective mood. MasterCard, sponsors of the World Cup, were deeply upset by FIFA's negotiating tactics in 2006. [67]

Kerry Packer's World Series Cricket led to shock headlines, bans – and litigation led by Tony Greig [68]

The US catamaran, *Stars & Stripes '88*, competes against New Zealand's *Big Boat* for the America's Cup – and for even longer in the courts. [69]

The great darts divide. Phil Taylor plays in the first 'break-away' WDC World Championships at Purfleet in 1994. [71]

Stephen Hendry at the Embassy World Championships in 2000 – and at the centre of a major dispute dividing snooker. [72]

Carlos Tevez in full flight for West Ham against Manchester United on the final day of the 2007 season. His goal, inevitably, would save West Ham from relegation – or would it? [75]

Ron Dennis, team principal of McLaren, (right) shakes hands with FIA president, Max Mosley, before the Belgian grand prix in September 2007.....and just after the verdict of the World Motor Sport Council in Formula One's 'Spygate'. [74]

Renée Richards playing at the US Open after her sex-reassignment surgery. It had been a difficult case for the New York courts. [78]

Wendy Toms leads out an all-female officiating team (left is Janie Frampton and right Amy Rayner) in 1999 at Kidderminster, the first in the Nationwide Conference. [79]

Jane Couch, the 'Fleetwood Assassin'. She won the WBF lightweight world title at the David Lloyd Club in Raynes Park, London in 1999 ... after becoming the first licensed professional female boxer in Britain. [81]

Could Casey Martin ride his golf cart on the US PGA tour? 'What is golf ?' His case would go up to the US Supreme Court. [82]

Darrell Hair, accompanied by co-umpire Billy Doctrove, examines the suspect ball with Pakistan captain, Inzamam-ul-Haq, at the Oval Test in 2006. [83]

Oscar Pistorius's carbon-fibre 'blades'. Could he race against able-bodied athletes? [84]

Slovakian handball player, Maros Kolpak, led to significant changes in many sports but especially English cricket. [88]

Belgian footballer, Jean-Marc Bosman, (right) who would become better known as a litigant in the courts of Europe, with his lawyer, Jean-Louis Dupont, after his landmark case. [87]

Crystal Palace chairman, Simon Jordan, (left) consoles manager Iain Dowie after relegation in 2005. He was less conciliatory in 2006 after Dowie's controversial move to Charlton just days after leaving Crystal Palace purportedly 'to go North'. [89]

Andy Webster's move from Hearts to Wigan would lead to 'doing a Webster' becoming part of the football lexicon. [90]

Welsh rugby legend, JPR Williams, never shirked a challenge on the field. An off-field challenge in 1979 would threaten his rugby future. [92]

Ian Botham and his wife, Kathy, leave the High Court during his libel case with Imran Khan in 1996. [93]

Australia's Ian Thorpe in the controversial 'long-john' swimsuit in 2000. Should it be permitted under FINA's rules in international competition? [98]

Scotland kick-off, and celebrate victory after three seconds, in an unusual World Cup qualifying match in Estonia in 1996. [95]

Sir Alex Ferguson with *Rock Of Gibraltar*, and jockey Mick Kinane, after victory in The St James Palace Stakes at Royal Ascot in 2002. [100]

Barry Bonds hitting his record 73rd home run in a season in 2001. The ball would end up in the stands – and in the US courts as two claimants fight over ownership. [99]

In the second half of 2005, the spotlight fell on Tim Montgomery. He was found guilty of taking performance enhancing drugs and banned by the Court of Arbitration for Sport for two years. Importantly, the ban was based on evidence gathered during the BALCO criminal investigation and not on a positive drugs test at an athletics event. The evidence at the grand jury into Conte had revealed a plan at BALCO to turn Montgomery into the world's fastest man: 'Project World Record.'

The plan included, it transpired, a regular programme of human growth hormone and the substance called 'the clear'. Montgomery's results since 31st March 2001, including the 100 metre world record he once held, were nullified from the record books. The 100 metres world record seemed cursed.

A continuing escapee was Marion Jones. She continued to assert that she was drug-free and threatened to sue if the US anti-doping agency imposed a sanction that was based on anything other than a failed drug test. In her autobiography, she said: 'I am against performance enhancing drugs. I have never taken them and I never will.'

But who sent the syringe that triggered all the investigations into BALCO? Who had the knowledge?

Jamaican-born athletics coach, Trevor Graham, was later identified. Was he acting for the good of the sport – or was it simply to gain revenge on Conte? He had once worked closely with athletes supplied by BALCO, including Marion Jones and, for a time, Tim Montgomery. There appears to have been a major row in 2002 between Graham, Conte and Montgomery, probably about money. After Montgomery broke the world record at Paris, many track observers noted that Graham's move to congratulate him at the track was rebuffed; a bitter argument was heard between them, with Montgomery saying it 'was nothing to do with' Graham.

But who sent the syringe that triggered all the investigations into BALCO?

Where did the syringe come from? Graham said later that he was given it by CJ Hunter who was trying to get a job as a coach with Graham at the latter's own Sprint Capitol track training and advisory clinic in Raleigh, North Carolina. CJ Hunter apparently said the syringe came from BALCO from whom he had now split. We will probably never know the truth.

In June 2006, another 100 metres world record holder had fallen. Olympic and world champion sprinter, Justin Gatlin, tested positive for THG. Gatlin was trained by ... Trevor Graham. Already having one offence on his record, Gatlin attempted to avoid a lifetime ban by helping anti-doping officials in their continuing investigations. An initial eight-year ban was reduced, on appeal, to four year. Now it was Graham's turn to be under the spotlight. Was Graham really thinking it through when he sent the syringe to USADA? Did he not realise that the investigation would eventually get round to his own camp of athletes?

Perjury is the charge which trapped them; perjury arising out of evidence under oath at the grand jury trial into the BALCO four in 2003. Graham now faces criminal charges. Similar charges of perjury were made against a number of others – including Marion Jones and baseball's Barry Bonds who, in 2007 broke past Hank Aaron's career record for home-runs in major league baseball – one of America's iconic sporting records. The tremors from the BALCO affair show no sign of ending – even if the major shocks have now passed.

Perjury is the charge which trapped them.

In October 2007 came the news that many had suspected. Marion Jones was facing criminal charges of perjury – lying to the BALCO grand jury in 2003 that she had not taken performance enhancing drugs and, separately, to federal investigators in a cheque fraud case involving her former boyfriend, Tim Montgomery. She finally broke down. She confessed that she had taken performance enhancing drugs before, during and after the 2000 Sydney Olympics.

'I have let have let my family down. I have let my country down and I have let myself down.' She blamed her choice of men in her life. She claimed at first that she did not take the drug knowingly and was told that it was just a supplement called 'flaxseed oil'. She accepted a two-year ban from US Track and Field although she promptly retired from athletics. All her results since September 2000 have been nullified. Jones has been stripped of her five Olympic titles and she has handed back the five medals from the 2000 Olympics.

In January 2008 Marion Jones was sentenced by US District Judge

Karas to six months in prison for perjury. He said there was a need to promote respect for the law.

> *Athletes in society have an elevated status, they entertain, they inspire, and perhaps, most important, they serve as role models. Nobody is above the legal obligation to tell the truth.*

Marion Jones, who 'survived' more than 160 drug tests (what does that say about the effectiveness of these drug tests?), became the first athlete to be convicted of a criminal offence for her role in the BALCO saga.

With hindsight, perhaps early signs were there. As a sixteen-year-old at high school, Marion Jones escaped punishment after missing a drugs test. She was defended by Johnnie Cochran, the lawyer who later successfully defended OJ Simpson.

Marion Jones became the first athlete to be convicted of a criminal offence for her role in the BALCO saga.

Victor Conte later summed up the temptation facing elite athletes:

> *I realised elite sport is about doing what you have to do to win. I've seen athletes ... forced to decide ... whether it's more painful for them to entertain the idea of giving up their dream than to use anabolic steroids.*

The BALCO affair became the biggest drugs scandal in sport. Sports bodies and governments have been forced to face the truth that elite athletes have routinely used steroids, growth hormone and other banned substances in their quest to succeed. BALCO educated the world about doping. BALCO stimulated the biggest shake-up worldwide in drug-testing regulations, testing and investigative procedures. It underlined the IOC's requirement that all nations wishing to participate in the Olympics at Athens in 2004 must have signed up to the World Anti-Doping Code promulgated by the World Anti-Doping Agency (WADA).

Many jurisdictions now apply criminal laws. In the UK, the debate is now commencing in earnest whether to make it a criminal offence to distribute or use performance enhancing drugs in sport – in order to provide more effective weaponry with which to tackle this major challenge to the integrity of sport before London's hosting of the Olympic Games in 2012.

In May 2008, Trevor Graham was found guilty in San Francisco on one count of perjury, lying to federal agents investigating BALCO. A jail sentence and a lifetime ban from athletics lie ahead.

The tremors from the BALCO affair show no sign of ending. And all triggered by a plastic syringe turning up anonymously in the post.

Victor 'Walkin' Fish' Conte himself is back in his laboratory in California running a successful business again selling and distributing nutritional supplements through his new company, Scientific Nutrition for Advanced Conditioning. The Tower of Power band is still playing.

---

53 MARIANO PUERTA – THE FRENCH OPEN AND A GLASS OF WATER

Was Mariano Puerta justified in challenging an eight-year ban, following a second doping offence, on the grounds that is was disproportionate when both offences involved no significant fault?

Was it in the glass of water? Another significant and difficult doping issue arose in tennis in 2005. In June the sporting world's attention was on the French Open at Roland Garros, one of the most famous venues in tennis and the scene of past triumphs of the game's greatest clay court players.

The slow, red clay courts were ideal for Mariano Puerta's game. The twenty-six-year-old unseeded Argentinian was in the form of his life. His tenacity and skill in a dramatic five-set semi-final over twelfth seeded Nikolay Davydenko had thrilled the lively Parisian crowd. He now faced the Spanish teenage sensation and hot favourite to win the final, Rafael Nadal.

It was a tense period before the final. After having some lunch, Puerta spent time sitting with his wife and other family members in the players' cafeteria. They sat together at a small table. Puerta drank coffee and mineral water. Time passed slowly.

Puerta's wife had for many years, on the advice of her doctor, taken the drug effertil during periods of hypertension and menstrual pain. This was one of them. Colourless and odourless, effertil could be purchased in pharmacies over the counter in Argentina without a prescription. Written information supplied with the drug stated that its active ingredient was etilfene, a stimulant prohibited under the anti-doping programme of the International Tennis Federation (ITF) which was consistent with the Code of the World Anti-Doping Agency (WADA) which had now been adopted in virtually all sports.

The atmosphere before the match became a little chaotic. Puerta left for the changing room. He was early and he heard that the start of the final might be delayed. He returned, unexpectedly, to his family in the cafeteria. His wife and her mother had left the table to go to the cloakroom. He sat in the same seat as before. He poured some water into a glass from a bottle he was carrying with him. He believed he was pouring it into the glass from which he had previously been drinking. He thought it was empty. Was it in fact the glass from which his wife had been drinking – containing a small amount of effertil?

Was it in fact the glass from which his wife had been drinking?

The final, nearly three and a half hours, was tough. Nadal won in four sets. Each finalist was then tested under standard ITF procedures. Puerta's sample was later found to contain a small quantity of etilfene.

Unfortunately for him, Puerta had a previous drugs' record. In 2003 he had tested positive for clenbuterol, a prohibited anabolic agent, which he had inadvertently taken at a tournament in Chile. He had served a nine month ban for this offence. As a result, even though the etilfene in his body in Paris was accepted as being too small to have any effect on his performance, the second offence meant that, under the ITF and WADA Code, a further mandatory ban of not less than eight years must be imposed. The ITF appeal tribunal imposed the mandatory period 'with a heavy heart'.

Puerta claimed that the fixed minimum eight-year penalty was excessive. It would effectively end his career. He appealed to the Court of Arbitration for Sport. It was the first time a player or athlete had challenged a WADA-compliant rule of a sport's federation.

Should Puerta be able to overturn the fixed minimum eight-year ban for a second offence when he was not aware that he was taking the drug, the source was probably his wife's medication and the quantity was too small to be in any way performance enhancing? It was a tricky one.

For: Puerta was not aware of the doping. He was not a cheat. He ingested the drug accidentally from his wife's medication. The quantity of etilfene was too small to be performance enhancing. (Indeed, if it had been ephedrine to which it was closely related, the quantity would have been too low to have even been an offence.) The penalty of elimination of the results of the French Open and subsequent tournaments and ranking points and a ban for eight years was unjust and disproportionate in the context of two inadvertent offences. It was tantamount to a lifetime ban and the severe consequences for the player's livelihood were excessive. **Against:** A doping offence had been committed under the ITF/WADA rules. This was a second offence. There must be a mandatory disqualification of Puerta's results obtained at the French Open. Puerta should not be able to claim a defence of 'no fault or negligence' – although a claim of 'no significant fault or negligence' may be agreed. If so, the mandatory ban under the rules for a second offence was eight years and this must apply. The contamination need not have occurred at all if Puerta had exercised the utmost caution. He knew of the risks and of his wife's medication. Every player was responsible for what he ingested. A strict approach was necessary in order to preserve the integrity of sporting competition. Uniformity and standardised penalties, even when they operate harshly in individual cases, are the necessary price in the fight against doping in sport.

Puerta's ban was reduced to two years.

The Court of Arbitration for Sport (CAS) decided that, yes, a minimum eight-year ban as required by the ITF Rules was 'unjust and disproportionate'. This was an exceptional case where both offences had been inadvertent and involved no significant fault. His degree of negligence in this case was 'slight'. The rules should allow discretion in these exceptional circumstances.

CAS was prepared to override the WADA rule in the interests of 'proportionality'.

> *The problem with any 'one size fits all' solution is that there are inevitably going to be instances in which the one size does not fit all. [There is] the very rare case that the imposition of the WADA-sanction will produce a result that is neither just nor proportionate. It is argued by some that this is an inevitable result of the need to wage a remorseless war against doping in sport, and that in any war there will be the occasional innocent victim ... [T]he Panel is not persuaded that it is necessary for there to be undeserving victims in the war against doping. It is a hard war, and to fight it requires external vigilance, but ... it is incumbent on those who wage it to avoid, as far as is possible, exacting unjust and disproportionate retribution.*

CAS, taking a bolder line than in the earlier Baxter case, felt able to fill what it considered a 'lacuna' and impose a sanction which was 'just and proportionate'. A difficult balance had to be weighed between 'strict liability' in the fight against doping and the extenuating circumstances of each individual case. 'The hard choice in sport is whether to have truly deterrent uniform sanctions for doping, or whether to have open-ended discretion in each case. The signatories to the WADA Code have chosen the former.' There was no intake here of a drug at a level which could be performance enhancing. It was accepted that there was no significant fault on Puerta's part. The WADA Code had allowed for some reduction in penalty in those circumstances but had not contemplated the circumstance of a second offence where both offences were accepted as not involving significant fault.

CAS reduced the ban to two years from the end of the French Open. Nevertheless, Puerta's individual results since the French Open should be disqualified and all prize money and ranking points forfeited.

Puerta resumed playing in June 2007. His ATP ranking at the end of the year was 261.

Argentinian tennis players have been particularly prone to falling foul of the strict anti-doping rules. Puerta's suspension came after suspensions in 2001 for two of his compatriots: Juan Ignacio Chela and Guillermo Coria for three and seven months respectively.

More recently, in February 2005, Guillermo Canas tested positive for hydrochlorothiazide at a tournament in Acapulco, Mexico. Initially suspended for two years, an appeal to the Court of Arbitration for Sport (CAS) reduced the ban to fifteen months on the grounds of 'no significant negligence' – Canas had been given the offending medication by a member of tournament staff at Acapulco although the tournament doctor had prescribed a different cold medicine. An important consequence followed. Canas successfully argued before the Swiss courts that CAS had not allowed him sufficient opportunity to present his case before the original tribunal. It was the first successful appeal in the twenty-three-year history of CAS.

The success of Canas was, though, short-lived. A reconstituted CAS tribunal reheard the case – and maintained his ban at fifteen months.

---

54 DAVID MECA-MEDINA – A CASE OF DOPING – OR A DIET OF WILD BOAR?

Marathon swimming was the background. The issue? Are disciplinary rules liable to challenge under European competition laws or does a 'sporting exception' apply?

David Meca-Medina was a professional long distance swimmer. In open water, the Spaniard was the world's best. Ranked number one, he started 1999 in fine form. He won the opening event of the FINA Marathon Swimming World Cup held in January 1999 at Salvador de Bahia in Brazil. Then ... trouble. But was his diet to blame?

Triumph turned quickly to disaster for Meca-Medina and second placed Igor Majcen from Slovenia. They tested positive for nandrolone, a prohibited substance under the rules of the International Swimming Federation (FINA).

Meca-Medina's tests revealed a nandrolone level of 9.7 nanograms per millilitre – substantially in excess of the permitted level of two nanograms under the anti-doping code. He joined a long list of athletes who have crossed the line with this substance. FINA's anti-doping panel suspended both Meca-Medina and Majcen for a period of four years in accordance with FINA's then penalty regime for a first offence.

In January 2000, Meca-Medina saw an escape route. Scientific experiments appeared to show that nandrolone could be produced endogenously within the human body (and therefore innocently) up to a level which could exceed the doping threshold of two nanograms per millilitre – particularly when certain foods, such as wild boar meat, have been consumed. Meca-Medina claimed that this could have been the case here; he had been eating a Brazillian speciality, sarapatel, a stew often based on wild boar meat!

Yes, he had been eating sarapatel, a stew based on wild boar meat!

Meca-Medina and Majcen appealed to the Court of Arbitration for Sport (CAS) for a review of FINA's penalty. They were partially successful. The penalty was reduced to two years suspension.

This was not enough for Meca-Medina and Majcen. They were determined to challenge the penalty further. They took the matter to the European Commission. They claimed that the permitted two nanogram level for nandrolone was too low and could catch innocent athletes. The penalties were excessive. FINA's anti-doping rules were generally anti-competitive and violated the European community rules on competition and freedom to provide services.

This was a new claim. This was the first time that the legality of anti-doping rules in sport had been challenged directly under European competition law. The European Commission itself had previously refused to intervene in sport's anti-doping measures on the basis that this was a matter for sport itself. But Meca-Medina and Majcen were persistent. They eventually brought an action before the European Court of Justice.

Were FINA's anti-doping rules contrary to European competition law? Were the penalties on the swimmers excessive and open to legal challenge as not being proportionate to the particular offence?

For: Anti-doping rules, even if based on sporting objectives of fair play, were capable of having a significant economic impact on the participants. They must therefore comply with European laws relating to competition. The rules and restrictions must be reasonable and proportionate. These were not. The permitted threshold of nandrolone fixed by FINA's anti-doping rules was set at an excessively low level which was not founded on any scientifically safe criteria. **Against:** Anti-doping rules were based purely on sporting considerations of integrity and fair play. They had nothing to do with economic activity. The rules should therefore not come within the scope of the European competition and economic freedom laws. The 'sporting exception' applied. Nandrolone was a substance which, in an athlete's body, was capable of improving performance and compromising the fairness of a sporting event. The two-year ban was accordingly justified in the light of the objective of anti-doping rules. FINA's rules were in accord with the WADA Code. There was no accepted scientific evidence to suggest that the threshold imposed on professional sportsmen was excessive. The penalties were not disproportionate to the offence.

The European Court dismissed the claims of the two swimmers.

Importantly, though, the European Court did agree that the anti-doping rules and penalties fell within the scrutiny of European competition law. Although the rules were based on sporting factors 'in order for competitive sport to be conducted fairly ... and to safeguard equal chances for athletes', they could have economic consequences. This was sufficient for the European competition laws to apply.

> *The penal nature of the anti-doping rules at issue and the magnitude of the penalties applicable if they are breached are capable of producing adverse effects on competition because, if penalties were ultimately to prove unjustified, [they could] result in an athlete's unwarranted exclusion from sporting events ...*

Their operation was not excluded because of a 'sporting exception'. Restrictions must be reasonable and penalties must be proportionate.

Meca-Medina won the skirmish but not the battle. The evidence at the time the rule was applied was that the maximum endogenous production of nandrolone by the human body was substantially lower than the two-nanogram threshold set by the anti-doping rules. The anti-doping rules and penalties in this case were not disproportionate. The length of the bans would not be overturned.

This is one for the lawyers. Dry stuff but an important decision. Although the European Court upheld the anti-doping rules and rejected the swimmers' claim, it did establish that the 'sporting exception' from European competition law is very narrow. Anti-doping rules, previously thought to be outside the scope of competition law, did fall within the ever pervasive jurisdiction of European law. Any restrictions on competition imposed by sporting bodies must be shown to be inherent in the pursuit of sporting objectives and proportionate to those objectives.

Many fear a further, and unnecessary, encroachment of European law into sport.

Meca-Medina and Majcen may have lost the battle but many fear that the law of sport has been changed by a further, and unnecessary, encroachment of European law into sport. The 'sporting exception' would appear to apply only in exceedingly narrow circumstances. European competition law hangs again, Bosmanlike, over rules and decisions of sporting bodies – particularly disciplinary decisions.

After his ban, David Meca-Medina resumed his successful swimming career. Awards culminated in a gold medal in the 25 kilometres at the 2005 World Championships in Montreal. He has also appeared regularly as an actor on American television and cinema.

In public protest at his original FINA ban and with an eye for drama, he once swam — with his feet in shackles — from the former prison island of Alcatraz across San Francisco Bay to the city. It took him thirty-six minutes.

---

55 FLOYD LANDIS – TOUR DE FRANCE AND YET ANOTHER SCANDAL

Floyd Landis was the 'winner' of the 2006 Tour de France. He became the first cyclist to be stripped of his title in his year of victory. The credibility of cycling, and of its most famous race, was hanging by a thread.

It was stage seventeen of the 2006 Tour de France which stunned the cycling world. Experts described it as one of the most epic days of cycling ever seen.

Floyd Landis, the thirty-year-old American who had been a close team-mate of Lance Armstrong at the end of his winning reign, had led the Tour overall by ten seconds after stage fifteen. The next phase, stage sixteen, was a disaster for Landis. He suffered badly on the last hill climb and, shoulders slumped, rider after rider passed him. He fell back from first to eleventh place overall and a full eight minutes behind the new leader, Spaniard Oscar Pereiro. His chances of winning the coveted title, with just three stages left, now seemed to be over.

The following day's stage was the last mountain climb of the Tour. Landis, leader of the Phonak team, had a bold plan. He decided to make an individual breakaway attack from the very first climb, fully 130 kilometres from the finish, and with four further tough climbs to follow during the gruelling stage. Landis broke the field as the chasing pack failed to react. It was an astonishing ride. He was the 'master of the mountains'. It was regarded as one of the most spectacular single-day performances in the history of the Tour. Landis eventually won the stage by nearly six minutes, a massive distance. He punched the air ecstatically in triumph. He had closed the gap with Pereiro by more than seven minutes and was now back in third place overall with a renewed chance of the title.

It was one of the most spectacular single-day performances in the history of the Tour.

Landis succeeded in making up the gap with the leader in the following two days' final stages. He proudly crossed the finish line, on the elegant cobbles of the Champs Elysées in Paris, a triumphant winner of the world's greatest cycling race. He was presented with the final yellow jersey.

The euphoria of victory drained away when, three days, later, it was reported that an 'adverse analytical finding' had resulted from a drugs test after stage seventeen. No name was given but the president of the International Cycling Union (UCI) said that it was the 'worst possible outcome'.

The Tour de France has a history riddled with drugs. It is a sporting event which perhaps calls upon human reserves of stamina, strength and endurance beyond any other. Drugs have probably been involved in one form or another from the earliest days. The saying even developed: 'No dope, no hope.' It has become the most 'suspect' sporting event in the world.

The problem was first brought to the front of the world's attention, sadly and dramatically, when Britain's Tommy Simpson died during the 1967 Tour. During stage thirteen, on a beating hot July day during a climb up Mont Ventoux and about two kilometres from the summit, Simpson began to zigzag across the road before collapsing. Two empty tubes and a third full of amphetamines were found in the pocket of his jersey. He, tragically, was so doped that he did not know he had reached the human level of endurance.

In 1978, having just claimed the leader's yellow jersey on a mountain stage, the Belgian Michael Pollentier and another rider went missing when they should have provided a urine sample. They turned up two hours later. One doctor was suspicious and tugged at Pollentier's shorts – revealing a tube linked to a rubber condom of pre-prepared urine under his armpit. Pollentier was thrown off the Tour.

Use of drugs was still, clearly, widespread in professional cycling.

Before the 1998 Tour, one of the managers of the leading Festina team, Willy Voet, drove across the Belgian-French border early one morning. A routine, but unexpected, examination of his official Fiat estate car by French customs officials revealed it to be full of illegal prescription drugs, erythropoietin (EPO), growth hormones, testosterone and amphetamines. At first, he said that they were for his 'own personal use'. French police raided the Festina team's hotel. The Festina team were just the first of seven to withdraw from the 1998 race as ever increasing evidence was found and criminal arrests were made. Use of drugs was still, clearly, widespread in professional cycling.

Following the Festina scandal, further anti-doping measures were put into effect. Rules were tightened and a more optimistic view was taken that the sport had become 'clean'. Yet, even before the start of the 2006 Tour, a criminal doping investigation in Spain – known as 'Operación Puerto' – into the activities of Dr Eufemiano Fuentes and his team at a Madrid clinic had involved many professional cyclists and led to the withdrawal from the Tour of two race favourites, Ivan Basso and Jan Ullrich.

Surely there would be no further scandal in 2006? Could the Tour and the dwindling reputation of cycling as a sport survive any more scandals?

On 27th July came the announcement from the Phonak team. It was Floyd Landis. He had tested positive after stage seventeen for an excessive level of the hormone testosterone – the ratio of testosterone to epitestosterone (the T/E ratio) was apparently 11:1 and far above the maximum permitted ratio of 4:1. The test on the A sample had been carried out by the French government's anti-doping clinical laboratory in Paris, the National Laboratory for Doping Detection (LNDD), a WADA accredited laboratory.The B sample later confirmed the finding. Past samples of Landis during the Tour were also tested. A number, but not all, revealed similar results.

First reactions were of bemusement. Why would he do it? How could he be so stupid as to get caught? It did not seem to make sense.

Why would he do it? How could he be so stupid as to get caught?

Tests on Landis two days before and two days after stage seventeen had shown no adverse findings.How did testosterone, a drug for developing muscle growth, really aid short-term recovery in the circumstances of the Tour? It was not blood manipulation or use of an oxygen enhancer, such as EPO. Or had he been taking something more regularly which had previously been 'masked'?

Testosterone is a difficult substance for the testers since it is naturally produced within the body. Tests have to establish whether its presence is natural or from the outside – is it from 'the body' or 'the bottle'? Different tests and studies are undertaken and the patterns analysed before a conclusion is reached. So, one test determines the T/E ratio to establish if that is abnormal. Another, performed after the T/E test, is a carbon isotope ratio test which establishes the measurement between two isotopes in a different way to discriminate between 'endogenous' (naturally produced) and 'exogenous' (synthetically produced) steroids such as testosterone.

Landis denied cheating and said high levels of testosterone must have occurred naturally in the body. He was, with approval, taking cortisone injections for a hip ailment which may have been a factor.

> *There are multiple reasons why this could have happened other than what they are saying ... there are possibly hundreds of reasons why the test should be this way ... The analysis is replete with fundamental, gross errors.*

For months afterwards – and well into 2008 – Landis sustained a vigorous and public attack on the procedures for testing at the LNDD laboratory. There were questions over some of the findings – even, at one time, a question whether the B sample had been correctly identified as that of Landis since it seemed to bear the wrong sample number. He later developed his defence by publicising many of the documents and facts on a website and appealing for 'the collective resources of cycling fans', particularly in relation to the deficiencies of the LNDD. It became known as the 'Wikipedia defence'.

Landis was charged with a doping violation by the US anti-doping agency (USADA) in September 2006. The case went to arbitration in Malibu, California in May 2007 under the auspices of the American Arbitration Association. Landis mounted a highly sophisticated, detailed and seemingly never-ending challenge to the procedures and testing at the LNDD.

In September 2007 the American arbitration panel decided, by a 2-1 majority, that Landis was guilty of a doping offence. His defence, costing an estimated $2 million, had failed. However, the decision was not straightforward. The panel acknowledged that: 'The practises of the [LNDD] in training its employees appear to lack the vigor the panel would expect ... given the enormous consequences to athletes.'

The panel concluded, first, that the charge of an elevated T/E ratio (the initial charge) from the sample 'was not established in accordance with the WADA International Standard for laboratories' and was dismissed. However, the panel by a majority did conclude that the charge of 'exogenous testosterone being found in the sample' by the carbon isotope analysis was established and this was an anti-doping violation. The UCI president commented: 'He got a highly qualified legal team who tried to baffle everybody with science and public relations, and in the end the facts stood up.'

Landis was banned for two years as from 30th January 2007. The UCI stripped him of his 2006 Tour de France title. He was the first 'winner' of the Tour de France to be stripped of his title because of a doping offence.

The problem of drugs continued to plague the Tour. In 2007, three riders and two teams withdrew following positive doping tests. Following stage sixteen, the race leader, Michael Rasmussen, was removed from the Tour by his Rabobank team who accused him of lying about the reasons for missing several drugs tests earlier in the year.

The saga of Floyd Landis was still not over. Landis appealed further to the Court of Arbitration for Sport (CAS). A cynical, and exhausted, public awaited the final verdict. It came in July 2008. CAS dismissed Landis' claim. The laboratory had used some 'less than ideal laboratory practices but not lies, fraud, forgery or cover-ups' as Landis had contended.

> *In summary, [Landis] failed to provide any credible evidence of a deliberate attempt to deceive or defraud the Panel or cover-up alleged data tampering... The Panel finds that the presence of exogenous testosterone or its precursors or metabolites in [Landis'] Stage 17 Tour sample... proves that [he] engaged in doping... Accordingly, [Landis'] result at the 2006 Tour is disqualified.*

The longest, most expensive case in anti-doping history was over.

---

56 DWAIN CHAMBERS AND CHRISTINE OHURUOGU – TWO BRITISH RUNNERS, BANS AND BEIJING

Two British athletes returned from bans for drug-related offences. Two potential medal contenders. Could Christine Ohuruogu or Dwain Chambers overturn the lifetime eligibility ban imposed by the British Olympic Association and go to Beijing?

Dwain Chambers settled into his starting blocks for the 100 metres final at the British Olympic trials in July 2008. This was his chance. Ten seconds later came his victory roar amid the sound of the crowd. Ten seconds dead, well within the Olympic qualifying time of 10.21 seconds for the 100 metres. He was Britain's top-ranked sprinter again. He was a potential medal contender. But would he be going to Beijing?

The British Olympic Association said 'no'. Chairman, Colin Moynihan, was adamant: 'There will be no room for cheats in the British team as long as I am involved with the BOA.'

The governing rule was bye-law No. 45 of the National Olympic Committee of the BOA, a bye-law first introduced in March 1992 under the chairmanship of Arthur Gold and promoted by Britain's leading athletes as 'Gold's law'. The BOA had failed to persuade the International Olympic Committee to adopt a rule generally. Britain would go it alone – although since then Norway and Romania have also adopted the rule.

'There will be no room for cheats in the British team as long as I am involved with the BOA.'

Any person who has been found guilty of a doping offence... shall not... thereafter be eligible for consideration as a member of a Team GB... in relation to any Olympic Games...

An exception could be made if the offence was 'minor' or there were 'significant mitigating circumstances'. There were none here. Chambers could only beat the ban by fighting it in court. Within a period of less than twelve months, two leading British athletes would stand before courts or tribunals challenging the BOA in their pursuit of places in Beijing. No wonder the BOA has a full-time Director of Legal Services.

First, Christine Ohuruogu. Born in east London and pride of Newham and Essex Beagles, her breakthrough came as a twenty-one-year-old at the 2006 Commonwealth Games in Melbourne when she stormed past the Olympic and World champion, Tonique Williams, to win a stunning gold in the 400 metres. Triumph turned to personal disaster later in the same year.

She fell foul of the random 'out-of-competition' drug testing rules introduced by the International Association of Athletics Federations (IAAF). Athletes registered in the testing pool with the IAAF were now obliged to provide 'whereabouts information' for one hour a day, five days a week – a measure to counter the activities of 'cheats' (athletes like Dwain Chambers himself in his BALCO-days) whose use of drugs was designed to be out the athlete's system by the day of competition itself. Three missed tests and severe sanctions apply.

Not difficult to comply? Twice over nine months during 2005 and 2006 a doping control officer from UK Sport had turned up at the location scheduled that day for Ohuruogu's training. She had been training elsewhere. She had forgotten to update her schedule. Two missed tests.

Ohuruogu's bad luck (or neglect) continued in July 2006. The Mile End Stadium was the declared location for her training that day between 11 a.m. and 12 noon. But there was a school sports' day! Her coach had called early that morning to say she would have to train at the Crystal Palace stadium instead. The doping officer turned up at the Mile End Stadium to conduct a test. It was a third missed test. She was in trouble.

Ohuruogu went before the disciplinary committee of UK Athletics and was found guilty of an anti-doping violation. She was suspended from competition for one year. This was now the fixed penalty for this offence under the rules of the IAAF.

Christine Ohuruogu was deeply upset. Her career was in jeopardy. She complained that it was unfair. Britain's world triathlon champion, Tim Don, had received a three-month ban only in 2006 under the triathlon association's rules for his missed tests. A one-year ban for Ohuruogu was disproportionate. It should be struck down. She appealed to the Court of Arbitration for Sport (CAS) to over-rule, or at least reduce, this ban. Should she succeed?

CAS upheld the one-year ban. The IAAF rules were clear and one year was within the range of punishment permitted by the WADA Code. CAS added that there was no suggestion that Ohuruogu was guilty of taking drugs to enhance her performance. Indeed, this case 'can be viewed in all the circumstances as a busy young athlete being forgetful'. Nevertheless, the suspension 'was proportionate and should not be disturbed'. It should serve:

> *... as a warning to all athletes that the relevant authorities take the provision of 'whereabouts' information extremely seriously as they are a vital part in the ongoing fight against drugs in the sport.*

Christine Ohuruogu was 'totally stunned by the decision'. (Echoes of Rio Ferdinand's reaction to his penalty for missing a drugs test at Manchester United while shopping at Harvey Nichols.) Beijing now seemed a distant dream.

Ohuruogu served her one-year ban. She returned to athletic competition in August 2007... and promptly caused a major upset when, in only her second meeting since the ban, she sensationally won the 400 metres at the World Championships in Osaka. The dream of Beijing was still there – except for the major obstacle of the continuing lifetime ban imposed by the BOA on athletes found guilty of a doping offence. So, back to a tribunal.

Christine Ohuruogu was totally stunned by the decision. Beijing now seemed a distant dream.

She appealed to an independent BOA Panel chaired by Nicholas Stewart QC. Could she show that there were 'significant mitigating circumstances'? She was optimistic. Surely there was a difference between an offence for, innocently, missing tests compared with actually being a drug cheat? Indeed, there had been a record of successful appeals – at least twenty-five athletes (including Tim Don) had previously satisfied the 'minor' or 'mitigating circumstances' criteria. But an offence carrying a one-year ban was of a different order.

The Appeals Panel decided 'yes'. There had been no intent to avoid the rules... but this was not enough on its own to support her appeal. The Appeals Panel nevertheless thought that, with hindsight, more could have been done to train and instruct athletes as to the vital role of 'out-of-competition' testing. It would be very difficult in future for any athlete to claim the benefit of 'teething problems'.

Christine Ohuruogu was fortunate. By such fine margins... She was free to race in Beijing. Perhaps the BOA was secretly relieved.

Thirty-year-old Islington-born Dwain Chambers knew that his case was more difficult. He had been a drug cheat. Former world junior record holder and bronze medallist in the 1999 World Championships, his talent was undoubted. He had struggled to fulfil his enormous potential at the highest level. He could not match the leading Americans, including in the 2000 Olympics in Sydney. He moved to California and linked in 2002 with a new coach, veteran Remi Korchemny, the Ukranian who coached Valery Borsov to double Olympic sprint glory in 1972. And then he became involved with nutritionist, Victor Conte, at BALCO... and a positive test for THG was exposed in August 2003.

The IAAF mandatory ban for a first offence was two years. (It had formerly been four years but reduced, primarily for legal concerns, to two by the IAAF in 1997. Linford Christie, somewhat ironically in view of his later failed test, led a British protest.)

Chambers had served his two-year ban by August 2005. His first athletic comeback had mixed fortunes. He needed to earn money. He dabbled, unsuccessfully, as an American football player and then, for a bizarre period early in 2008, had a month's trial as a rugby league player with Castleford Tigers. He now wanted to re-establish himself in top-class athletics. His performance at the British Olympic trials, and earlier in the World Indoor Championships, had proved that he was fast enough.

He was also reformed. He wanted to help in the campaign against drugs. He persuaded Victor Conte to detail his drugs regime. John Scott, head of UK Sport's anti-drug unit, was enthusiastic:

> *This is priceless information. What Dwain is giving us is a unique, detailed and honest account of exactly how*

sophisticated drug use in athletics has become. The manual of a drug cheat.'

What did it show? Not only had Chambers taken THG but a whole cocktail of performance enhancing drugs including also: a testosterone/epitestosterone cream, blood-boosting drug EPO, human growth hormone, insulin, a 'wakefulness agent' called modafinil and liothyronine, a synthetic form of thyroid hormone. It was indeed 'the full enchilada' of performance enhancing drugs. Conte also explained how athletes were continuing to use 'duck and dodge' tactics to get away with cheating.

Sympathy for Chambers was low. For people like Sir Steve Redgrave, the position was clear:

Every athlete that competes for Great Britain knows the BOA's rules. If an athlete takes the risk of cheating they have to accept the penalties that go with this.

And yet there was disquiet in some circles. Dick Pound, former president of the World Anti-Doping Agency and noted 'hard man', expressed his concern:

The sanction for a first offence is a two-year suspension. Chambers has served his ban and I think, depending on your view of criminal justice, if you serve the penalty that was deemed appropriate – for whatever the offence was – you are entitled to be reintegrated into society. The additional penalty of never representing Britain again can be seen as a sanction that is over and above what is in the [World Anti-Doping] Code.

Emotions ran high. The legal and moral arguments became inter-mixed. Many of the comments seemed personal to Chambers, fuelled by some of his less diplomatic remarks. (Carl Myerscough, 'the Blackpool Tower', a shot-putter who had also served a drugs ban, had not received the same criticism when selected to represent Britain in various events.) To side with Chambers' case was to appear 'soft on drugs'.

Chambers finally made his move. He initiated proceedings on 3rd July. His High Court hearing came on 16th July, four days after his victory in the British Olympic trials and just days before the BOA's final nomination of the team for Beijing. He sought a temporary injunction requiring the BOA to suspend its eligibility rule. Should Dwain Chambers succeed?

For: He had served the two-year ban imposed under the IAAF's code. No lifetime ban was imposed by the International Olympic Committee. There was no further sanction imposed by WADA. Britain was virtually the only country with such a rule and athletes from other countries would be competing in Beijing despite similar previous bans. The ban would greatly affect Chamber's income and future. A lifetime ban was disproportionate and an unlawful restraint of trade. **Against:** There was no right to represent GB at the Olympics. The Olympics offered no monetary prize. The rule did not prevent Chambers competing in other non-Olympic events. The BOA were entitled to take a lead against doping and set its own eligibility rule. Chambers might still be benefiting, physically or by experience, from his former 'cheating'. His selection would affect Team GB morale and management. To take him to the Olympics could deprive another clean athlete of his place – particularly if the injunction was later dropped at full trial. Chambers had left it too late to challenge the rule for Beijing.

Justice McKay gave his judgment on 18th July. The issues were complex. There were arguments on both sides. A full hearing could be held in March 2009, after Beijing. But, in short, Chambers had left it too late. He could have made his legal challenge much earlier than the 'eleventh hour' and enabled the court to assimilate more fully the difficult arguments. On the evidence, he had not yet proved an unreasonable restraint of trade. Justice McKay summed up:

Chambers looked across at his legal counsel who mouthed simply: 'We've lost.'

> *'In my judgment, it would take a much better case than the claimant has presented to persuade me to overturn the status quo at this stage and compel his selection for the Games.'*

Chambers looked across at his legal counsel who mouthed simply: 'We've lost.'

Outside the court, the BOA Chairman, Lord Moynihan, was pleased but restrained:

> *The BOA will continue to send a powerful message that nobody found guilty of serious drugs-cheating offences should have the honour of wearing GB vests at the Olympic Games.*

Chambers would not be going to Beijing.

Ironically, the International Olympic Committee – perhaps influenced by the BOA's leadership – has introduced a new eligibility rule to apply from 1st July 2008 for future Olympics after Beijing. Any athlete banned for more than six months for a doping offence will not be eligible to compete in the next Olympics following the end of his or her suspension. It provides a tough sanction but a universal one. If this rule had been in force for Beijing, Dwain Chambers would not have been eligible under IOC rules... nor would Christine Ohuruogu.

Immediate reaction to the High Court decision was triumphant. Nobody wants to be 'soft' on drugs. But a suspicion remains that the door is still open for a sustained legal challenge to the bye-law. The BOA quietly confirmed that, after Beijing, it will commission a survey of all British athletes for their views. It will not be a surprise to many if the lifetime ban is changed to reflect the IOC's rule of missing the next Olympics.

Had Dwain Chambers been in Beijing and run 10.00 in the final, he would have come seventh – well behind Usain Bolt's stunning world record of 9.69 seconds.

As for Christine Ohuruogu... Olympic glory. 400 metres champion. Her thrilling, surging finish clinched Great Britain's only track victory. The gold medal was presented to her by Lord Coe.

CHAPTER SEVEN

SPORT AND BUSINESS

Business and sport, particularly professional sport, have become inextricably linked.

Leading companies spend substantial sums in promoting their products or corporate image through an association with major sporting events, teams or personalities. Significant commercial arrangements are made including television and other broadcasting deals, sponsorship and 'official' supplier arrangements, licensing and merchandising contracts. Corporate hospitality has become a significant source of income. Individual sporting stars have become 'hot' property, able to exploit their reputation and image through profitable sponsorship, product endorsement and merchandising deals.

This explosion of commercial activity has inevitably led to numerous legal disputes which have been fought in the courts. Our journey takes us to an evocative range of sporting events including horseracing in Australia, Formula One motor racing, Euro 2000 football in Holland, souvenir selling outside Highbury stadium and golf at Augusta.

---

57 AN OUTSIDE RADIO BROADCAST – AN UNUSUAL HORSERACING COMMENTARY POSITION

Should a racecourse owner be entitled to prevent broadcasting from private land opposite the course?

George Taylor lived in a road opposite the Victoria Park racecourse on the outskirts of Sydney. His front lawn was the unlikely scene for a dispute in 1937, in the early days of sports broadcasting, which would significantly affect the legal basis for the commercialisation of sport.

The course at Victoria Park had been opened in 1908 by Sir James John Joynton Smith, a keen sportsman. Built on reclaimed land, it had become a leading centre for horse and pony racing with significantly better facilities than those at the previously disreputable pony tracks. Prior to the 1930s, Victoria Park had also been the scene of historic aviation activity. In December 1909, an Englishman, Colin Defries, made an attempt there at the first powered air flight. His flight only reached an altitude of fifteen feet. It ended in a crash landing after one hundred yards when he lost control grabbing for his hat which was blown off in the wind.

Most of the racecourse at Victoria Park was in 1937 surrounded by an eleven foot high weatherboard fence. It was bounded on the east side by Dowling Street. George Taylor owned a cottage and land on Dowling Street on the opposite side from the racecourse. With a canny eye on some useful income, Taylor allowed a broadcasting company, the Commonwealth Broadcasting Corporation, to build a platform on scaffolding, about sixteen feet high, on his front lawn.

From the platform on Taylor's land, a person could see the whole of the racetrack including the notice boards showing the names and positions of the competing horses. An employee of the broadcasting company watched the races through his field glasses and gave a running commentary into a microphone connected with a transmission station. The commentary, mingled with advertisements, was broadcast 'live' to the public in Sydney and surrounding districts.

... he allowed a local broadcasting company to build a platform on scaffolding ...

The racecourse owners of Victoria Park were outraged. No permission had been given for this broadcast. They did not want any outside broadcasting from the course. It encouraged betting to take place off course rather than at the track. It could seriously damage spectator attendances at the racecourse and admission receipts. It violated their 'rights'. But what rights?

The racecourse owners brought a legal action to stop this broadcasting from Taylor's land. It became a major case. It would go to the High Court of Australia. Should the racecourse owners be entitled to prevent broadcasting taking place from facilities constructed outside the territory of the racecourse itself?

For: No permission had been given for the broadcasting. It could prejudicially affect the owner's business at the racecourse. Attendances were likely to be affected. The activity, which was not a natural use of Taylor's residential property, interfered with the proper use and enjoyment of the racecourse. The racecourse owners had spent considerable sums building up the business and goodwill in the racecourse as a sporting venue. The activities on Taylor's land violated the rights which the racecourse owners had in the business and its commercial exploitation.
Against: The construction of the platform on Taylor's land and its use was perfectly lawful. There was nothing to make the broadcasting unlawful. There was no exclusive right or property in the races, or any of the information being displayed, which prevented an outsider simply describing what he could see. There was no trespass onto the racecourse. It was simply exploitation by Taylor of his own land. The broadcasting should be allowed to continue.

The court decided in George Taylor's favour. He could not be stopped.

The activities of Taylor and the broadcasting company had not infringed any legal right of the racecourse owners. There was no wrong in describing what took place on the racecourse. Chief Justice Latham set out the position succinctly: 'I am unable to see that any right of the plaintiff has been violated or any wrong done to him.' He added, critically: 'A 'spectacle' cannot be 'owned' in any ordinary sense of the word.' There was no proprietary right in a sporting event.

There was no proprietary right in a 'spectacle' or sporting event.

George Taylor could continue with his activities. The owners of the Victoria Park racecourse would have to build a higher fence.

This case arose in the early days of broadcasting and the commercialisation of sport. It was an important decision since it denied any general 'property' right in a sporting event as such. English and Commonwealth law was forced to take a different direction from that taken in certain other countries – including the USA where the courts have been much readier to establish rights for sports events organisers.

As a result, a sports event organiser in the UK can only create valuable 'rights' by a series of measures mostly centred on the right to control entry to the venue itself and the contract conditions which apply to those who do enter – whether spectators, participants, broadcasters, sponsors or others. For instance, it is only by the contract of admission, the all-important ticket, that spectators and others can be restricted from unauthorised broadcasting, photography, sponsorship activity and merchandise selling.

Would the analysis in 1937 have been different if the court could have foreseen the explosion in sports broadcasting which would take place later in the century? Little did George Taylor know that he was shaping the law of sport.

---

58 THE PGA – HOSPITALITY AT THE RYDER CUP

Could the PGA prevent an unauthorised company using the term 'Ryder Cup Hospitality Village' to cash in on the event?

The Ryder Cup has become one of the great sporting events of the world. The golf competition is held on a biennial basis between professional golfers from the USA and Europe. The competition involves many of the best players in the world.

The Ryder Cup at Muirfield Village golf course in Columbus, Ohio in 1987 had seen the first victory for Europe on American soil. The next match was due to be held in September 1989 at the Belfry course near Birmingham in England. The tournament was being organised by the Professional Golfers Association (PGA). Interest in the event had never been greater.

Hospitality at the Ryder Cup, as with other major sports events, was much in demand. As the High Court later noted, long gone were the days when 'a cup of hot soup on a cold wet day and perhaps some shelter at midday' was all that was required. Hospitality operations and services offered to customers had become extensive: food, refreshment, seating and marquees along with highly prized admission tickets. The provision of hospitality had become a profitable business activity. The PGA had appointed Keith Prowse to be the sole agent for the provision of hospitality on the course and for the sale of tickets for the 1989 match at the Belfry.

Brochures, however, started in early 1988 to be issued by another company, Ryder Cup Hospitality (RCH), founded by Marcus Evans. These offered tickets to potential customers and advertised special facilities described as 'the Ryder Cup Hospitality Village' located at a 'prime course site location'. Potential customers were invited to enquire at the 'Ryder Cup Hospitality sales office'.

The PGA and Keith Prowse, alarmed at these advertisements, brought legal action to prevent RCH from using the expression 'Ryder Cup Hospitality' in their promotional offerings. They alleged that RCH were, in effect, parasitically taking advantage of the business goodwill built up by the PGA in the Ryder Cup. It was a form of what has since been termed 'ambush marketing'.

Interest in the Ryder Cup had never been greater. The PGA appointed Keith Prowse as sole agent for on-course hospitality.

Should the PGA be able to prevent the use of 'Ryder Cup Hospitality' by RCH in its advertisements?

For: The provision of hospitality was part of the business of the PGA in staging the Ryder Cup. It had built up substantial goodwill in that business. RCH's brochure was a form of 'ambush marketing' by RCH: deliberate promotion of its commercial services to suggest an 'official' association with the tournament and so take advantage of the PGA's goodwill. It was misleading and potentially harmful to the official hospitality providers, Keith Prowse, who could lose business and reputation. The PGA should be able to take action to protect the exclusivity which it offered its official suppliers.

Against: 'Ryder Cup' was not a registered trademark. It was simply a description of the event. There was nothing to prevent RCH providing hospitality facilities at a location alongside the course. It was not breaching any condition of entry on to the course. RCH had since made it clear in a revised version of the brochure that RCH was an independent company and not associated with the PGA.

The PGA won.

A preliminary injunction was granted by the court to restrain Evans and RCH from using the name 'Ryder Cup Hospitality Village' in their promotions. The court was satisfied that the use of these terms would create 'a serious risk that the hospitality services offered will be associated by those to whom they are addressed with [the PGA] and Keith Prowse'. There was a material risk of potential customers being confused or misled. This is the kernel of what the lawyers quaintly call 'passing off'.

RCH's brochure was a form of ambush marketing. There was a material risk of confusion.

Evans and RCH were also stopped from reselling tickets in breach of the original ticket conditions.

Keith Prowse and the PGA were happy. The match at the Belfry was another great contest, resulting in a 14-14 tie. Europe retained the Ryder Cup.

'Ambush marketing' takes a variety of forms and on many occasions it is difficult to assert that it is wrongful. Sports event organisers try to protect against unauthorised activity of third parties by registering trademarks and by use of copyright logos and designs. Enforcement is then easier. 'Ryder Cup' itself was not then a registered mark. (It now is.) Although this was only a temporary injunction pending a full trial, this decision was important. It did demonstrate a willingness of the courts to intervene to prevent 'ambush marketing' where it crossed the line.

The remedy, though, is not quick or certain. As far as the Olympics are concerned, legislation exists to give stronger and more specific protection. A new, exceptional 'London Olympics Association Right' has been created. Broad in scope, this prohibits the use of any visual or verbal representation in a manner which is likely to create in the mind of the public an association with the 2012 London Olympics. It covers, specifically, use of words such as 'games', '2012', 'gold' and 'medals'. Many other major events would greatly welcome similar protection.

Marcus Evans himself was not deterred, however, in his ambitions to expand his hospitality empire. It later evolved into an international business events, training, hospitality and services business and a personal fortune for Evans. Part of that fortune has, to some people's surprise, recently been used to acquire a controlling interest in Ipswich Town.

---

59 TIGER WOODS – A MASTER OF AUGUSTA

Should Tiger Woods be entitled to prevent the commercial sale of a painting exploiting his image at Augusta?

The fairways of Augusta National were their usual glorious emerald green in April 1997 for The Masters. The course was set majestically; the cathedral in the pines. As ever, a sense of history pervaded this wonderful event – the first of the golf majors and the one where the previous winners of the coveted 'green jacket' are invited to return each year. This was destined to be Tiger Wood's year.

Eldrick 'Tiger' Woods, aged twenty-one, was playing for the third time in The Masters. After a glittering amateur career, Woods was marked out for sporting greatness. The previous year, his first as a professional, he had failed to make the halfway cut. In 1997, though, he was a sensation. After a shaky start, he played superb golf over the last three-and-a-half rounds and destroyed the

In 1997, Woods was a sensation at The Masters.

field – winning by twelve shots over his nearest rival. He became the youngest ever winner. His score of 270 was, and still is, the lowest in the history of the tournament.

Rick Rush is an artist from Alabama. He has become known as 'America's Sports Artist'. In 1998, he produced a painting commemorating Woods' 1997 victory. Entitled 'The Masters of Augusta', the painting consisted of three distinctive perspectives of Woods in front of the Augusta National clubhouse. Depicted against a light blue background were shadowy images of Arnold Palmer, Sam Snead, Jack Nicklaus and other previous great winners of The Masters. Behind them could be seen The Masters' leaderboard. The painting was to be sold commercially as a limited edition print including a set of five thousand lithographs. The narrative accompanying the print said that the painting featured Tiger Woods 'displaying that awesome swing' and 'flanked by his caddie and final round player partner's caddie'.

Woods had not been involved in any of this. He had not given permission for any painting. Were any of his rights infringed? Woods' licensing company, ETW Corp, complained that the painting, without Woods' permission, wrongfully exploited the rights of Woods in his image or his right of publicity under Ohio law. They sought to prevent any commercial sale of the painting.

It became a classic case. It encapsulated a significant, and difficult, issue. What should the law favour? Protection of the rights of a sportsman against the unauthorised commercial exploitation of his image – or freedom of expression? One of the world's richest sportsmen and his commercial machine against the 'little' man, the creative, small town painter.

Rick Rush said: 'I believe these events are in the public domain. I want to capture the sporting lifestyle.' Media organisations lined up to back the artist. 'Mr Wood's extraordinary accomplishments give rise to many benefits and a few burdens. One of the burdens ... is having to see himself depicted in words and pictures by people who have things to say about him.'

Lawyers for Woods countered: 'When a painting is done and hung on the wall, that may be acceptable but when you commercialise that person's image, you cross the line.' Some of Wood's supporters actually included other sporting artists: 'Why should an artist just looking for a hot market not do something about having an arrangement [with the player]. The player is entitled to a cut.'

Was it freedom of expression – or protection of a sportsman's rights against unauthorised exploitation of his image?

The issue was fought, ultimately, to the US Court of Appeals in Cincinnati. Should Tiger Woods be able to prevent the commercial sale of a painting which exploited his image?

For: The painting depended on the image of Woods for its basic subject matter. It used the name of Tiger Woods in the accompanying description to assist the selling of the painting. The painting was for commercial sale, designed to produce a commercial benefit utilising the image of Woods. The commercial benefits would be solely for the publishers and the painter, not Woods. This should not be permitted without his consent.
Against: This was an artistic work. The painting was a collage of images which described the majesty of a newsworthy sports event. Woods had no copyright in the painting. The use of his name was a description and not use as a trademark. The concept of a sportsperson's 'image rights' did not extend to prevent all commercial use of his image. In this case, any such concept should not override the general principle of freedom of expression, particularly for an artistic work.

Woods lost.

The US Court of Appeals decided, by a 2-1 majority, against Woods. Woods could not assert trademark rights in every photograph and image of himself. He had no 'image rights' which outweighed the freedom of artistic expression which was a principle of US law. Judge James Graham concluded:

Wood's right of publicity was outweighed by society's interest in artistic freedom.

> *Rush's work consists of a collage of images which combine to describe an historic sports event and to convey the significance of Wood's achievement in that event ... After balancing the societal and personal interests embodied in the First Amendment against Woods' property rights, we conclude that the effect of limiting Wood's right of publicity in this case is negligible and*

> *significantly outweighed by society's interest in the freedom of artistic expression.*

Rick Rush could sell his paintings.

This decision, controversial in many quarters, was based specifically and narrowly on US law which emphasised the priority of the First Amendment to the US Constitution over the 'rights of publicity' of an individual under Ohio law. However, it was significant because the law in most US States has a more developed concept of a 'right of publicity', an exclusive right of a celebrity to exploit commercially his or her image, than exists under English law.

No separate 'image right' exists as such under English law despite attempts by some celebrities, including Michael Douglas and Catherine Zeta Jones, to expand the boundaries of English law. Remedies here depend on particular situations – such as a misleading suggestion that a particular sportsman has endorsed a product or service (see the later case involving Eddie Irvine below). Woods would not succeed under English law as presently developed.

For the enthusiasts, the final round playing partner of Tiger Woods at Augusta in 1997 was Costantino Rocca.

---

60 BSKYB'S BID FOR MANCHESTER UNITED – A MARRIAGE OF BROADCASTING AND FOOTBALL?

What could stop Rupert Murdoch's BSkyB from acquiring Manchester United?

Sport attracts investment by 'big business'. Football clubs, in particular, have since the early 1990s been a magnet for the attention and money of major investors – both individual and corporate. None more so than Manchester United.

Perhaps Rupert Murdoch envied the position of Italy's Silvio Berlusconi, head of his own television and media empire and majority owner of AC Milan. Or possibly Murdoch's thoughts were first stirred by the memory of Michael Knighton on the pitch at Old Trafford in 1989 celebrating, he thought, a successful deal with Martin Edwards to acquire Manchester United for £20 million.

With hindsight, if it had gone through, Knighton's bid would have been the deal of the century. It failed. Manchester United's shares were instead floated publicly on the London Stock Exchange in 1991. The club had entered the world of high finance, stock exchange regulation and exposure to a potential takeover bid. The duties of the parent company's directors were now to enhance 'shareholder value'. Manchester United was no longer simply a football club.

Manchester United was no longer simply a football club.

In 1998, Murdoch spotted his opportunity. As principal shareholder in News Corporation which in turn owned BSkyB, Murdoch recognised clearly how the fortunes of football and subscription television were closely connected. The FA Premier League, founded in 1992, was thriving on the revenues from its TV broadcasting deal with BSkyB. BSkyB was thriving on the millions of subscribers attracted to its packages by the 'battering ram' of its exclusive live TV access to premier football.

On 7th September 1998, to an unprepared and astonished sporting world, BSkyB and Manchester United announced that they were involved in takeover talks. Two days later, Manchester United's board of directors announced that they were recommending the acceptance of BSkyB's bid of £623 million to its shareholders. The offer was too good to refuse.

Murdoch was, to many outside observers, being as shrewd as ever. BSkyB already had the exclusive rights to live screenings of Premier League matches until 2001. Ownership of Manchester United would strengthen BSkyB's influence and position in any future negotiations with the FA Premier League for the sale of its broadcasting rights. Indeed, as owner of Manchester United, BSkyB would share directly in a proportion – a relatively significant proportion – of the revenues which it itself paid for the rights!

In addition, there was a real possibility that the system of collective sale by Premier League clubs of broadcasting rights centrally through the FA Premier League might be broken up – in favour of each club being free to negotiate independently the sale of broadcasting rights to its own home matches. The system was being reviewed by the Office of Fair Trading and the Restrictive Trade Practices Court. If the decision went against the collective sale system established by the existing rules, what better position for BSkyB to be in than owner and controller of the rights to Manchester United, the club with the greatest support and commercial reach in the country? The bid for Manchester United appeared to be a classic 'each-way bet' for BSkyB.

The bid for Manchester United appeared to be a classic 'each-way' bet for BSkyB.

The press, and the fans, reacted with astonishment – many with considerable anger and fury. Protests mounted. Fans attempted to campaign through the Independent Manchester United Supporters' Association. But it was now in the world of corporate takeovers. What could effectively be done to stop the sale? A majority of the shareholders seemed to favour the bid which the board were recommending. Success of the bid appeared certain.

Then, to the surprise of many, the UK Government decided to intervene through the Secretary of State for Trade, Peter Mandelson. He used powers under legislation which enabled significant acquisitions and mergers to be referred to a body called the Monopolies and Mergers Commission (MMC) and, if necessary, blocked on the grounds of the public interest. During the next four-and-a-half months, the panel of the MMC investigated the proposed acquisition taking evidence from more than 350 parties.

Should the BSkyB's proposed acquisition of Manchester United be blocked on the grounds of the public interest?

For: If successful, the bid would consolidate BSkyB's already dominant position in the market for live football broadcasting. It would become more difficult for others to make inroads into the industry. In addition, Manchester United's decisions might no longer be based principally on footballing considerations. The club would become a bargaining and marketing tool for a broadcasting company intent on enhancing its dominant position in the pay-TV market. Decision-making would not have sufficient regard to the interests of the local community as a key stakeholder in the football club. **Against:** Manchester United's shareholders should be free to decide what was in their own best interests. The risk of a takeover bid (and the opportunity for shareholders to realise value from a sale of their shares) was an inevitable consequence of the club being listed on the Stock Exchange. BSkyB's acquisition would substantially strengthen the club's financial position and ability to buy players and compete as a football club. The market should be allowed to operate freely. The adverse risks were exaggerated. They could, if necessary, be mitigated by undertakings given as to the independent management of the football club.

The MMC reported in March 1999. They concluded that the proposed merger might reduce competition for the purchase of broadcasting rights to Premier League matches. This would lead to less choice for the Premier League. It would reduce competition in the market for sports premium television channels.

On the wider front, the MMC judged that:

> *...the merger would reinforce the existing trend towards greater inequality of wealth between clubs, weakening the smaller ones. The merger would give BSkyB additional influence over Premier League decisions relating to the organisation of football. On both counts, the merger could have an adverse effect on English football. This adverse effect would be more pronounced if the merger led to other mergers between broadcasters and Premier League clubs.*

The only way of dealing with the full range of public interest concerns, in the view of the MMC, was to prohibit the merger.

Four weeks later, the Secretary of State, by now Stephen Byers, accepted in full the findings and recommendation of the Monopolies and Mergers Commission.

> *The MMC's findings ... concluded that the merger would adversely affect competition between broadcasters. But they also examined wider public interest issues, concluding that the merger would damage the quality of British football. I accept these findings.*

The takeover was stopped. Murdoch had been foiled at the last minute.

Who would have thought Peter Mandelson and Stephen Byers would be heroes in the football homes of Manchester?

Collective selling of broadcasting rights of clubs centrally through the Premier League continues. The Restrictive Trade Practices Court found that the system was not contrary to the public interest. England has not yet gone the way of certain other countries, such as Italy, where each club in Serie A sells its own rights individually. But the European Commission is hovering and may review this structure. The issue is not yet finally resolved.

BSkyB and other broadcasting companies might have been prevented from building up controlling interests but the dynamics of football club ownership were changing. Entrepreneurs and wealthy investors from across the world have taken a much closer interest in the financial prospects of owning Premier League clubs. Nearly half the clubs in the Premier League are now under foreign ownership.

Manchester United itself fell into the hands of the family of Texan oil billionaire, Malcolm Glazer, for £790 million in 2005.

---

61 EDDIE IRVINE – A RADIO AND A DOCTORED PHOTOGRAPH

Could Eddie Irvine, leading motor racing driver, stop a radio company using a photograph doctored to suggest he was using its radio?

Eddie Irvine was a shrewd businessman. Evidence before the court later suggested that he 'would not get out of bed for less than £25,000'. It was a dispute over a cheeky commercial promotion. The decision would have a major effect on a sportsman's 'image rights' in the UK.

The Ulsterman was one of the characters of Formula One racing. In only his second grand prix, he was lapped by the great Ayrton Senna in his McClaren – and, deciding that Senna was then going too slow as Irvine was chasing another back-runner, Irvine overtook Senna and unlapped himself. Senna later let Irvine know that he was not amused! Eddie Irvine was always a fierce competitor.

Eddie Irvine was always a fierce competitor.

By 1999 Irvine was a major force in Formula One and was partnering Michael Schumacher at Ferrari. Irvine enjoyed the limelight and it was his most successful racing season. He won four grand prix races and was destined to finish a close second to Mika Hakkinen in Formula One's drivers' championship.

This challenge before the courts, though, was not about a race at Monaco or Monza but a leaflet distributed during that 1999 season by Talk Radio to potential advertisers. Talk Radio, later to become Talksport and a not infrequent visitor to the courts, was a commercial radio station. Its chairman and chief executive was Kelvin McKenzie, former editor of *The Sun*, and it was beginning to make its mark. It had acquired radio broadcasting rights to a number of major sporting events including the Formula One championship. It was trying to build its profile. McKenzie was not afraid of some lively marketing techniques.

Talk Radio sent a promotional pack to around one thousand advertising executives. It was intended to be humorous in nature. Each pack included, for instance, a pair of boxer shorts with a skid mark of the kind a racing car might make. An accompanying leaflet contained pictures of a number of grand prix drivers – and the front cover featured a photograph of Eddie Irvine. The photograph had been obtained legitimately. There was no breach of copyright in the use of the photograph.

But the photograph had been 'doctored'. In the 'doctored' version, instead of holding a mobile phone to his ear, Irvine appeared to be listening to a radio bearing the words 'Talk Radio' and the company's logo. The strapline was 'we've got it covered'.

Irvine complained. The original photograph was of him with a mobile phone. He had not agreed any commercial deal with Talk Radio.

The misleading and unauthorised use of his image was wrongful. Talk Radio agreed not to distribute any more of the 'doctored' leaflets. But that was not enough for Eddie Irvine. He proceeded to bring a legal action against Talk Radio seeking damages. The claim came before the High Court.

Was it just simple, innocent fun? Or were Talk Radio wrongfully taking advantage of Irvine's reputation for its own commercial use? Should Talk Radio be liable to pay damages to Irvine on the grounds that the leaflet wrongfully implied that he was endorsing the Talk Radio service? If so, what should be the amount of damages?

For: Irvine had built up valuable goodwill and reputation in his name and image. He had various existing commercial deals to endorse certain products. Talk Radio's leaflet was designed to deceive members of the public to whom it was sent into believing that Irvine was endorsing Talk Radio. This constituted 'passing off' (the legal term for commercial misrepresentation). As to damages, Irvine produced evidence that his endorsement fee, whilst depending on the size of the deal, would normally be substantial; he 'would not get out of bed for less than £25,000'.
Against: The photograph had been lawfully obtained. Its publication was not in breach of copyright. It was clearly a humorous promotion. The leaflet was only sent to a very limited number of recipients. There was no evidence that it would have any effect on Irvine's reputation or his ability to enter into other endorsement deals. In any event, no-one would have paid more than £500 for such a small campaign. It was inappropriate to base damages, if any, on 'fancy' sums which Irvine might secure in a commercial endorsement deal.

Irvine won.

The High Court decided in his favour. The promotional leaflet was a form of misrepresentation, implying wrongfully that Irvine was endorsing Talk Radio. There was a further dispute about damages. The court initially awarded just £2,000. On appeal, Irvine was more successful. The Court of Appeal agreed that £25,000 was the appropriate measure based on Irvine's other endorsement deals. What mattered was the fee which Talk Radio 'would have had to pay to obtain lawfully that which it in fact obtained unlawfully' – and, possibly, Irvine's assertion as to the amount required to get him out of bed.

The amount of money at stake may have been relatively small, but this was a breakthrough case in sporting law. The courts showed that they were prepared to prevent the commercial use by a third party of an association with a sporting star where that was done without the star's consent. It gave sportsmen stronger rights to prevent or get money from product advertisements which 'wrongfully' implied their endorsement.

One of the first sportsmen to take advantage of the 'new' right was Ian Botham who sued Diageo over an advertising campaign during the cricket World Cup for Guinness which (without his consent) featured images of Botham's exploits as a backdrop. Botham reportedly obtained a substantial payment in settlement. Boris Becker won a similar claim for damages in Germany. More recently, Oliver Khan and Michael Ballack brought a legal action against a German sex toy manufacturer for unauthorised promotion of 'Olli K' and 'Michael B' sextoys. There was a 'David B' version but the England player decided not to sue after he apparently 'saw the funny side of things'.

In the meantime, Talk Radio had changed their name to Talksport. They were soon back in the courts.

---

62 EURO 2000 – TALKSPORT AND AN AMSTERDAM HOTEL ROOM

Could the BBC stop Talksport from broadcasting a 'live' match at Euro 2000 from a hotel room?

Back to broadcasting and a lively court case involving a broadcaster's attempt to protect its 'exclusive' commercial position. And a reappearance in the courts of the innovative, but somewhat provocative, Talksport. The setting was Euro 2000 – or was it an Amsterdam hotel bedroom?

The European football championships were taking place in Belgium and the Netherlands. England were playing Portugal, a key first round match in Group A. The match was being played in Eindhoven. Millions of English fans were watching on television or listening on the radio. Most were tuned into the BBC.

Many, though, were listening to Talksport, a UK radio broadcaster focusing heavily on sports coverage. The commentator described the gripping action – Paul Scholes scoring for England after just three minutes but England going down in a dramatic 3-2 win for Portugal. Listeners heard the noise of a football crowd and the ambient sounds of the match.

The BBC were up in arms at this coverage. Why? Unlike the BBC, Talksport was not an authorised broadcaster in the stadium itself. Talksport was operating 'off tube'. The commentator was not in the stadium. He was not even in Eindhoven – but simply commentating from the television footage, transmitted by another broadcaster, shown in an Amsterdam hotel room which had become Talksport's studio for the tournament. The ambient crowd sound was not from the match itself. Every ten minutes or so, an announcement was made: 'This is Talksport, not the BBC, with unofficial full match commentary on Portugal v England on Talksport, courtesy of our TV monitors at the Talksport Amsterdam Studio.'

The commentator was not in the stadium. He was commentating in an Amsterdam hotel room.

The BBC strongly objected to Talksport advertising its Euro coverage as being 'live'. The BBC, as the only UK radio broadcaster authorised by Euro 2000 in the stadium, argued that the occasional disclaimers did not bring home to listeners that the commentators were located many miles from the action. The BBC brought a legal action in the English courts to stop Talksport describing itself as providing 'live' coverage. The dispute came before the High Court.

Was this just a domestic spat? Or did it raise a serious issue? When a broadcaster is appointed by an event organiser and pays substantial sums for 'exclusive' rights, can it prevent an 'off tube' broadcaster from muscling in on the event?

Should the BBC be entitled to prevent Talksport describing itself as producing 'live' coverage? Should the BBC be able to claim damages for this misrepresentation by Talksport?

For: The BBC was the UK radio broadcaster 'authorised' by Euro 2000. The Talksport coverage was misleading. Listeners did not really appreciate that the commentators were not at the ground. The BBC had a long-established reputation as a broadcaster of live sporting events. Talksport's claim that its coverage was 'live' devalued the reputation of live coverage of sporting events and could cause damage to authorised broadcasters, such as the BBC, who were providing a superior and proper live coverage. The BBC might also lose listeners in due course as a result. **Against:** 'Live' simply meant coverage at the same time as the event. The disclaimer made it clear that Talksport was coming from its Amsterdam studio. In any event, the BBC had no separate interest which was being damaged. It was simply describing its own activities as a broadcaster. There was no separate goodwill which the law should protect. There was no real risk of financial damage to the BBC and the legal action should fail.

The court rejected the BBC's action. It would not intervene.

The court did not condone Talksport's coverage. It considered that the coverage was 'deceptive', although it did in a literal sense provide a blow by blow account of what was going on at the scene of play. Importantly, though, the court decided that the BBC had no separate interest or goodwill to support an action of this kind. Whilst the BBC has 'a widespread and long established reputation as a broadcaster of live sporting events', the court did not consider there was 'any protectable goodwill simply in what it does' to found an action. In addition, there was no real risk of financial damage to the BBC. Any such claim seemed 'fanciful'. The court decided that the BBC's claim was not sufficient to justify the court's intervention.

In a sense, this was a narrow point. It was technically an application for injunctive relief which was always in the court's discretion. More generally, this case illustrates again the hurdles which event organisers have to overcome in order to protect 'exclusivity' for their authorised licensees. Authorised licensees demand properly protected exclusivity if they are to pay significant sums for these rights.

For Talksport, the case provided some excellent publicity!

---

63 UP THE GUNNERS! – MATTHEW REED AND HIS ARSENAL MERCHANDISE

Matthew Reed had sold his 'unofficial' souvenirs and merchandise on the street outside Highbury for over thirty years. Could Arsenal stop him now?

Highbury stadium, in north London, was the home of Arsenal FC until 2006. The club had a tradition and following as strong as any club in London. Highbury was the home of 'the Gunners'. It was also the site of Matthew Reed's trading stall.

Reed had been a lifelong supporter. He was also a street trader, one of many lining the streets outside Highbury on match days. He had worked his pitch there for more than thirty years, selling hats, scarves, shirts and other football merchandise.

He had celebrated through his merchandise the great Arsenal stars and triumphs. A number of the scarves and other items bore the legend 'Arsenal', 'Arsenal Gunners' and the club's distinctive shield and cannon design. All part and parcel of the football stadia scene on match days?

Reed had a large sign on his market stall stating that his goods were 'unofficial goods'.

> *The words or logos ... are used solely to adorn the products and do not imply or indicate any affiliation or relationship with the manufacturer or distributor of any other products. Only goods with official Arsenal merchandise tags are official Arsenal merchandise.*

Obviously written by a lawyer!

Arsenal were unhappy with this type of activity. 'Arsenal', 'Arsenal

Gunners' and the shield and cannon design were registered in 1989 as trademarks of Arsenal FC. Most of Reed's products, though, were not manufactured by any authorised licensee of Arsenal. Arsenal decided to crack down on sellers of 'unofficial' merchandise such as Matthew Reed. The club wanted to exercise full control over the sale of 'Arsenal' merchandise. They wanted to stop Reed trading in these goods and in January 1999 started proceedings against him.

But Reed was stubborn. He strenuously fought the action. 'I might as well go all the way as this will affect a lot of small traders around the country,' said Reed. Indeed, the dispute occupied the time and attention of numerous courts including, extraordinarily, the European Court of Justice. The contest swung to and fro, the result uncertain until the end.

Should Arsenal be entitled to prevent Matthew Reed trading, without permission, in souvenir goods bearing the marks 'Arsenal' and the registered shield and cannon design?

For: The merchandise sold by Reed used the registered marks and logos of Arsenal. The products were not manufactured or sold by any 'official' licensee of Arsenal. They could mislead buyers into thinking that they were buying 'official' merchandise with the approval of Arsenal (and that some of the funds would find their way back to the benefit of the football club). In any event, they were not manufactured by any person authorised to use the trademarks. It was as simple as that. Reed, and other offending traders, should stop.
Against: Matthew Reed had been trading outside Highbury for more than thirty years. Customers did not buy the goods because they thought the Arsenal club was the origin of manufacture. They bought them solely because of their support and allegiance to the club. The marks on this sort of merchandise had nothing to do with the source of manufacture; they were simply a 'badge of allegiance'. In legal terms, this was not 'trademark use'. Also, Reed had a placard clearly informing people that the goods were not 'official' merchandise. Arsenal made millions of pounds out of merchandising; this was a pin-prick in terms of revenue. Reed should be allowed to continue.

Losing initially in the UK courts, Arsenal were rescued by a surprising victory in the European Court. The court decided that the type of use by Reed could constitute an infringement of Arsenal's trademark. Whilst the court admitted that the use of the marks in this case may not strictly indicate source or origin of manufacture, a number of potential buyers may be confused. Over time, the confusion could damage the marks and weaken their ultimate function as an indication of origin.

The final result in Europe was a victory for Arsenal. But there was still 'extra time' to be played back in the UK courts. One judge thought that the European Court had exceeded its remit. But the Court of Appeal disagreed. It followed the European Court's guidance. Reed's type of use of the marks on his merchandise was an infringement and should be stopped.

Arsenal had been more successful in the courts of Europe than on the football field.

Some commentators remarked that Arsenal had been more successful in the courts of Europe than the club's campaigns in Europe on the football field.

This was an important decision, a verdict welcomed by major football clubs and sportswear manufacturers. It gave football clubs and other sporting event organisers control over the sale of merchandise bearing 'official' marks. It indicated a move by the courts to prevent this form of 'ambush marketing'. Whilst the result was clear, the reasoning is still disputed. Also, the case has its limitations. It only applies to the use of official marks. It does not extend to use of marks or indicia which have not been registered – where a claimant has to overcome the stricter tests of 'passing off'. Event organisers and clubs still have much work to do to prevent 'ambush' forms of marketing which benefit from an association with the club or event but which do not employ the use of registered marks or copyright material.

Enthusiastic Arsenal fans who follow the trademark news were pleased to note that, their own club having been successful in registering 'Arsenal' as a trademark, the trademark registry subsequently refused to register 'Tottenham' as a trade mark for their north London rivals. In their case, 'Tottenham' was not sufficiently distinctive of the football club rather than the geographical area.

---

64 THE FOOTBALL LEAGUE – ITV DIGITAL AND THE POT OF GOLD

When its TV broadcaster went bust, could the Football League sue the broadcaster's parent shareholders, Granada and Carlton?

Commercial deals relating to sport, as in other fields of business life, depend – or at least their enforcement depends – on contracts. The Football League would discover, much to its cost, that contracts are important.

No source of revenue is more lucrative to football than the sale of TV broadcasting rights. The fortunes of the FA Premier League have been founded on the vast sums paid by Rupert Murdoch's BSkyB. In 2000, there was growing competition in the market for subscription TV. The Football League, comprising the seventy-two clubs in the English first, second and third divisions outside the Premier League, was keen to increase its broadcasting income. It was attracted by the prospect of enjoying some of 'the pot of gold'.

The Football League put its broadcasting rights out to tender. It was excited by the interest shown, particularly by ONDigital. ONDigital (later branded as ITV Digital) had been launched with great fanfare in 1998. It was jointly owned by two major media companies, Granada and Carlton Communications, with each having a fifty per cent share. ONDigital was seeking to challenge BSkyB. As with its rival, it saw football as being a major attraction to pull in subscribers. It hoped in due course to get rights to show Premier League matches. In the meantime, it was prepared to bid high to secure TV rights to the Football League. Very high.

In April 2000, ONDigital proposed an initial bid of around £80 million a year for the TV rights to the Football League. Further discussions took place. On 7th June a bid document, expressed to be 'subject to contract', was submitted by ONDigital with a bid worth around £240 million for a three-year deal. The non-binding bid document included a statement that 'ONDigital and its shareholders will guarantee all funding to the FL outlined in this document.'

The tendering process intensified. The Football League thought it could get even more. More negotiations took place. Eventually a deal was done later in June. A binding contract (the June Contract) was entered into with ONDigital – a three-year deal worth in total around £315 million: the payments were £12 million on signature; £35.25 million payable within three months; and three annual payments of £89.25 million. The Football League and its member clubs were overjoyed. It did seem that they had found, in effect, a 'pot of gold'. The June Contract did not include any guarantee by the two shareholders, Granada and Carlton.

The commercial world can be tough. The ITV Digital service never really took off. Subscribers could not be found or retained in sufficient numbers. The sums payable for the Football League broadcasting rights were crippling for the new company. It had overpaid. The plug had to be pulled. ITV Digital (as now named) went into administration in April 2002. It gave up its broadcasting licence. Payments to the Football League ceased.

ITV Digital had overpaid. The plug had to be pulled.

Where did that leave the Football League? Chasing, fruitlessly, the money.

Mitigating its loss, the Football League managed to sign up a replacement deal with BSkyB worth £95 million over four years – substantially less than the deal with ITV Digital. The Football League sought compensatory payments from ITV Digital's two shareholders. Granada and Carlton reluctantly offered a compromise £74 million. The Football League, in a major tactical error, rejected it. It argued that Granada and Carlton were liable, as guarantors, to pay the full amount – in effect, a claim to recover the Football League's 'loss' of £178.5 million being the additional sums which would have been received by the Football League if the ITV Digital contract had lasted. The Football League decided to take legal action against Granada and Carlton before the High Court.

The High Court dismissed the Football League's claim. There was no guarantee. The original bid document was clearly made 'subject to contract'. There had been extensive subsequent negotiations. The June Contract did not contain a guarantee and neither Granada nor Carlton were parties. Granada and Carlton were not liable to pay the Football League. Justice Langley was withering in his comments, saying: 'In my judgment the Football League's case remains just as unpromising at the finish as it looked at the start.'

The Football League ...had learnt a tough commercial and legal lesson.

The Football League was left to count the cost. A substantial cost.

The consequences of the ITV Digital collapse were significant. Many clubs in the Football League had overspent in the first year of the deal – using funds expected to be received as their share of the ITV Digital deal which had not yet arrived. Many came close to going out of business. Hundreds of players were transfer listed across all clubs in an effort, particularly, to reduce wage bills. The Football League – along, no doubt, with other sporting bodies watching the League's precedent – had learnt a tough commercial and legal lesson. Commercial deals can only be enforced if there is a binding contract. And parties can go bust!

The Football League tried to sue its lawyers and recover some of its loss. It claimed damages of £150 million – one of the biggest professional negligence claims ever. It lost. The judge found two minor breaches of duty and awarded damages of just £4. The Football League was also liable for virtually all legal costs.

Heads rolled at the Football League. Although not in office at the time of the original deal, both the chairman (Keith Harris) and the chief executive (David Burns) resigned in August 2002. They paid the price for the way the case had gone. The new chairman was Lord Mawhinney. He remarked simply: 'The collapse of ITV Digital marked a watershed for the Football League and its clubs.'

---

65 BRITISH HORSERACING BOARD – HOW VALUABLE WAS ITS PRE-RACE DATABASE?

Could the BHB charge William Hill for using pre-race information derived from BHB's computer database?

The future of the horse betting levy and the funding of British racing would, in 2004, come to depend on an obscure point of law and the European Court. The lawyers scratched their heads – and the British Horseracing Board and the UK Government groaned.

Horseracing and betting have always been close companions. The bookmaking fraternity in Britain thrives on horserace betting. In turn, since the early 1960s – after the legalisation of off-course betting shops – the British Horseracing Board (BHB), then the governing body for horseracing in the UK, had been primarily funded by a levy on bookmakers collected by the Horserace Betting Levy Board. The levy was agreed with representatives of the bookmakers or, failing agreement, settled by the UK Government.

In March 2000, the Government announced that the levy should be abolished. BHB should look after itself. The Government, and BHB, believed that future funding of BHB could come from its own commercial arrangements. These would include television access to the racecourses and the sale to bookmakers and the media of 'rights' to racing's fixture list and BHB's other pre-race data. This data was a unique source of information – information regarding runners, riders, past form, weightings, pedigrees and other details which BHB compiled and issued in its 'official' capacity to the racing industry.

BHB saw a commercial opportunity to charge bookmakers for use of its pre-race information.

BHB spent around £4 million a year in its efforts to obtain, maintain and update this data which was crucial to the racing world. It had been developed by BHB into a computerised database which BHB could now license on a commercial basis to the media, bookmakers and other users.

How valuable was this database? One potential group of customers were the bookmakers. Online betting was increasing rapidly. William Hill, one of the country's biggest bookmakers, were keen to publish online for their customers lists of runners, riders and pre-race data which included certain information originating from BHB. BHB saw a commercial opportunity to charge the bookmakers substantial sums for the use of this information – a substitute for the lost income from the betting levy.

William Hill did not see things that way. The particular information they proposed to use was already obtainable, without any need for William Hill to go directly to BHB itself, from newspapers and from an online licensee of BHB with whom they had a subscription service – although subscription was only for access and not online re-use. The information could be freely used. William Hill did not, they argued, need to pay for a 'licence' from BHB to put the information online.

The battleground had been set. BHB brought a legal action to prevent William Hill using the lists of runners and associated information which it had obtained from newspapers and other media licensed by BHB. BHB chose a clever legal ground on which to proceed; at least it seemed clever at the time – and appropriate. European law, for once, seemed to have helped sporting event organisers and governing bodies. BHB alleged that this use by William Hill infringed BHB's 'database right' – a new right, akin to copyright, which was introduced to English law in 1998 as a result of a European Directive. If William Hill wanted to use the information, they would have to pay for it. The issue went first to the High Court.

Should BHB be able to prevent William Hill using pre-race information derived, directly or indirectly, from the database developed by BHB?

For: BHB spent considerable sums each year collecting its information and compiling the database. It should be protected by the law against 'free' use by others for their commercial purposes. The new 'database right' provided that protection and William Hill could not use the data without BHB's consent.

Against: The 'database right' did not apply here. William Hill were not copying BHB's original data. They were simply using information legitimately obtained from newspapers and other third parties.

It was litigation which would occupy the courts, in the UK and the European Court, for years as the lawyers wrestled with the interpretation of the new law. The points of law in dispute became ever more dense and esoteric. But BHB seemed to have the clear advantage. BHB won its first action in the High Court. The court decided emphatically that the use of the information by William Hill did infringe BHB's 'database' rights. William Hill should either stop or agree licence terms with BHB for its use.

BHB and the Government were delighted. Plans were on track. BHB subsequently agreed terms with the principal bookmakers for a 'licence' to use this pre-race data for a five-year period. The agreed fee? Ten percent of the bookmakers' gross winnings from bets taken on British horseracing. At around £150 million per annum, this was a large sum. This was almost exactly the same amount as the betting levy. Payment would, seamlessly, replace the levy when abolished by Government. In October 2004, the Horserace Betting and Olympic Lottery Bill was passed. It gave the Secretary of State formal power to abolish the levy system. The future funding of British racing seemed in place.

Then, in November 2004, just twelve days after the Government's Bill had received Royal Assent, came a legal bombshell. Certain technical aspects of the BHB/William Hill case had been referred to the European Court for clarification since they were relevant to the interpretation of the European Directive generally. All indications, including the influential advisory opinion of the Advocate-General to the Court, were that the European Court would confirm the view of the UK's High Court.

The European Court delivered its judgment. To much surprise in both legal and racing circles, the European Court – and subsequently the English Court of Appeal – ruled against BHB.

It was a narrow, and obscure, argument. The Court decided that, in effect, the new computer database right should be construed narrowly. It did not apply to the collection and computerisation by BHB of information which formed its own 'official' lists of runners, riders and pre-race data. It only protected a database which was compiled from material held 'independently' and where significant investment was incurred in compiling the material into a computer database rather than in the original collection of the information itself. It was a distinction even the lawyers struggled to understand. But it ruined

BHB's plans. It spelled the death knell for BHB's hopes of a substantial income to replace the levy. Not only were William Hill free to use and profit from this data, the Government's plans for abolishing the levy were in turmoil.

A Government review body, chaired by Lord Donoghue, formally had no answer. It required more time to study the problem. In December 2006 the Government announced that the levy would continue indefinitely 'until such time as a secure alternative commercial funding arrangement can be identified'. The law had come to BHB's aid – and then crushed its hopes.

---

66 DAVE BEDFORD – 'I'VE GOT YOUR NUMBER'

To the surprise of many, advertisements appeared in 2003 featuring two comic runners bearing a close resemblance to the figure of Dave Bedford, an athlete of the 1970s. Could Bedford stop them?

Dave Bedford was one of Britain's most colourful athletes of the 1970s. No one would have predicted that in 2003, thirty years after his heyday, he would find himself in a challenge to protect his 'image rights'.

A fine middle distance runner, Bedford once held three British records over three different distances. He set a world record for the 10,000 metres in 1973 at Crystal Palace – a record which has been reduced by barely more than one minute over the intervening thirty-year period. With lengthy black hair and sporting a drooping moustache, the London-born athlete was a distinctive figure on the running tracks of the world and on television. He frequently wore red socks, sky blue shorts with gold braiding and a running vest with two hoops.

Forward to 2003. The UK Government had opened up to the private sector the telephone directory enquiry service previously run by BT. One of the new licensees, The Number, operated under the number '118 118'. To the surprise of many, on advertising hoardings and television screens around the UK suddenly appeared two runners, in rather comic strip and actions, advertising the service – and bearing, to those with memories of the 1970s, a close resemblance to the figure of Dave Bedford as remembered by many: the hairstyle, the drooping moustache and similar running kit.

On advertising hoardings appeared two runners, in comic strip, bearing a close resemblance to Dave Bedford...

The Number claimed that the advertisements were not specifically based on Bedford: 'During the Seventies all the runners had moustaches and long hair, even the footballers did.' A great many felt, nevertheless, that the figures did deliberately represent a caricature of him. Bedford was unhappy. He had certainly not been consulted or approved the advertisements. Could Bedford claim that his image rights were being infringed and stop the use of the advertisements?

For: The advertisements clearly bore a close resemblance to the distinctive figure of Dave Bedford, with his drooping moustache and running kit. They were taking commercial advantage of his 'image'. The fact that it was an amusing caricature made no difference. Bedford's consent was required before such an advertising campaign could be run.
Against: The advertisements were not directly based on Bedford. They were a caricature of runners at that time, not a copy of his image. There was no suggestion that Bedford was endorsing the service. Bedford had not suffered any financial harm.

The route Bedford chose to make his challenge was not a direct legal action against The Number but to make a formal complaint that the commercials contravened the Advertising Standards Code. The Independent Television Commission upheld Bedford's complaint. The Number appealed to Ofcom, the regulatory body which ultimately supervised the Code.

Ofcom decided that the 118 118 advertising campaign did 'caricature Bedford by way of a comically exaggerated representation of him looking as he did in the 1970s sporting a hairstyle and facial hair like his at the time'. Since the caricature was published without Bedford's consent, it constituted a breach of the Code.

However, it was a doubtful victory for Bedford. Ofcom did not ban the adverts. Bedford had delayed for about six months before making a complaint and The Number had committed itself to substantial expenditure in continuing the successful advertisements for the 118 118 service and its brand image. There was no evidence that Bedford had suffered any financial harm as a result of the caricature.

Ofcom decided, on balance, that to ban the advertisements: 'would be disproportionately damaging to The Number compared with any harm to the feelings or reputation of David Bedford as a result of the advertisements.'

This could be addressed by an announcement that there had been a breach and, importantly, that Bedford had not endorsed the 118 118 service.

Many observers were critical of Ofcom's decision not to punish the breach of the Code by banning the advertisements. This did not prevent Bedford from bringing a personal claim in the courts – although it is doubtful whether such a claim would be successful under current English law.

Since the decision, observers will note that The Number has subtly changed the appearance of the comic runners. They have developed a new image. They have kept their moustaches but their hair is now shorter and has been restyled in a somewhat more contemporary look.

Dave Bedford, who is race director of the London Marathon, said that he was not seeking 'greedy' damages. He was pleased that Ofcom had vindicated his claim that The Number had 'ripped off my image'. He had decided eventually to pursue the matter when he 'would go into pubs and people would shout: 'I've got your number'.'

---

67 MASTERCARD AND FIFA – FIFA PLAY THEIR CARDS UNFAIRLY

FIFA's negotiators tried to be clever. Unknown to MasterCard, they were also negotiating with VISA for sponsorship rights for the World Cup. It would prove a costly tactic.

FIFA have a slogan: 'fair play'. A judge in the US District Court felt obliged to comment, as the case unfolded, that FIFA 'does not govern itself by its slogan'. It was a case which became an embarrassment for soccer's world governing body – and provide another lesson in the importance of contracts in the world of business and sport. A costly lesson. A $90 million lesson.

A US judge would comment that FIFA does not govern itself by its slogan 'fair play'.

Sponsorship of the World Cup is one of the most valuable commercial properties in the whole of sport – both for the organisers, FIFA, and for the sponsors. It enables the sponsors to get their name and product to an audience of hundreds of millions of viewers and spectators. MasterCard had held the advertising and sponsorship rights as official credit card sponsor for all World Cups since 1990. The terms for the period 2003/06 were governed by a contract signed in 2002. It was, they thought, a strong relationship. In the 2002 contract they had negotiated a term which, in effect, required FIFA to give MasterCard a 'first right' to acquire the sponsorship rights offered for the succeeding 2007/10 period. If MasterCard decided not to take up the offer, FIFA were then free to grant comparable rights to a different sponsor. All very commercial, dry and legalistic.

FIFA moved the goalposts a little for the new contract. They decided that it should be an eight-year deal covering both the 2010 and 2014 World Cups and that it should cover a broader range of financial services. It would be more expansive in scope – and more valuable – than the previous deal. Was this sufficient for the new contract to fall outside the 'first refusal' right of MasterCard? The US District Court would later say 'no'.

Negotiations took place over a new contract. By the end of March 2006, MasterCard were ready to sign. But FIFA's negotiators were being clever – or, at least, so they thought. At the same time, they had been negotiating with MasterCard's great commercial rivals, VISA. They did not reveal to MasterCard that they were double-dipping with VISA – but, in the words of the judge later in court, VISA were being given 'blow by blow descriptions of the status of the FIFA/MasterCard negotiations'. Encouraged by FIFA, VISA increased their bid to match MasterCard's offer plus $15 million of nebulous 'marketing in kind value'. FIFA's Executive Committee, apparently not informed of the 2002 undertaking and persuaded by FIFA's marketing director, Jerome Valcke, decided to go with VISA. FIFA notified MasterCard of this decision on 5th April, saying that they had signed a deal with VISA.

MasterCard were angry. This was commercial skulduggery. They went to the American courts to assert the legality of FIFA's existing commitment to MasterCard and the failure of FIFA to negotiate in good faith. MasterCard sought an injunction to prevent FIFA from proceeding with the sponsorship deal with VISA.

Judge Loretta Preska of the US Southern District Court of New York heard the case and all the arguments. She gave judgment in December 2006. It was a humiliating verdict for FIFA:

> *FIFA's negotiators lied regularly to MasterCard including when they assured MasterCard that FIFA would not sign a deal for the post-2006 sponsorship rights with anyone-else unless it could not reach an agreement with MasterCard.*

They had characterised their breaches as 'white lies', 'commercial lies' and 'bluffs'. They had not negotiated in good faith as required under Swiss law which governed the contract. She ordered FIFA to abide by the terms of the 2002 contract and award the agreed package of advertising and sponsorship rights to MasterCard.

Heads rolled. Four senior FIFA executives, TV and marketing director Jerome Valcke and three other marketing executives, were dismissed – or at least so it appeared. FIFA admitted embarrassingly:

> *The FIFA employees who had conducted negotiations ... were accused of repeated dishonesty ... and of giving false information. FIFA's negotiators breached its business principles. FIFA cannot possibly accept such conduct amongst its own employees.*

FIFA, as a Zurich-based institution, tried to bypass the verdict by starting separate proceedings for arbitration in Switzerland. They also appealed to postpone the implementation of the US court decision. It had all become a bit of a fiasco for FIFA. One of their 'top tier' sponsorships was in court – and in limbo. The Second US Circuit Court of Appeals did not assist. In May 2007 the appeal court ruled that Judge Preska should reconsider certain aspects of her original decision to award the deal to MasterCard, including being more specific as to which contracts were in force at that time. Now it was VISA as well as FIFA who were up in arms at the court's judgment. More lawyers, costs, arguments and uncertainty.

In July 2007, MasterCard decided that they had had enough. But at a price. It would cost FIFA $90 million. In exchange for this payment to MasterCard in settlement, all legal proceedings – both in the USA and Switzerland – would be dropped. Perhaps not surprisingly, MasterCard decided that they no longer wanted to work with FIFA. There had been 'irreparable damage' to their trust in the relationship with FIFA. A company spokesman declared that 'substantial financial compensation ... along with severing the relationship ... was in the best interest of MasterCard's customers and shareholders.'

FIFA were relieved. They could at least proceed with a new deal with VISA. In June it was announced that they had signed up with VISA for an eight-year deal worth around $170 million. But it had been at a high cost and considerable embarrassment to the reputation of FIFA. Sepp Blatter said the settlement 'was a weight off my shoulders. The divorce has taken place, but every divorce costs money.'

'The divorce has taken place, but every divorce costs money.'

Or perhaps Sepp Blatter and FIFA were not particularly embarrassed. In June 2007, just one month after the US appeal court decision, FIFA announced that former marketing director, Jerome Valcke, had not only been re-instated – he had been promoted. He was appointed the new General Secretary in place of Urs Lins who had recently resigned. Valcke was now Blatter's right-hand chief executive in charge of day-to-day operations.

CHAPTER EIGHT

LEAGUES, COMPETITIONS AND TEAMS

Competitive sport requires the framework of a league, tournament or other competition in which teams or individuals can compete against each other – with the outcome of the competition depending upon the results of each match or contest. It is the significance of the result within the context of the particular league or competition, coupled with the prior uncertainty of that result, which provides sport with much of its excitement, fervour and tension – both for players and spectators.

Success in leagues and competitions leads to rewards for participants (individuals or teams) and their managers and owners. Major sporting disputes have come before courts or tribunals involving the organisation of leagues and competitions and the right of individuals and teams to participate in them. Many have centred on the formation, or attempted formation, of new leagues or competitions and their potential effect on the 'old order'. Deep conflicts in the organisation of cricket, football, snooker and darts have led to disputes before the courts. Many have been critical to the future of the particular sport. Some of the decisions have changed the face of sport in this country.

This chapter also includes two recent disciplinary cases involving alleged misbehaviour by teams, McLaren in motor racing and West Ham in football, which have significantly affected title or relegation issues in a leading competition. It ends with Argentina's wish to select its star soccer player for the Olympics.

---

68 TONY GREIG AND KERRY PACKER – STARTING A REVOLUTION IN CRICKET

Kerry Packer, with the support of Tony Greig and many leading test players, was planning a new 'World Series' cricket tour. Could it be stopped by the established cricket authorities?

The Centenary Test Match between England and Australia was being played at the Melbourne Cricket Ground in March 1977. The enthusiastic spectators were enjoying a classic encounter. Extraordinarily, the result was exactly the same as that first Test one hundred years previously. Australia won by 45 runs. In the background, though, a thunderous political storm was brewing.

Tony Greig was the England captain. The 6ft 7ins all-rounder loved being at the centre of the action. Born in South Africa to a South African mother and a Scottish father, he moved to England aged twenty and qualified to play for Sussex. Now thirty-years old, he was not only thinking about the match, he was also thinking of his future. He hoped to play Test cricket for a few more years but, planning ahead, some work as a television commentator would be welcome. Greig had arranged to meet Kerry Packer at his home in Sydney on 20th March.

The Australian broadcaster was an ambitious and forceful character. He had a strong interest in Australian sport, particularly cricket. One of his channels was the Channel 9 Network. Packer had taken over the running of Channel 9 after the death of his father. He was determined to turn around the fortunes of the network with an aggressive strategy centred on more sports programming. He had already secured rights to the Australian golf open. Packer wanted to acquire the exclusive rights to televise Test matches in Australia. He made a strong bid. Despite Packer's higher offer, the Australian Cricket Board stayed loyal to their existing broadcaster. Packer was deeply upset by the decision. He planned his next move.

Packer and Greig met. Packer put forward a striking, and secret, proposition to Greig. He said he planned to launch a new tour, a 'world series cricket' tour to be held in Australia during a season from 1st September to 30th March. It would be televised exclusively on

Channel 9. Offering significant financial reward, Packer had already secured the promised participation of many of the leading Australian cricketers. He wanted Greig to join and help build the new tour.

Just five days later, on 25th March, Greig signed a three-year contract with Packer's organisation. 'It was a purely financial decision, and a very easy one to make.' He planned to continue playing cricket in England in the summer but, along with the other recruits, he committed to Packer's programme. More than that, he undertook to assist in the recruitment of other top-class players. Recruits already signed up included Sussex's former English fast bowler, John Snow and South African captain of Gloucestershire and world class all-rounder, Mike Proctor, as well as many of the existing Australian test team. The duration of their individual contracts varied from one to three years. All had been done in 'cloak and dagger' secrecy in order to facilitate recruitment.

Packer put forward a striking, and secret, proposition to Greig.

It was not until 9th May that the news of Packer's plans became public – and then by some loose remarks at a press conference when the Australian team were visiting England. The news caused immediate and great consternation among the cricket governing bodies of all the Test playing countries. Their fear was that the well paid 'private' series run by Packer would greatly damage the structure of Test cricket which had historically been the foundation of the sport. The condemnation was severe.

Tony Greig was sacked as England captain for his role in the new tour. A spokesman pronounced: 'This was considered to be a breach of the normal trust which is expected between the captain and the England team and the authorities.'

Steps to fight the rebel organisation were taken by 'the establishment'. It was civil war. Two constitutional measures, in particular, were enacted:

On 26th July, the International Cricket Council (ICC) passed a resolution changing the qualification rules for playing in Test matches. In effect, any person who played in the 'Packer circus' after 1st October 1977 would be disqualified from playing Test cricket unless specific consent was given by the ICC.

Shortly afterwards, the Test and County Cricket Board (TCCB) imposed an even more drastic resolution applicable to English county cricket (where many overseas players, such as Mike Proctor, played during their 'winter' months). Any player who was subject to an ICC Test ban would be disqualified for two years from playing in any competitive English county cricket match.

The Packer 'rebels' would be ostracised. The battle for the future of cricket was on. The battleground moved to the courts.

Tony Greig, John Snow and Mike Proctor, as representatives of the new 'World Series' contract players, brought a legal action in the English courts to declare invalid the resolutions of the ICC and TCCB. They alleged that the resolutions were an unlawful restraint of trade. Each of them wanted to continue to play county and, if selected, Test cricket. The outcome of the litigation would be critical to the future of World Series Cricket (WSC). If they lost, the 'old order' would prevail. The dispute went to the High Court.

Should the resolutions of the ICC and TCB be declared invalid on the grounds that they were unreasonably in restraint of trade – by unjustifiably restricting the ability of professional cricketers to earn their living? Should Greig, Snow and Proctor be entitled to overturn the ban which would otherwise apply to them?

For: The immediate threat to the Test-playing countries was exaggerated. Players like Greig and Snow would still be available for English county cricket. The impact of World Series Cricket would be to stimulate greater general interest in cricket and thereby bring financial benefits to the game. The ban would apply to players (like Greig) who had already signed contracts with Packer – as well as being a disincentive to prevent other players 'deserting' in future. This retrospective application of bans to players who had already signed contracts was indiscriminate, unfair and unjustifiable.

Against: The ICC and TCCB were entitled to protect the long-term interests of Test and county cricket. World Series Cricket (WSC) constituted a very grave threat to the economic viability of Test cricket throughout the world. WSC was, in effect, a parasitic organisation 'creaming off' star players from conventional first-class cricket when it had incurred no expense in training and preparing them for stardom. Television viewers might well watch WSC matches and diminish the future viewing of official Test matches. Retrospective application of the ban was necessary in order to give credibility and act as a deterrent in order to prevent WSC ruining existing Test and county cricket.

The case began in September 1977 before Justice Slade in the High Court. Evidence was given, on both sides, by leading figures in the game of cricket. Erudite legal submissions were made. After seven weeks of evidence and argument, the High Court made its decision.

Greig and the WSC won this vital battle. The High Court decided that both bans were unreasonable and unlawful.

Justice Slade recognised that 'cricket has traditionally been regarded by many as embodying some of the highest professional standards in sport'. However, the ban deprived professional cricketers of the opportunity to make their living. The resolutions were retrospective in effect. They were designed to encourage players to withdraw from or breach their existing contracts with WSC. This was the major flaw. Justice Slade found it:

The High Court decided that both bans were unreasonable and unlawful.

> *...impossible to see how resolutions in this extended and wider form [could] be adequately justified on any rational and objective grounds... To deprive, by a form of retrospective legislation, a professional cricketer of the opportunity of making his living in a very important field of his professional life is ... both a serious and unjust step to take.*

The ban was contrary to the public interest since the public would be deprived of a great deal of pleasure and the opportunity to watch these talented cricketers – including in the many official Test matches which would not clash with World Series Cricket. The ICC had not discharged the burden on it to show that its resolution was reasonable.

The TCCB resolution was, in the view of the High Court, even more unreasonable since it prevented players from playing county cricket – the principal means by which players could supplement their incomes outside Test cricket. It would deprive the cricket-going public in England from seeing talented players like Greig, Snow and Proctor in first-class cricket.

The Test and county bans on the players could not be implemented. Players were free to join Packer's organisation and they did so – in numbers. Greig and Packer had won on all fronts. The World Series Cricket would go ahead. It was a vital victory.

Greig, although no longer captain, retained his position for five Tests under his successor, Mike Brearley, before his Test career ended at the Oval on 30th August 1977.

The first WSC match, between the Australians and the West Indians, was held at VFL Park, an Australian rules football stadium in Melbourne, on 2nd December 1977.

For lawyers, this was an important decision. A rule of a sports governing body had been struck down again on the grounds of restraint of trade. This had become a major legal weapon with which to attack the rules and decisions of sporting bodies and tribunals. Many legal actions in other sports based on this ground were to follow.

For cricket, this was an even more momentous decision. Greig himself, following Packer's death in 2007, summed up the impact of Packer's revolution: 'Packer was a colossal man, wonderful Australian and of course, a great friend of cricket.' He applauded the role Packer played in changing the face of cricket:

> *The most important thing, I suppose, was night cricket – that got cricket to a wider audience. The second most important thing is that cricketers are paid what they should be paid. Every cricketer would be grateful, I am sure, for the involvement of World Series Cricket, because it got them a better deal. Also, he certainly improved cricket on television beyond recognition. He just took it to another level. Associated with that was the one-day game, played at night, which required a white ball and if you have a white ball you need coloured clothing. All sorts of things like that were directly as a result of Kerry Packer.*

The chairman of Cricket Australia added: 'One-day international cricket is now an international phenomena as a result of Kerry Packer.

He has left a lasting legacy in the way the game is played, administered and presented to the public.'

In 2008, more than thirty years later, echoes of the Packer case reverberate as the ECB and other cricket authorities respond nervously to the heady financial attractions being offered to players to join the Twenty20 competitions of the Indian Premier League and the unauthorised Indian Cricket League.

---

69 THE AMERICA'S CUP – THE SAGA OF THE BIG BOAT AND THE CATAMARAN

Tradition and custom were being set aside by the New Zealand club's proposal to fight the America's Cup with a ninety-foot boat. It was an extraordinary challenge. How would the San Diego Yacht Club react?

It should have been a friendly lunch. The Commodore of the San Diego Yacht Club, the holders of the America's Cup, was entertaining Michael Fay from New Zealand's Mercury Bay Boating Club on his visit to San Diego in July 1987. Then, over coffee, came the challenge.

The America's Cup is one of the most prestigious sports events in the world – and one of the oldest. The competition is named after the New York Yacht Club's schooner *America* which won the trophy, an ornate silver cup, offered to the winner after defeating fifteen British yachts in a race around the Isle of Wight in 1851. The race was watched by Queen Victoria and held in conjunction with Prince Albert's Great London Exhibition. Queen Victoria asked: 'Who is first?' '*America* has won,' she was told. 'Who is second?' asked the Queen. The famous reply came back: 'Your Majesty, there is no second.'

The America's Cup became the most sought-after trophy in international sail boat racing. It is a competition which has involved many protests, court actions and arbitral proceedings. No dispute has been bigger than the one triggered by that lunch in 1987.

First, a little more background. The cup was donated to the New York Yacht Club on the terms of a Deed of Gift drafted in 1857 – a two-page trust deed which, although amended in part over the years, still formed the underlying basis for the competition. The trophy was to be 'preserved as a perpetual Challenge Cup for friendly competition between foreign countries'. It set out the terms for challenges to be made against the defending club, generally thought to favour the defending club. Indeed, for over one hundred years until the 1960s, the Cup became a series of failed attempts by the British to gain the Cup from the New York Yacht Club. Then, the Australians joined in.

No dispute has been bigger than the one triggered by that lunch in 1987.

In 1983, the Royal Perth Yacht Club of Australia, financed by Alan Bond and led by skipper John Bertrand, won the Cup with their famous winged keel yacht. The America's Cup left America for the first time. In 1987, skippered by Dennis Connor, the Cup was reclaimed for America by the San Diego Yacht Club. San Diego were preparing for their first defence – anticipating a regatta for 1991, since the Cup was now usually held every four years with a prior qualifying competition for challengers from many nations.

Then, at that lunch in July 1987 came the dramatic surprise. Michael Fay said that the San Diego Yacht Club would be receiving a challenge from New Zealand's Mercury Bay Boating Club. Michael Fay, a boyish, bespectacled, millionaire banker, was, in the words of American Dennis Connor, planning a 'backdoor assault' on the Cup. 'If the America's Cup is sport's most contentious contest, this had to be its singular most combative act.'

Fay and his legal advisers had read closely the terms of the Deed of Gift under which the trophy was originally donated. No one else had for years. Mercury Bay's challenge broke with tradition in three major respects. First, they challenged for a race on just ten month's notice. Secondly, it was to be a single challenge without the now customary pre-Cup qualifying race between multiple challengers. Thirdly, and most significantly of all, Fay specified a challenge with a giant sloop with a length of ninety-feet at the water line. Although the original Deed of Gift referred to a maximum water line length of ninety-feet, the race had by mutual consent and tradition for nearly thirty years been run with twelve-metre boats about forty-four feet long at the water line. Mercury Bay had already been working on its design of a challenger boat.

San Diego promptly rejected a challenge involving a boat more than twice the traditional size. There was no way that, on ten month's notice, they could design, finance and build a similar long boat even if they were prepared to change the traditional format of the race. It was clear that the longer the boat, the greater the sail area and the faster it would go. San Diego considered it a rogue challenge.

Mercury Bay pressed ahead. They went to the courts. Eleven weeks later, in August, they sought a declaration from the New York Supreme Court that the challenge was valid under the terms of the Deed of Gift and that the race should proceed. Mercury Bay won their claim before Justice Carmen Beauchamp Ciparick (another splendidly named US judge). ' … Mercury Bay Boating Club has tendered a valid challenge and … San Diego Yacht Club must treat it as such in accordance with the terms of the Deed.' The race was on.

What could San Diego do? If Mercury were going to play 'clever' by the rules, so were they. Dramatically, San Diego responded with an announcement that they would defend by racing with a sixty-foot catamaran. As Dennis Connor would later say: 'It was an alley fight. He jumped us, and I turned round and decided to fight to the death.' Sometimes termed 'biker boats', it was well-known that a catamaran, a multihull boat, would be faster than a monohull, however big. Mercury Bay realised that they no longer stood a chance of winning the Cup at sea if this went ahead.

Dramatically, San Diego announced that they would defend by racing a catamaran.

So, back to the courts. Mercury Bay brought a second action claiming that sailing a multihull catamaran against a monohull would no longer be a 'match' under the Deed of Gift and should be prohibited. They argued that San Diego's actions amounted to a contempt of court following Mercury Bay's previously successful legal action. Justice Ciparick refused, however, to hear the case at that time. The court deferred the hearing until after the end of the Cup. The race would go ahead.

The race was held on 7th and 9th September 1988 in the waters off San Diego. The result was predictable. It was a strange duel. Connor's catamaran *Stars & Stripes '88* easily won the first two races with victory margins of eighteen and twenty-one minutes respectively over Mercury Bay's giant sloop *New Zealand KZ1*. Connor was reported to have gone slowly so as not to make the victory margin even greater. It was a gross mismatch.

Michael Fay and Mercury Bay returned to the courts in New York. They contended that the use of a catamaran by San Diego had been unsportsmanlike and contrary to the basic concept of a 'friendly competition between foreign countries'. It was not a 'match'. San Diego's actions broke the 'spirit and intent' of the Deed of Gift. How should the court decide?

For: The Deed of Gift contemplated a 'match'. Mercury Bay's original challenge was within the rules and had been recognised as such by the courts. A catamaran was completely different. It was no longer a 'match' within the terms or spirit of the Deed. **Against:** Use of a catamaran was within the specification permitted by the Deed of Gift. If Mercury Bay could use the literal terms of the Deed with a ninety-foot boat, San Diego could respond by also employing a 'literal' approach.

The initial court, before the same Justice Ciparick, decided in favour of Mercury Bay. It had not been a 'match' as contemplated by the Deed of Gift. San Diego forfeited the Cup.

But that was not the end of the litigation. It rarely is in America. San Diego lodged an appeal to the Appellate Division of the Supreme Court. This court, by a bare majority, decided in favour of San Diego. There was no provision, or implied term, in the Deed of Gift that multihulls should be prohibited. Chief Judge Wachtler stressed:

> *This case ... has caught the public eye like few cases in this court's history. Much of the reason ... is the supposition that here at stake are grand principles – sportsmanship and tradition – pitted against the greed, commercialism and zealotry that threaten to vulgarise sport. In the end, however, the outcome of the case is dictated by elemental legal principles.*

The Deed did not require that vessels be evenly matched or raced with 'like or similar' boats. The Cup was re-awarded to San Diego.

Mercury Bay tried once more by appealing further to the Court of Appeals of the State of New York. This final appeal was heard in April 1990. Was there to be a further twist in the saga? No, by a majority, the court upheld the decision that San Diego's catamaran was a valid defence. It criticised heavily '...the most distasteful innovation of all – resolution of the competition in court.' 'No one wishes to see the competition debased by commercialism and greed. But if the traditions and ideals of the sport are dependent on judicial coercion,' the court continued, 'that battle is already lost.'

The America's Cup stayed in San Diego. The 1988 contest and the litigation were finally over.

The litigation tarnished the image and reputation of the America's Cup for a number of years. It led to changes in the rules of the competition in order to prevent such a mismatch again. Importantly, revised procedures were agreed for any disputes to be resolved by an arbitration process. Never again should there be a year and a half battle in the courts to decide a yachting race. Until 2007, when a challenge to the Swiss holders, Alinghi, took the rules of the America's Cup back into the courts of New York for a heated battle – if shorter than that triggered by the 1987 challenge.

San Diego successfully defended the Cup three times before losing it in 1995 – to New Zealand's Royal New Zealand Yacht Squadron.

---

70 FA PREMIER LEAGUE – FA AND FOOTBALL LEAGUE FIGHT OVER THE BIRTH OF A NEW LEAGUE

The FA was supporting the breakaway of the first division clubs into a new Premier League. Could it be stopped by the Football League?

The years 1990 and 1991 were turbulent for football. Sir Bert Millichip, the genial chairman of the Football Association, and Graham Kelly, his chief executive, had many uneasy moments in the offices of the FA at Lancaster Gate in London as they considered the future.

At that time, the first division was simply one of the four divisions within the Football League. The major first division clubs, led by the 'big five' (Manchester United, Liverpool, Arsenal, Tottenham and Everton), were threatening to break away and form a 'super league'. The leading clubs were convinced that they were the major attraction for the growing commercial interest in the game. They believed they were entitled to a greater share of the ever increasing revenues available from broadcasting and sponsorship. They also wanted a greater say in the running of their own league and associated affairs. Sir Bert was under pressure. How should the FA react to the increasing pressures for change? Was the structure of professional football in England about to break apart?

Was the structure of professional football in England about to break apart?

The Football League, founded in 1888, sought valiantly to keep its current structure together. The Football League was, along with around two thousand other leagues and competitions in England, formally run under the ultimate sanction and authority of the FA, the governing body and rulemaking authority for football in England. The Football League applied annually for the sanction of the FA to run its league. It had always been a formality.

The Football League's leaders were very concerned. Broadcasting revenues were shared, in agreed proportions, between all members of the League. Income for the lower clubs in the Football League would be vastly reduced if the major clubs left the League. Worried by the threat of a total breakaway by the top clubs, the Football League had in 1988 adopted a regulation requiring any club to give at least three full season's notice if it intended to leave the Football League. The time period was actually inconsistent with the FA's own regulations which provided for annual renewal but nothing was said by the FA until 1991 – when the FA decided to act.

Sir Bert Millichip and Graham Kelly decided that a breakaway in some form by the top clubs was inevitable. The FA published its own *Blueprint for the Future of Football* in June 1991. The FA considered that it would be in the best interests of football if the new League were created with substantial autonomy for the clubs but still kept under the auspices of the FA. Plans were developed with the major clubs for the formation of the FA Premier League.

Events moved quickly to pave the way for the new league. The FA decided in May 1991 to amend its conditions for sanctioning leagues. The revised condition said that any rule of a league which required a member club to give longer notice to leave than that required under the FA's own rules would not be acceptable. The league would not be sanctioned. This condition for sanctioning the Football League for 1991/92 would enable the first division clubs to leave the Football League at the end of that season and the new FA Premier League to commence in the 1992/93 season.

The Football League continued to fight. They brought a legal challenge in the High Court.

The Football League continued to fight. They brought a legal action to challenge and overturn the FA's decision. It was a last-ditch attempt to prevent the formation of the FA Premier League. If the Football League succeeded, the FA Premier League could not proceed – certainly not in the proposed form or timescale. The matter was heard urgently in the High Court in July 1991.

Should the FA's decision, in effect to impose new conditions on the sanctioning of the Football League and to facilitate the birth of the FA Premier League the following season, be open to legal challenge?

For: The FA was a body which regulated an important aspect of national life. Its decisions should be open to judicial review in the same way as other government and administrative bodies. It was obliged to act impartially, as a regulatory body, but it would have a serious potential conflict of interest if it entered into competition with the Football League by running its own league. The FA was not intended to have the function of running its own league. The new rule had the effect of inducing a breach of contract between the Football League and its clubs since the three-year notice rule was well-known to the FA. Changing the rules should be struck down as an abuse of power by the FA.

Against: The FA was a domestic body and its decisions

should not be open to legal challenge in the same way as a government department. In any event, the FA was acting in good faith in the best interests of the game. Its role was not simply supervisory. It already ran the FA Cup and was involved in commercial matters. Its role in relation to the FA Premier league would not result in a conflict of interest. The Football League's requirement for three years' notice for a club to leave the league was inconsistent with the scheme of annual sanctioning of leagues. There was nothing to prevent the FA from insisting on compliance with its rule for the following season as a condition of sanctioning the Football League. Its role was bona fide to make decisions in the best interests of the game.

The Football League lost.

Justice Rose stressed that 'it is no part of my job to decide whether the creation of a premier League will or will not be a good thing for English football.' He then decided that the FA was not a body susceptible to legal challenge in this way. It was a domestic body and the issue was simply a matter of private law between the FA and the Football League based on the contractual terms of the annual sanctioning of the Football League. The court would not intervene.

The formation of the FA Premier League could go ahead.

Even if the FA's decision were open to judicial review as a governmental type body, the court expressed the view that it would still not have intervened. 'The challenge mounted would, in my view, fail,' said Justice Rose. The FA's decision was fairly within the scope of its function to govern football in England.

The Football League's resistance was quashed. The formation of the FA Premier League could go ahead.

This was a momentous decision for football. The decision cleared the way for the birth, in the following 1992/93 season, of the Premier League, more formally entitled 'The Football Association Premier League'. On 20th February 1992 all first division clubs gave notice en masse of their resignation from the Football League at the end of the

1991/92 season. Each of the clubs in the new Premier League became a shareholder in the company which would run the new Premier League. The FA would have a 'special share' with certain supervisory rights in relation to the England team and the FA Cup.

Although transitional payments were established to soften the blow for the remaining clubs in the Football League, the die was cast. The FA Premier League opened the way for the leading clubs to benefit from the explosion in commercial revenues – led significantly by the television revenues from BSkyB. Football in England would never be the same again.

The first matches in the new Premier League were held on 15th August 1992, with the first goal being scored by Brian Deane of Sheffield United in a 2-1 win against Manchester United. The sale by the Premier League of UK television rights to Sky and Setanta for the four-year period, 2007-2011, will raise £1.7 billion – with another £625 million being paid for overseas television rights.

---

71 THE GREAT DARTS DIVIDE – A BITTER BATTLE

Phil Taylor, Eric Bristow and other leading players were threatening to break away to form a new organisation. Could the British Darts Organisation prevent a major split in darts?

The Embassy World Darts Championships final between Phil Taylor and Mike Gregory at the Lakeside Country Club, Frimley Green, in 1992 was one of the finest darts matches ever played, a classic encounter which went right down to a tie-break in the final set of the match. Phil Taylor won his second title and was beginning an ascendancy which would lead commentator, Sid Waddell, later to remark: 'If we'd had Phil Taylor at Hastings against the Normans, they'd have gone home!' The standard of darts had never been higher. And yet, behind the scenes, a deep division was developing within the world of darts.

A year later, at the 1993 Embassy Championships, the division had become apparent. There was heavy political tension in the air. John Lowe was destined to be the last winner of a unified world championship. A bitter dispute was coming to the boil. Darts would be split into two factions and there would be two separate world championships. How did this all come about?

A deep division was developing within the world of darts.

The background was a declining popularity in darts from its high point of the early 1980s. Some attributed this in part to image. Players drinking alcohol and smoking cigarettes during matches had not helped the reputation of the game – an image reinforced by an unforgettable sketch on *Not the Nine O'Clock News*. Many sponsors had dropped out. The number of televised events in the UK had virtually ceased except for the Embassy Championships. Many players who had earlier turned professional now found less prize money on offer and lack of TV exposure led to a reduced living from exhibition matches.

The historical governing body of the game in the UK was the British Darts Organisation (BDO). It had been formed in 1973 by Olly Croft in the front room of his house in Muswell Hill. The BDO was a founder member of the World Darts Federation. It comprised sixty-four member counties in Britain and organised tournaments for grass roots players all the way up to the professional level. This is how many of the leading players had developed 'up the pyramid'. The BDO set the rules which governed the game, such as the height of the board and size of the throwing oche. It organised the first World Professional Darts Championship in 1978 which, for many years under its sponsor, became known as the Embassy World Championships. All players were, until 1993, members of the BDO.

Many of the leading players now thought that not enough was being done by the BDO to attract new sponsors. A group of players wanted the BDO to appoint a public relations consultant. They decided to form a new organisation to be known as the World Darts Council (WDC). The group included Phil Taylor, Eric Bristow, John Lowe, Dennis Priestley, Jocky Wilson and all the other world champions still active in the game. They became the sixteen 'rebels'.

The tension was felt by all at the 1993 Embassy Championships. As a mark of their campaign, the WDC players wore a distinctive insignia bearing the initials 'WDC' on their sleeves during practice sessions of the tournament. They were told by the BDO to remove the badges. The WDC players objected to an arrogance with which they were being treated. They decided that, if the BDO was not going to recognise their organisation, the WDC players would not in future play in the Embassy Championships.

The BDO, like any governing body, wanted to keep control of the game. It tried to quell the rebels. It wanted all players to stay within 'the family' of darts. The BDO sought to prevent players defecting to the WDC. The BDO did so by passing resolutions which would have the effect of banning players who belonged to the WDC from playing in any events organised by the BDO including all county darts and its super league competition. Indeed, also banned by the BDO would be any players who played in exhibition matches, even for charity, with WDC players. A civil war in darts had begun.

The WDC players decided that, if the BDO was not going to recognise them, they would not play in the BDO World Championships.

The WDC players retaliated by taking legal action against the BDO. It was reminiscent of the days of Tony Greig and the Packer revolution in cricket. They argued strongly that these bans by the BDO were in restraint of trade and illegal. They sought damages for loss of earnings over the previous four years of the ban. A claim was brought in the names of Phil Taylor, Eric Bristow, Jocky Wilson ('what an athlete': Sid Waddell) and the other professional members of the WDC.

It was a bitter and protracted battle, lasting more than three years, and an expensive one for both sides. Eventually, a settlement was reached at the end of June 1997 after three days of negotiation before the start of the court hearing. The settlement was approved by the High Court. Basically, the WDC 'rebel' players had won:

The bans imposed by the BDO were dropped. Each player was free to enter into such 'open' events as he wished. Eric Bristow said: 'For the first time in four years I am free to play in darts competitions all over the world.' In exchange, the WDC players dropped their claims for damages.

The new WDC accepted that the World Darts Federation should continue to be the sport's regulatory body responsible for the rules.

The WDC also agreed to drop 'World' from its name and were renamed the Professional Darts Council (PDC).

A further term protected each party's lead championship event. Whilst both the BDO and the new PDC could hold its own 'world' championship, the top sixteen players in each event in a particular year would not enter into the other organisation's event in the following year.

The court settlement did little to prevent the great darts divide. It effectively confirmed it. There would still be two world championships. Players would, in effect, have to choose to join one body or the other.

The first WDC world championships were the 1994 Skol World Championships which commenced in late December 1993, a week before the BDO World Championships, and were held at the Circus Tavern in Purfleet. This started the unusual practice of the yearly championships of the WDC/PDC being commenced in December of the previous year. The first winner of the 'new' 1994 WDC world championships was Dennis Priestley who defeated Phil Taylor.

Darts followers still argue as to which tournament is the more prestigious. The overall average three-dart score in each championship is remarkably similar. Generally, though, leading players have continued to join the PDC. The most significant transferee in recent years has been Raymond van Barneveld, the Dutchman, who had won four BDO world titles including in 2006. Despite the agreed term in the 1997 court settlement, he played in the 2007 PDC World Championships. He won a dramatic sudden-death tie-break at five legs each in the final set to beat the previously invincible Phil Taylor 7-6 to win the PDC world title. It was a match to rank alongside that great 1992 final.

One potential sign of greater harmony was the announcement of a planned thirty-two-man 'Grand Slam of Darts' competition in November 2007 which would feature players aligned with both organisations. Would this be a first step in closing the great darts divide? Barely. The BDO/WDF subsequently altered the date of one of their world 'masters' events so that there was a clash. Several leading BDO players, including their world champion Martin Adams, did not play in the Grand Slam of Darts – won by Phil Taylor. The divide continues.

---

72 STEPHEN HENDRY – WORLD SNOOKER IN TURMOIL

A bitter divide in snooker was threatened as the prospect grew of a rival tour being established which would divide the players. Could the rival tour be stopped?

In December 2000 it was the turn of snooker to become embroiled in an ugly dispute destined for the courts.

The administration of the game was in a state of turbulence. As with the divide in darts, many leading players were not satisfied with the way the game was being run. The players were led by Stephen Hendry and Mark Williams. Hendry was probably snooker's greatest ever player. The thirty-two-year-old Scot had been ranked number one on eight occasions. In 1999 he won the world championship at the Crucible Theatre in Sheffield for a record seventh time, defeating the rising Mark Williams in the final. In the spring of 2000 it was Williams who became world champion at the Crucible and ended the season as the game's number one ranked player.

Behind both Hendry and Williams was their manager, Ian Doyle. Doyle was a tough, ambitious Scotsman ready to take on 'the establishment'. From his offices at a snooker club in Stirling, Doyle had for many years been fighting for a better deal for the players with the game's governing body, the World Professional Billiards & Snooker Association (WPBSA). In 2000, he saw his chance to apply further pressure. He agreed to merge his sports management agency with a new internet company, The Sportsmasters Network (TSN), which was keen to invest in snooker. Doyle became chairman of TSN.

Doyle, Williams and Hendry were dissatisfied, they said, with the 'amateurish' way in which the WPBSA was being run. The association had virtually all the leading players among its members. In effect, only tournaments run or sanctioned by the WPBSA counted towards world ranking points. Chaired by former player, Rex Williams, its board had no professional management with expertise in marketing or sponsorship affairs. Doyle was forthright: 'I don't believe that the sport can move forward with players or ex-players running the game. They've got a part to play but we need professional management. The problem is people on the board don't want to give up their own little fiefdoms.'

'I don't believe that the sport can move forward with players or ex-players running the game.'

Doyle thought that the WPBSA was too dependent on tobacco companies for sponsorship; this source was destined to disappear. New sponsors should be found. Doyle complained that, as a regulatory body, the WPBSA should not also be the sole promoter of major televised tournaments.

With £10 million investment support from City backers, Doyle approached the WPBSA during September 2000 with an offer to invest £3.3 million over three years in promoting four tournaments with new sponsors, in exchange for rights to transmit over the internet live pictures of WBSA events. A deal seemed possible but negotiations became protracted. The WPSBA failed to give its backing – partly because the new sponsors did not want to be involved with a sport with its existing tobacco sponsors. Doyle and TSN became frustrated and walked away.

On 6th December 2000, TSN issued a declaration of civil war. A press release pledged a 'fresh vision for snooker' and announced an intention to mount a rival ten-event global tour. New sponsors were planned with a significant increase in prize money. Events were planned in Dubai, Thailand, Malta and China. TSN announced in February that there would be a new world championship in 2002 to be staged in the National Indoor Arena in Birmingham with dates which would, deliberately, clash with WPBSA's World Championship at the Crucible. BBC snooker correspondent Clive Everton commented: 'This looks like a fight to a finish between competing tours each with its own World Championship.'

Many leading players committed to participate in the new tour. They included Stephen Hendry, Mark Williams and Jimmy White. Hendry was the first to back the breakaway tour. 'The circuit has become jaded because nothing has developed in the last five or six years.' He signed a three-year contract to promote the organisation and its events. TSN proposed that, in the new world, the WPBSA should become solely a regulatory body. It was, in effect, an attempted takeover of the marketing of the professional game at the top level.

It was an attempted takeover of the marketing of the professional game.

The WPBSA retaliated. Its main potential weapon was the BBC. The WPBSA's £20 million existing contract with the BBC for televising certain major events, including the world championship at the Crucible, still had several years to run. Pressure was applied to persuade the BBC to continue to honour its contract to televise WPBSA events despite the loss of the TSN players. The BBC confirmed that it would do so.

The WPBSA's second main defence was Ronnie O'Sullivan. He was then ranked only number four in the world but he was already one of snooker's major attractions. A substantial offer was made to Ronnie O'Sullivan to remain loyal to WPBSA tournaments and stay within the fold. After initial doubts, he eventually agreed to do so. Other leading players who stayed with the WPBSA included Steve Davis, John Parrott, John Higgins and Peter Ebdon. The professional ranks were being split. O'Sullivan won his first World Championship at the Crucible in 2001.

The snooker civil war escalated. The WPBSA decided in March 2001 to make a number of rule changes for the 2001/02 season. These included rules enabling the WPBSA to exercise greater control over players' promotional activities such as the number of logos which could be worn on players' waistcoats. A principal change, though, was a rule specifically designed to block the new rival tour. The new rule provided, in essence, that WPBSA members could not enter into or play in any snooker tournament, event or match without the prior consent of the board of the WPBSA.

The WPBSA indicated that this consent would not be given for a player to compete in an event being televised in any country at the same time as a WPBSA tour event being held in that country. The aim, clearly, was to prevent the rival tour being attractive for TV or commercial sponsors. If this rule were implemented, it would either kill off the rival tour or lead to the creation of two separate snooker circuits. This became the legal battleground.

Civil war had broken out. Hendry, Williams and other leading players in the TSN camp fought back. They brought a legal action challenging the validity of the WPBSA's rule changes. The crux of their case was that the WPBSA was abusing its dominant position as a governing body and imposing anti-competitive conditions on the players. It was very reminiscent of the fight by Tony Greig and Packer's 'world series' tour against the established cricket governing bodies.

In March 2001, TSN relented. It announced that, at least for now, it was abandoning plans to form a new snooker tour. It did not wish, it said, to split the game. TSN complained:

> *Since our announcement [in December] the world governing body have done all they can to undermine our genuine attempt to offer a real choice for the player. They have denied us access to the players, banned our journalists from the venues, and used their dominant position in the market to deny any form of competition.*

The TSN players would return to the WPBSA tour with 'considerable reluctance.' In practice, the BBC decision had been a particularly important commercial blow. WPBSA also backed down by withdrawing its principal rule change for the 2001/02 season.

However, it was not peace. TSN would still proceed to challenge the WPBSA's 'monopoly position' in the High Court which they maintained was an 'unfair restraint of trade'. Fearing that the rule could always be re-introduced unless challenged and seeking to overturn the WPBSA's dual role as regulator and commercial promoter, Hendry and Williams decided to press ahead with their legal action. It was fought in the High Court.

The principal issue for the court was: should the proposed WPBSA rule, which would have had the effect of preventing Stephen Hendry and others from competing in televised events run by the new tour, be declared invalid as being unlawful and in restraint of trade?

For: The rule affected the ability of a snooker event organiser to recruit players. It effectively restricted the ability of any rival organisation to gain a foothold. Taken with the rule that only WPBSA sanctioned-events counted for ranking points, its effect was to limit significantly the events in which players

could compete in order to earn their livelihood. It was contrary to UK and European competition laws. The WPBSA's interests should solely be as a regulator. The rule should be declared void.
Against: The WPBSA was acting in good faith to protect and further the interests of all its members. Many of the rival tour events were likely to have restricted fields and so, in practice, would not be open to many WPBSA members. WPBSA events, on the other hand, were generally open to all members. Money made by the WPBSA from its tournaments was re-invested in the sport as a whole. The rule was necessary to support the broadcasting and sponsorship revenue of the WPBSA. It was therefore in the best interests of the sport.

The High Court hearing lasted six weeks. Judgment was given on October 2001.

On the major point, Hendry and Williams won. Justice Lloyd decided that the rule, requiring the WPBSA's consent for players to compete in other events, was too wide and was unreasonable under competition laws. It was declared invalid. Justice Lloyd explained: 'The WPBSA had market power and was in a dominant position.' The effect of the new rule was to 'prevent competition – by limiting the sources to which the players can have recourse in order to earn their livelihood'. He did not consider this restriction could be justified.

As to the complaint that other rule changes and actions of the WPBSA in the commercial field were an 'abuse of its dominant position' as a governing body, TSN failed. Both sides came away claiming victory. The WPBSA's chief executive welcomed the court's overall decision: 'This is a victory for the Association's right to protect the players and their assets against commercial predators.'

Both sides came away claiming victory.

Hendry was happy with the result in court. 'All the big points we have won – and the other minor issues like logos and rankings were all peripheral anyway. Mark and I feel that we are very much vindicated in our decision to go to court.'

Each side had to bear its own substantial legal costs. It had been an exhausting battle. Very little in fact had been achieved.

At the legal level, the case was important. It was the first judgment of the High Court to uphold a claim under English law that a sports governing body's exercise of its regulatory powers could amount to 'an abuse of a dominant position' in breach of competition law. It re-emphasised that decisions by a governing body must be 'proportionate'. If measures are introduced which restrict the ability of players and athletes to earn their living, those measures must be limited to the minimum reasonably necessary to protect the sport's interests.

'an abuse of a dominant position'

It is a case which will continue to be cited in many future actions against sports governing bodies.

For snooker, there was an uneasy aftermath. Some organisational changes were made in the WPBSA which changed its name to the World Snooker Association. A new chairman, Sir Rodney Walker, was appointed in 2003. Prize money was increased. Tobacco sponsorship was forced by law to end in 2003 – except for the Embassy World Championships which had an extension to 2006. Some new sponsors were found. TSN changed its name to 110sport and Doyle continued to seek change.

At least snooker had avoided the position which emerged in darts of having, confusingly, two different circuits and two different world champions. But it has been an uneasy truce.

---

73 THE DONS: WIMBLEDON OR MILTON KEYNES? – A PASSIONATE AFFAIR FOR SUPPORTERS

Wimbledon FC proposed a controversial move seventy miles north to Milton Keynes. Should it be permitted by the football authorities?

By 2002, the great days of Wimbledon FC were in the past. The finest hour for Wimbledon's 'crazy gang' was the 1-0 defeat of Liverpool in the FA Cup Final in 1988 with a memorable winning goal from Lawrie Sanchez. It was now a fading memory.

It had been a rapid ascent for 'the Dons', founded in 1889 as Wimbledon Old Centrals, who had spent most of their history in non-league football. The club had only been elected to the Football League as recently as 1977. Fourth division champions in 1982/83, successive promotions saw the club reach the heady heights of the first division in 1986. Wimbledon FC became a founder member of the FA Premier League.

By 2002, however, the club was in disarray. Relegated from the Premier League on the last day of the 1999/2000 season following a defeat at Southampton, Wimbledon's finances and fortunes were collapsing. What could the club do? It was an unexpected and bold solution. Move seventy miles north to Milton Keynes!

Wimbledon were 'homeless'. Its home ground had for nearly seventy years until May 1991 been Plough Lane in Merton, south London. This was a spartan ground and did not meet the requirements of the Taylor Report enacted following the Hillsborough disaster. Plans to relocate to a new all-seater stadium in Merton failed. The FA had granted permission in 1992 for the club to play their 'home' matches at Selhurst Park in Croydon, sharing Crystal Palace's ground. Plough Lane was redeveloped as a supermarket. Wimbledon were losing, on one estimate, around £3 to £4 million per annum in commercial income through not having their own ground.

Wimbledon toyed with the idea of being bought by an Irish consortium and 'moving' to Dublin. This idea was stamped upon by the Irish FA who would not allow a team based in Ireland to play in the English league. It went no further.

It was an unexpected and bold solution. Move seventy miles north to Milton Keynes!

Then, along came the Milton Keynes proposal in 2001. The man behind the proposed move to Milton Keynes was Pete Winkleman. A well-known music entrepreneur and football fan, he wanted top-class football for Milton Keynes. A number of possibilities were considered. There was an opportunity with other backers to build a modern new stadium as part of a large commercial development in the town. Starting a new club there would not, though, be enough to attract the necessary financial backing. Could an existing professional club be brought in from another town? Since 1998, Winkleman had been approaching without success other clubs in financial trouble, reputedly including Barnet, Luton and Queens Park Rangers. But Wimbledon FC, desperately looking for a new home, were a more promising proposition. A deal was agreed in principle.

Wimbledon applied, as required under the rules of the Football League, for permission to relocate to Milton Keynes – around seventy miles from Wimbledon itself. This was the first time permission had been sought in England for a league football club to make a significant geographical move of this nature. There was passionate opposition to the move from many Wimbledon supporters. The move broke the important bond between a club and the fabric of its local community. It was tantamount to an American-style of 'franchising' prevalent in baseball and other sports. This was not America. It was a concept alien to English football.

Such a geographical move of a club was unprecedented in English football – but not without some precedent in Scotland. In 1996, the Scottish Football League allowed Meadowbank Thistle FC to relocate permanently from central Edinburgh to a 'new town' more than eighteen miles away, Livingstone, and to change its name. And in 2002 Airdrie United were, in effect, permitted to acquire Clydebank FC, taking its league position but playing at Airdrie's old ground.

There was passionate opposition to the move from many Wimbledon supporters.

The Football League rejected Wimbledon's application in August 2001. Wimbledon persisted. The matter was referred to an independent Commission jointly appointed by the Football League and the Football Association. The Commission met in May 2002.

Should the football authorities permit a league club to make such an unprecedented move of this nature away from its 'home' roots? If so, should 'Wimbledon' be regarded as the same club and keep their position in the first division of the Football League?

For: Football must be commercial. There was no land site in Merton or south London where it was viable to construct a major football stadium. Wimbledon FC were a secondary tenant at Selhurst Park and there was no or little opportunity to promote their own colours, branding and marketing at the ground. Wimbledon were already playing a fair distance from their 'home'. A majority of the club's supporters came from outside Merton. There had been a steady decline in attendances. Milton Keynes offered a new stadium, excellent infrastructure and a potentially large fan base. A move was necessary to save the club. **Against:** A football club had its heart in the community. Wimbledon 'belonged' to south London. Long-standing Wimbledon supporters would not be able to associate with the new venue. Permitting a club to be bought and moved in this fashion would be to allow a 'franchise' system to be introduced for owning professional football clubs, contrary to the English tradition. It would, in effect, become a 'new' club and should not be permitted to retain its league position as if it were the same club. It would go against the core principle of football's pyramid structure whereby rises up and down the league should be governed solely by results, promotion and relegation.

Exceptional circumstances existed. The Commission noted that, in this case, the club's links with Merton were 'not so profound, or the roots go so deep, that they will not survive a necessary transplant to ensure the club's survival'. The Commission decided by a narrow majority it was better that the club was saved. This, the Commission stressed vainly, should not be regarded as a precedent.

Wimbledon could, though, move to Milton Keynes – and remain in the first division of the Football League. The FA were not happy:

> *The Commission reached its conclusions despite evidence presented by the FA opposing such moves in principle. The Commission has made it clear that their decision is based on exceptional circumstances. They see Wimbledon as a one-off. This is not the beginning of a franchise system.*

2002/03 became Wimbledon FC's last full season at Selhurst Park. Fans deserted the club in protest. Average attendances fell to fewer than 3000. In October 2002 only 849 fans turned up for one league match against Rotherham, and 227 of them came from Rotherham! It was the lowest attendance ever recorded at a match in the Football League. Wimbledon FC subsequently went into financial administration.

Wimbledon played their first match in Milton Keynes in September 2003. It was against Burnley and ended in a 2-2 draw. Matches were played initially at the National Hockey Stadium in Milton Keynes. In Spring 2004, Pete Winkleman led the purchase of Wimbledon out of bankruptcy. A new 28,000 all-seater stadium was planned. On the pitch, results were poor. The club dropped to two divisions below where they were when they last played, as Wimbledon, at Selhurst Park. They were relegated to Coca-Cola League Two in 2006 but, in 2008, promoted as champions back to League One.

In June 2004, despite the FA Commission's recommendations, Winkleman announced that the club would change its name to Milton Keynes Dons FC.

Back in Wimbledon itself, the club's supporters formed a new club, AFC Wimbledon, which they saw as the direct descendant of Wimbledon FC and the 'true' club of the people of Wimbledon. The new club started at the bottom of the football pyramid and enjoyed sizeable support from the start. In 2008 the club played in the Ryman Isthmian League Premier Division before average home crowds of more than 2,500. The season ended with another promotion in their short history.

In late 2006, agreement was reached whereby the replica of the FA Cup, so proudly won in 1988, together with other club papers and memorabilia gathered under the name of Wimbledon FC were returned to the London Borough of Merton. They were handed over by Pete Winkleman in a ceremony at Merton Civic Centre on 2nd August 2007.

All that remained in Milton Keynes was the name 'Dons'.

---

74 McLAREN AND 'SPYGATE' – ALLEGATIONS OF ESPIONAGE IN FORMULA ONE

We finish this chapter with two recent disciplinary cases, relating to the misbehaviour of teams, which have significantly affected championship and relegation issues. In the first, 780 pages of technical information, derived from Ferrari, were found in the possession of a senior McLaren engineer. What would be McLaren's penalty?

It was a visit to a photocopying shop in Walton-on-Thames which triggered it all.

Months later, Lewis Hamilton waited nervously for the judgment of the FIA World Motor Sport Council. Would the British-based McLaren team be banned from racing for the remainder of 2007 or indeed for 2008? Would Hamilton retain his lead in the individual drivers' championship or would McLaren team drivers be docked points and Hamilton's chances of sensationally winning the title in his 'rookie' year be dashed?

Ferrari and McLaren were the two top teams in Formula One during 2007. Each team kept a close eye on their rival's developments. Finding out as much as possible about rival teams, studying race photographs and videos and listening to gossip were everyday occurrences. But had McLaren overstepped the mark? Were they, in effect, guilty of industrial espionage?

But had McLaren overstepped the mark? Were they, in effect, guilty of industrial espionage?

It was Ferrari, no doubt unwittingly, who started the saga. Nigel Stepney, their test and technical manager, had been with the Ferrari team since 1992. He was part of the 'dream team', with driver Michael Schumacher, credited with the success of Ferrari in the late 1990s. But times moved on. Ferrari announced a change in team structure in February 2007. Stepney had a different role. He was not happy. He thought about getting away from Ferrari. There were allegations of a 'white powder' and sabotage of a Ferrari car at the Monaco Grand

Prix. Ferrari investigated and called in the Italian criminal authorities. Stepney was dismissed by Ferrari on 3rd July 2007.

The story widened. Ferrari announced, on the same day, that they were taking action in the High Court against an engineer from the McLaren team – later named as Mike Coughlan, their chief designer. A search warrant had been obtained. Coughlan's home had been searched in the UK. He was found to be in possession of 780 pages of Ferrari technical documentation and two computer discs on which the documents had been copied. The material originated from Ferrari's Maranello factory. Where did the lead come from? Coughlan's wife, Trudy, had taken the material to a photocopying shop in nearby Walton-on-Thames. An observant employee at the shop had spotted that the documents were marked 'confidential' and appeared to belong to Ferrari. He decided to contact the team's headquarters in Italy.

A few days later, Ferrari dropped their action against Coughlan in return for a promise of full disclosure and co-operation. With a senior engineer at McLaren knowingly in possession of detailed confidential information relating to Ferrari, they had McLaren in their sights instead. The sport's governing body, the FIA, investigated. Were McLaren in trouble – or was this a minor spat?

The pressure was on McLaren. Team boss, Ron Dennis, fighting for his reputation for integrity and fair play, announced that a full investigation had taken place and that 'no Ferrari intellectual property has been passed to any other members of the team or incorporated into [our] cars'. Coughlan had acted without their knowledge and on his own. Indeed, there was a strong suspicion that Stepney and Coughlan were colluding not to benefit McLaren but to offer themselves to another team. Honda had even interviewed both of them.

'No Ferrari intellectual property has been passed to any other members of the team or incorporated into our cars.'

After an internal hearing in Paris, the FIA's World Motor Sport Council found that McLaren had been in possession of confidential Ferrari information and therefore technically in breach of the motor racing's International Sporting Code – but, since there was no evidence that they had used the information, no punishment was levied. The FIA reserved, however, the right to reconvene if any new evidence emerged.

Ferrari were furious. 'Ferrari find it incomprehensible that violating the fundamental principle of sporting honesty does not have, as a logical and inevitable consequence, the application of a sanction.' The Ferrari machine moved into gear. Pressure was brought to bear and the FIA (sometimes known as Ferrari's Internal Agency) decided to refer the matter to the FIA International Court of Appeal.

And then another disaffected employee critically entered the story. None other than McLaren's own twice-world champion, Fernando Alonso. Alonso was in open conflict with Ron Dennis. He thought Britain's Lewis Hamilton was now getting favoured driver's treatment at McLaren. Incidents occurred during qualifying at the Hungarian Grand Prix and an angry exchange took place between Alonso and Dennis. During that exchange, Alonso threw in a verbal grenade. He threatened to send to the FIA details of certain email exchanges between himself and Pedro de la Rosa, McLaren's test driver, clearly linking the two drivers with information provided by Mike Coughlan.

Was this the 'smoking gun'? Ron Dennis himself called FIA chief, Max Mosley, and informed him of the exchanges. He claimed that there was nothing in them – but was this an indication that disclosure, and possible use, of the Ferrari information had gone further into the McLaren organisation than previously imagined?

The FIA decided to reopen its investigation. The three McLaren drivers (Alonso, Hamilton and de la Rosa) were asked to provide all relevant evidence against an assurance that, if there was full disclosure, no action would be taken against the drivers personally. Mobile phone records were examined. These revealed that, during the period from 11th March to 3rd July, no fewer than 288 text and email messages and thirty-five telephone calls were exchanged between Coughlan and Stepney. Some information was passed on to de la Rosa and Alonso. It was clear, as the World Motor Council later stated, that both drivers 'knew that this information was confidential Ferrari information and was being received by Coughlan from Nigel Stepney'.

The data received by McLaren covered such detailed matters as Ferrari's brakes, weight distribution, aerodynamic balance and tyre inflation. There was an exchange, for instance, in which de la Rosa asked Coughlan if he knew the weight distribution of the Ferrari because he wanted to test it in McLaren's simulator. But did de la Rosa know about the specific Ferrari documents – or simply that Coughlan and Stepney spoke together as long-term friends?

This was a disciplinary case 'within the sport'. McLaren were charged again under a provision of motor racing's International Sporting Code which made it an offence to commit 'any fraudulent conduct or any act prejudicial to the interests of any competition, or to the interests of motor sport'. There was no requirement that a party must have been advantaged by the use of documents – although this would undoubtedly aggravate the offence.

Was Ferrari's anger justified? Should McLaren be heavily penalised? Should points be deducted from the McLaren team in the constructor's championship and from their drivers in the drivers' championship?

For: Ferrari argued that it was clear that significant technical information, known to be confidential, had been received by a senior engineer in McLaren. It had been deliberately passed to at least two of McLaren's drivers. There was evidence that it was being reviewed and used – even if not incorporated specifically in McLaren car design. McLaren's top level assurances given at the previous hearing were incorrect. This was a serious breach. The integrity of the sport required a severe penalty.
Against: There was no evidence that any of the technical information had been used in any McLaren car. All 140 McLaren engineers had sworn that no Ferrari intellectual property had been incorporated in the McLaren cars. McLaren had acted promptly when they learnt of the material. The dossier did not actually contain much useful information. The exchange about Ferrari was no more than the usual talk about rival teams.

McLaren were found guilty by the World Motor Sport Council (WMSC).

An extraordinary meeting of the WMSC was held in Paris in September. They concluded that 'some degree of sporting advantage was obtained, though it may forever be impossible to quantify that advantage in concrete terms'. What would be the penalty? The WMSC decided to inflict a heavy punishment on McLaren because 'there was an intention on the part of a number of McLaren personnel to use some of the Ferrari confidential information in its own testing'.

The WMSC announced that McLaren would lose all points in the 2007 constructors' championship – but not in the drivers' championship. Hamilton retained his three point lead in the title race. The team would also be open to examination to prove that there was no Ferrari 'intellectual property' in their cars next year before racing.

In addition, to initial gasps, McLaren were fined $100 million. It was the largest fine ever imposed in sporting history. In practice, the fine included the loss of around $40 million in prize and television money which McLaren would have earned from the constructors' championship – but it would still create a huge hole in their budget. Also, they would be much further back at the track, with a reduced number of garages and fewer VIP paddock passes for sponsors and guests – a blow to their prestige and reputation.

It was the largest fine ever imposed in sporting history.

Bernie Ecclestone later said that McLaren were 'minutes away' from being thrown out of the World Championships of 2007 and 2008. 'A few of us sort of battled on and campaigned for the fine instead.' Conscious, no doubt, that Hamilton's success and the dramatic battle for the drivers' title were of enormous commercial value to Formula One as a sport.

Legally, the punishment could have been challenged if it was clearly disproportionate. McLaren claimed that it was and threatened to appeal. Ron Dennis could 'not accept that we deserve to be penalised or our reputation damaged in this way'. After a few days, McLaren announced that they would not do so – further actions and hearings would be damaging to the sport. The show should go on – on the track.

This was a classic case of a disciplinary issue being dealt with 'within the sport'. It resulted in the largest fine ever imposed in a sporting disciplinary action. To many, including former champion Jackie Stewart, the punishment does indeed seem harsh when weighed against the fact that there was no concrete evidence that McLaren benefited in any significant way from the Ferrari information. And why weren't Ferrari also to blame for the actions of Stepney who disclosed the information? But sport's ability to decide for itself in its own best interests is what the 'autonomy of sport' means.

Without, though, an initial search by criminal authorities and the 'arm of the law' the case would not have developed. Italian prosecutors still have their files open. We may not have heard the end of this saga.

The world drivers' championship in 2007 went to the last grand prix of the season in Brazil. By an irony (or was it justice?) the championship was won by Ferrari's Kimi Raikkonen who won the last two races to clinch the title by one point ahead of both Lewis Hamilton and Fernando Alonso.

In 2008 racing resumed on the track. Ferrari settled their differences with McLaren. The parties 'agreed to bring the various disputes between them in relation to this matter to a final conclusion'.

Attention turned to the FIFA President Max Mosley and his off-track activities.

---

75 THE BLADES ATTACK THE HAMMERS – BREACH OF RULES AND A RIVAL'S RELEGATION

West Ham signed Carlos Tevez under transfer arrangements which breached the rules of the Premier League. Should they be 'docked' points? The decision would greatly affect which club was to be relegated.

The odds on it happening seemed extraordinarily high. But that's football. It was the last day of the 2006/07 season in the Premier League. West Ham to win away at champions Manchester United and Sheffield United to lose at home against relegation rivals Wigan – it was the only combination of results which would relegate Sheffield United and keep up West Ham. At Old Trafford, Manchester United pressed on the attack relentlessly against West Ham. Then, a counter-attack; the ball was played through and West Ham snatched a winning goal – and the scorer, inevitably, was Carlos Tevez.

Should Tevez have been stopped from playing for West Ham? Should West Ham have been 'docked' points for a breach of the rules? Should Sheffield United be spared relegation? Did Sheffield United have a legal claim against West Ham for breach of the duties owed by one competitor in a league to another? These questions occupied the attention of commentators, fans and the media – and courts and tribunals – for months afterwards.

Should West Ham have been 'docked' points for a breach of the rules?

Tevez, an Argentinian international and once described by Diego Maradona as the 'Argentine prophet for the twenty-first century', was signed by West Ham from the Brazilian side Corinthians at the end of August 2006 along with fellow countryman, Javier Mascherano. West Ham were cock-a-hoop. The players were duly registered with the Premier League and started playing, not that successfully, for West Ham.

Rumours spread that Kia Joorabchian's MSI Group still had 'economic rights' to the players under arrangements not uncommon in South America. Tevez could be transferred during a transfer window if and when the MSI Group said so and MSI would receive the fee – West Ham did not have full control. This 'third party agreement' had been hidden from the Premier League when West Ham obtained his registration. It was almost certainly in breach of Rule U18 of the Premier League Rules which prohibits a contract which 'enables any [third] party ... to acquire the ability materially to influence' the policies or performance of a club.

The Premier League investigated but West Ham, through its managing director at the time, gave an emphatic assurance in September that there was no such agreement. The club lied to the Premier League. This was the real 'crime'. In late November 2006 West Ham came under new ownership and management, bought by an Icelandic consortium then led by Eggert Magnusson. The new management volunteered the true position regarding Tevez to the Premier League and in January 2007 handed over a copy of the agreement with the MSI Group.

Disciplinary charges were laid against West Ham by the Premier League for breach of the duty of 'utmost good faith' (Rule B13) and for the 'third party agreement' (Rule U18). A hearing of the Premier League's disciplinary commission took place at the end of April. West Ham pleaded guilty. They were fined a total of £5.5 million – £3 million in respect of the breach of Rule B13 and £2.5million for Rule U18. Crucially, the disciplinary commission did not deduct any points from West Ham. They decided it would not be a 'proportionate punishment' in the circumstances. The club was under new ownership and management.

Moreover:

> *A points deduction in, say, January ... would have been somewhat easier to bear than today which would have consigned the club to certain relegation.*

Actually, with West Ham lying nineteenth in the table and virtually certain of relegation in any event, many thought that the monetary fine was a severe punishment to go with the cost of inevitable relegation.

As far as the continued registration of Carlos Tevez was concerned, the disciplinary commission were weak. They did not require his de-registration but left it to the Premier League to be satisfied that the 'third party agreement' had been terminated. Given hurried and not very convincing assurances that it had been terminated by West Ham and that West Ham would resist any claim that it was still active, the Premier League allowed Tevez to continue playing.

And play he did! West Ham won their final three matches of the season – against Wigan, Bolton and Manchester United – with Tevez having a significant role in each match. He created two of the goals in the away win against Wigan. He scored twice against Bolton and scored the only goal in the away victory against Manchester United. Remarkably, and totally against the odds, West Ham finished above Sheffield United who were relegated along with Charlton and Watford.

Did Sheffield United have any hope left? They launched a legal campaign to the effect that the disciplinary commission should have docked West Ham points – and that the Premier League should have been required to de-register Tevez for the final three games of the season. The issue came before an independent three man arbitration tribunal of the Premier League in June 2007. The tribunal had limited scope. It could not itself change the decision – but it could order the disciplinary commission to re-consider its decision.

The arbitration tribunal said 'no'. It would not order a fresh disciplinary hearing. The tribunal could only do so if it concluded that the original decision of the commission was 'irrational or perverse'. 'This is a very strict test and is very difficult to satisfy on a question very much of judgment and discretion.' Tantalisingly, the arbitration tribunal had 'much sympathy' for Sheffield United's grievances and

> *... would in all probability have reached a different conclusion and deducted points from West Ham.*

But they could not say that the decision was irrational or perverse.

On the continued registration of Tevez, the arbitration tribunal recognised that, despite apparent termination, the MSI Group might still assert rights. That possibility was 'not entirely excluded'. It certainly wasn't! However, there had been no attempt in practice so far by the MSI group actually to influence the club's policies or performance.

But they could not say that the decision was irrational or perverse.

'The arrangement may not have been legally watertight but it was a practical and workable solution to a difficult situation' and, again, the decision not to de-register Tevez was not 'unreasonable in the sense of ... being perverse or capricious'. All a bit weak.

Time had virtually run out for Sheffield United to have any chance of staying in the Premier League for the following 2007/08 season. One last attempt was made to go to the High Court to appeal the arbitration decision. The High Court stamped on that last chance attempt. No leave was given to appeal to the court. It was the Championship next season for Sheffield United and an opening home match against Colchester United.

The row over Carlos Tevez's contract continued after the end of the

2006/07 season. Not surprisingly, the MSI Group claimed that they were entitled to any transfer fee – not West Ham – and that West Ham could not hold on to his registration. Further litigation was threatened. In the end, agreement was reached without further reference to the courts. West Ham did receive a small part of the transfer fee, the MSI Group received the lion's share and Carlos Tevez was transferred ... to Manchester United.

Sheffield United were still angry. They faced a heavy financial loss of TV and other income as a result of relegation – a cost estimated in excess of £30 million. Could they claim compensation by way of damages in a civil claim directly against West Ham? It was worth a try. They would argue that West Ham broke the rules of the Premier League, including the duty of 'utmost good faith' which each club owed the others – and this had resulted in the club's relegation and financial loss. West Ham would counter that the Premier League's disciplinary regime should be the sole mechanism for punishing any breach of the rules. Surely, in any event, Sheffield United's own play on the pitch was the main cause of their downfall?

The lawyers found a route under the FA's rules, not previously used for claims directly between clubs, to an independent tribunal chaired by Lord Griffiths, former president of the MCC. Sheffield United's chances of success seemed small. Or would the story have one last sting?

...would the story have one last sting?

Yes, it would. The tribunal announced its decision in September 2008. The Hammers were legally liable to pay compensation. Critically, if later discovered evidence of the club's assurances to Joorabchian's advisers had been known to the Premier League at the time, they 'would have suspended Mr Tevez's registration as a West Ham player'. The tribunal had 'no doubt that West Ham would have secured at least three fewer points over the 2006/7 season if Carlos Tevez had not been playing for the club.' The amount of compensation, likely to be multi-millions, would be assessed later.

Many were astonished at this unprecedented leap from the rulebook to compensation directly between clubs – and its implications for future disputes. Sheffield United felt 'vindicated'. West Ham, facing forced sales of players, were stunned. It was now their turn to seek, despairingly, an appeal route. But the outcome was probably now for the accountants rather than the lawyers.

Back to the football. At the end of the 2007/08 season, West Ham finished a comfortable tenth in the Premier League, Carlos Tevez collected a winner's medal with Manchester United ... and Sheffield United lost away at Southampton on the final day and failed to reach the play-offs.

---

76 BEIJING OR BARCELONA? CLUB, COUNTRY AND ARGENTINA'S LIONEL MESSI

Lionel Messi was one of the world's top footballers. Argentina wanted him in their Olympic team. But Barcelona wanted him to play in a Champions League match. Were they bound to release him for the Olympics?

Were Sepp Blatter's fears justified? Could it end up as 'beach football' or a 'five-a-side competition'?

Lionel Messi was showing all his skills on the practice pitch in China. The close ball control, the pace, the deadly finishing... and the Latin smile. The right-sided forward was widely regarded as one of the world's best footballers. And still only twenty-one. Argentinian coach, Sergio Batista, looked on admiringly. He was preparing his side for Argentina's opening match in the 2008 Beijing Olympics in defence of their soccer gold medal won in Athens – won with a goal from Carlos Tevez in a 1-0 final victory over Paraguay. Argentina naturally wanted to select their best team. But would Messi be available for Beijing ?

It was club versus country. A club competition versus the Olympics.

Or would he be in Barcelona? FC Barcelona president, Joan

Laporta, was unhappy. Barcelona paid Messi's substantial wages. They were a club with the highest ambitions. They faced an important European Champions League third round qualifying match against Wisla Krakow during the same period. They wanted Messi for Barcelona.

It was club versus country – another country. A club competition versus the Olympics. An individual's desire to represent his country versus his duty to his club. And Messi was in the middle.

Barcelona had spotted early the talent of Messi as a young player with River Plate in Argentina. He had been diagnosed with a growth hormone deficiency. Barcelona signed him and offered to pay his medical bills if he emigrated to Spain. His family moved with him and Messi became a hero at the Nou Camp. His reputation grew worldwide. He was voted World Soccer Young Player of the Year for both 2006 and 2007.

His international start for Argentina in 2005, in a friendly against Hungary, was unusually memorable ... and a record. He came on as a substitute in the sixty-third minute. His debut lasted forty seconds. He was sent off for elbowing a defender who tugged his shirt! He became, though, the youngest player to represent Argentina in the World Cup and soon a talisman figure for his national side. The latest 'new Maradona'.

Perhaps at the heart of the dispute was the status of football in the Olympics. Was it a 'real' Olympic sport? Dropped initially from the Olympics after FIFA launched the World Cup in Uruguay in 1930 but re-instated in 1936, an uneasy reputation in the soccer world existed for the tournament even after professionals were admitted for the 1984 Los Angeles Games. (Great Britain, incidentally, had ceased to enter after 1972.)

FIFA were anxious that the Olympics should not rival their own World Cup. That was 'the real one'. After 1984, the 'strong' nations were initially only allowed to pick players who had not played in the World Cup. Teams became relatively young. Since 1992, the rule instead has been that players in the men's soccer competition at the Olympics must be aged under-23 – with three 'over-age' players being allowed. There was no special effort to adjust football's calendar in Olympic year. The Beijing Olympics clashed with the start of the European club season.

Two other European clubs, Germany's FC Schalke and SV Werder

Bremen, took a similar stance in relation to the release of their young Brazilian stars, Rafinha and Diego. This had developed into a major issue. Were the clubs obliged to release their under-23 players? They said 'no'. The dispute went to FIFA's Players' Status Committee and on 30th July a judge said 'yes'. Barcelona and the two German clubs promptly appealed to the Court of Arbitration for Sport (CAS).

CAS was readying itself for the Beijing Olympics, and busy. Many of the disputes related to a country's right to select particular individuals. Could Germany nominate Ranier Schuettler for the men's singles tennis even though, at the relevant time, he was ranked below other players not selected? (Answer, said CAS, was 'yes'.) Could the Philippines nominate Hawaiian-born swimmer Christel Simms, also a US national, although it was not clear that the nationality rules had been fully satisfied. (Again CAS said 'yes'.) Could swimmer Octavian Gutu represent Moldova having previously represented Romania ? (No.) And, most controversial of all, could Argentina insist on Barcelona releasing Messi to play in the Olympics?

Could Argentina insist on Barcelona releasing Messi to play in the Olympics?

A CAS panel met urgently in Zurich on 5th August, two days before Argentina's opening match against the Ivory Coast. CAS was in an interesting position. Set up and still in part funded by the IOC, CAS had nevertheless long proved its independence as an arbitral body. But would the panel support the Olympic movement on this one ? Would it support FIFA and the Argentina FA and require the player's release ?

For: The Olympics were an ambition for most players and athletes. Messi wanted to play for Argentina. The established custom, well-understood by the leading clubs, was that top under-23 players would be released. It was only right and fair, to the player and the country, to support the Olympic movement.
Against: There was no legal commitment. The Olympics were not part of the official FIFA 'calendar' for this purpose. Messi was a Barcelona employee. They paid his substantial wages. They ran the risk of injury to a valuable player. It was not the World Cup. Barcelona could suffer in an important competition if he was not available for their European Champions League qualifier.

CAS said 'no'. Barcelona were not bound to release Messi. The German clubs, Schalke and Werder Bremen, were not bound to release Rafinha and Diego. FIFA's position was based on custom not law. The Olympics were not included in FIFA's Co-ordinated Match Calendar and there was no specific decision establishing the obligation to release players under-23.

> *The requirements to justify a legal obligation of the clubs to release their players on the basis of customary law are not met.*

Barcelona were entitled to re-call Messi. Argentina could not insist on him playing.

CAS added hopefully:

> *In view of FIFA's recommendation made to clubs to release their players as well as the Olympic spirit, the CAS call upon the good will and good sense of FIFA and the clubs to find a reasonable solution with regard to players who wish to represent their country in the Olympics.*

FIFA were 'surprised and disappointed'. Indeed, president Sepp Blatter was furious. 'This could have a snowballing effect. Other players could now be withdrawn from the tournament. We will then simply not have an Olympic tournament. We could of course revert to a beach football or five-a-side competition.'

'We could of course revert to a beach football or five-a-side competition'

Barcelona president, Joan Laporta, was satisfied. '[T]he tribunal... have accepted the position of Barcelona. We had the right to decide whether to release the player to the Argentina national team. We have now set a precedent which is very important to the football clubs.'

What would happen with Messi? In less than twenty-four hours, Argentina would be playing the Ivory Coast. Would they defy Barcelona and CAS ? Would they reach a compromise with the club? Or would they concede ? No word from Barcelona. Match day arrived in Shanghai. The teams were announced... and huge cheers went up around the ground, both from the small band of Argentinian supporters and the many thousands of Chinese fans. Messi was playing.

Barcelona had relented. They had won the legal battle – but taken a pragmatic view in the end. Their relationship with Messi was vital. Barcelona's sporting director commented: 'It's the best decision as, although with Leo we're a better side, these are exceptional circumstances. We want the player to be happy and his happiness is there for all to see.'

Importantly, Barcelona had also done a deal. The Argentina FA had agreed to fund an insurance plan, no doubt an expensive one, to pay substantial compensation in the event of an injury to Messi during the Games. The twenty-one-year-old would also be exempt from certain friendly matches involving Argentina, allowing him to remain in Spain with the Barcelona squad. Schalke and Werder Bremen made similar insurance deals in respect of their players. The clubs had extracted their price.

There will be repercussions flowing from this decision. FIFA will review their regulations. But the leading clubs now recognise their negotiating strength in relation to the Olympics. There are clear analogies with the row (see later in this book) between the leading European clubs wanting compensation from FIFA and UEFA for players released for international duty.

Back to the football. After forty-three minutes against the Ivory Coast, Argentina took the lead with a neatly clipped left-foot finish ... from Lionel Messi. The South Americans went on to retain their Olympic title with a gold-winning 1-0 final victory over Nigeria. The goal came from Angel di Mario after a well-timed through ball from ... Lionel Messi.

Barcelona duly won their Champions League qualifying tie against Wisla Krakow.

Who won in this dispute in the end? Club, country, the Olympics? More consequences, one suspects, to flow from this issue before the London Games in 2012.

CHAPTER NINE

SEX, DISCRIMINATION AND PARTICIPATION

An athlete or player cannot win unless he or she can participate in the competition. Several of the most significant legal challenges in sport have concerned the right of a particular individual to play in a sport or to compete in an event.

It is fascinating how many of the cases have reflected changing attitudes or sensibilities in society at large as the courts have encountered challenges for alleged discrimination on the basis of gender, youth, disability or race.

Groundbreaking cases involve transsexual tennis player Renée Richards, the fight of Florence Nagle to become Britain's first female holder of a horseracing trainer's licence, Belinda Petty's wish to referee in an all male judo competition, Jane Couch's campaign for a professional boxing licence in Britain, Theresa Bennett's wish to play junior football with similarly aged boys, Casey Martin's battle to be permitted to use a golf cart in professional competition and the challenge of disabled athlete, 'the blade runner', Oscar Pistorius. We also follow Darrell Hair's claim for racial discrimination when dropped from the elite cricket umpiring panel.

---

77 FLORENCE NAGLE AND THE JOCKEY CLUB – A WOMAN'S FIGHT FOR A TRAINER'S LICENCE

Florence Nagle wanted a licence to be a racehorse trainer. Was it unlawful for the Jockey Club to deny her a licence because of a 'men only' policy?

The cause of women in sport has, as far as the courts have been concerned, had no stronger champion than Florence Nagle.

Licences to train horses for racing in Great Britain were issued by the Jockey Club. No horse could race in meetings under their auspices unless trained by a licensed trainer. No trainer's licence had previously been issued to a woman. Florence Nagle owned and ran a racing stable at Westerlands, near Petworth in Sussex. She had extensive knowledge and experience of racehorses and, by 1966, she had trained them for more than thirty-five years. It was in her blood. How were Florence Nagle's stables licensed for her horses to run? The Jockey Club had issued a licence to her 'head lad'.

She was a proud and determined woman. Seventy-year-old Florence Nagle now sought a trainer's licence in her own right. It was refused. The Jockey Club said simply that it was a private institution and had complete discretion to decide to whom it issued a licence. Nagle decided to take on the Jockey Club, alleging that the decision was based on sex discrimination and was an unlawful restraint of trade. She took the claim to the High Court. The Jockey Club tried to stop the claim.

Seventy-year-old Florence Nagle now sought a trainer's licence in her own right.

Should the Jockey Club's decision be declared invalid as an unlawful restraint of trade contrary to public policy?

For: The Jockey Club's decisions affected people's livelihoods. It must act reasonably in the issue of licences. Its general practice, clearly based on sex discrimination, was to refuse to grant a trainer's licence to a woman in any circumstances. There was no objection on the grounds of Nagle's capacity

and fitness as a trainer. The issue of a licence to her 'head lad' was an artificial arrangement. Nagle was not applying for membership of a club but for a licence to train. The Jockey Club's practice was contrary to public policy and an unlawful restraint of trade. It should be declared invalid.
Against: The Jockey Club was a private organisation. There was no contract or obligation to issue a licence. The sex discrimination legislation (as then existing) did not apply to the issue of licences by the Jockey Club. It was well established that a private club had complete discretion to decide whom to admit as a member. The discretion was absolute and could only be challenged for bad faith. It was for the Jockey Club to decide its own policy. The courts were not entitled to interfere.

Florence Nagle won her battle. This was despite losing in the first round. On appeal, the Court of Appeal allowed her claim to go ahead.

It was a landmark case. Although there were no applicable sex discrimination laws in force at that time, the court said that the general practice of the Jockey Club in refusing a trainer's licence to a woman was contrary to public policy and an unlawful restraint of trade. The Jockey Club had adopted, in effect, an unwritten rule. Lord Denning, one of the country's leading and most reforming judges, said:

' ... arbitrary and entirely out of touch with the present state of society in Great Britain.'

> *... this unwritten rule may well be said to be arbitrary and capricious ... It is not as if the training of horses could be regarded as an unsuitable occupation for a woman ... We are considering an association which exercises a virtual monopoly in an important field of human activity.*

Lord Justice Danckwerts added:

> *Her application is not considered [by the Jockey Club] simply because she is a woman. That is arbitrary and entirely out of touch with the present state of society in Great Britain.*

The decision seems straightforward today but it was revolutionary at the time. Note that Florence Nagle even lost when the issue first came to the courts. It was only her perseverance and determination in pressing the case, and appealing, which won this famous victory. The decision was a clear warning that, even though sporting governing bodies may be private bodies, they affect peoples' livelihoods by making decisions such as whether or not to issue a licence to a particular individual. Decisions cannot be taken arbitrarily.

The Jockey Club capitulated. A trainer's licence was issued to Florence Nagle. In 1969, she became the first woman trainer in Britain to saddle a winner under the rules of racing.

The gates had opened for the cause of equality of women in sport – but not fully open. The Jockey Club continued to resist calls for women to be allowed to ride as jockeys in races until 1972. The first woman to ride a winner in Britain was Meriel Tufnell on *Scorched Earth* at Kempton. It was eleven years after Florence Nagle's victory, 1977, before women were admitted as members of the Jockey Club.

The first woman to ride a winner in Britain was Meriel Tufnell.

Subsequent female horseracing trainers of distinction have included Jenny Pitman (trainer of Grand National winners, *Corbiere* in 1983 and *Royal Athlete* in 1995), Jessica Harrington, Auriol Sinclair, Mercy Rimell and Henrietta Knight (trainer of *Best Mate* which won three consecutive Cheltenham Gold Cups).

Florence Nagle is a name which should feature strongly in the history of women in sport.

---

78 RENÉE RICHARDS – PLAYING IN THE WOMEN'S SINGLES AT THE US OPEN

Renée Richards had undergone gender change surgery to become a woman. Should she be permitted to play in the women's singles at the US Open?

Renée Richards was a fine tennis player. She wanted to play in the women's singles event in the 1976 US Open at Forest Hills in New York. Her standard was good enough. The United States Tennis Association (USTA) denied her entry. The reason? She was born a male, Richard Raskind.

Richard Raskind went to Yale University and captained the men's tennis team there in 1954. After Yale, he went to medical school and then served in the Navy. He pursued a career as an eye surgeon. He married and fathered one son. He continued to play amateur tennis and, in 1974, was ranked thirteenth in the US men's 35-and-over division. Nevertheless, he had for many years a troubled sexual identity and was increasingly uncomfortable, psychologically, as a male. In the mid-1960s, he travelled Europe dressed as a woman, intending to have sex reassignment surgery. Finally, in early 1975 at the age of forty, he did go ahead and had successful sex reassignment surgery.

She was denied entry. She was a transsexual.

As Renée Richards, she re-established her ophthalmology practice in California and started playing tennis seriously again. She played in a few local amateur tournaments. Indeed, she played some before her gender change was discovered. It was after a prestigious amateur tournament at La Jolla, California, which she entered under the name of Renée Clark, and won, that her past became public knowledge following a local media 'exposé '.

Inevitably, the question arose. What should the tennis authorities do? For the next year or so, Renée Richards played various US tennis tournaments. Some tournaments accepted her entry with knowledge of her transsexual background and indeed invited her. Some refused her entry. At one tournament, twenty-five women players withdrew in protest, claiming that she still maintained the muscular advantages of a male and genetically remained a male. The issue came to a crunch with her wish to play in the 1976 US Open.

The International Tennis Federation (ITF), when considering the issue of transexuality for events under its jurisdiction, decided to invoke sex chromatin tests which the International Olympic Committee had adopted in 1968 to test gender eligibility for the Olympic Games. The Barrbody test analysed membrane cells, taken by a smear test inside the mouth, for the presence of 'female' genes. The test was not without its critics. The USTA decided to require the same eligibility for entry into the women's events at the US Open.

Prior to 1975, no sex chromatin test had ever been asked of any competitor in the history of the US Open nor had Richards been requested to undertake any such test for any event sanctioned in the USA. Although she had once passed the test, she had failed it (secretly) at two tournaments in Europe. She knew it was unlikely she would satisfy the test for the US Open. She considered that it was being introduced specifically in order to exclude her.

Richards questioned the validity of verifying gender through a genes test and insisted that 'bodily, psychologically and sexually' she was female. She had been issued official papers such as a passport and a certificate to practice medicine. 'In the eyes of the law, I am female.' She said: 'It's a human rights issue. I want to show that someone who has a different lifestyle or medical condition has a right to stand up for what they are.'

She rejected the theory that 'the floodgates would be opened and through them would come tumbling an endless stream of made-over Neanderthals who would brutalise Chris Evert and Evonne Goolagong'.

'How hungry for tennis success must you be to have your penis chopped off in pursuit of it?' This was 'sheer nonsense'. She had the support of Billie Jean King and many other leading players.

Richards spent a year battling in the courts. She brought a legal claim against the USTA to prevent them relying on a sex chromatin test for determining whether or not she was female and to require the USTA to permit her entry. The primary legal basis of her claim was that the test breached the anti-discriminatory code which was part of the equal opportunities legislation in the State of New York.

It was a unique and challenging case. It came before the New York Supreme Court. Should she succeed?

For: Richards had undergone medically approved sex reassignment surgery. This was not a case of fraud. Her passport and other official documents legally recognised her as a woman. The sex chromatin test was introduced by the US tennis authorities solely in order to exclude Richards. It had never been required as a condition of entry previously or required of any other players. It was discriminatory. **Against:** Although a difficult issue, in fairness to all female competitors, it was reasonable for the US Open to apply the same sex chromatin test as applied to events under the jurisdiction of the International Olympic Committee.

After hearing conflicting medical and tennis evidence, the New York Supreme Court upheld Renée Richard's claim.

The court decided that the requirement for her to pass the sex chromatin test in order to be eligible to participate in the tournament was 'grossly unfair, discriminatory and inequitable' and violated Richards' rights under the human rights law of New York.

Renée Richards was free to play as a woman in the US Open.

When sex testing was first introduced by the IOC in 1968, several Eastern bloc shot putters and discus throwers suddenly disappeared from women's sport. The only athlete known to have failed a femininity test at the Olympics is Ewa Kłobukowska, a Polish sprinter, in Tokyo in 1964.

The issue of transexualism has led to continued medical and legal attention. The Barrbody test was actually phased out by the IOC during the late 1970s in favour of different and technically preferable tests. In the UK, specific legislation now governs the position, the Gender Recognition Act 2004. This sets out medical criteria and evidence required to support certification of a 'new' gender which, once certified, must be recognised. Discrimination in sport is then only permitted if the sport is a 'gender-affected sport' – which means one where the physical strength, stamina or physique of average person[s] of one gender would put them at a disadvantage to average person[s] of the other gender and the prohibition or restriction is 'necessary to secure fair competition or the safety of competitors'. That would, almost certainly, include tennis.

Renée Richards did play in the 1977 US Open. She lost 6-1 6-4 in the first round to the third seed, Britain's Virginia Wade. Partnered by Betty Ann Stuart, she however reached the final of the ladies' doubles where they lost to Pam Shriver and a youthful Martina Navratilova.

Renée Richards played in further US Opens until 1981 with moderate success, reaching the quarter-finals of the singles in 1978 and, in 1979, winning the US Open thirty-five-and-over singles event. In 1981 Richards retired from professional tennis and returned to her other profession, ophthalmic surgery.

Perhaps fortunately for the British tennis authorities, when Renée Richards came to Wimbledon it was not as a player but during a successful two-year stint as coach and adviser to the future Wimbledon champion, Martina Navratilova – climaxed by Navratilova's dramatic three set victory over Chris Evert-Lloyd in the 1982 Wimbledon final.

---

79 BELINDA PETTY – THE FIGHT TO REFEREE A MEN'S COMPETITION

Belinda Petty wanted to be a full judo referee. Why couldn't she referee a men's competition at senior level?

A female referee of a men's competition? It was a case which could, if it succeeded, break through another barrier of male-dominated sporting practices. But would it?

By 1977, Belinda Petty had practised judo for nearly twenty years. She was a full member of the Budokwai and had the qualification known as a Second Dan. In 1974 she obtained the British Judo Association's club coach award. She had been employed as a part-time judo instructor at various schools and clubs. She had also qualified as a judo referee, passing the national referee examination in 1976. The certificate did not differentiate between men's competitions and women's competitions. She had refereed competitions at club and area levels including men's competitions.

She was proud of her qualifications. They assisted her job as an instructor. In October 1977 she was a referee in the national All England Men's Competition. Then, she suffered a blow to her aspirations. The president of the Judo Association intervened and stated that she should not have refereed in a men's national competition. It was not the Association's policy. Since then, she had never again been selected to referee in men's competitions at national level. The Association believed that 'it was not in the interests of the sport and not in the interests of women that they should referee male events'.

The president of the Judo Association intervened ... she could not referee in men's national competitions. It was not the Association's policy.

Belinda Petty was very upset. She was determined. She decided to fight the policy, alleging sex discrimination. The Sex Discrimination Act 1975 had by then been passed – but the Act exempted discrimination in sport 'where the physical strength, stamina or physique of the average woman puts her at a disadvantage to the average man' and the discrimination 'relates to the participation of a person as a competitor' in a sporting event. The scope of this so-called 'sporting exemption' was now in question.

Belinda Petty took her case against the Judo Association to an industrial tribunal in London where she won. The Judo Association appealed to the Employment Appeal Tribunal.

Should Belinda Petty be permitted to referee in men's national judo competitions? Did the Judo Association's policy amount to unlawful discrimination? Florence Nagle had won her case as a female trainer. Could Belinda Petty now achieve a similar result as a referee?

For: The policy of not selecting women to referee in national men's competitions was clearly discriminatory. Belinda Petty had plenty of experience and full qualifications. The sporting exemption in the 1975 Act only applied to discrimination relating to participation as a competitor, not as a referee. The national referee's qualification did not distinguish between men's and women's events. There were no physical reasons justifying the discrimination. The

Judo Association's policy should be declared unlawful. **Against:** The Judo Association should be free to decide, in its view, the best policy for selection of referees for national events. Refereeing fell within the sporting exemption since the role of referees related, in a general sense, to participation in competition. Discrimination was justified since women would not have the necessary physical or vocal strength, if necessary, to break apart two hefty male combatants in such an event. The policy was reasonable and consistent with the exemption in the 1975 Act.

Belinda Petty won her case.

The Employment Appeal Tribunal decided that the sporting exemption in the 1975 Act only applied to the issue of who could, or could not, take part in the contest as a competitor. This did not extend to refereeing. A referee was not a competitor. 'We cannot see how provisions as to referees relate to the 'participation' of the competitors in the contest.' said the tribunal. Belinda Petty's qualifications for selection as a referee should be considered by the Judo Association on their merits. A general policy of excluding women from refereeing in senior men's competitions was unlawful.

The case was another significant step forward for women in sport. Any practice of excluding women from refereeing in sport, even in an all male competition, was blown away.

Even the sight of a female assistant referee (no longer called a linesman) at football matches, and indeed as principal referee, has now become frequent – if not popular with all football managers. Wendy Toms became, on 27th August 1997, the first woman to officiate in the Premier League – as an assistant referee in a match between Arsenal and Newcastle. She was not daunted. Before refereeing earlier in a Championship match, she was reported as saying: 'If the players want to make it hard for me, I am happy to make it twice as hard for them.'

---

80 THERESA BENNETT – WHY CAN'T I PLAY WITH THE BOYS?

Theresa Bennett was an eleven-year-old girl who loved playing football. She wanted to play with the boys in a local league. She was prevented. Was this sex discrimination?

Theresa Bennett was a good young footballer and played with the boys at school. She wanted to play more and join a boys' team which played in a local league run by the Nottinghamshire FA. They said 'no'. It was 1978. Why could she not play in the same team as boys of her own age?

The rules of the regional Nottinghamshire FA and the national FA did not permit mixed teams. They stated in effect that, except for matches in a playing season in age groups up to the age of ten, 'players in a match must be of the same gender'. Theresa Bennett, or those acting on her behalf, challenged this rule. She was good enough to play in the 'boys' team. This was sex discrimination. Her case was supported by the Equal Opportunities Commission.

The FA claimed that the rule was there for the safety of women and was justified under the Sex Discrimination Act which had a 'sporting exemption'. This permitted single sex competitions 'where the physical strength, stamina or physique of the average woman puts her at a disadvantage to the average man'. The FA wanted to encourage girls and women to play football but age eleven was an appropriate cut-off point for mixed football.

Should Theresa Bennett succeed and be able to play in a mixed team at age eleven in the local league?

For: The physical differences, in terms of strength and stamina, between girls and boys at that age were not so great as differences between individuals of the same sex. To prevent girls aged eleven playing with boys in a mixed team was discrimination and not the intention or policy of the Act.
Against: The rules were reasonable for the safety of girls and women. The 'sporting exemption' in the Act applied. The test was not based on individual attributes but whether

the 'average woman' would be at a physical disadvantage compared with an 'average man' when playing football and the answer was 'yes'. The rules were permitted by the Act.

The case went first to the county court. Evidence was given of Theresa Bennett's skill and prowess as a young footballer. One witness said that 'she ran rings round the boys'. Another witness recalled that she 'was a vicious tackler and once tackled a fifteen-year-old so hard he had to be supported and taken from the field'. She won her case there but the FA appealed.

Theresa Bennett lost in the Court of Appeal. Despite the strong evidence about Bennett's individual position, the court decided that discrimination under the Act was permitted where 'the average woman' was at a disadvantage in the particular sport compared with 'the average man'. An average woman was, in the opinion of the court, at a disadvantage to the average man in football because she has not got the physique to stand up to 'the rigours of mixed football'. And, importantly, 'woman' for this purpose should be interpreted as a woman of any age – and not by reference alone to girls aged eleven. One judge commented: 'We do not enquire about the ages of ladies.'

The court (which included Lord Denning, one of the country's most reforming judges) had sympathy for Theresa Bennett – but allowing her to play would be 'stretching the bounds of judicial creativity beyond breaking point'. No further appeal was allowed. So, she lost her case.

'We do not enquire about the ages of ladies.'

In Australia, the High Court of Victoria recently took a more robust view in the case of Australian Rules Football – admittedly on slightly different legislative wording. The court decided that mixed teams could not be excluded at under-14 level (but could at the under-15 level). The Australian court was persuaded by strong evidence that, at the earlier age, relative physical differences between the sexes in terms of strength and stamina were not sufficiently great – and less than differences within each gender.

Perhaps Theresa Bennett did have some partial success in that the cut-off point for mixed football was subsequently raised by one year.

Nearly thirty years later, she also had a fine successor and campaigner in ten-year-old Minnie Cruttwell. Minnie was a key member of the Balham Blazers in south London. She wanted to continue to play for them when her age group included twelve-year-olds. 'Girls are just as good as boys and if you've been with a team for a long time, you know them well and you don't want to have to make new friends.' She wrote to Tessa Jowell, Secretary of State for Culture, Media and Sport, who went to see them play. 'Women's football is England's fastest-growing sport and I'm concerned that we are the only country in Europe who have a blanket ban in place for mixed football at this age level.'

The result? In May 2007 the FA announced that it was reconsidering its age limit for mixed sex teams and might raise the level to under-14s. In the meantime, there would be a one year pilot in specified leagues to see how older mixed sides work before the FA decided on a long-term policy. One of these allowed Minnie to continue to play for the Balham Blazers. Her father said: 'Minnie is the toughest tackler. I am glad the FA has decided to rethink.'

---

81 JANE COUCH – THE 'FLEETWOOD ASSASSIN' FIGHTS FOR A UK BOXING LICENCE

Are there sports or events in which women should not participate? Is boxing one of them?

Jane Couch was born in Fleetwood, England in 1968. She later became known as 'the Fleetwood Assassin'. Expelled from her Blackpool school as a teenager, she lived what she later described as a 'life of booze, drugs and street fighting' until she was aged twenty-six. Then she saw a TV documentary about women's boxing in the USA. She decided she could do that. 'It all looked so easy and feeble compared with some of the street fights I had been in.'

She saw a TV documentary about women's boxing in the USA. She could do that.

Her first official fight was against a female policewoman. Couch knocked her out in the second round. 'It was brilliant to flatten one and get paid for it.' She burst on to the world professional boxing scene in May 1996 when she travelled to Copenhagen and outpointed French kick boxing star Sandra Geiger over ten rounds to win the Women's International Boxing Federation (WIBF) welterweight title. The fight attracted a peak TV audience across Europe of 3.5 million viewers. Geiger reportedly spent three days in hospital recovering after the fight with a broken nose and cracked ribs. Couch successfully defended her title in New Orleans in March 1997.

All her professional fights had been abroad. By 1998, Jane Couch, who trained at a gym near Bristol with her manager, Tex Woodward, wanted the opportunity to box professionally in Britain. She sought the additional income which she could earn from fights held in her home country. It was her livelihood. The British Boxing Board of Control (BBBC) refused to give a licence to Couch, or any other female boxer, to box in Britain. It caused many emotions. The BBBC justified their policy on the grounds that, if permitted to box professionally, women were more likely to suffer life-threatening blows to head and breasts and that premenstrual tension would make a female more liable to injury. One British promoter minced no words and put it another way: 'The only reason for women to be in the ring is as ring card girls.'

Couch decided to fight her cause with the BBBC. She alleged unlawful sex discrimination. She had the strong backing of the Equal Opportunities Commission. She took the BBBC to an industrial tribunal.

Was the policy of the British Boxing Board of Control, in refusing to award boxing licences to women, unlawful sex discrimination? Should Jane Couch be entitled to box professionally in Britain?

For: The sex discrimination laws only justified discrimination in circumstances where men would be competing against women. The 'sporting exception' was not relevant to single-sex competition. The BBBC's refusal to sanction female boxing in the UK was costing Couch money in lost earnings. Not to issue licences to women for boxing amounted simply to unlawful sex discrimination. **Against:** The refusal by the BBBC to award a licence was based on objective and justifiable grounds. The risks of injury for women in boxing were greater than for men. There was medical evidence that women were potentially accident-prone and unstable emotionally when suffering from pre-menstrual tension. Professional boxing was inappropriate for women.

Jane Couch won another victory.

The industrial tribunal in Croydon, after a two day hearing, upheld her argument. The policy of the British Boxing Board of Control, in refusing to award any licences to women to box in Britain, amounted to unlawful sex discrimination. The 'sporting exception' did not apply.

The policy of the British Boxing Board of Control amounted to unlawful sex discrimination.

Jane Couch received her licence. She made British boxing history at Caesar's Palace Casino in Streatham, London on 25th November 1998 when she fought eighteen-year-old Simona Lukic from Germany in the first licensed professional women's fight in Britain. Couch won by a technical knockout when the referee stopped the contest in the second round.

In February 1999, at the Thornaby Pavilion in Teeside, she took part in the first female title bout in Britain to be sanctioned by the BBBC. Jane successfully defended her WIBF welterweight title with a unanimous ten-round decision over European champion, Marischa Sjauw of Holland. Later in 1999, at the David Lloyd Tennis Centre in Raynes Park, London, Jane won the vacant WBF women's lightweight title with a ten-round decision over Sharon Anyos of Australia.

Jane Couch carried on her personal fight with the BBBC in 2001 when she sought a licence to fight an exhibition bout at Wembley with one of her male sparring partners. This was refused.

In 2007, Jane Couch was awarded the MBE in the Queen's Birthday Honours. 'I've been all over the world boxing in some of the biggest shows in front of millions of people and this is the biggest shock ever.'

---

82 CASEY MARTIN – A GOLF CART AND THE QUESTION: WHAT IS GOLF?

Casey Martin suffered from a blood disorder. He needed a golf cart to play. Could he be denied a place on the US PGA Tour?

Casey Martin holed his putt for a bogey on the 18th hole in the final round of the Nike Tour Championship. It was a disappointing 78 and he was slipping from his overnight position on the leaderboard. He waited nervously as other players finished. Would he remain in the top fifteen of the money list on the Nike Tour and qualify for the main 2000 US PGA Tour?

Yes. PGA Commissioner, Tim Finchem, presented Martin with his tour card, shook the golfer's hand and patted him on the back. But would he be allowed to play on the US PGA Tour in the same way as he was now competing – using a motorised golf cart? That would depend, finally, on the verdict of the US Supreme Court.

Martin, born in Eugene, Oregon, was educated at Stanford University where he was briefly a team-mate of Tiger Woods. A promising golfer, he turned professional in 1995. His ambition was to play on the US PGA Tour. But he suffered from a birth defect in his left leg, a circulatory problem known as Klippel-Trenauny-Weber syndrome. This resulted in bleeding from blood vessels and difficulty in walking. He wore a special pressure stocking on his leg so that he could stand and walk. The constant tightness of the stocking had weakened his leg muscles. He could not walk the distances involved in PGA Tour events. He needed a golf cart between shots. He argued that he was entitled to a golf cart by reason of the disability legislation in the USA, the Americans with Disabilities Act. 'I just want to be given the chance to play.'

Would he be allowed to play on the US PGA Tour with a golf cart?

The US PGA said 'no'. They maintained that use of a cart would give him an unfair advantage and take away a fundamental aspect of the athleticism and stamina involved in top flight tournament golf. Many top golfers agreed. Jack Nicklaus was among those who took issue with the opinion that walking was not a fundamental part of the sport. 'I think we ought to take them all out and play golf. I think they'd change their minds. I promise you, it's fundamental.'

Martin filed a lawsuit in 1977 challenging the US PGA Tour's decision and obtained a ruling from a US magistrate that a golf course during a tournament was indeed a 'place of public accommodation' within the US disability legislation. The US PGA agreed that Martin could use his cart for the time being during the appeals process until the issue was finally decided. He continued to do so on the secondary Nike Tour.

In 1998, Martin won a Nike Tour event, the Lakeside Classic. He also achieved a career highlight that year by qualifying for and finishing twenty-third at the US Open at the Olympic Club in San Francisco, briefly contending for the lead before falling back. He was the first player to use a cart in US Open history. Now, in 1999, he had qualified and was ready for the full US PGA Tour for the 2000 season.

In January 2000, at Indian Wells Country Club in the Bob Hope Chrysler Classic, twenty-seven-year-old Casey Martin teed off as a tour 'rookie' and, the first time for a professional golfer on the US PGA Tour, went to his golf cart – an EZGO. He finished with a four under par 68. The marshalls carefully guarded his golf cart during the round.

But could he continue? The appeals process finally reached the US Supreme Court. In May 2001, the US Supreme Court would decide whether he could compete, using a golf cart between shots, in US PGA Tour events. Could he overcome the US PGA's objections?

For: A golf course during a tournament was a place of public accommodation covered by the US disability legislation. Martin was disabled and entitled to a reasonable accommodation – which would include a cart. He didn't want a special advantage, just a chance to ride to the tee. The cart did not give any advantage in golfing terms; if anything, it disturbed his rhythm.
Against: It gave Martin an unfair advantage over everyone else who must walk. A golf cart was an 'outside agency'. It violated the spirit of competition. It took away a fundamental aspect of athleticism and stamina that walking brings to top-flight tournament golf. The area inside the ropes was no different from a playing field in any other professional sport. The disability legislation was not designed to apply to

competitions in professional sporting events. In elite athletics, certain rules must apply equally to everyone.

One of the nine judges of the US Supreme Court (yes, nine judges to decide this issue), Justice Antonin Scalia, summed up the question before the court – perhaps with 'tongue in cheek' humour – in these polemic terms:

> *It has been rendered the solemn duty of the Supreme Court of the United States ... to decide What Is golf. I am sure that the Framers of the Constitution, aware of the 1457 edict of King James II of Scotland prohibiting golf because it interfered with the practice of archery, fully expected that sooner or later the paths of golf and government, the law and the links, would once again cross, and that judges of this august Court would some day have to wrestle with that age-old jurisprudential question, for which their years of study in the law have so well prepared them: Is someone riding around a golf course from shot to shot really a golfer?*

By a 7-2 majority, the US Supreme Court decided in Casey Martin's favour.

A golf course for a US PGA Tour event was indeed a 'public' place for the purposes of the US disability legislation. It was reasonable for Martin to use a golf cart in such a 'public' place. Justice Stevens commented: 'The purpose of the walking rule is ... not compromised in the slightest by allowing Martin to use a cart.' Accommodating Martin with a golf cart would not fundamentally change the game, said the court. 'What it can be said to do, on the other hand, is to allow Martin the chance to qualify for and compete in the ... events [the PGA Tour] offers to those members of the public who have the skill and the desire to enter.'

As for Casey Martin, he could only finish 179th on the money list in the 2000 season and failed to keep his elite level US PGA Tour card through his earnings. In the qualifying school for the following year, he narrowly failed to keep his spot (finishing tied for 37th when only the top 35 qualified) relegating him to the Nike Tour again. Playing only a limited number of events, he failed in subsequent years to regain his US PGA Tour card.

In May 2006, he decided to retire from professional tournament golf and was named coach of the University of Oregon's men's golf team in his hometown of Eugene.

---

83 DARRELL HAIR – RACIAL DISCRIMINATION AND A CRICKET UMPIRE

Darrell Hair was one of two umpires who decided that Pakistan had forfeited a Test match. He was later disciplined but not his co-umpire. Was it racial discrimination against him?

Darrell Hair was a no-nonsense, straight-talking Australian. He was an international cricket umpire. He called it as he saw it. Did he call it once too often?

Born in New South Wales, Hair was a useful right-arm fast-medium club bowler in Sydney grade cricket until a knee injury cut short his playing career. He became a Test match umpire in 1991 and was appointed to the ICC elite umpire panel in 2002 when the International Cricket Council (ICC) introduced a policy that both umpires should come from nations not participating in the match.

Hair, a big man with a commanding presence, was not short of self-belief in his umpiring. This was evident at the Melbourne Cricket Ground in December 1995 when Australia were playing Sri Lanka. Hair – unusually, remarked *Wisden*, from the bowler's end – called Muttiah Muralitharan seven times in three overs for throwing. This, accompanied by other incidents and decisions involving Asian subcontinent nations, meant that he was always viewed with suspicion – and more – by India, Pakistan and Sri Lanka. No one was prepared, though, for the events of the fourth Test between England and Pakistan at the Oval in August 2006.

Hair was not short of self-belief in his umpiring.

Pakistan, behind two-nil in the series, were in a strong position with a first innings lead of 331 runs. Play began quietly on the fourth day with England on 78 for 1. After the dismissal of Alistair Cook by Umar Gul in the fifty-second over of the England innings with a 'reverse swing' delivery, the umpires inspected the ball in customary fashion. Play continued.

At the end of the fifty-sixth over, just four overs later, Hair again inspected the ball and judged that, showing various scratches, it had been altered unfairly by human intervention – it had been tampered with. He reported this to fellow umpire, West Indian Billy Doctrove. Hair wanted the ball changed. Doctrove agreed although his initial preference had been to play on and try to identify the person responsible. A box of replacement balls was brought on. Hair signalled to the scorers that five penalty runs should be added to the England score.

Play continued in the afternoon until bad light intervened and tea was taken. The umpires decided to resume play at 4.45 p.m. They returned to the field of play. But the Pakistan team did not. Indignation had turned to anger. The team, led by captain Inzamam-ul-Haq, decided to protest. The decision on ball-tampering was an allegation of cheating. It was, they considered, a direct and unfair challenge to their honour. The umpires left the field of play, leaving the bails intact. They went to see the Pakistan team in their dressing room. The exact verbal exchange is in dispute. The umpires stated that they were returning to the field of play – but it is not clear that any warning was given that the match could be forfeited.

Hair and Doctrove walked out again on to the pitch at 4.53 p.m., along with the England batsmen and to the cheers of the bemused crowd. The Pakistan team did not follow. Wicketkeeper, Kamran Akmal, was seen on the balcony taking his gloves off and reading a paper. At about 4.56 p.m., the umpires symbolically removed the bails and awarded the match to England. They were applying Law 21 which, in effect, stated that a match shall be lost by a side which in the opinion of the umpires refuses to play.

Hair symbolically removed the bails and the umpires awarded the match to England.

Chaos ensued. The 23,000 crowd jeered, with no idea of what was going on. Had the match really been forfeited? Crisis meetings took place involving senior cricket and match officials. In a surprising twist, the covers were seen coming off the pitch. The Pakistani team had apparently indicated, after their initial protest, that they would now take the field. They did indeed set out on to the pitch – but the umpires would not. It was a farce. It was not until 10.30 p.m. that an announcement was made that the Test had been forfeited as an England win. It was the first time ever, in 129 years of Test cricket, that a Test match had been forfeited.

It was a public relations disaster for cricket. Recriminations abounded. The Pakistani team and management expressed outrage at the charge of ball-tampering. Others said it had only been a matter of time. The public perception was that the whole issue had been a shambles and handled badly. The conduct of the umpires was heavily criticized. Hair's past record of controversy involving Asian subcontinent teams was raised by many commentators. Imran Khan called Hair an 'umpiring fundamentalist' and commented that 'such characters court controversy'. Wasim Akram called for Hair to be sacked. Michael Atherton said: 'The whole sorry mess was caused by the crassest and most insensitive piece of umpiring I have ever seen.'

The first official action, though, was a disciplinary action against Pakistan captain, Inzamam-ul-Haq, under the ICC Code of Conduct. The tribunal found that there was insufficient evidence to support the charge that his team had been guilty of ball-tampering. A turning point was dramatic evidence given by England's own Geoffrey Boycott. Holding aloft the infamous ball, he declared: 'That's a good ball, not just a playable ball.' Inzamam was, however, found guilty of bringing the game into disrepute by deliberately refusing to lead his team back on to the field of play when called to do so by the umpires.

The ICC then turned to fifty-three-year-old Hair. The problem was that the decision to award the match to England, when the Pakistan team failed to return to the field of play, was in accordance with the laws of cricket. Hair knew his cricket laws. However, many considered that the umpires had acted insensitively and that much greater effort should have been made to continue the game in the interests of cricket. The growing swell of opinion was strongly anti-Hair. Hair recognised this and did his cause little good by secretly offering to resign in return for a healthy payment of $500,000 (USD).

Holding the infamous ball aloft, Boycott declared: 'That's a good ball, not just a playable ball.'

In November 2006 the ICC formally met in Mumbai. After a short hearing by a three-man sub-committee who then reported to the full ICC, Hair, whose contract was due to run until March 2008, was banned from officiating in international matches. He was no longer a member of the ICC panel of umpires. Hair's umpiring career appeared to be at an end.

Hair, though, did not take the decision meekly. In February 2007 he dramatically announced that he was suing the ICC on grounds of racial discrimination. 'I believe that if I had been from the West Indies, India or Pakistan, I might have been treated differently.' It was an extraordinary and ironic claim given past accusations against Hair himself. Was Hair just trying to get his revenge? Yet, one could see his point. Why had he been disciplined and not co-umpire West-Indian Billy Doctrove? Hair claimed that, as a result of the premature termination of his contract, his lost earnings would be in the region of $4 million (USD).

Should Darrell Hair succeed in his claim for racial discrimination against the ICC? The claim was heard in the Central London Employment Tribunal in October 2007.

For: No one questioned Hair's technical competence. He was accepted as being one of the ICC's best umpires before that incident. He acted in accordance with the laws of cricket in forfeiting the match. The decisions in the Test at the Oval were taken jointly with his co-umpire, Billy Doctrove. There was no such position as 'senior' or 'lead' umpire. No disciplinary action had been taken against Doctrove. The action against Hair was due to the pressure of the Asian cricket representatives. It was racial discrimination. **Against:** Race was never mentioned in the deliberations of the ICC board or sub-committees. The decision was solely taken in the interests of cricket. Hair had clearly taken the lead in the decision to forfeit the match. Insufficient warning was given. He acted insensitively and contrary to the broader interests of est cricket. The ICC had lost confidence in him. His actions and lack of judgment had damaged the reputation of cricket and could properly be taken into account in the decision to drop him from the international umpiring panel.

Several days of mud-slinging and cross-accusation took place in the tribunal. Hair's counsel ripped into the ICC and their witnesses. It was revealed that the members of the three man sub-committee had summarily rejected the recommendation of ICC chief executive Malcolm Speed that Hair should be retained on the elite panel. This three man panel was made up of representatives from Pakistan and Zimbabwe and Sir John Anderson from New Zealand who described Hair's actions at the Oval as 'appalling'. As Hair's counsel said, 'Hair didn't stand much of a chance did he?'

But no evidence of racial discrimination in making the decision really emerged. The ICC asserted that: ' ... exactly the same decision would have been reached had Mr Hair been black or brown or even green.' Billy Doctrove himself found a reason not to attend.

Then, on the seventh day of the tribunal, the hearing was abandoned. Talks had taken place. Hair withdrew his claim for racial discrimination. He would be re-instated as an umpire with the ICC. He could umpire certain second tier matches but not Test matches as a member of the elite panel. Hair agreed to work with ICC management during a six month 'period of rehabilitation'. The ICC would review his status as an umpire in March 2008 but must give him at least twelve months' notice of non-renewal. No financial settlement was made. The ICC would bear their own legal costs – which were, by then, probably more than the $500,000 payment Hair sought for his resignation in the previous November.

After the Oval incident, Hair was voted Umpire of the Season in the annual poll carried out by *The Wisden Cricketer* magazine, with more than one-third of the votes.

What were the consequences of the saga? Serious damage was caused to the reputation of the world cricket authorities both as result of the original incident and the revelations of the ICC's decision making process and administration. For Hair, the possibility remained of a return to top-class umpiring – realised when, in March 2008, the ICC reinstated Hair to the full international panel of umpires. It is not known whether he will officiate in matches involving Pakistan.

In July 2008, the ICC officially re-designated the Oval Test in 2006 as a draw.

---

84 OSCAR PISTORIUS – DISABILITY, ABILITY AND THE BLADE RUNNER

Oscar Pistorius had both his legs amputated as a child. He could run with the use of prosthetic legs. He was fast. Was he eligible to compete internationally against able-bodied athletes – even in the Olympics?

A more extraordinary question in sport can never have been before a court or tribunal. Could a man with no legs run against the fastest able-bodied athletes in the world and qualify for the Olympics?

Oscar Pistorius was born with a congenital defect. He had no fibula (calf) bones in either of his legs. His parents made the heartrending decision, when Oscar was just eleven-months-old, that his legs should be amputated below the knee. Oscar himself did not grow up thinking he was disabled. He knew no different. 'I just didn't have any legs.'

He knew no different. 'I just didn't have any legs.'

From an early age, the South African turned to sport. He attended the boys' high school in Pretoria where, with the help of prosthetic limbs, he played rugby in the school's third XV team. He also played water polo and tennis. Then he suffered a bad knee injury playing rugby. He was introduced to sprinting in January 2004 as part of his rehabilitation. At seventeen, using carbon-fibre 'legs' designed for disabled athletes and after just two months training, he ran his first competitive race in his hometown of Pretoria. He broke the paralympic world record for 100 metres. In his own words, he 'never looked back'. He was a natural athlete.

Just eight months later, he represented South Africa in the 2004 Athens Paralympics. He was a sensation. He took the bronze medal in the 100 metres – and won gold in the 200 metres, breaking the world record with a time of 21.97 seconds. Watching him with his father was the surgeon, Dr Gerry Versveld, who undertook the original amputation operation. With tears in his eyes, Versveld exclaimed: 'Thank you! Thank you! This is the most amazing thing I will probably ever witness.' In 2005, he won gold in both the 100 and 200 metres in the Paralympics World Cup in Manchester in record times, triumphs that he repeated in the 2006 World Cup. He enjoyed competing in Manchester. He was a keen United supporter.

His thoughts turned seriously to competing against able-bodied athletes in open competition. Why should he not do so if he was fast enough? In March 2005, he competed in the South African National Championships for able-bodied athletes. He proved he was fast enough. He came sixth in the 400 metres in 47.34 seconds. With the aid of his high-tech carbon-fibre legs, he was almost as fast as the best able-bodied runners in the world over that distance. Was qualification for the Beijing Olympics within his reach?

Attention turned to the rules. How should the authorities react? The International Association of Athletics Federations (IAAF) were uneasy. Were they to become the 'villains' in the piece? In March 2007, partly one suspects aimed at Pistorius but possibly other forms of running shoes, the IAAF adopted a new rule to regulate the use of technical devices. It prohibited:

> *... use of any technical device that incorporates springs, wheels or any other element that provides the user with an advantage over another athlete not using such a device.*

Pistorius, for running, uses a J-shaped prosthesis known as the Cheetah Flex-Foot supplied by an Icelandic company, Ossur. It is the 'Ferrari' of its kind. The model has been used by many single and double amputees, almost unchanged, since 1997. Despite admiration for his extraordinary achievements, many – including many within the IAAF – thought that it should be regarded as a 'technical device' and that it did provide an 'advantage' compared with an able-bodied athlete. Sentiment must not be carried too far. Fairness to all athletes required a strict approach to the rules.

In the meantime, the IAAF did permit Pistorius to run in 'open' competition including a British Grand Prix event at Sheffield. In wet conditions, he was last of the finishers and was actually disqualified for running outside his lane. But his dreams were still alive.

How should the controversy be resolved? Pistorius agreed to participate in tests planned by the IAAF. He ran in a specially staged race in Rome in July 2007 videotaped by an Italian sports laboratory using several high-definition cameras from different angles. The video appeared to show that Pistorius was slower than other runners off the starting blocks and during the next fifty metres, the acceleration phase, and also around the first bend – but faster over the back straight where he appeared to have a longer stride than the able-bodied athletes.

The test was inconclusive. Further biomechanical studies were undertaken, on behalf of the IAAF, by Professor Brüggemann at the Institute of Biomechanics and Orthopaedics at the German Sport University in Cologne. The studies looked at his sprint movement, oxygen intake, blood lactate metabolism and various other measures agreed with the IAAF. On the basis of this study, Professor Brüggemann concluded that Pistorius' oxygen intake was twenty-five per cent lower than for the able-bodied athletes and that the 'energy return' to his artificial joints was higher than for human ankle joints. In other words, he used less energy and could run with less vertical motion and mechanical work than an able-bodied athlete. In total, he 'received significant biomechanical advantages by the prosthesis in comparison to sprinting with natural human legs'.

In January 2008, on the basis of this report, the IAAF Council concluded that the Cheetah Flex-Foot was a 'technical device' which gave the user an 'advantage over valid athletes'. Pistorius was declared ineligible to compete in IAAF-sanctioned events for able-bodied athletes. Were his Olympic dreams over?

Pistorius was not one to give up. He appealed to the Court of Arbitration for Sport (CAS). He claimed that he should be permitted to participate in competitions held under IAAF Rules, including the Olympics if he qualified, using his Cheetah prosthetic limbs. Should he succeed?

For: The Cologne tests concentrated solely on the 'advantages' for Pistorius. By excluding the start and acceleration phases, the results were distorted and did not consider the effect on his performance over the entire 400 metres race. Overall, there was no net advantage. The test was incomplete and the process was not fairly conducted. The IAAF, by not searching for an appropriate accommodation for Pistorius' disability to permit him to compete on an equal basis with able-bodied athletes, had denied him his fundamental human rights and were guilty of unlawful discrimination. **Against:** There was no discrimination by the IAAF. It was simply a question of applying a fair rule to prevent athletes, any athletes, having a technical advantage. If a technical device is used which provides an athlete with any advantage, in any part of a competition, the device must render that athlete ineligible to compete regardless of any compensating disadvantages. The tests showed that Pistorius did have certain advantages, through the device, which able-bodied athletes did not. The Cheetah device was therefore contrary to the IAAF rule.

Pistorius won.

Or, more realistically, the IAAF lost. It was a carefully-argued and sensitive judgment given in May 2008. It was a lawyers' judgment. The CAS panel accepted that the IAAF were not guilty of discrimination – it was indeed a question of applying the Rules. However, CAS judged that a proper interpretation of the Rules, in the case of a passive device such as the Cheetah Flex-Foot, required the IAAF – and now CAS – to determine if it provided 'an overall net advantage'. In the context of sport, this should be the vital test.

> *If the use of the device provides more disadvantages than advantages, then it cannot reasonably be said to provide an advantage over other athletes, because the user is actually at a competitive disadvantage.*

Crucially, CAS decided that the burden of proof was on the IAAF. The evidence was therefore not sufficient. It had concentrated solely on particular advantages without assessing the effect of disadvantages. It did not demonstrate, on the balance of probabilities, that there was an overall net advantage for Pistorius. CAS noted that the IAAF appeared to accept that the rule would not prevent Pistorius from running in 100 metre or 200 metre races since such distances did not allow Pistorius to catch up from his slower start.

Moreover, the CAS panel was not persuaded in any event, on the evidence, that there were metabolic or biomechanical advantages in favour of a double amputee using the Cheetah Flex-Foot. The fact that Pistorius used less vertical force than an able-bodied athlete might actually be a disadvantage; many sprinters sought more 'spring' in their actions. The scientific evidence did not discharge the burden of proof.

CAS was influenced by the fact that the Cheetah Flex-Foot prosthesis had been in use for a decade, and yet no other runner using them – whether a single or double amputee – had run times fast enough to compete effectively against able-bodied runners until Pistorius.

CAS stressed the limitations of the panel's decision. This was not carte blanche for disabled athletes and other equipment. The decision was limited solely to be eligibility of Pistorius using the specific Cheetah prosthesis. Any other athlete or device would have to be assessed on a case-by-case basis. Moreover, it was possible that further and more definitive scientific evidence might be produced in due course to prove that Pistorius did have an advantage over other athletes. If all this imposed a new burden on the IAAF, 'it must be viewed as just one of the challenges of 21st Century life'.

The 'fastest man on no legs' could compete in open competition. 'I think this day is going to go down in history for the equality of disabled people,' he said. The twenty-one-year old's quest for a place at the Olympics was no longer a dream. It was for real.

Although Pistorius would, if he qualified, be the first leg-amputee to run in the Olympics, he would not be the first disabled athlete to do so. America's Maria Runyan was legally blind when she finished eighth in the 1500 metres in the 2000 Sydney Olympic Games. Since Pistorius began his quest, Natalie du Toit, another extraordinary South African – an amputee swimmer who races without a prosthesis – earned a place in the open water swim event when she finished fourth in the 10-kilometre race in Seville, Spain.

For Pistorius, the challenge was now to lower his personal best of 46.34 seconds for the 400 metres and reach the Olympic qualifying time for Beijing of 45.55 seconds. It was too tough a challenge. But, if not Beijing, possibly London in 2012?

In June 2008 Oscar Pistorius was listed by *Time* magazine as one of the 100 most influential people in the world. His sporting motto echoes throughout his story:

> *You're not disabled by the disabilities you have. You are able by the abilities you have.*

CHAPTER TEN

SPORT AND EMPLOYMENT

Disputes between employers and employees have always been a common source of litigation. Disputes in the sporting workplace are no different. Tensions arise if a player (or team manager) performs badly or is guilty of serious misconduct or if one party wishes to end the relationship for some other reason. Tension is exacerbated, in sports such as football, if a player wants to transfer his employment to another club.

Some disputes here are of lighter interest including the rise of Mirabel Topham at Aintree and Crystal Palace's dispute with Iain Dowie. Groundbreaking claims include Newcastle's George Eastham, Belgian footballer Jean-Marc Bosman and Slovakian handball player Maros Kolpak. This area, more than any other, has been deeply affected by the all-pervasive scope of European law into which sport has, however unwillingly, been drawn. And 2008 started with two major football cases – one affecting international transfers and the other a club's entitlement to compensation if a player is injured on international duty. Each could significantly shape the game.

---

85 MIRABEL TOPHAM – THE QUEEN BEE TAKES OVER AT AINTREE

A boardroom struggle after the death of the long-serving clerk of the course, EAC Topham, would have a major effect on the future of Aintree. It led to the reign of Mirabel Topham.

The judge in the civil court would later sum up: she was 'a person of dominating and masterful character and personality and no doubt of considerable business acumen ... Not only did she dominate everyone with whom she came into contact, but she completely dominated her husband.'

Mirabel Hillier was an actress. She had a number of smallish parts in West End and provincial shows. She was for a time a Gaiety girl. In one showing of a musical comedy, *The Cinema Star*, at the Royal Court Theatre in Liverpool in 1914 she captured the eye and heart of Ronnie Topham. They married eight years later. She had no racing background. Indeed, it was not until the death of EAC Topham in 1932 that Mirabel started to take a closer interest in Aintree, the racecourse leased to the family company from the Earl of Sefton.

The Tophams had been associated with Aintree since 1843 when Edward William Topham (the 'Wizard') became the official handicapper for the Grand National. He also became the lessee of the racecourse land. 'Wizard' Topham was succeeded by his sons and the family company was established in 1899. EAC Topham took over in 1905. 'EAC' was a great figure. The Grand National grew in popularity and became a national institution. A boardroom struggle after his sudden death in 1932 would determine his succession and the future of Aintree.

A boardroom struggle would determine the future of Aintree.

Captain Douglas Wood was his natural successor as clerk of the course. Wood had known the Topham family for thirty-one years. He had been a director and secretary of the company since 1919. He had assisted EAC as clerk of the course for many years. He was very close to Bill Topham, EAC's brother. Together they ensured that Wood was appointed his successor as clerk of the course at a short board meeting held just one day before the funeral of EAC. Wood was one of the directors and his friend, Bill Topham, was the other. A little later, a written agreement was signed appointing Wood deputy managing director of the company, and confirming his position as clerk of the course, for a seven-year period from 1st January 1934.

All was relatively calm on the surface during 1933 and 1934.

Behind the scenes, Mirabel was planning her move. She did not like Wood. She decided to take over. She had plans, in effect, to oust Wood and to bring the company and Aintree under firm Topham family control again. Cleverly, she joined the board in 1935 and, by a surprise voting manoeuvre initiated by Mirabel, a 'tame' cousin was appointed as chairman in place of Bill Topham. Life at Aintree was never the same again. Certainly not for Douglas Wood.

The first big row with Wood arose over the distribution of complimentary badges. Wood considered, as clerk of the course, that official and complimentary badges were his responsibility. He was not going to have any interference on race meeting matters from management of the company. They could let him know how many they wanted personally; he would deal with all others. That was not the only issue. Even more emotionally, Mirabel wanted Wood's name removed from the race card and the name of Topham to have far greater prominence. Wood considered that, as clerk of the course, he was solely responsible to the stewards of the Jockey Club for the arrangements for the meetings and official race cards.

Senior figures of the racing world, including Lord Derby, expressed support for Wood. Lord Derby tried to broker peace with the board. He met them. He said that Topham's had no right to dictate to the clerk of the course in this way. The authority of the stewards must be obtained before anyone else was appointed in his place, as Mirabel Topham clearly wanted. 'In my opinion, from a sporting point of view, [Wood] is a most admirable clerk of the course.' Asked later whether these views were accepted, he replied: 'There was only one director who spoke, and that was Mrs Topham. She didn't agree.'

Once on the board, there was only going to be one winner of this boardroom struggle. In 1937, within two years of Mirabel Topham joining the board, she pushed through a board resolution to dismiss Wood as an employee and deputy managing director of Topham's Ltd with immediate effect on the grounds of misconduct. Wood was sent a cheque for £220. He claimed, instead, damages for wrongful dismissal and breach of his seven-year employment contract. Should he succeed?

For: Wood had signed a seven-year contract of employment with the company. The complaints against him were trivial. He had not committed any act of misconduct. He was a highly respected clerk of the course. He was entitled to damages for wrongful dismissal and breach of contract. **Against:** Wood had not carried out the instructions of the board. He had failed to advise the board properly about racecourse matters. He was acting beyond his authority. That was misconduct.

The litigation came before the Civil Court at Liverpool Assizes in June 1936. Proceedings were widely reported in the Liverpool and national press. It was the 'Aintree Racecourse Lawsuit'. The racing fraternity were captivated. It became a daily show with Mirabel sweeping into court each morning in a variety of elegant outfits and hats, an actress in a star role.

The case was notable for the leading legal teams involved, Maxwell Fyfe KC leading for Tophams and Norman Birkett KC for Wood. Birkett KC, for Wood, argued that the matters relied on by the defence were 'trivial and trumpery'. All along, Mirabel Topham had secretly plotted to get Wood out of the company.

> *The real trouble is that Wood is not a Topham. All was harmony until Mrs Topham joined the board. Mrs Topham is the chief cause of all this trouble. She must be a very remarkable woman. Certainly it is plain from the evidence that she dominates her husband.*

Lord Derby, called as a witness, noted:

> *There was a vast difference between the position when EAC Topham was clerk of the course and the present directorate. There was nothing EAC did not know about racing. Old Topham knew it all but the present directors know nothing about it.*

Lord Sefton gave similar evidence to the court: 'Mr Topham, one of the directors, married a lady, an actress, who had no knowledge of racing.'

One often quoted moment arose in the court proceedings when Ronald Topham was called to give evidence. Birkett KC asked: 'You have heard your wife say that she was the dominating mind in your marriage?' Topham replied: 'Well, most men are influenced by their wives. I use my own commonsense in some matters.'

'Well, most men are influenced by their wives. I use my own commonsense in some matters.'

Justice Lewis considered his judgment. It was no surprise when he decided in favour of Douglas Wood.

The company was ordered to pay Wood £3,250 damages plus the substantial costs of the case. And there were harsh words for Mirabel. It was clear to Justice Lewis that 'certain members of the Topham family' were determined to wrest management control out of the hands of Wood.

> *The ringleader was Mrs AR Topham, a person of dominating and masterful character. Not only did she dominate everyone with whom she came into contact, but she completely dominated her husband.*

Wood was not, though, reinstated. Mirabel Topham had made sure that control of Aintree would not pass out of the Topham family. She was now in control. She arranged for herself to be appointed managing director in 1938. She would be in sole control for the next thirty-five years.

Mirabel Topham would play a crucial role in determining the destiny of the course and its most famous race, the Grand National. She led the restoration of Aintree immediately after the war and the staging of the first postwar National in 1946. In 1949, she bought the freehold of the course from Lord Sefton and consolidated her power. She initiated the short-lived attempt to create a motor racing circuit at Aintree. She determined to keep the Grand National alive, despite financial problems. But in 1964, to great uproar, she announced she was selling Aintree – returning to court and winning a battle in the House of Lords to overturn a restriction, on the sale from Lord Sefton, that the land should only be used for horseracing or, in part, for agriculture. Mirabel wanted the Grand National to continue as a first-class event but run on another course. Eventually, in 1973, the course was sold for £3 million but on the basis that the National would continue to be run there for at least five years.

It was, perhaps, fitting that Mirabel Topham's last Grand National was in 1973, the first victory for the great *Red Rum* – two figures forever associated with the Grand National.

---

86 GEORGE EASTHAM – A LANDMARK CASE FOR PROFESSIONAL FOOTBALLERS

George Eastham wanted to leave Newcastle. The club refused to release him under the 'retain and transfer' rules of the Football League. Could Eastham challenge them as being invalid?

Newcastle's George Eastham was an elegant, skilful inside forward with superb ball control and an edge for the penetrating pass. In April 1960, he decided he wanted to leave Newcastle. He made the first of several unsuccessful requests to be released. They would lead to a fundamental challenge to football's transfer system.

Eastham simply wanted to earn more money. In 1960 the maximum wage was £20 per match day during the season and £17 in the summer. He wanted a job outside football in the afternoons.

> *We only trained in the mornings so I wanted something to occupy me rather than just wasting money on becoming a better snooker player. They [Newcastle] said they'd get me a job but nothing was forthcoming, so I went down to London and started selling cork.*

Eastham had joined Newcastle in 1956 from Ards, a club in Northern Ireland managed by his father. In 1960, he was on the verge of the England team. He was a firm favourite at St James' Park. Newcastle refused to release him. 'If Eastham wants to play football, it will be at Newcastle,' said the combative chairman, William McKeag.

'If Eastham wants to play football, it will be at Newcastle.'

In 1960, the Football League still operated a so-called 'retain and transfer' system established at the turn of the century after professional pay for footballers had, somewhat reluctantly, been allowed by the football authorities. Players were engaged on yearly contracts with clubs. Under Football League rules, a player was registered with a club and, while it held that registration, he could only play for that club. A club decided at the end of each season whether to 'retain' a player by offering a new contract (and, at that time, there was a maximum wage). If the player did not resign, he would not be paid. A club could decide to place a player on the 'transfer' list. If he was not on the transfer list, he could not be transferred and the club retained his registration. The club, in effect, decided whether a player would stay or go; it controlled the player's employment future.

Eastham was stubborn. He refused to resign for Newcastle. Crucially, he was supported by the Professional Players' Association (PFA). The PFA was becoming active under new chairman, former Fulham player, Jimmy Hill and secretary Cliff Lloyd. The fight for a better lot for professional footballers was underway. Eastham decided, with PFA support, to challenge the system. In October 1960, having been out of the game for three months, he issued a writ against Newcastle, the Football Association and the Football League claiming that the retain and transfer rules of the Football League were 'an unlawful restraint of trade'. The Football League defended the existing system on the basis that it maintained stability and was in the best interests of the game, particularly for the smaller clubs. The system prevented poaching of players. The law should leave football alone. It had no place interfering in rules which had served football well for over half a century.

Newcastle actually relented in the face of Eastham's persistence and, shortly after the start of legal proceedings, agreed that Eastham could transfer to Arsenal for a substantial transfer fee of £47,500. Eastham made his debut for Arsenal against Bolton Wanderers in December 1960 and scored twice. The PFA, however, had the scent of a breakthrough. They agreed to fund Eastham if he was prepared to continue his action as a test case against the Football League. He was. The challenge was on. The case went to the Chancery Division of the High Court.

Was the retain and transfer system operated by the Football League an unreasonable restraint of trade? Should Eastham, no longer in employment with Newcastle, have been free to move to another club?

For: The existing system treated players like chattels as if a relic of the Middle Ages. Eastham had been shut out from professional football for over three months. The retention system deprived him of his opportunity to earn his livelihood after his employment with a particular club had ended. It was an unreasonable and unlawful restraint of trade.

Against: The rules provided stability. If a player could do as he liked, the wealthier clubs would at once snap up all the best players (particularly when the maximum wage bar had been lifted). Smaller clubs would cease to survive or offer high-class football. Clubs would find it difficult to build up and maintain a consistent team. They would be discouraged from investing substantial sums in training and developing young players. It helped maintain competition and spectator interest. The system was not unreasonable. It was no more than was necessary to ensure a stable league.

Eastham won his case.

The High Court decided that the retain and transfer system operated by the Football League was an unjustifiable restraint of trade. The 'retention' rules deprived an individual, no longer in employment, of his reasonable opportunity to play professional football. If a player wanted to leave at the end of his contract, he should be permitted to do so. Justice Wilberforce said starkly:

> *Any system that interfere[s] with the player's freedom to seek other employment at a time when he was not actually being employed by another club would seem to me to operate substantially in restraint of trade.*

The court considered the Football League's justification of the existing system but was not persuaded. 'The system is an employers' system, set up in an industry where the employers have succeeded in establishing a united monolithic front all over the world.' The rules were more restrictive than necessary to protect the interests of the parties. The rules were invalid.

Eastham had won a landmark case for the employment rights of professional footballers.

It was a breakthrough for the PFA. While the Eastham dispute was in progress, the PFA also challenged – and, with a threat of a players' strike, succeeded in 1961 in removing – the maximum wage limit. The Eastham case, combined with the lifting of the maximum wage, broke the barriers. The best players were now free to negotiate longer and more lucrative contracts. Johnny Haynes of Fulham became the first £100 per week player. Clubs could no longer 'retain' players, after their employment, and in effect bring a player's career to an end if a player refused to accept the terms offered. The transfer rules were changed. If a player did not want to resign on the offered terms, the dispute could be referred to a new independent transfer tribunal for arbitration. The balance of power was no longer held solely by the clubs.

Eastham also claimed another 'first' in English football history in 1963 when he made his international debut for England against Brazil. His father George 'Diddler' Eastham having represented his country in 1935, he became part of the first father and son combination to play for England. Since then, Brian and Nigel Clough and Frank Lampard senior and junior have also joined this 'two generation' club.

Eastham played nineteen times for England. He was part of the England squad in 1966 which won the World Cup although he did not play during the tournament. He played a bigger role in helping his later club, Stoke City, to win the 1972 League Cup when, at the age of thirty-five, he scored the winning goal against Chelsea in the final.

Eastham was awarded in 1976 the OBE for services to football. Rightly, he was given pride of place at the launch of the PFA's centenary in 2007.

---

87 JEAN-MARC BOSMAN – A DECISION THAT TRANSFORMED FOOTBALL IN EUROPE

Jean-Marc Bosman, a Belgian footballer, wanted to leave his club at the end of his contract and move to a French club. His club prevented his move taking place. Did this infringe the 'freedom of movement' rules of the European Union?

It all happened, perhaps, because his parents lived a few doors away from the girlfriend of an intelligent and adventurous young lawyer.

Jean-Marc Bosman was, in 1990, a twenty-five-year-old midfield player with Belgian first division side, RC Liege. His early promise as a youth international footballer had not been fulfilled. As a litigant before the European Court of Justice, though, he succeeded in changing fundamentally the employment rights of footballers in Europe.

He succeeded in changing fundamentally the employment rights of footballers in Europe.

Bosman's contract with RC Liege, under which he received an average monthly salary of Bfr 120,000, expired at the end of June 1990. The club offered him a new contract for one season but at a substantial, seventy-five per cent, drop in salary to Bfr 30,000. Surely, RC Liege knew this was asking for trouble?

Bosman refused to resign for RC Liege. He was placed on the transfer list. No Belgian club showed any interest at a fee fixed according to Belgian FA rules. However, Bosman made contact with US Dunkerque, a club in the French second division. This led, fruitfully, to a proposed transfer. His monthly salary would be around Bfr 100,000 and he would receive a substantial signing-on bonus. A fee of Bfr 1,200,000 would be payable to RC Liege on receipt of the transfer certificate which needed to be issued by the Belgian FA, with the approval of RC Liege, before the transfer could take place. It was initially a one year transfer. US Dunkerque would have an irrevocable option for full transfer of the player on payment of a further Bfr 4,800,000 by the beginning of August. All seemed well for Bosman. It was a good deal for him.

But RC Liege scuppered the deal. They had doubts about the French club's ability to pay the full fee. They refused to support the issue of the transfer certificate before the start of the season, as US Dunkerque wanted. The transfer could not go through. Since Bosman refused to resign, RC Liege then suspended Bosman but kept his registration, preventing him from playing for any other club without their approval. It was reminiscent of the 'slavery' ended, in the UK, thirty years earlier by the Eastham case.

Not surprisingly, Bosman was upset and commenced a claim. A Belgian court made a preliminary judgment in his favour, ordering RC Liege not to impede Bosman's transfer. In fact, Bosman did then sign yearly deals with successive lowly French and Belgian clubs but each of these arrangements came to an end. Bosman was eventually signed by Olympic de Charleroi, a Belgian third division club. All these subsequent contracts were on personal terms less favourable to Bosman than the original proposed deal with US Dunkerque. If he hadn't been such a mediocre player, Bosman's claim for compensation would not have arisen.

The saga was, therefore, not over. Bosman was determined to pursue a claim for compensation to recover the income he had lost over the years as a result of the original refusal of RC Liege to allow him to join US Dunkerque. It led to a protracted battle before the courts.

How should Bosman argue his case? His parents knew a young lawyer, Jean-Louis Dupont, whose girlfriend lived a few doors away. He wanted to have a go at the case. He was bright and seemed full of enthusiasm and ideas. He knew that the European Commission had started giving warnings to UEFA that football's rules needed attention in order to satisfy the EU's rules for a 'single European market' after the Maastricht Treaty. UEFA had ignored these warnings.

Bosman's claim was on the dramatic new ground of 'free movement of workers' under European law.

Bosman, with his new young lawyer, brought an action against RC Liege, the Belgian FA and UEFA in the Belgian courts. Bosman's claim was not made on grounds of restraint of trade (or its Belgian law equivalent) but on the dramatic groundbreaking basis that RC Liege's actions were in breach of the rules relating to 'free movement of workers' under European law.

The Belgian appeal court took the crucial step of referring the case to the European Court of Justice for certain preliminary rulings. The European Court took the opportunity to address two critical issues which went to the heart of the organisation of football in Europe. It was no longer a 'one-off' dispute. It would dramatically change football.

First, was it unlawful for a club to require the payment of a transfer fee in respect of an 'out of contract' player like Bosman? Did the rules contravene European law on 'free movement of workers' by preventing him, a European national, from moving and being employed elsewhere in the European Union?

Secondly, were the existing 'quota' rules invalid, under the same European law principles, which in a number of national leagues restricted the ability of clubs to select more than a specified number of 'foreign' nationals for matches in certain competitions?

These were major issues. UEFA may have ignored the European Commission in the past. Did UEFA consider 'buying off' Bosman to prevent these issues finally going to court? Apparently not. Critical policy issues affecting the future of football in Europe were now in the hands of the European Court.

For: Each of these rules restricted Bosman's freedom, as a national of an EU member state, to join a club in another EU member state. A transfer fee was inappropriate and unlawful since Bosman was no longer employed 'under contract'. He should be free to negotiate his own employment as in any other industry. The nationality limit also restricted a club's ability or willingness to sign a 'foreign' player. Bosman had lost significant income as a result of the refusal to permit his transfer to US Dunkerque. The rules were an obstacle to freedom of movement of EU workers contrary to the Treaty of Rome. The rules should be declared invalid.
Against: The courts should respect the autonomy of the football authorities in establishing rules for the best organisation of their sport. The rules aided stability within football. The transfer fee rules were needed to maintain a financial and competitive balance between clubs. Transfer fees supported clubs searching for talent and training young players (which would be discouraged if players could move freely at the end of the contract period without any compensation or transfer fee). The nationality clauses were also justifiable on sporting grounds. They helped to maintain the traditional link between each club and its country. They were necessary to create a sufficient pool of national players to provide teams in each national league with top players from the 'home' country. They also helped to maintain a competitive balance between clubs by preventing the richest clubs from simply acquiring services of the best players.

Bosman won.

The decision was handed down by the European Court in December 1995. The European Court decided that both the transfer and nationality rules constituted an obstacle to freedom of movement for workers in a manner prohibited by the Treaty of Rome. Efforts to argue that football should be exempt from European competition and employment law had failed. The football authorities had been putting their heads in the sand. Football was an 'economic activity' and the football industry was required to comply with EU law in a way similar to any other industry. As the Advocate General advised the Court:

> *The right to freedom of movement and the prohibition of discrimination ... are among the fundamental principles of the Community order. [The quota rules] represent an absolutely classic case of discrimination on the ground of nationality. [They] limit the number of players from other Member States whom a club can play in a match. Those players are thereby placed at a disadvantage with respect to access to employment compared with players who are nationals of the [home] Member State.*

The arguments in favour of the rules were not sufficiently strong. The Court said, if not convincingly, that the same aims could be achieved at least as efficiently by other, less restrictive means – such as the redistribution of broadcasting funds to clubs on a more equitable basis. The existing rules were invalid.

In December 1998, Bosman eventually accepted damages of Bfr 16 million (around £312,000) from the Belgian FA.

The Bosman decision had a major impact on football in Europe. Transfer fees for 'out of contract' players now became illegal where an EU national was moving between one EU member state and another.

Although the Bosman judgment was not strictly applicable to transfers between clubs within a single EU state, the European football authorities – including the Premier League – quickly accepted that free movement for 'out of contract' players should apply to transfers between clubs within each EU country, with no fee being payable when players' contracts have expired. The principle of the Eastham case, removing certain obstacles to transfers for 'out of contract' players, had been taken an important and vital step further.

The dynamics of the transfer market changed significantly. Clubs started signing players on longer contracts in order to avoid losing them on free transfers. Smaller clubs started to lose out on transfer fees unless they could commit younger players to sign long-term contracts. 'Out of contract' players could negotiate substantially increased salaries since the new employer club would no longer be paying out a transfer fee. Leading players recognised their significant bargaining power as contract periods came to an end and renewal contracts were negotiated. Club loyalty could actually be financially disadvantageous. A very large proportion of the new TV income in football has ended up in players' salaries rather than as club profits or money to be reinvested into the football business.

No single court decision has had a greater effect on the game of football.

The invalidity of the nationality limits has had equally significant repercussions – and went far wider than the circumstances of the Bosman case itself. Clubs became free to sign and play as many EU players as they wished. Quota systems, limiting the number of foreign players who could play in a particular match, could not survive (for example, the previous rule in UEFA club competitions whereby only three foreign players plus two 'assimilated' foreign players could play for a team).

Top clubs now look elsewhere for footballers, especially to continental Europe. The option of going for a cheaper, proven foreign footballer is often more attractive for Premier League clubs than relatively overpriced young players from lower divisions. By opening the doors to an influx of non-national players by the abolition of the home player quotas, richer clubs were free to create virtual multinational super teams.

History was made on Boxing Day 1999 when Chelsea became the first English side to field an 'all-foreign' starting eleven. Chelsea visited Southampton and came away with a 2-1 victory.

Now FIFA's Sepp Blatter seeks to stem the tide by introducing a 'six-plus-five' principle which would limit a team's foreign players to five. He has little support from European clubs and none with the European Commission.

What does Bosman himself now think? He is a little sour: 'I contributed to the enrichment of a whole host of players, but they did not, in turn, give me much recognition.'

---

88 MAROS KOLPAK – A SLOVAKIAN HANDBALL PLAYER AND THE GAME OF CRICKET

Rules restricted the number of non-EU players who could be selected in a German handball league team. Should they apply to players from a country, such as Slovakia, which had a special 'association' relationship with the EU?

Seven-and-a-half years after Jean-Marc Bosman's court victory, another case before the European Court slipped quietly through the legal system. Who could have anticipated that a Slovakian handball player would lead a legal challenge which would transform the rights of players and athletes from Eastern Europe, South Africa and many Caribbean islands to compete in Europe – and substantially affect the organisation of cricket in England?

Germany ran a strong professional handball league. Maros Kolpak was a national of Slovakia but resident in Germany. Since March 1977 he had played as a goalkeeper for the German second division handball team, TSV Ostringen. His contract of employment was renewed, for a three-year fixed term, in February 2000. But he wanted a better chance to play in the team.

His problem was that the German national handball federation (DHB) placed certain restrictions on foreign players. Teams could not, in league or cup matches, field more than two foreign players – who, for this purpose, were players with a player's licence (issued by the federation) which regarded them as a national of a non-EU member country without, in effect, equal employment rights. Kolpak had been issued with a foreign player's licence. This

He wanted a better chance to play in the team.

potentially restricted Kolpak's ability to play in German league or cup matches.

Kolpak challenged his player categorisation. He considered that his selection should not be subject to any restrictions based on nationality. He wanted to be treated for this purpose in the same category as an EU national. How could he argue this? Kolpak (or his studious lawyer) based his argument on the 'association agreement' which Slovakia had with the EU by which the EU agreed a principle of nondiscrimination on grounds of nationality in relation to employment and related matters. It was a clever argument. The issue was referred to the European Court.

Should Kolpak be free of any discriminatory rules based on nationality? Even though he was not an EU national, was he entitled to be classed for employment purposes in Germany in the same category as an EU national?

For: Kolpak was already lawfully employed in Germany. He should not be subject to any barriers of employment or selection based on nationality. The association agreement between Slovakia and the EU prohibited discrimination in employment matters based on nationality. He should have the same opportunity as EU nationals to participate in cup and league matches as part of his professional activity. This principle was directly binding on sporting bodies in EU countries. Kolpak was entitled to a 'level playing field' and to be treated in the same way as EU nationals. The classification by the German association was invalid.
Against: It was going too far to equate a non-EU national with an EU national for all employment purposes. The EU rules should only apply to countries who enjoy complete equality of treatment vis-à-vis EU nations in respect of free movement. The association agreement with Slovakia did not create legally enforceable obligations in this way. It was proper for a sporting body to restrict the number of non-EU nationals who could play. This was reasonable on sporting grounds. It safeguarded the training of young players by German clubs and also helped to promote the German national team.

In a landmark judgment, the European Court decided in favour of Maros Kolpak.

The European Court agreed that, because of Slovakia's association agreement with the EU, he should indeed be treated in the same category as EU nationals for the purposes of eligibility to play in league and cup handball matches. The restriction in the rules of the German handball association was invalid. The Court considered, but rejected, the association's attempt at a 'sporting' justification to exempt the application of this principle.

The Bosman principle established that no EU national should be prevented by sporting rules from working in another part of the EU. Quotas or restrictions on selection of players from other EU countries were banned. The Kolpak ruling extended this principle so that it applied not only to EU nationals but also nationals of a wide range of countries merely having 'association' or similar relationships with the EU. Whilst the wording of many of these agreements may vary, similar 'rights' could now be claimed by nationals of countries such as South Africa and numerous countries in Eastern Europe, the Caribbean and the Pacific.

The European Court decided in favour of Kolpak. He should be treated in the same category as EU nationals for the purpose of eligibility.

There was one significant qualification in the Kolpak ruling. Kolpak was himself already validly working in the EU. The question whether a particular country's governmental authorities should issue a work permit (where required under national laws) in any particular case was a separate matter for that government. However, it was now clear that the rules of a sporting body could not themselves discriminate against non-EU nationals from these countries.

It is difficult to believe that the diplomats negotiating these 'association agreements' could ever have contemplated their effect on sport!

What has the decision meant in practice?

In Britain, the greatest effect has been on cricket. The decision has enabled English county cricket clubs to sign up a multitude of overseas cricketers. The earlier Bosman ruling had little effect on cricket, unlike football, since there were no other strong cricket nations within Europe. However, Kolpak opened the way for cricketers from countries with strong cricket backgrounds such as South Africa, Zimbabwe and a number of West Indian islands – all of whom have association agreements with the EU containing anti-discriminatory employment provisions. So long as they possessed or obtained a relevant work permit, cricketers from these countries could now be classed as domestic and not 'overseas' players. Any restrictions limiting the number of 'overseas' players would not apply to them.

English counties have not been slow to take advantage. The first 'Kolpak signing' in county cricket was South African Claude Henderson signed by Leicestershire in 2004. At first, the ECB imposed a requirement that the player must not have represented another country for twelve months prior to the signing. More recently, the ECB has acknowledged that this is not enforceable and has permitted Yorkshire's signing of Jacques Rudolph who had played for South Africa six months previously. Glamorgan were, by 2007, the only county side never to have used a 'Kolpak' or EU-qualified player.

The effect on international cricket has been considerable and, in many respects, damaging. There has been a significant trend for counties to recruit 'Kolpak' players, not always of the highest quality, rather than spend money on coaching and developing young, home-grown players. Many argue that the national English team is suffering as a result of the smaller pool of talent available in county cricket. Other nations, such as South Africa, complain that their Test sides suffer because of 'Kolpak' players playing abroad who are not available for the national team.

There has been a significant trend for counties to recruit 'Kolpak' players.

The other sport deeply affected by the Kolpak decision in the UK has been rugby. The ruling has enabled rugby teams (union and league) to sign players not only from South Africa but also Fiji, Tonga and Samoa. In France, up to 150 South Africans are playing rugby union.

Will the situation change? As a result of a campaign by the ECB and supported by the French, the European Commission has recently altered its stance in relation to the EU's Cotonou Agreement with many African, Caribbean and Pacific states. The latest ruling, in July 2008, indicates that the treaty should in future be regarding as applying only to free trade in goods and services and not free movement of labour. The ECB is studying the implications. The tidal wave of 'Kolpak' players may have ended — or we may be heading for another legal fight.

Ironically, if the situation of Maros Kolpak had arisen now, there would be no need to extend the principle of nondiscrimination to non-EU countries. Slovakia became a full member of the EU in May 2004.

---

89 IAIN DOWIE – A CONTROVERSIAL MOVE IN SOUTH-EAST LONDON

Crystal Palace's manager, Iain Dowie left and joined local rivals, Charlton. Was Palace's chairman, Simon Jordan, misled?

Simon Jordan, owner and chairman of Crystal Palace, would remember the remark.

It was the last match of the 2004/05 season. Crystal Palace were playing away at Charlton Athletic, desperately needing a win to avoid relegation from the Premier League. A late equaliser from Charlton made it 2-2. It meant that Palace returned to the Championship after just one season in the top flight. Charlton's fans delighted in Palace's plight. There was no love lost between the two local rivals in south-east London. Richard Murray, largest shareholder and deputy chairman of Charlton, turned to Jordan and remarked: 'Enjoy the Championship, tosser.'

Crystal Palace's manager was forty-one-year-old Iain Dowie. Dowie had been an old-fashioned centre-forward with West Ham, Southampton and Crystal Palace in his playing days. He was born of a Belfast father and played a record fifty-nine times for Northern Ireland. Dowie joined Crystal Palace as manager in December 2003 when the team were languishing in nineteenth spot in the Championship.

Memorably described by a witness later in court as 'not photogenic but hard-working and disciplined', Dowie showed inspirational skills as a manager. A sensational run of form had led them to the promotion play-offs. Crystal Palace then clinched promotion to the Premier League with a 1-0 victory over West Ham in the play-off final.

But now, in 2005, it was back to the Championship again for Crystal Palace. And, in May 2006, it was back to the promotion play-offs for a place in the Premier League. This time Crystal Palace played Watford. They were well beaten and lost 3-0 over the two legs. They had failed in their promotion bid. Another year in the Championship lay ahead.

It was a frustrating time for the club – and for Simon Jordan. He returned to his home in Spain before telephoning Iain Dowie the following day. The 'parachute' payment from the Premier League would be reduced the following season. There would need to be cuts in the budget. Players would need to be sold. It was a fraught telephone call with Dowie. It was a call which was to lead to a bitter and personal dispute in the High Court.

It was a telephone call which was to lead to a bitter and personal dispute in the High Court.

It is unclear exactly what was said but the relationship between chairman and manager was deteriorating fast. Dowie claimed that Jordan was highly critical and often abusive. He felt that he was being encouraged to resign. It was a 'vulgar and abusive attack on him and the team'. Jordan said that he wanted Dowie to stay but that Dowie had ended by saying that, if a job came up with a club in the north, he would like the opportunity to speak to the club. His family were in Bolton and he would like to be nearer his wife and two young sons. Maybe, also, it was time for a different challenge. In Jordan's view, this conversation changed everything. He could not plan ahead if his manager was not one hundred per cent committed to the club.

As for the language, Jordan explained later to the court:

> *'It was common for both of us to use swear words frequently. Swear words were used without intending to cause any particular hostility or aggression.'*

A critical clause in Dowie's contract was that, if he joined another Premier League or Football League club before 30th June 2008, Palace were to receive a compensation payment of £1 million. In practice, this payment would have to be met by the new club. It was a deliberate hurdle to make it difficult for Dowie if he wanted to move early to a new club. Dowie knew that Jordan had a reputation for enforcing contracts. Back in 2001 he had gone to court successfully to enforce a six month 'garden leave' contract clause against Steve Bruce to delay his move to rivals Birmingham City after resigning as manager with Crystal Palace. Jordan was a tough litigator.

Events moved swiftly after that telephone call. Jordan assumed that Dowie wished, and intended, to go north. A few miles away in south-east London, Charlton by this time were also seeking a new manager after Alan Curbishley had brought to an end his fifteen-year reign there. Despite rumours, Dowie assured Jordan that 'he had had no contact whatsoever with Charlton.' Jordan stressed: 'You can't go to a club that was dancing on our f****** graves when we got relegated.'

Jordan agreed to enter into a 'compromise agreement' with Dowie. Palace would waive their entitlement to the £1 million compensation payment and Dowie's employment contract would be terminated by mutual consent. A press conference was held by Crystal Palace on 22nd May to announce Dowie's departure. Jordan gave, as the main explanation, Dowie's wish to move to the north to be closer to his family.

Jordan felt that he had been made to look a fool.

Just eight days later, on 30th May, Charlton unveiled Dowie as their new manager. Jordan was furious. He felt that he had been made to look a fool.

Jordan, on behalf of Crystal Palace, promptly brought a legal claim against Dowie for deceit. He even tried to have the writ served at the Charlton press conference. He wanted damages and his £1 million compensation payment reinstated.

Should Crystal Palace succeed in getting damages from Dowie for misrepresentation and deceit?

For: Dowie had represented that a primary reason for leaving was that he intended to move north and he represented, as fact, that he had had no contact with Charlton. Jordan would not have entered into the 'compromise agreement', waiving the £1 million compensation payment, if he had known Dowie had been in contact with and intended to move to Charlton. Crystal Palace were entitled to damages. **Against:** Dowie's defence was simply that he had made no such representations. He was a 'free' agent after the end of his contract with Crystal Palace.

A bitter court battle ensued before Justice Tugendhat in the London High Court during the summer of 2007. Essentially, the question was: who should be believed? Evidence given in the court was often contradictory. Mobile phone records were examined. After hearing all the evidence, Justice Tugendhat made his findings. He accepted Jordan's case and did not believe Dowie's story. He found it 'unconvincing' and 'confusing'. It became clear that:

Dowie did represent that he intended to move to the north to be nearer to his family.

Dowie did have contact with Charlton on 17th May and again on the morning of 22nd May. Dowie had alleged that the discussion with Charlton's Richard Murray was principally about players. The judge disagreed. He said that it was part of the football 'courting ritual' and 'they were showing to one another their interest in Mr Dowie being a candidate for the Charlton job.'

Jordan had spoken to Dowie on 20th May following rumours that he might be going to Charlton. Dowie replied that Jordan's source was wrong. 'I have had absolutely no contact whatsoever with Charlton.'

Even if Dowie's original statement that he intended to move north was true, he came under a duty to correct that representation when it became untrue by the time of the signature of the 'compromise agreement' on 22nd May.

Dowie intended to induce Jordan to sign the compromise agreement on the basis of those misrepresentations.

Dowie was guilty of deceit. The court would not tear up the compromise agreement. The last thing anyone wanted was for Dowie still to be under contract as manager at Palace! Damages would be awarded – but whether Palace were owed £1 million or another amount was to be determined another day. Dowie was obliged to bear the costs of the case, thought to be in the region of £400,000.

Jordan remarked: 'It's a good day for football. A judgment has been found in favour of contracts. The allegations made were not put forward in as dignified manner as I would have wanted but I'm delighted they were proved.'

Football offers many twists and turns. Dowie became the first Premiership manager to be sacked in the 2006/07 season. He lasted only twelve Premier League matches at Charlton. With just two wins, he was sacked in November 2006. Charlton were later relegated back to the Championship.

Jordan and Dowie continued their legal wrangle in 2007. Jordan claimed that he reached a 'peace settlement' with Dowie in September for the payment of £350,000 in place of pursuing the £1 million compensation claim. Dowie did not acknowledge any such agreement and appealed the original verdict. In April 2008, the parties announced that a satisfactory out-of-court settlement of all issues had been reached. Shortly after, Crystal Palace, under manager Neil Warnock, were back in the Championship play-offs ... but failed to gain promotion.

A particular highlight of the evidence at the High Court for many was the existence of a computer presentation on Iain Dowie's laptop entitled 'Advancing tne Addicks' (misprint in the title) setting out a script of plans which Dowie proposed to implement if appointed manager of Charlton. The fact that he came to the interview with Charlton, ready with this presentation, on 23rd May made a favourable impression. Subsequent investigation revealed that the document had been created earlier on 19th May – under a different title 'Reinvigorating the Rams', the nickname of Derby. He had simply changed the title for his Charlton interview! Similar versions appeared under different headings when he was looking for a job in early 2007 and, apparently, a version for use in 2004 when Blackburn were looking for a manager.

He had simply changed the title for his Charlton interview!

---

90 ANDY WEBSTER – A NEW BOSMAN FROM SCOTLAND?

Andy Webster moved from Hearts to Wigan. Was it an 'international' transfer? He was the first player to exercise new rights under the FIFA transfer regulations.

It was the move from Hearts to Wigan in September 2006 which did it. Such a move probably made football history in itself – but it was also the first time a player had used a right to terminate his contract early under the new FIFA transfer regulations.The implications were significant. Was Andy Webster to become a Scottish 'Bosman'?

Andy Webster joined Heart of Midlothian in the Scottish Premier League from Arbroath in March 2001. The transfer fee for the centre-half was £75,000. It was a good move and, in June 2003, he signed a four-year contract. Webster won several Scottish international caps. At the end of the 2005/06 season, though, he had a disagreement over contract matters with Hearts' owner, Vladimir Romanov, and was left out of the team. No one anticipated the next steps.

No one anticipated the next steps.

After Bosman, it was no longer possible for a club to require a transfer fee for a player at the end of his contract. This did not affect transfer fees paid during the period of a player's contract. However, the European Commission were also dubious whether an employer club should, during a player's contract, be able to require a fee for transfer of a player's registration if the fee represented substantially more than the salary which would have been payable during the remainder of the player's contract term. Why – in the interests of 'free movement' of workers – could not a player (or the club to whom he wanted to transfer) 'buy out' the remainder of his contract in the same way as employees moving in any other industry and, it might be said, in the same way as football managers? The 'football' argument was that clubs need contract stability to build up and maintain teams.

With the European Commission applying pressure on FIFA and UEFA, new transfer regulations for international transfers were adopted by FIFA in 2001 with minor revisions coming into force in July 2005.

They provided for greater player mobility. Amongst the regulations, Article 17 entitles a player to terminate his contract after a 'protected period' – which for a contract entered into when the player is still under age twenty-eight is, in effect, a period of three years. (For a contract entered into after age twenty-eight, the period is down to two years.) A player cannot be held to a long-term contract. There are three basic provisos:

First, he must exercise his right to terminate (if he wishes) by notice within fifteen days of the end of the season.
Secondly, the right only applies to a transfer between clubs in different countries – it applies to international transfers but not (at least not yet) domestic transfers since the underlying objective of the rule, legally, is to prevent undue restraints on 'free movement' of workers within the EU.
Thirdly, a player and his transferee club are jointly obliged to pay compensation to the former employer club unless the termination is for 'just sporting cause'.

That's the legal background. How did it apply here? Andy Webster was the first player to invoke this right when, three years into his contract, he left Hearts to join ... Wigan Athletic. A transfer from Scotland to England was an 'international' transfer for this purpose. With still a year to go on Webster's agreed contract, many regarded this as exploiting a 'loophole'.

The transfer was duly ratified by FIFA. (There was a nice initial point whether Webster's notice had been given within fifteen days of the end of the season – since it had been given after the Scottish Cup final rather than the closing day of the league season. For this, Webster was suspended for two matches at the start of the following season but otherwise the transfer was allowed.) A dispute arose over the amount of compensation payable to Hearts. The small print in the FIFA regulation made it clear that (unless the contract was specific) compensation was based on the player's salary for the residual term of his contract and an element based on his original transfer cost. No one had really done the sums before in an actual case. Webster was the first.

A transfer from Hearts to Wigan was an 'international' transfer.

The transfer became even more controversial when at the beginning of January 2007, just four months after his transfer to Wigan for whom he made just five appearances, Webster moved to Glasgow Rangers on a loan deal. Hearts contended that Webster should not be able to play for another Scottish club within twelve months of leaving them. But FIFA ruled that the move was in order.

Webster was now back playing for a key Scottish rival!

Back to the issue of compensation. Hearts were deeply upset. Here was a player whom they valued at around £4 million or £5 million in the transfer market. He had taken advantage of a 'loophole' which assisted a transfer between Scotland and England well before the end of his contract. Not only had Hearts not benefited from his full transfer value – but Webster was now back playing for a key Scottish rival! Hearts pursued their claim against Webster and Wigan (the transferee club) for compensation in accordance with FIFA's regulations. The issue went to the FIFA Dispute Resolution Chamber.

Should the compensation be fixed by reference to Webster's transfer value in the open, domestic market – or by reference to the value of his salary for the remaining period of his contract?

The FIFA tribunal decided that the amount payable was not the full transfer value of Webster on the domestic market but £625,000 – a sum calculated by reference to the residual value of Webster's contract with Hearts and his salary in the first year of his contract with Wigan, multiplied by a factor of 1.5. In effect, Webster and Wigan were able to buy out his contract at substantially less than his full transfer value.

Hearts were furious. There was a major issue here with overtones of Bosman. Hearts believed:

> *If allowed to stand, the effect on clubs caught in similar situations worldwide will be highly damaging. This matter is about the good of football and preserving the interests of clubs that invest in players and youth development in order to reap the rewards of those investments.*

There was, equally, a strong counter-argument by Wigan that the compensation fee fixed by the FIFA tribunal was, under the FIFA regulations, too high – and that it should not have taken into account the salary paid by Wigan and based the calculation solely on the

Hearts' salary. And why was a multiple of 1.5 used to increase the compensation figure?

All parties appealed, in accordance with the FIFA regulations, to the Court of Arbitration for Sport. Judgment was given in January 2008. Hearts lost. It was a shattering judgment for them. The compensation figure was revised, downwards, to just £150,000 – in effect the value of the remaining term of Webster's contract with Hearts.

The compensation figure was revised, downwards, to just £150,000.

The implications began to dawn on the international football community. Star 'players' could become available across Europe, for much reduced transfer fees, before the end of their contracts. It is another boon for the 'big' players (and their agents). They will have even stronger bargaining power when negotiating renewal contracts. Tony Higgins of Fifpro, the worldwide players' union, declared 'This is the most significant case since Bosman.' 'Doing a Webster' may become part of the football lexicon.

£150,000 for Andy Webster. £13.6 million for Adrian Mutu – but in rather different circumstances. The record award, highly contentious, was made against Mutu by a FIFA tribunal in August 2008 to compensate for Chelsea's loss (including loss of transfer value) after the highly-valued Romanian striker was sacked by the club for misconduct (cocaine use). Mutu had otherwise been picked up 'for free' by Juventus. Another appeal to CAS is likely.

As for Webster, he suffered a knee injury in his first training session with Rangers and missed the rest of the season. His loan deal was extended. He played his first match for Rangers in September 2007 scoring in the win against Gretna. It was his only appearance that season. His knee was injured again shortly afterwards.

---

91 AN INTERNATIONAL INJURY – A BELGIAN CLUB, A MOROCCAN PLAYER, THE G14 AND FIFA

Abdelmajid Oulmers was injured playing for Morocco. He was a key player for his Belgian club. Could they claim compensation?

'It would be the end for international football. A World Cup would take place with only Spain, Germany, Italy, France and England and that would be the end.' A spokesman for UEFA, soccer's European governing body, expressed the fears of many if the case was decided against FIFA. It was a dispute which would change, perhaps fundamentally, the relationship between 'club' and 'country' in football in the twenty-first century. And all triggered by a match between Morocco and Burkina Faso.

It was a Belgian league club, Sporting Charleroi, who started it. Always in Belgium! Charleroi were going well in the 2004/05 season, heading the first division table until November 2004. Abdelmajid Oulmers, a left-side midfielder, was one of their best players. Twenty-six-year-old Oulmers was a Moroccan. He was called up for his first international cap for a friendly between Morocco and Burkina Faso. Charleroi wanted Oulmers to pull out on medical grounds claiming, not convincingly, that he was not fit. FIFA overruled and insisted that he should be made available for international duty under the FIFA rules for compulsory release of players for international matches. Oulmers came on as a half-time substitute, scored and then was seriously injured – tearing ankle ligaments in an injury which kept him out of the game for eight months. Morocco, incidentally, defeated Burkina Faso 4-0.

All triggered by a match between Morocco and Burkina Faso.

Charleroi were angry. Oulmers was not insured against injury by Morocco. Charleroi, as his employer, had to bear the full cost of his continuing wages, the cost of surgery and of a replacement player. Moreover, the team's form dipped and Charleroi eventually finished fifth in the league – failing to win a place in the UEFA Champions League. They felt 'mugged'. The loss of Oulmers had severely damaged their league chances. Charleroi decided to bring a legal claim against FIFA for compensation for Oulmers' injury whilst on international duty.

Why does it always seem to be Belgium at the centre of these European legal disputes? Perhaps because Jean-Louis Dupont, the young lawyer who acted for Jean-Marc Bosman, was behind it again. He was now acting for Sporting Charleroi. He developed a claim that FIFA's regulations on release of players breached European law. It was a Bosman-like attack on well-established footballing rules of FIFA.

Crucially, Charleroi were backed by the powerful G14 group of clubs in Europe. (Only in football could this body keep the same name and comprise 18 clubs! Arsenal being one of the clubs added to the original 14 who included Manchester United and Liverpool – but not Chelsea.) The G14 was a body which UEFA had once described as a 'self-appointed group of clubs ... only interested in protecting themselves and their economic interests and in dictating their conditions on others'. Oulmers was the case that the G14 had been looking for in their quest to challenge FIFA's rules. The G14 latched on to similar claims by French club Olympique Lyon and Spanish club Atletico Madrid following injuries to their players during international fixtures. The G14 would cause FIFA's rules to be broken up.

The G14 would cause FIFA's rules to be broken up.

It had been a long-running sore with the G14. They wanted more power for the clubs. They maintained that, since they paid the wages (and very high wages) of their employees, they should have a greater say in when they were released for international matches – and should be compensated if their employees were injured whilst on international, not club, duty. If the national associations would not bear responsibility, FIFA itself should do so and pay at least a proportion of the player's wages and/or give the clubs a greater share of the profits from competitions such as the World Cup and the European Cup in which 'their' players are performing.

Sporting Charleroi (or Jean-Louis Dupont) and G14 developed this frustration into a legal argument that demanding the obligatory release of players without some form of compensation (particularly in the event of injury) amounted to an 'abuse of a dominant position' by FIFA under European law.

FIFA responded that this was a narrow and largely selfish view by the big G14 clubs. International football enhanced the experience and value of the players themselves. Clubs benefited from their players being internationals – both in terms of publicity and value. Importantly, the clubs were fully aware of the rules and the possibility of players being selected for internationals when they bought or developed players – including a 'foreign' player representing a country such as Morocco. England might be able to afford insurance (or at least partial insurance) for an injury to Michael Owen – but a major fear of FIFA was that many national associations, particularly those in regions such as South America, Africa and Eastern Europe, simply could not afford to pay compensation. Could Ghana afford to pay compensation for injury to Michael Essien or the Ivory Coast for injury to Didier Drogba? Could they risk playing them in international football?

Could Ghana afford to pay compensation for injury to Michael Essien?

The legal claim went first to a commercial court in Belgium, the Charleroi Tribunal of Commerce. The court decided in May 2006 that it would refer four key issues to the European Court of Justice for guidance before it could judge on Charleroi's claim. They sought guidance on four rules which went to the heart of the 'club-versus-country' relationship in football. Were they valid – or did they infringe European laws on competition? The four were in effect:

the obligation on clubs to release players for international duty;
the rule which meant clubs received no financial reward in return for releasing their players;
the provision that insurance cover was a matter for the clubs themselves (and could not be imposed on national associations as a condition for release by clubs of their players);
the rule requiring clubs to be bound by FIFA's international calendar.

All were fundamental rules. All central to international football. The legal issue would turn on whether FIFA could successfully argue that the rules were reasonable, and proportionate, in the interests of maintaining a structure of international football – an objective which was good for the game and all football followers. It would be necessary to justify each rule separately. It would be a long haul.

FIFA argued strongly that these rules should not be put under the legal spotlight of the European Court. These were matters which should be dealt with 'within football'. FIFA failed to persuade the Belgian court. Once again, fundamental matters affecting football would be in the hands of the lawyers and judges of the European Court. The legal battle-lines were drawn. The political issues were, though, much wider than the specific situation of the injured Oulmers.

Could a compromise be found 'within football'? Was there still time? Would FIFA and UEFA decide that it was preferable to work out a detailed 'football' solution, even if it involved some compromise, than face the stark possibility – as in Bosman – of the rules being swept aside entirely?

In January 2008 FIFA, UEFA and the G14 announced the basis for a peace deal.

Yes. On 15th January 2008 in Zurich, before the European Court had given its judgment, FIFA, UEFA and the G14 announced the basis for a peace deal:

FIFA/UEFA agreed in principle that they would make 'financial contributions for players' participation in the European Championships and World Cups'.

The G14 would in due course disband and a new independent European Club Association would be formed comprising over 100 clubs with membership across Europe determined 'solely on sporting achievements'.

The G14 clubs would drop any court cases they have against FIFA and UEFA.

Initially there was simply a letter of intent. The parties would work towards a 'memorandum of understanding'. A little more flesh to the deal was announced a few days later. UEFA and FIFA would pay clubs a daily rate for each player involved in the final stages of the European Championships or the World Cup. UEFA would pay €43.5 million in respect of Euro 2008 (around €4,000 per day per player). The cash would be shared among any clubs for whom a player has played in the previous two years. FIFA had earmarked €40 million for the 2010 World Cup in South Africa with the sum rising to €70 million for 2014. FIFA also agreed that clubs will only have to release players for one friendly a year played outside their own continent.

Michael Platini, president of UEFA, told a news conference:

> *There is no winner here apart from football itself. It was utterly unthinkable for us that players might not have the right to play for their national team but of course we could see it was also logical the clubs who provide these players should also share in the profits from the competitions.*

As far as the Charleroi case was concerned, strictly it remained in limbo. A G14 spokesman said that: 'As a sign of their commitment and goodwill, member clubs will take the formal decision to dissolve G14 and to withdraw its claims in court.' Karl-Heinz Rummenigge, chairman of the new European Club Association added: 'The lawsuits will be dropped ... and the many misunderstandings and legal actions are now a part of the past.'

Many uncertainties remain. Indeed, the peace deal barely addressed the specific issues in the Charleroi case. The proposed payments will not include any additional element of compensation for injury – insurance will be a matter for the clubs or their national associations. Will the rules remain for compulsory release for tournaments such as the Africa Cup of Nations for which no compensatory payments are mentioned? What about friendlies or qualifying matches? Will the new arrangements need, in effect, the approval of the European Commission – or is there a continuing risk, even if diminished, that elements of the new rules could still be challenged by a determined club under European competition laws?

Where will the funds for compensation payments come from? The cynics point out that this will mean a reduction in the profits from these tournaments available to FIFA/UEFA (for the benefit of the game as a whole) and more money diverted to the already successful clubs who will be supplying most of the players. Was it, in reality, just another shift in favour of more power, influence and money for the major clubs?

If many loose ends remained, at least FIFA/UEFA appeared to have learnt one of the lessons of Bosman – that it is preferable to reach a solution 'within football' rather for such fundamental matters to depend on the decision of the European Court. But it probably would not have happened without the trigger of a legal claim – and an injury to a twenty-six-year-old Moroccan midfielder.

CHAPTER ELEVEN

A CLOSING COCKTAIL

We end with a few diversions away from the main path. The chapter starts with libel actions fought by two sporting titans, JPR Williams and Ian Botham. We continue with a collection of sporting cases and incidents which have not changed the course of the law or the direction of sport – but which may provide some amusement or interest to the sports observer.

Perhaps there is a theme here. In many of the stories in this last 'cocktail' the claims have been somewhat unusual or optimistic in nature. They include a Scotland supporter's hopeful claim after a rather strange match against Estonia, a Leicester City fan seeking damages for shock after a referee's decision, two American fans fighting over a ball and Sir Alex Ferguson taking on a leading racing tycoon over the ownership of a racehorse.

And we finish with a warning for the sports fan from the divorce courts. No claimant in this last chapter succeeded – except for this final one.

---

92 JPR WILLIAMS – 'ALL THE MEN ... MERELY PLAYERS'?

John Williams, legendary rugby full-back, rarely shirked a challenge. He was Welsh captain in 1979 when a newspaper article accused him of 'shamateurism'. Was it libel?

JPR Williams, as Cliff Morgan remarked when commentating during that classic Barbarians match against the All Blacks at Cardiff Arms Park in 1973, ' ... never ever shirks not only a tackle but any situation at all.' In 1979, it was a serious off-field challenge he had to confront – an article in the *Daily Telegraph* that threatened his entire rugby future.

By 1979, John Peter Rhys Williams (one of the few world sportsmen instantly recognisable by his initials – originally, and usefully, to distinguish him from his similarly named and very fine Welsh winger, JJ Williams) was at the zenith of his rugby career. Aged twenty-nine, captain of Wales, already holder of more than fifty caps and three Grand Slam titles, the finest full-back of his and arguably any other era, JPR was enjoying the final international season of his legendary rugby career – planning to finish with the Triple Crown match against England at Cardiff Arms Park in March.

Then, in February 1979 and just weeks before the England match, the *Daily Telegraph* published a shattering article by journalist John Reason. JPR had been working on an autobiography which had been given some pre-publication publicity. The article in the *Daily Telegraph* was blunt. It alleged that JPR had infringed his amateur status by writing the book for money contrary to the rules of the International Rugby Football Board (IRFB). He was no longer an 'amateur'. He should no longer play for Wales. The article threatened his future in rugby.

The article in the Daily Telegraph threatened his entire rugby future.

Rugby union was still, proudly, an amateur sport. It was more than eighty years earlier, in 1895, when representatives of more than twenty prominent northern rugby clubs had met in Huddersfield to form the breakaway Northern Rugby Union which would permit payments to players – and lead to a changed rugby code, the 13-player per side Rugby Football League. The dispute about JPR's book may now seem from another age but, to use JPR's words, in those days 'rugby union players walked on egg shells'. If found guilty of the charge, JPR would have been banned from any formal involvement in the game of rugby union – whether as an international or club player, a coach or on a committee.

The distinction between amateurs and professionals, between gentlemen and players, had already been removed in many leading spectator sports. The Football Association had permitted payments, initially up to a maximum wage, since 1885. The distinction in cricket was removed in 1963 – although high performing amateurs (including, notoriously, WG Grace) had previously found ways of being compensated. Tennis, led by Wimbledon, had been open to all players since 1968. The Olympics were now largely 'open' in most sports. Yet, rugby union in the UK remained firmly and determinedly amateur – even if the walls were crumbling a little around the edges. Some players quietly received 'boot money', cash payments from footwear suppliers for wearing their products. (In fact, the term originated in the late 1880s in football, before professionalism was permitted, when it was not uncommon for players to find a half crown in their boots after a game.) But these payments were usually fairly small, often shared and a 'blind eye' was turned.

What about an autobiography – which could involve more substantial sums? Three of the Welsh greats, Gareth Edwards, Phil Bennett and Gerald Davies, had published autobiographies at the end of their careers. These had caused a stir but the players knew they had become 'professionalised' as they accepted work in the media. But JPR was different. He wanted to keep his amateur status. He wanted, after retirement at international level, to continue playing at amateur club level while he pursued another career. He had trained to be a doctor and planned a career as an orthopaedic surgeon. It was a 'real' job. Indeed, two years earlier, he had even missed a British Lion's tour to New Zealand. 'My consultant told me to buckle down for my forthcoming surgeon's exams. Medicine had to come first.'

What were the rules? The IRFB rule said:

> *No person shall ... for remuneration ... whether direct or indirect write a book or write an article ... on the game or related matters. A person may be exempted ... if he donates all such remuneration ... through his Member Union ... to a club or charity which should in no way benefit the person or his dependants.*

John Reason's article raised a storm. *The Sun* also joined the campaign. The Welsh Rugby Union (WRU) was forced to start an investigation. JPR's career was in serious danger, including his hopes of completing a final international season for Wales ending at the Arms Park. The rugby world held its breath.

The rugby world held its breath.

The WRU investigated. JPR was summoned to a meeting. JPR explained that he was not going to receive any of the money personally. He was going to give it all to a charity, a proposed new sports clinic in Bridgend. The legalities were complex and taking time. In the meantime, he had appointed an agency to receive any money from the book – and so he should remain an amateur provided he did not receive personally the money paid to them. The WRU accepted JPR's argument – and decided in his favour. He could finish his glorious career in style. He would play in yet another Welsh victory over England – JPR did not lose a single game in his ten matches against the English opposition.

But, off-field, John Reason was not satisfied. The *Daily Telegraph* published a further article in March bearing the heading 'BOARD SHOULD ACT NOW TO HALT SHAMATEURISM'. It claimed that the WRU had got it wrong. They had misinterpreted the regulations. The article alleged that JPR had infringed his amateur status under the rules by contracting in the first place to write his autobiography for money without getting prior exemption from the WRU or having established the charity or any binding arrangements to pass over the money. A simple intention (even if genuine) to give money away in the future was not sufficient. The article went further. It seemed also to suggest that JPR may already have indirectly benefited from some proceeds and implied that he may never have intended to give them to charity until the first of the newspaper articles appeared.

JPR had had 'a gutful of the innuendo in the newspapers'. He promptly served a writ alleging defamation. The defendants were the *Daily Telegraph*, journalist John Reason and editor Bill Deedes. A similar writ was brought against *The Sun*. The latter settled but not the *Daily Telegraph*. JPR was not prepared for a long drawn-out legal battle but, true to his nature, he refused to back down.

JPR had had a 'gutful of the innuendo in the newspapers'. He served a writ for defamation.

His claim eventually came before the High Court in February 1982. The hearing became a 'slanging match' between JPR and the journalist. The first leg of the libel match went well for JPR. After four days of the hearing, the judge directed the jury in a manner favourable to JPR's argument. The jury found that the articles in the *Daily Telegraph* had libelled him. He was awarded £20,000 in damages. JPR was satisfied.

But that was not the end of the saga. The *Daily Telegraph* appealed. The Court of Appeal, perhaps a little reluctantly, decided that the original judge went 'seriously wrong' in his direction to the jury. The judge should have given a different interpretation of the 'amateur' rule. The later court thought the more technical interpretation of John Reason and the *Daily Telegraph* had been correct. A new trial would be ordered before a new judge and jury. And, worse for JPR, new evidence could be asserted about the practice of 'boot money' which had now become available. Although not relevant to the specific question of an autobiography and amateur status, the Court of Appeal decided that it was relevant to the *Daily Telegraph*'s plea of justification when the 'sting' of the libel was based on a claim of 'shamateurism and hypocrisy'. It should be left to a new jury to decide whether the newspaper was justified: 'Did [the evidence] compel the conclusion that this outstanding rugby football player, the idol of his native Wales, had stooped to make money while posing and playing as an amateur?' There would have to be a new trial if JPR wished to pursue his libel claim.

JPR was 'furious at the outcome' but, by this time, just 'wanted an end to it all'. He wanted to complete his surgeon's qualifications in London and then go back to Wales to practise. He called an end to the litigation. He had not lost – but he had not won. It was 'very hard to walk away'. But it was over.

JPR became 'Mr Williams', consultant surgeon at the Princess of Wales Hospital in Bridgend. In 1994 the Sports Injury Clinic in Bridgend finally opened with financial help from the Mid-Glamorgan health authority. Sideburns and hair a little shorter but socks still at half-mast, JPR continued to play club rugby – first for the St Mary's B team in London and then, for sixteen 'wonderful' seasons until the age of fifty-four, for the second and third teams of Tondu in Wales. Perhaps he really was 'one of the last of the Corinthians'.

Perhaps he really was 'one of the last Corinthians'.

On 26 August 1995, the IRFB declared rugby union an 'open' game and removed all restrictions on payments or benefits to those connected to the game. The issue of shamateurism had become irrelevant. To adapt the words of Lord Justice Stephenson in the Court of Appeal in JPR's case:

> *... the distinction between 'gentlemen' and 'players' [was now] dead and buried, not only on the cricket field, and, to give a new meaning to the words which Shakespeare's Jaques spoke in a theatrical context (As You Like It II. vii. 140), ' ... all the men and women merely players.*

JPR published a second autobiography in 2006. He offered some advice to sports people tempted to bring a libel action: 'Think carefully ... and think twice about what your lawyers say. Remember, they are the only ones who are certain to make money out of it.'

Advice that should have been heeded by Bruce Grobbelaar ... and perhaps by Ian Botham?

---

93 BALL-TAMPERING IN THE HIGH COURT – BOTHAM, KHAN AND AN INFAMOUS LIBEL CASE

Ian Botham was deeply offended by newspaper articles by Imran Khan. Botham thought he was being accused of ball-tampering and lack of class. It would become one of sport's most infamous libel actions.

In July 1996 an England Test match at Lord's was about to begin. Two of the world's greatest cricket all-rounders were facing up to each other. But this was not a contest on the cricket pitch but in the High Court. It was a saga which lasted longer than any Test series. A judge would end up describing it as litigation 'which does no credit to anybody.'

Ian Botham was not popular in Pakistan. He did not like touring there. Once, during a radio commentary, he joked: 'Pakistan is a place to send one's mother in law, all expenses paid.' Matches between England and Pakistan in the early 1990s had been fraught including Pakistan's victory in the World Cup final in 1992 at the Melbourne Cricket Ground. Botham was out for nought. One of the Pakistani players is reputed to have told him to send his mother-in-law in next to bat since she couldn't do any worse! More seriously, accusations or hints of 'ball-tampering' were constantly in the air as Pakistan's bowlers carved through the English side.

Imran Khan, Pakistan's captain, added to the friction. He was interviewed for an article in *India Today* in 1994 in which he discussed the issue of ball-tampering. He had previously admitted that he himself once tampered with a ball, using a bottle-top, in a Sussex county match in the early 1980s. The article reported Khan as saying that 'the English media and a certain section of cricketers' had been motivated by 'racism' when they kicked up such a storm over Pakistani bowlers. The article continued to quote Khan: 'Look at people who have taken a rational stand on this. Tony Lewis, Christopher Martin-Jenkins, Derek Pringle. They are educated Oxbridge types. Look at the others, Lamb, Botham and Trueman. Class and upbringing makes a difference.'

Shortly after, Khan followed up with an interview for *The Sun* in England when he appeared to assert that ball-tampering in certain forms was commonplace in world cricket. 'The greatest and most famous bowlers from England and around the world have been guilty of ball-tampering. The biggest names of English cricket have all done it. And when I say big names, I mean as big as you can get.'

'The biggest names of English cricket have all done it. And when I say big names, I mean as big as you can get.'

No name in English cricket came bigger than Botham. He claimed that the article in *The Sun* was calling him a 'cheat' and was a libel. He had never tampered with the ball contrary to the rules of cricket. He demanded a public apology. He also threatened to sue Khan for libel for the other article alleging that Khan was calling him a 'racist' and 'lacking in education, class and upbringing'. Lamb joined him in this claim – but Trueman did not bother.

Khan tried to quell the row. He said that he had been misquoted and was only trying to defend himself. He asserted again that he did not regard certain forms of ball-tampering as 'cheating'. He regarded Botham as a 'worthy opponent' and not a 'cheat'. But the apology was not sufficiently public or unequivocal for Botham. Perhaps Pakistani pride would not permit Khan to go that far.

So, the feud was taken to the courts. Khan first tried to get the claim based on *The Sun* article struck out – on the grounds that, taking the article as a whole, it was clear that Khan was saying that the practice of lifting the seam and scratching the ball was commonplace and not, in his view, 'cheating'. 'To me, they are within acceptable limits.' This issue went to the Court of Appeal. On this point, Botham won a partial victory. Whilst the jury should look at the article as a whole and it may not have been asserting that Botham was a 'cheat', it could still be viewed as damaging Botham's reputation.

So, on 15th July 1996, the stubborn cricket rivals found themselves facing up to each other in a libel action before a jury in Court 13 of the High Court in the Strand. It would be an unpleasant battle – perhaps more fiercely fought than the Lord's Test beginning later that week. Khan even changed his defence to add a plea that the claim that Botham had been involved in ball-tampering was justified.

Witnesses from the world of cricket were called. Michael Atherton and England coach, David Lloyd, were forced to miss a day's training session for the Lord's Test to attend. David Gower and Robin Smith were called. Brian Close and Geoffrey Boycott, as usual, were on different sides – Boycott arousing Botham's wrath by a 'bravado' performance suggesting that ball-tampering had become as common as speeding. Charles Gray QC fought the case for Botham and Lamb. They were up against the legendary George Carman QC whose courtroom tactics managed suggestively to include stories of Botham's past off-field exploits. Khan, nine days into the proceedings, did at least drop his defence that the allegations of ball-tampering against Botham were justified. It was a thirteen-day hearing which came to a climax on 31st July.

The jury retired to consider its verdict. The courtroom was tense when they returned. By a margin of 10-2, the jury decided in Khan's favour. It was not libel. Botham and Lamb were left to pick up most of the costs of the case, estimated at around £400,000. Khan would bear a portion. The verdict came as a 'great shock' to Botham. He later said in his autobiography: 'And to the day I go to my grave I will never understand how they reached it.'

The verdict came as a 'great shock' to Botham.

Botham and Lamb would not give up the feud. They appealed and were set to return to the court in May 1999. The case was suddenly dropped. 'The parties believe that in the best interests of cricket their differences should not continue to be argued in the courts.

Any remaining issues between the parties will be resolved between them.'

The case was over – if not happily resolved.

In 2000, Botham did go to Pakistan to commentate on a series there. He took his mother-in-law. He recalled his earlier comment as something silly said in his youth. He said that she had a great time on the 'all-expenses paid' trip, especially shopping for carpets. Perhaps it represented some sort of closure.

But not fully. In November 2004, more than ten years after the article which triggered the feud, Botham and Khan – or their advisers – were back in court fighting over costs. No negotiated settlement had been reached. Both parties had been guilty of delay. The judge allowed Khan's claim for assessment of costs to continue but he 'deplored' the reactivation of court proceedings between them. He expressed the 'very strong hope' they would end.

---

94 A CARIBBEAN FARCE – WHICH WAY IS THE GOAL?

It was an extraordinary end to a match in the Caribbean. Grenada were trying to score at both ends of the pitch – and failing!

It did not reach a court or tribunal – we are allowed one exception in this book – but it was an example of a basic sporting doctrine, 'rules are rules', which should be retold. It was a match for the mathematicians and the lawyers. It ended in a farce.

Barbados were playing Grenada in a preliminary group match in February 1994 in the Shell Caribbean Cup, the soccer championship of the Caribbean. Grenada went into the match with a superior goal difference which meant that Barbados needed to win by two clear goals to progress to the final phase of the competition.

Under the rules of the tournament, if a match was level at the end of normal time, extra time would be played until a sudden-death winner. In order to encourage teams to attack for that winner rather than wait for penalties at the end of extra time, the rule makers introduced a rule that a sudden-death winner would be worth two goals. It seemed like a good idea at the time – but what trouble it would cause!

Back to the match. Barbados were playing well and took a 2-0 lead. They had the necessary two-goal advantage. They held this lead until the eighty-third minute. Then Grenada scored, making it 2-1. A frantic finish was in store as Barbados pressed forward trying to clinch the extra goal – but they could not get past Grenada's packed defence.

Suddenly, with around three minutes remaining, the Barbadians passed the ball – and deliberately kicked the ball into their own net. It was an own goal to tie the game. They had worked out that their best chance of getting a two-goal advantage was now to score in extra time!

Barbados deliberately kicked the ball into their own net.

Bewildered, Grenada did not know which way to turn. There followed the extraordinary sight of one group of Grenadian players trying to attack for a winner – and another group trying to score an own goal themselves to restore the one goal difference for Barbados which would be sufficient to see Grenada through. But, equally extraordinary, Grenada could not score at their own end – Barbados were defending both ends of the pitch. The full-time whistle blew. Football being football, Barbados scored the sudden-death winner in the fourth minute of extra time and were awarded a 4-2 victory. Grenada were out.

Grenada complained. But there was no remedy. Barbados were playing within the rules of the tournament. Moreover, they could not be accused of trying to lose the match – they were trying to win. Rules are rules. So it was all the fault of the rule-makers, and no doubt the lawyers, who drew up the rules!

Barbados' success was short-lived. They were eliminated in the next phase. Trinidad and Tobago, the hosts, went on to win the title.

---

95 A DISAPPOINTED SCOTTISH SUPPORTER – 'THERE'S ONLY ONE TEAM IN TALLIN'

The floodlights at the stadium in Tallin were poor. The time of Scotland's match with Estonia was changed – with unusual consequences.

John MacDonald was an enthusiastic Scottish supporter. It was October 1996 and Scotland were due to play Estonia in a group qualifying match for the 1998 World Cup. It was a 6.45 p.m. evening kick-off in the Kadriorg Stadium in Tallin, the Estonian capital. MacDonald was with a group of travelling Scottish fans. He was looking forward to the match.

Then, the arrangements changed. On the day before the match, temporary floodlights were erected at the Kadriorg Stadium. After testing, the Scottish FA claimed that the floodlights were unsuitable for such an international fixture. FIFA agreed. They decided that the kick-off time should be brought forward to 3 p.m. in the afternoon. Estonia were upset by the decision – perhaps because the revised time would interfere with the arrangements, and fee, agreed for live television transmission.

The kick-off time of 3 p.m. arrived. Six hundred Scotland supporters, including John MacDonald, were allowed into the ground and took up position. A farce ensued. With the tartan army singing 'There's only one team in Tallin', the fully-kitted Scotland eleven kicked off. Some say the Scottish team never put a foot wrong throughout the match! The match was abandoned after one pass. The Estonian team had failed to turn up. FIFA awarded the match to Scotland 3-0 by default.

John MacDonald was frustrated by his wasted journey and expense, despite the apparent Scotland victory. He wanted compensation. Who could he sue? He brought a claim against FIFA alleging that FIFA were under a duty not to alter the kick-off time so close to a game that the Estonian team would not turn up. He also claimed that the Scottish FA should have taken reasonable care to ensure that the match could be played at the original time. His claim for compensation came before Judge McEwan in a Scottish court.

John McDonald lost. The Scottish FA had only made representations to FIFA and had no control over the decision to re-arrange the match or the adequacy of the floodlights. As for the claim against FIFA, a spectator simply had no legal redress against the organisers for this kind of disappointment. A spectator could have no claim unless personal injury was caused. 'If the present kind of claim were allowed, it would open the way to many claims by an indeterminate class of people disappointed at the outcome or organisation of a sporting event.'

Perhaps it was a sign of our litigious times that the claim could get as far as the courts in the first place.

To make matters worse for the Scottish supporters, FIFA changed their minds after a successful appeal by Estonia and, instead of awarding victory to Scotland, ordered the match to be replayed at a neutral ground. It was duly replayed, four months later, in Monaco – where it ended in a 0-0 draw. Scotland failed to qualify.

---

96 WHAT A REFEREE! – A LEICESTER FAN'S SHOCK AT A LAST-MINUTE PENALTY DECISION

A Leicester fan tried to sue for damages as a result of a bad refereeing decision in a FA Cup match. Did he have any chance?

All football fans have suffered it. The refereeing decision which has cost 'our' team the match.

This one was at Stamford Bridge in February 1997 during the final few minutes of extra time in the fifth round of a FA Cup replay between Chelsea and Leicester City. The match up at Filbert Street had ended in a 2-2 draw. The score now was still 0-0 after 115 goalless minutes. A penalty 'shoot-out' was looming to settle the tie.

Chelsea's Erland Johnsen moved into the Leicester penalty area in a final attacking attempt. He appeared to clash with two Leicester defenders. Johnsen fell to the ground. Was it a dive? The referee, Mike Reed, awarded a highly dubious penalty. Chelsea scored. The final whistle blew and Leicester were out of the FA Cup. Leicester's manager, Martin O'Neill, was apoplectic. He attacked the decision as a 'disgrace'.

Leicester's supporters were in uproar. One, Tom Tyrrell, was so upset he later decided to take legal action. He issued a claim for damages against the Football Association as being responsible for the referee's alleged negligence. The basis of his claim was novel. His loss, he claimed, was having to miss work for two days due to the trauma and shock he had suffered as the result of witnessing such a negligently-given penalty decision. He claimed lost earnings of £100, travelling expenses and the cost of his ticket.

Tom Tyrrell was so upset by the penalty decision he issued a claim for damages against the FA!

The FA applied to have the claim struck out. The case was duly heard in the Central London County Court in April 1997. It was a lost cause for Tyrrell. He was no more fortunate than his team. The court dismissed his claim. There was no reasonable cause of action. The referee, even if he was incompetent, owed no duty of care of this kind to a spectator. Tyrrell went away empty-handed – except for a bill for costs.

It is fundamental to sport that the decision of a referee, made in good faith in the course of the playing of the game, must be accepted – however reluctantly – both by players and also by spectators. The implications would be mind-boggling if a referee, or a sports governing body such as the FA, could be liable in law for financial consequences of a mistaken, but honest, decision in the course of play. Put legally, the risk of a referee making a mistaken decision is an inherent risk which a spectator takes when attending a match. Tom Tyrrell's claim was ill-founded in law. It had no prospect of success. But all football fans knew how he must have felt!

It was of little consolation to Leicester City fans that Chelsea went on to win the FA Cup in 1997. After beating Portsmouth in the semi-final, they defeated Middlesbrough 2-0 in the final.

---

97 UNSEATED AT NEWCASTLE – A SUPPORTER CLAIMS HER SEAT AT ST JAMES' PARK

Jane Duffy paid £500 to guarantee 'her' seat at St James' Park. Could she be moved ?

The promotional leaflet in 1994 featured Newcastle legend, Kevin Keegan, endorsing the offer: 'Your place at St James' Park is secure well into the next century ... As a United bondholder your name ... will be fixed to your personal seat.'

Newcastle were offering season ticket-holders, on payment of £500, a 'bond' which would guarantee them a seat for the next ten years at the applicable season ticket prices together with complimentary home cup tie tickets for three years. Jane Duffy was a loyal supporter of Newcastle United. A forty-four-year-old City Council education adviser, she had been a season ticket holder for many years. These were exciting times at St James' Park and she wanted to continue to be part of it. Waiting lists for season tickets were building up.

'Your place at St James' Park is secure well into the next century ... '

Jane Duffy took up the offer together with one for her father. 'I was, simply, scared of losing my seat.'

Jane Duffy enjoyed 'her' seat in the centre of the Milburn Stand. Then, just six years later, Newcastle notified her that they were moving her. Around 4,000 season ticket-holders were being moved to a different place in the ground. The club needed the original seat positions as part of 'top-class' facilities to be offered to corporate clients in a new fundraising scheme to support a £42 million redevelopment at St James' Park which would increase the ground capacity to 52,000. The club said, if they were not willing to pay the substantially increased prices for the 'corporate' seats, Duffy and other season ticket-holders would have to move to the newly-built upper tier. Jane Duffy insisted that the alternative seats 'up in The Gods' were inferior and destroyed the ambience built up among loyal season ticket-holders over the years.

She and many others were deeply upset. They set up a 'Save Our Seats' campaign. They claimed that the literature and advertising gave a clear impression that £500 would guarantee the same seat for a decade. 'Fans are incensed,' said a spokesman. 'The snub to ordinary season ticket-holders, shifted for corporate entertainment, is bad enough. But for those who bought bonds, this is an absolute disgrace.' Jane Duffy said: 'I feel totally conned.' She brought a legal claim against Newcastle to prevent 'her' seat being moved. Five other fans brought similar actions – together they became known as the 'Newcastle Six'. The actions came to court.

Justice Blackburne praised the fans 'unswerving loyalty, even fanaticism' but ruled in favour of the club. The Six appealed.

While the rest of football was absorbed with Euro 2000, the appeal was heard in London. Led by Lord Justice Woolf, the Court of Appeal confirmed that, in the end, this was a matter of interpretation of the contract terms of the bond. The club's lawyers had protected the position in the small print. Unfortunately for Jane Duffy, those terms did allow Newcastle to make this change. She would have to watch from another seat.

Newcastle, desperately trying to rebuild their public image, eventually agreed not to pursue Jane Duffy and the other members of the Newcastle Six for legal costs.

---

98 SWIMMING LIKE A SHARK – CONTROVERSY OVER THE 'LONG-JOHN' SWIMSUIT

Sporting manufacturers had produced an extraordinary full bodysuit for competitive swimmers. It was designed to mimic sharkskin. Should the new swimsuit be allowed?

You wouldn't wear it at the beach – but in the Olympic pool?

Swimwear had moved a long way from the woollen suits of the

1930s. With modesty less of a concern, swimsuits became more brief. Fabric turned to silk, nylon and then Lycra. But in 1999 two manufacturers came up with perhaps the biggest change of all for competitive swimwear ... a full-body skintight suit covering the whole body from neck to ankle. The 'long-johns' left uncovered only the face, feet and hands. They looked more appropriate for deep-sea diving than Olympic swimming. The theory? To swim like a shark.

It had been a 'eureka' moment for Speedo, the sporting goods manufacturer. Consultant swimming coach Gennadi Touretski declared: 'We have finally produced the swimsuit of a new generation.' The fabric was light and rigid – rigid to 'eliminate all the vibrations of the system'. Speedo called it 'Fastskin'. It mimicked the 'dermal denticles' of a shark's skin. These enabled surrounding water to flow over the body more effectively and reduced drag. The super-stretch quality of the fabric increased body-shape retention. It was like a second skin. Speedo claimed that the new suit could improve times by up to three percent. Competing manufacturer, Adidas, also had a similar full bodysuit which they were developing. They were more influenced by the aerodynamics of an aeroplane and would later call their model JETCONCEPT.

For many, this was a step too far. Reactions to the bodysuits were varied and lively. Should they be banned on fashion grounds alone? The debate was, in some circles, termed 'Baywatch v Stopwatch'. For others, this was an excessive intrusion of commercial interests into the sport. The change should be resisted in order to preserve swimming as 'a pure sport'. The swimsuits were designed significantly to alter performance. They should no longer be classed as 'costumes' but 'equipment'. Would gold medals go to the swimmer with the best performance enhancing suit rather than the best ability and training? Were swimsuits simply becoming an advertising campaign for swimming manufacturers? Feelings ran high.

The debate was, in some circles, termed 'Baywatch v Stopwatch'.

Or should this simply be regarded as technical progress? Just part of the remorseless advance of technology in sport? Was this for swimming the equivalent of the fibreglass pole vault, the oversized racket in tennis or the titanium golf club? Many sports were struggling to strike the appropriate balance – and, in the background, lurked the 'carrot' of increased sponsorship monies and the 'stick' of possible legal action from sporting manufacturers if profitable products were not permitted into the marketplace by rules which were unduly restrictive or wrongly interpreted by the governing bodies.

More immediately, were the new bodysuits allowed under the existing rules of FINA, the world governing body for swimming? FINA's rules aimed to prevent artificial aids. Under Rule 10.7:

> *No swimmer ... shall use or wear any device that may aid his speed, buoyancy or endurance during a competition (such as webbed gloves, flippers, fins etc.). Goggles may be worn.*

The new bodysuit was clearly aimed to improve speed or buoyancy. Was it a 'device'?

Did it really matter? Well, a particular problem here was that the Sydney 2000 Olympics were rapidly approaching. USA Swimming initially imposed a ban on the new suits. The Australian Olympic Committee were also very concerned. Trials for Olympic selection were to be held shortly. If some swimmers wearing the new suits were selected after the Olympic trials ahead of swimmers not sponsored by full bodysuit suppliers, could the 'disadvantaged' swimmers have a legal claim? As for the Olympics themselves, could swimmers missing out on medals bring a legal claim against the organisers that winners had been using equipment 'unlawful' under FINA's rules?

FINA duly considered – and declared in October 1999 that the new bodysuits were permitted. They were not 'devices'. (Unlike certain previous examples. In the late 1980s, for instance, an American named Moriarty had tried to use a 'device' at the starting blocks in order to prevent the feet from slipping. That was not permitted.) But the Australian Olympic Committee (AOC) were not convinced by FINA's ruling. John Coates, president of the AOC, said: 'They have misinterpreted their own rules.' It did not, as far as they could see, remove the potential threat of litigation from deprived, and disgruntled, swimmers not using the new suits. The swimming world was still divided.

In order to resolve the controversy, the AOC referred the issue to the Court of Arbitration for Sport (CAS) – not in a full-blooded two-sided hearing but by seeking an 'advisory opinion' from an arbitrator, one of the facilities provided by CAS. So, it was over to a highly respected Canadian law professor, Professor Richard McClaren, to opine for

CAS. Had his years of legal training prepared him for this? It was his role to judge the 'long-johns'. Should the Fastskin and other full-body swimsuits be allowed in the Olympics?

The CAS arbitrator issued his opinion in May 2000. He backed FINA's ruling. In the fine legal print, he avoided giving a direct opinion whether or not the swimsuit was a 'device' for the purposes of the FINA rules. But he did conclude that FINA could properly be the final judge of that decision within its own rules – and that FINA's approval for the new bodysuits had been 'validly granted'.

Should the Fastskin and other full-body swimsuits be allowed in the Olympics?

The swimsuits could be used in the Olympics. The debate had been resolved in favour of the stopwatch.

Speedo's Fastskin was worn by eighty percent of the swimming medal winners in Sydney 2000. Australia's seventeen-year-old sensation, Ian Thorpe, wore the Adidas JETCONCEPT and went on to win three gold medals in his five-medal haul at his first Olympic Games. Many world records were shattered.

And now the manufacturers are looking at further improvements – a cap that conforms better to the shape of the head or streamlined or even strapless goggles. All in search of that extra tenth of a second.

---

99 'IT'S NOT A CATCH IF YOU DROP THE BALL' – TWO FANS FIGHT OVER A BASEBALL

Barry Bonds hit a record-breaking home-run into the stands. Baseball fans fought for the ball. Who would own it?

It was the last day of the 2001 US baseball season in October at PacBell Park in San Francisco. It was a record-breaking season for Barry Bonds, lead hitter for the San Francisco Giants. He had already broken the major league record for home-runs in a single season. He was about to smash his seventy-third, and final, home-run of the season into his favourite right-field stands.

The event was widely anticipated. Fans, in American tradition, were at the ready to catch and claim the historic ball. Many had come prepared with baseball gloves. The ball flew into the stands. Alex Popov, the owner of a healthfood restaurant in Berkeley, was the first to get to the ball, thrusting his gloved hand above the swarm of fans. Extraordinarily, the scene was caught on videotape by a cameraman. Popov held the ball very briefly, for less than a second, before disappearing under an unruly mob of excited and grasping fans. A minute later, Patrick Hayashi, a software engineer from Sacramento, emerged from the scrum with the ball in his hand. He smiled and showed it to the cameraman. Hayashi said he found the ball rolling free in the melée.

Was Hayashi entitled to retain the ball? Popov claimed that he had possession and that it had wrongly been taken from him. He was entitled to the ball. No, said Hayashi: 'It's not a catch if you drop the ball.' Popov started a lawsuit to reclaim the ball. Did it matter financially? Well, a previous record-breaking home-run ball, Mark McGwire's home run in 1998 which was the first to reach the magic seventieth in a season, was purchased for $3.2 million by a major baseball memorabilia collector, Todd McFarlane. After months of wrangling between Popov and Hayashi, the dispute could not be resolved outside the courtroom – so to the Californian Superior Court.

'It's not a catch if you drop the ball.'

Judge McCarthy presided over this unusual trial. It became an intense and often surreal three-week court battle. It raised deep theoretical questions. What constituted possession of a baseball landing in the stands? What was the nature of 'possession' in law? Did it require full 'dominion and control'?

Four distinguished law professors gave their views to the court. They all disagreed. Arcane arguments and precedents were drawn from pursuits such as whale hunting, fox hunting and the salvage of sunken vessels. Reference was even made to Herman Melville's 1851 novel *Moby Dick* and the customs and practices of whalers when a whale had been harpooned and subsequently captured – distinguishing between 'fast fish' and 'loose fish'. It was all very erudite and no doubt profitable for the lawyers – but frankly inconclusive.

After all the arguments Judge McCarthy finally came to his decision, a twenty-minute ruling in the mould of King Solomon. Both men, he said, had an equal claim under the law. He settled on a principle of 'equitable division' discovered in the roots of ancient Roman law. He ordered the ball to be sold and the proceeds to be shared equally!

Popov did not, he judged, achieve full control of the ball but did attain something Judge McCarthy termed 'pre-possessory rights' before he was attacked by the swarming crowd. It would never be known whether Popov would have been able to retain control of the ball if the crowd had not interfered. It was 'an out of control mob, engaged in violent, illegal behaviour'. Judge McCarthy saw here, in the midst of America's national game, a need to assert a fundamental principle underlying American history and culture – the rule of law:

'an out of control mob, engaged in violent, illegal behaviour'.

> *Judicial rulings, particularly in cases that receive media attention, affect the way people conduct themselves. This case demands vindication of an important principle. We are a nation governed by law, not by brute force.*

As a result, Judge McCarthy decided that 'each man has a claim of equal dignity as to the other'. The result? With the aid of a sports memorabilia agent, the ball was auctioned. It fetched $450,000, bought by Todd McFarlane for his prestigious collection.

The litigation could surely only have taken place in America. As one consequence, Popov faced a legal bill for over $470,000 – twice his share of the proceeds from the auction of the ball in dispute.

---

100 *ROCK OF GIBRALTAR* – FERGUSON AND MAGNIER: TWO TITANS CLASH

Sir Alex Ferguson thought he had rights to stud fees from Rock Of Gibraltar, *which ran successfully in his colours. Had he hit the jackpot? Or had he made a mistake in taking on John Magnier?*

Manchester United had just lost against Arsenal in February 2003. Now it was the Ferguson 'hairdryer' treatment for his team in the changing-room. He kicked at a boot. It flew and struck David Beckham in the face above his left eyebrow. Beckham could barely be restrained. Was this the match that hastened Beckham's departure to Real Madrid? Sir Alex Ferguson had seemed under strain for several days. Was one reason for Ferguson's mood that he had, earlier that week, heard from the Coolmore stud?

Was one reason for Ferguson's mood that he had, earlier that week, heard from the Coolmore stud?

It became a battle between two titans of sport: Sir Alex Ferguson and John Magnier. One, football's most famous and successful manager; the other, a dominant force in racing and head of the outstandingly successful stud farm, Coolmore. One, Scottish; the other Irish. Both highly focused, proud, determined and driven men. It was a dispute which would threaten Ferguson's job as manager of Manchester United – and affect the ownership of the club itself.

The story started back in 1997 at Cheltenham. Alex Ferguson was introduced through a mutual friend, a bookmaker, to John Magnier who, with business associate JP McManus, held a small but significant shareholding in Manchester United. The two men clicked and soon became friends. Ferguson visited Coolmore. The two men shared a love of red wine – and Ferguson's growing interest in the racing world became even greater.

Under a loose but friendly arrangement, various horses – including *Heritage Hall, Zentsor Street* and *Juniper* – were jointly registered in the names of Ferguson and Magnier's wife, Sue. They carried Ferguson's red and white colours, the colours of Manchester United, but there appeared to be no talk of training fees, insurance or vet's bills. The horses were not particularly successful. But it seemed a good public relations exercise for Coolmore. Ferguson certainly enjoyed it.

Then, along came *Rock Of Gibraltar*, a two-year-old trained by Aiden O'Brien at the Ballydoyle stables, partly owned by Coolmore. *Rock Of Gibraltar* had a good pedigree and had won his first race. Magnier suggested that Ferguson should become a co-owner. A joint racing registration was lodged in August 2001, again in the names of Ferguson and Sue Magnier, shortly before the Gimcrack Stakes at York. But on what terms? Was Ferguson offered a real share of 'ownership' or was it still a loose, friendly arrangement to enable the horse to run in Ferguson's colours and for both parties to enjoy the publicity? There appears to have been no written documentation and no payments. The facts remain very, very unclear.

Ferguson's hobby had now become, so he might have thought, his biggest earner. Had he hit the jackpot?

It seemed to matter little while *Rock Of Gibraltar* was racing – with enormous success. He won eight of his ten races in Ferguson's colours. He won his first Group One race at Longchamp in France, and then proceeded to win seven consecutive Group One races in a season – including both the English and Irish Guineas. It was a record which surpassed even the great *Mill Reef*'s record of six victories at the highest level in 1971/72. *Rock Of Gibraltar* was retired to stud at the end of 2002 after failing, by a narrow margin, to win the Breeders Cup in America. Ferguson would say:

> *As a relative newcomer into ownership I cannot adequately express the pleasure I have derived from the association with such a great horse. I owe an eternal debt of thanks to everyone associated with Ballydoyle.*

Financially, the horse's stud value had rocketed. *Rock Of Gibraltar* was conservatively estimated to be worth at least £50 million or more in potential stud fees. Ferguson's hobby had now become, so he might have thought, his biggest earner. Had he hit the jackpot?

But, in racing, it is quite common for stud ownership of a horse to be different from its registration while racing. *Rock Of Gibraltar* was now registered by Coolmore with Weatherbys Ireland in its stud book simply under '*Rock Of Gibraltar* Syndicate'. Ferguson apparently believed that he was entitled to a one-half share of the stallion's earnings.

In early 2003, Ferguson's advisers contacted the Coolmore stud to discuss the implications and how Ferguson would be paid. The fundamental misunderstanding became apparent. Magnier denied any such arrangement. Magnier made it clear that his recollections were very different from Ferguson's. He simply offered one stud nomination a year – an arrangement commonly reached with an established trainer or jockey. Some speculate that this conversation became known to Ferguson in the second week of February 2003 – shortly before that match against Arsenal.

Ferguson was hurt. He decided, stubbornly, to commence legal action against Magnier in the High Court in Dublin. It was a bold move – questioning the word of one of the giants of British racing on his home turf. It would have serious consequences for Ferguson and for Manchester United.

Magnier and McManus, in the meantime, stepped up their shareholding in Manchester United. Was this solely a financial investment? Were they seeking to acquire control of the club? No one was sure. Other investors, including an American Malcolm Glazer, were also building stakes. Magnier and McManus increased their stake to twenty-five per cent. They stepped up the pressure on Ferguson through this shareholding.

Ferguson's life became very difficult. Magnier made it clear that negotiations between the club and Ferguson for a long-term renewal of his contract as manager should be halted. A probe should be carried out into the club's recent transfer deals and use of agents, including of Ferguson's son, Jason. Magnier and McManus submitted a list of sixty-three questions to the United board. Another, and even longer, list was to follow. It was civil war. Many of the club's dealings came to a halt.

Ferguson's son, Jason, lodged a formal complaint with Cheshire police that his mail and rubbish had been tampered with. Magnier filed court motions to seek further disclosure from Alex Ferguson about his claim. A possible defamation claim was in the air. The prospects of any settlement seemed a long way off. Supporters of Ferguson threatened to demonstrate against Magnier's horses at the Cheltenham Festival. The saga was turning really nasty. The potential damage to Manchester United was high.

Supporters of Ferguson threatened to demonstrate against Magnier's horses at the Cheltenham Festival.

Finally, at the beginning of March 2004, Ferguson suddenly relented. Perhaps he could see that he would not win or that the cost of victory would be too high. He was given a settlement offer from Magnier of four stud nominations a year for *Rock Of Gibraltar* – or a one-off tax free payment of £2.5 million. He is reputed to have accepted the latter. Peace had been achieved. Both Ferguson and Magnier have kept a confidential silence over the affair.

Magnier and McManus eventually sold their stake, at a considerable profit, to Malcolm Glazer – thus paving the way for him to acquire full control of Manchester United. Ferguson was able to agree a new contract as manager with Manchester United and further triumphs, including two Premier League titles, followed on the field. What would have happened if the legal action had not been settled?

---

101 'GOLF WAS HIS MISTRESS' – A WARNING FROM THE DIVORCE COURTS

Ken Lane was a keen golfer. Perhaps he spent a little too much time at the golf club.

We finish our journey with a warning for the avid sports fan from the divorce courts. Carol Lane was fed up with her husband's behaviour. The couple had been married for fourteen years. Ken Lane's passion for golf was too much for her. The couple still shared the same home in Middlesex – a short drive from Moor Park Golf Club.

Carol complained that if her husband was not on the course, he could be found at the nineteenth hole, drink in hand. 'It was an obsession with him. You have heard of the golf widow? I am it,' she declared. 'I hate golf and because of it I just never saw my husband.'

They had three children, the oldest was thirteen and the youngest was five. 'She obviously needed and deserved the support of an understanding husband. I do not think she got it,' Judge Goodman said when her claim for a divorce came before the Family Division of the High Court in June 1987.

Forty-six-year-old Ken Lane saw things differently. A former county player, he enjoyed his golf. He was a film technician and mostly worked at nights. Sometimes he went straight to the course in the mornings. He denied his wife's allegations and believed their marriage had not irretrievably broken down. 'I have done nothing wrong. Okay, I played golf on Saturday afternoons followed by drinks at the clubhouse. Then I would be out at 6 a.m. on Sunday mornings and I occasionally played in the week. But I did not play or drink as much as they said.'

Carol Lane told the court. 'Golf was his mistress. It was never another woman. I always knew where he was – out on the course. A woman I could handle, but not the sport.' She added: 'I did go to a golf "do" with him once and went up to him while he was chatting with his mates and said: "Do you know who I am?" His friends did not even know he was married.'

'Golf was his mistress. It was never another woman.'

Judge Goodman granted her a decree nisi.

BIBLIOGRAPHY

A number of books have provided background to many of the stories included here. For the enthusiast I would mention, in particular, the following:

Chapter 1:

The Life of Senna by Tom Rubython (Business F1 Books, 2004)

Chapter 2:

Soccer in the Dock by Simon Inglis (Willow Books, 1985)

Setting the Record Straight by Peter Swan with Nick Johnson (Tempus, 2006)

The Hansie Cronjé Story by Garth King (Monarch Books, 2005)

... And Nothing but the Truth by Deon Gouws (Zebra, 2000)

The Final Score by Han Segers with Mel Goldberg and Alan Thatcher (Robson Books, 1998)

Calcio: A History of Italian Football by John Foot (Fourth Estate, 2006)

Chapter 3:

St Leger Goold: A Tale of Two Courts by Alan Little (Wimbledon Lawn Tennis Museum, 1984)

Back Home: England and the 1970 World Cup by Jeff Dawson (Orion, 2001)

Lester by Lester Piggott (Partridge Press, 1995)

Chapter 5:

The Second Mark by Joy Goodwin (Simon & Schuster, 2004)

Chapter 6:

The Tour de France 2006 by John Wilcockson (VeloPress, 2006)

Chapter 7:

Tony Greig: My Story by Tony Greig (Stanley Paul, 1980)

The America's Cup by Dennis Connor & Michael Levitt (St Martin's Press, 1998)

Bellies and Bullseyes by Sid Waddell (Ebury Press, 2007)

Chapter 9:

Second Serve by Renée Richards (Stein & Day, 1983)

Jane Couch: Fleetwood Assassin by Jane Couch and Tex Woodward (Blake Publishing, 2000)

Chapter 10:

Aintree's Queen Bee by Joan Rimmer (SportsBooks, 2007)

An Aintree Dynasty by John Pinfold (Trafford, 2006)

From Boot Money to Bosman: Football, Society and the Law by David McArdle (Cavendish, 2000)

Chapter 11:

JPR: Given the Breaks by JPR Williams (Hodder & Stoughton, 2006)

Botham by Ian Botham with Peter Hayter (Collins Willow, 1994)

Rock Of Gibraltar by Martin Hannan (Cutting Edge, 2004)

The law's application to sport has become a recognised subject for serious academic and practical study. Helpful texts and sources include:

Sport: Law and Practice by Adam Lewis & Jonathan Taylor (Tottel, 2008)

Sports Law by Simon Gardiner (Cavendish, 2001)

Sport and the Law by Edward Grayson (Butterworths, 2000)

Sports Law and Litigation by Craig Moore (CLT Professional, 2000)

Law and Sport in Contemporary Society eds Steve Greenfield and Guy Osborn (Frank Cass, 2000)

Digest of CAS Awards Vols, I, II & III ed. Matthieu Reeb (Kluwer Law International)

INDEX

Numbers refer to the number of the relevant story in the book